ЯED
ARMY

Also by Aaron Klein and Brenda J. Elliott

The Manchurian President: Barack Obama's Ties to Communists, Socialists and Other Anti-American Extremists

By Aaron Klein

The Late Great State of Israel: How Enemies Within and Without Threaten the Jewish Nation's Survival

Schmoozing with Terrorists: From Hollywood to the Holy Land, Jihadists Reveal Their Global Plans—to a Jew!

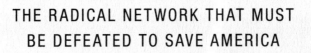

RED ARMY

THE RADICAL NETWORK THAT MUST BE DEFEATED TO SAVE AMERICA

AARON KLEIN

AND BRENDA J. ELLIOTT

BROADSIDE BOOKS
An Imprint of HarperCollins*Publishers*
www.broadsidebooks.net

HarperCollins books may be purchased for educational, business, or sales promotional use. For information, please write: Special Markets Department, HarperCollins Publishers, 10 East 53rd Street, New York, NY 10022.

Broadside Books™ and the Broadside logo are trademarks of Harper-Collins Publishers.

FIRST EDITION

Designed by William Ruoto

Library of Congress Cataloging-in-Publication Data
Klein, Aaron.
    Red army : the radical network that must be defeated to save America / by Aaron Klein, Brenda J. Elliott.—1st ed.
       p.   cm.
    ISBN 978-0-06-206924-5
    1. United States—Politics and government—2009– .
2. Radicalism—United States—History—21st century.
3. Obama, Barack. I. Elliott, Brenda J. II. Title.
E907.K54   2011
973.932—dc23   2011028734

11 12 13 14 15   ov/og   10 9 8 7 6 5 4 3 2 1

America is like a healthy body and its resistance is threefold: its patriotism, its morality, and its spiritual life. If we can undermine these three areas, America will collapse from within.

—JOSEPH STALIN

CONTENTS

Appendixes:

ЯED
ARMY

INTRODUCTION

When Senator Barack Obama, a few days before his inauguration as our forty-fourth president, promised an adoring crowd "the fundamental transformation of the United States of America," few realized that he was not speaking merely of himself or of his own role as the country's incoming chief executive. Behind the avatar of "hope and change" lies a left-wing "progressive" movement waiting to come to power.

At first, we knew very little about this clandestine Red Army, whose goal is the transformation of America into a socialist system. As a matter of strategy, the "progressives" had quietly and patiently perfected the art of creating innocuous-sounding front groups, and the promotion of its policies in the guise of moderation, in the rhetoric of modest-sounding social ideals.

Before the candidacy of Obama—whose entire political career has been spent under the tutelage of the "progressives," including some of its leading figures—this radical network had already succeeded over the decades in infiltrating major institutions of American power. But with his election to the presidency, it reached the highest levels of our government.

Along the way, the progressives hijacked an entire spectrum of important social causes, from feminism and race relations through environmental and antiwar activism, each of which, we will demonstrate, became subordinated to an agenda having very little to do with the actual cause at hand and everything to do with the underlying agenda of the radical reconstruction of our society.

This Red Army, as we will show, has taken over not merely the largest worker unions, but also the mainstream of the Democratic Party.

It has deeply penetrated the United States Congress, forming one of the most powerful caucuses on Capitol Hill. Key legislation, including President Obama's health care and stimulus bills, was crafted by the network's various branches—operating both inside and outside the government. The same network is now pushing other major measures, including defense, economic, and immigration policies.

Like a conventional army, the progressive Red Army is an organized network consisting of numerous branches and divisions, deploying an appropriate battalion for a specific goal or battle at hand. As you will see, many of the activists described herein are openly hateful of America, or at least of the American capitalist system, including its basic document and compact, the United States Constitution. Many others, to be fair, genuinely love this country while believing that socialism would pave the road to a better society. Still others are merely along for the ride, and pursue personal power and profit in the service of a new order.

While this radical network played a major part in the nomination and election of Barack Obama, as we show, it runs far deeper than the slew of "czars" in the Obama administration or the extremist personalities demonstrably tied to our president. It is much larger than Obama himself, and will far outlast however many months of the Obama presidency yet remain. Indeed, as you will see, it is already planning how to advance its agenda following the 2012 elections, regardless of which candidate is victorious.

We believe the story of this radical network, this "progressive" army, is the most important political story of our time. By design it has been concealed from the American public. Even the few voices of independence and dissent in our news media have largely missed it. But if we, as Americans, are to resist this radical campaign that has already caused so much damage to our economic and political system, and to our foreign relations, this story must be fully exposed and understood. For this "Red Army" shows no signs of relenting.

With the dramatic erosion of his poll numbers and the ascension of Republicans in the 112th Congress, Obama's mandate for change may have for the time being run thin. But, as you will see, these radical groups demonstrate an uncanny ability to wait patiently, like sleeper cells, for years or even decades, for the next opportunity to push their nefarious agenda while updating and perfecting the details of their well-planned, multilayered assault.

I first started to investigate Senator Barack Obama in January 2008, when the Democratic primary was getting into full swing and the largely unknown junior senator from Illinois emerged as a serious contender. So many questions should immediately have been raised about Obama's complex and unusual, not to mention exotic, background. And yet I watched from five thousand miles away—as a Jerusalem-based reporter who was supposed to be focusing on the Middle East—as most in the Washington press corps remained mysteriously uninterested in any real investigative reporting into the politician who would soon become the world's most powerful person.

In February 2008, I first pieced together Obama's extensive relationship with unrepentant Pentagon bomber Bill Ayers, including their having served together on the board of a Chicago nonprofit that funneled money to far-left causes. I was surprised that this tie was not being reported by the "watchdogs" in the mainstream news media, so I penned an article on Obama's extensive relationship with Ayers at WorldNetDaily.com. In that article, which broke into a major issue of the 2008 presidential campaign, I first documented Obama's personal and professional ties to the PLO-connected, anti-Israel professor Rashid Khalidi.

Much more was soon to emerge. I continued to uncover and report shocking facts about Obama's nearly lifetime ties to radical groups and anti-American personalities, including the Nation of Islam; the Association of Community Organizations for Reform Now, or ACORN; the SEIU union; as well as the strident radicalism of Obama's place of worship for nearly twenty years, the Trinity United Church, and its incendiary pastor, the Reverend Jeremiah Wright.

In April 2008, in a now-notorious WABC Radio interview with myself and cohost John Batchelor, a top official of the Palestinian terrorist organization Hamas "endorsed" Obama for president, speaking to us from the Gaza Strip. Our interview made world headlines and became a prominent theme of the 2008 presidential campaign, with Obama and Senator John McCain repeatedly trading barbs over Hamas's "endorsement."

Later, as his presidency took shape, I continued to research Obama and White House officials. I was one of the first to report that Obama's "Green Jobs Czar," Van Jones, had founded a communist organization—a theme later picked up by Fox News Channel's Glenn Beck and that led to Jones's resignation.

I also released a video, circulated nationwide, in which White House Communications director Anita Dunn boasted that Obama's presidential campaign had focused on "making" the news media cover certain issues while rarely communicating anything to the press unless it was "controlled." Dunn stepped down weeks later, but she continued to serve the White House in an advisory role.

During the course of my initial investigations, I befriended historian Brenda J. Elliott, who was running a blog and copiously documenting Obama's extremist ties. Brenda soon became the mainstay of my research team. As we both began to comprehend the scope of Obama's radical associates and mentors—most of whom traveled together in the same far-left circles—we decided to assemble the pieces of the puzzle for a book. Brenda contributed hugely to the research and writing of what became our *New York Times* best-selling title, *The Manchurian President: Barack Obama's Ties to Communists, Socialists and Other Anti-American Extremists* (May 2010). Her research has remained so central to my own investigations that I asked her to serve as a full co-author on the book you now hold.

Our first book-length effort focused on unmasking Barack Obama and his radical associations. But even before its publication, as we continued to delve into Obama's administration, it became clear that we were uncovering a larger world of radical organizations, which are not only the force behind Obama's "fundamental transformation of America" but also are now so well entrenched in the institutions of American power that their influence can hardly be overstated. In other words, in peeling off the layers of the onion that is the radical network, Brenda and I have unearthed something much larger and far more disturbing than even we, as seasoned political observers, could have anticipated.

We researched the communist and socialist origins of the "progressive" movement and of some of its most influential American affiliates, finding how later generations of militant socialists worked their way into positions of influence, to the point where they are today able to shape key aspects of the White House agenda and the legislation that comes before Congress.

The book begins by exposing how one of the most important groupings within Congress is a "Marxist-socialist" bloc that works actively with these outside radical groups to advance the "progressive" agenda.

High on that agenda is the complete socialization of health care, an aim the radical network moved vastly closer to achieving with the passage of Obama's comprehensive health care reform. We show how Obamacare, masked by moderate, populist rhetoric, was crafted and perfected by a coalition of socialists. A few other authors have endeavored to identify those responsible for the legislation, with some peripheral success. In these pages, however, we finally lay bare Obamacare's thoroughbred radical origins.

Another "progressive" policy goal is the sweeping reconstruction of the rest of the American economy. We disclose the radical network behind Obama's economic policies, including the crafting of the president's massive "stimulus" legislation, as well as these radical groups' legislative and executive plans for future economic "reform." In just one of many revelations, we document how "stimulus" money funded an education group now tied to unrepentant Pentagon bomber Bill Ayers. For Ayers and others, the radical transformation of America's education system is the key to a "progressive" future. We therefore devote two extensive chapters to showing how the Obama administration colludes with these radicals to promote an unprecedented left-wing assault on our already overliberalized public education system.

One of the most immediate dangers we face as a nation is the multipronged policy offensive aimed at disarming America as a superpower by emboldening our enemies, spurning our allies, and systematically dismantling the greatest military the world has ever known. We show how the nexus of radical groups, working with the Obama administration, has also crafted the now-institutionalized government policy of minimizing the threat of Islamic terrorism, even as the administration maintains close associations with Islamic groups of questionable intent and character, both inside America and in the Middle East.

In the contentious matter of massive illegal immigration—along with border control, an aspect of foreign policy—we unmask the personalities and organizations behind the perfecting of "immigration reform" proposals. A few of immigration reform's radical advocates even admit that their aim is not only to transform America's social fabric, but to secure long-term "progressive rule" by permanently altering the composition of the American electorate.

The radical socialist network influencing the president's environmental policies is also uncovered here. They aggressively promote a national "green campaign" to hijack the legitimate environmental movement, their true objective being the use of an environmental crisis "cover story" to conceal their agenda of redistributing our country's wealth and assaulting the U.S. business system. Remarkably, we discovered that even after he was forced to resign as "Green Jobs Czar" in 2009, the erstwhile communist Van Jones continues, as we complete this manuscript, to serve in leadership positions of several groups now advising the White House.

By now it is no secret that from the time Barack Obama was first propelled onto the national stage until the publication of this book, most of the news media surround the politician in a cocoon of protective silence. So-called news reporters are mysteriously uninterested in shedding any light on the president's radical associations while almost openly lobbying for his "progressive" socialist policies. Here we detail how the news media are not only colluding with some of the same radical groups we endeavor to expose, but how, in some cases, the news outlets and personnel are actual members of the very radical organizations they ought to be investigating.

In closing, we must take up the extremely loaded question of conspiracy. Conspiracy is a very serious offense in the U.S. legal system, and of course this applies to conspiracy to commit a crime. Yet the "Red Army" of which we write employs mostly legal means to pursue its radical agenda. In fact, the largest part of its nefarious genius lies precisely in its employment of legal and quasi-legal stratagems to "fundamentally transform," and even overthrow, the American system.

In uncovering what is mostly a legal conspiracy, the question of intentionality must inevitably be addressed, for the existence of a conspiratorial motive is what lies at the heart of this form of corruption. As noted above, many of the "progressive" activists described herein are openly hateful of the American system, including the United States Constitution, while others are patriots who do not realize that the well-worn road to socialist hell is paved with their good intentions. Still others, as we note, are merely along for the ride. And often it is impossible to distinguish where true conspiracy ends and mere corruption begins. But these, in the final analysis, are distinctions without a difference.

There is a conspiracy—albeit a mostly legal one—behind Obama's promised "fundamental transformation of America." As you will see, it is the radical socialist network behind the president that relentlessly pushes this agenda. What we call the Red Army has devised the means to seize enormous instruments of political, economic, and cultural power in our country, from the very presidency itself on down. To be sure, the American people have begun awakening from their slumber, rousing from their acquiescence, and seem eager to reclaim their great, free, and prosperous nation from this clutch of radical operatives. But in order to prevail, in order to save our nation from the designs of these operatives, we must first comprehend—and then defeat—the radical network that has seized the reins of American power.

Aaron Klein

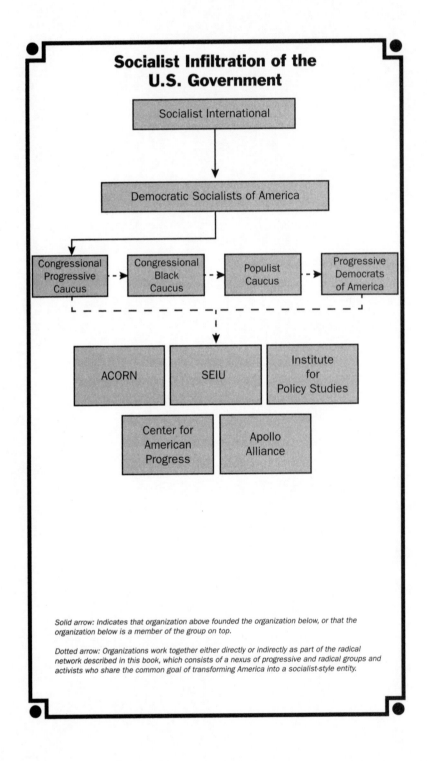

Socialist Infiltration of the U.S. Government

Socialist International

Democratic Socialists of America

Congressional Progressive Caucus

Congressional Black Caucus

Populist Caucus

Progressive Democrats of America

ACORN

SEIU

Institute for Policy Studies

Center for American Progress

Apollo Alliance

Solid arrow: Indicates that organization above founded the organization below, or that the organization below is a member of the group on top.

Dotted arrow: Organizations work together either directly or indirectly as part of the radical network described in this book, which consists of a nexus of progressive and radical groups and activists who share the common goal of transforming America into a socialist-style entity.

chapter one

CONGRESSIONAL RED ARMY

Marxist thought becomes even more relevant after the collapse of communism in the Soviet Union and Eastern Europe than it was before.
—CORNEL WEST, RACE RELATIONS PROFESSOR AND BARACK OBAMA ADVISER[1]

You might think that the collapse of the Soviet Union would have left the radical network in disarray, searching for relevance in a world suddenly much less friendly to the socialist agenda. One might even surmise that the radical network would begin to rethink its agenda after the collapse of yet another utopian experiment so closely tied to its ideology.

Ironically, however, it was during the period following the dissolution of the Soviet Union, a hopeful time during which our country seemed to relax its vigilance, that the radical left matured into a highly organized nexus of progressive organizations and groups that finally breached the walls of power in Washington, D.C.—including penetrating Congress, where the network began to craft and perfect policies and legislation that would wait for a vehicle like Barack Obama to push them through.

Many tend to think of the United States as one of the few democratic countries that does not have an official socialist party. In reality, however, socialists not only grace the leadership of highly influential political groups backing our president, but also form one of the most powerful coalitions in Congress, a "Marxist-socialist" bloc that is working to help the radical network advance a transformative progressive agenda. Indeed, the Congressional Progressive Caucus was originally founded as the sister to the U.S. socialist group, the Democratic Socialists of America, or DSA. Many current congressional Democrats have a close working relationship with the DSA.

The radical socialist network wasn't always so well entrenched within the Democratic Party and U.S. politics. Its ideology permeated our country's academic institutions decades ago. There were numerous failed attempts to form U.S. socialist parties. For a time, radicals attempted to overthrow the U.S. capitalist system through revolution, as the country witnessed in the 1960s, with the Students for a Democratic Society, or SDS, and its splinter, the Weathermen terrorist group.

Those revolutionary tactics were staunchly opposed by Michael Harrington, founder of the Democratic Socialists of America. Harrington rose to socialist stardom when he was elected leader of the SDS's less openly radical precursor, the League for Industrial Democracy. He was a student of the Fabian school of socialism, which held to the idea that social reforms and permeation of existing political institutions would naturally bring about the development of socialism.[2]

The DSA was established to gradually transform our capitalist enterprise into a socialist entity through democratic means.[3] Later, the DSA took heed to the Fabian socialists' earlier warnings that the appearance of *socialism* in an organization's title might turn many people off, so it dropped socialist terminology from the Congressional Progressive Caucus. It is far more effective to infiltrate a political system using innocuous-sounding titles and stealthy tactics.

Those tactics were later employed by some of the 1960s radicals themselves, many of whom reemerged in the 1980s to join the Harrington style of activism—boring from within. For example, extremists such as Bill Ayers, Mike Klonsky, and Bernardine Dohrn discovered that they could better combat capitalism from within the halls of academia. Others, such as Wade Rathke, who founded ACORN, and Heather and Paul Booth and Steve Max, cofounders of the Midwest Academy, which we will discuss later, emerged as reformers and attacked capitalism via Saul Alinsky–style community organizing.

For Harrington, however, infiltrating the Democratic Party was the primary goal. He argued for a party within a party within the Democratic Party, which he believed included "all of the important 'progressive' elements." The Democratic Party, Harrington continued, would "serve as 'the arena' for the development of the new policies." Socialist ideology, he argued, would "work within the party, acting as the 'left wing of the possible.'"[4]

In March 1982, Harrington, then a professor of political science at Queens College in New York City, officially formed the DSA, a group that would succeed where most other radical organizations until that point had failed, not only infiltrating the Democratic Party but forming a congressional gang whose individual members most Americans are inclined to ignore, but this group has served as a conduit for the introduction and passage of radical legislation aimed at fundamentally transforming our country.

The DSA is still the principal U.S. branch of the Socialist International, one of the planet's most influential socialist organizations, with democratic socialist party members from around the world. Since the Socialist International's 1962 congress, party members, including many major world leaders, have called for universal membership in the United Nations. SI has never wavered from its goal of global governance and worldwide socialism. It proudly boasts the Socialist International is the successor to the so-called First International of Karl Marx founded in London in 1864.[5]

Credit for the creation of the Progressive Caucus is due to the efforts of Vermont senator Bernie Sanders. Then the only avowed democratic socialist and Independent in Congress, Sanders writes that the

Black Caucus "had long been, in effect, *the* progressive caucus in the Congress."[6] Sanders planned to rectify that. Because not every progressive was black, Sanders said it was important to create a caucus that "brought all progressives together—white, black, Hispanic, Asian, male, and female—so that we could stand together in fighting for rational priorities." Sanders first took his idea to then California Democratic representative Ron Dellums and Representative Peter DeFazio (D-Ore.), who was one of the two people who had endorsed Sanders's 1990 run for office. Representative Barney Frank (D-Mass.) was the other. He next approached Representatives Lane Evans (D-Ill.) and Maxine Waters (D-Calif.). Sanders and Waters had served together on the House Banking Committee.[7]

In 1992, through its intermediary, the Democratic Socialists of America, the Progressive Caucus was one of the programs of action the Socialist International realized. The DSA helped to organize the members into the House Progressive Caucus, as the CPC was originally known.

There is no mistaking the significant role the DSA played in organizing the Congressional Progressive Caucus. It is clearly spelled out in the January/February 1998 issue of Chicago DSA's *New Ground*. Ron Baiman identified Sanders and Frank as leaders of the Progressive Caucus in Congress, which the DSA openly admitted it had helped organize.[8] The CPC's website was originally hosted by the DSA, but was later moved to an official congressional website as part of a larger effort to reimage the caucus, similar to the rebranding methods employed by the radical network—the same radicalism, but a different front.

The relationship between the DSA and CPC was also evident on the DSA website, which listed Caucus founders as members, including Sanders, DeFazio, Evans, and Waters. Other named members are Representatives Cynthia McKinney (D-Ga.) and Maurice Hinchey, Major Owens, and Nydia Velazquez (all D-N.Y.). Leading DSA member, retired representative Dellums, and his replacement in the House and political protégée, Representative Barbara Lee (D-Calif.), are also named.

The DSA-CPC files were subsequently removed from the Internet, although some remain accessible in the Internet Archive. For example, one file, dated July 1997, names the CPC executive committee: De-Fazio, Dellums, Evans, Owens, Sanders, Velazquez, and Waters. Both Dellums and Owens are identified as also being DSA members.[9]

A separate linked page in the archive, also dated July 1997, provides a list of thirty-three additional Caucus members, many of whom still serve in Congress. None of them carries a DSA identifier after their name.[10]

Two more noncongressional DSA members were identified in 1997 as a by-product of the Teamster scandal about how insiders were looting the union and laundering money through campaign fund-raisers, allegedly for Bill Clinton's campaigns. These members were AFL-CIO president, previously SEIU president, John J. Sweeney, and Citizen Action executive director Ira Arlook. Both were former members of the 1960s radical group Students for a Democratic Society. It was under Sweeney in September 1997 that the AFL-CIO ended its fifty-year ban on communists holding top positions in the union.[11]

In November 1998 the CPC portion of the DSA website included such phrases as *economic redistribution* and *social and environmental justice*.[12] Heretofore, these concepts were foreign to the majority of Americans. During the Obama administration, however, these socialistic terms became all too familiar.

The DSA-CPC connection was accurately described in March 1999 as a "consortium of radical congressional collectivists." Of the 58 CPC listed members, 55 had run for reelection in 1998, with every one of them successful. The fact that they were socialists had not mattered. It is possible they won due to the symbiotic relationship the CPC shares with the DSA, and vice versa. Then, as today, this relationship has largely been ignored by the mainstream media.[13] The DSA, however, has never been hiding. Rather, it has been hiding in plain sight, if at all. DSA's influence in Congress is clearly seen through an October 14, 1987, observance by Senator Edward M. Kennedy's Senate Committee on Labor and Human Resources. On that date, the committee celebrated the twenty-fifth anniversary of Michael Harrington's landmark book, *The Other America*, with a hearing "on poverty and policy in the 1980s and beyond."[14]

The close relationship between members of Congress and the DSA was clearly evident again on July 2, 1988, when Harrington was honored at the Roseland Ballroom in Manhattan. An estimated six hundred friends from around the country, some wearing buttons proclaiming boycotts and causes, were described by the media as a "nostalgic assembly of the old and new left including trade unionists, environmentalists, feminists and moderate Socialists."[15] The occasion was the publication of Harrington's new autobiography, *The Long-Distance Runner.*[16]

Among those who attended were Senator Kennedy and D.C.'s Eleanor Holmes Norton, head of the Equal Employment Opportunity Commission under Jimmy Carter. Both spoke on Harrington's behalf. Kennedy said Harrington, who worked on his 1980 presidential campaign, had "made more Americans more uncomfortable for more good reasons than any other person I know."[17] Kennedy's words are most revealing, signifying, for those who did not know, that he stood clearly in the progressive (liberal, socialist) camp even though he was never a member of the CPC. "I see Michael Harrington as delivering the Sermon on the Mount to America. When it comes to the Kennedy brothers, he bats three for three. Among veterans in the war on poverty, no one has been a more loyal ally when the night was the darkest," Kennedy said.[18]

Another senator, CPC's leader Bernie Sanders, drew the ire of then Republican National Committee chairman Jim Nicholson a little more than a decade later. In a December 1990 press release, Nicholson described as "outrageous" House Democrat leader Dick Gephardt's suggestion that Sanders should have a seat on the powerful House Appropriations Committee.[19] Nicholson spoke directly about the CPC, which then had thirty-seven members closely allied with the DSA. Included in the press release was the CPC's specific address within the DSA website. In other words, at the time the CPC took no great pains to hide its association with the DSA. Nicholson added that the Democrat Party's "unholy alliance with self-proclaimed socialists" had escaped notice for too long. Saying this should become an issue for the upcoming election, Nicholson challenged Democrats to "talk openly with voters" about their alliance with the DSA if they believed there was nothing wrong with it.

The issue of the CPC being hosted on the DSA website emerged again in June 2000 in connection with a heated dispute on the House floor between Republican California representative Randy "Duke" Cunningham and Democratic representatives DeFazio and David R. Obey (Wis.) over the merits of the F-22 fighter plane. When Cunningham stood to defend himself, he threw into his argument the fact the DSA website had a link to the CPC, which DeFazio then led.[20]

The DSA-CPC relationship was again in the open at the 2000 Democratic National Convention when the DSA kicked things off with a panel on elections. Panel members included DSA leaders Harold Meyerson of *LA Weekly*; Barbara Ehrenreich, who was then stumping for Ralph Nader; Cornel West, who had served as cochair of the Bill Bradley primary campaign (and would later advise Barack Obama's 2008 presidential campaign); and DSA youth organizer Daraka Larimore-Hall.[21] The DSA-CPC Web presence continued until at least April 2002, when the CPC still had not moved to its own website. When asked hypothetically whether there were any socialists in Congress, journalist Balint Vazsonyi responded in the *Washington Times* that there were dozens of them. He detailed his response by linking the CPC to the DSA and the Socialist International. In support of his claim, Vazsonyi included the DSA-CPC Internet address, and said the details of their individual programs were indistinguishable. "To their credit," he remarked, "they make no secret of it. Only the rest of us prefer not to believe it."[22]

In a November follow-up article, Vazsonyi questioned the constitutionality and the ramifications of the relationship. He carefully traced the lineage of the Socialist International from its roots, listing the roles played by Karl Marx and Friedrich Engels, coauthors of *The Communist Manifesto*, and Vladimir Lenin, Leon Trotsky, and Joseph Stalin.[23] Most significantly, Vazsonyi pointed out to his Beltway readers, Congress swears an oath to preserve, protect, and defend the U.S. Constitution. Unspoken for the reader was that this oath is in direct defiance of the tenets of the Socialist International and its U.S. member, the DSA, CPC's socialist partner.

The DSA is a dues-paying member of the Socialist International. Documentation shows that every year since 2006, when DSA's political action committee began reporting to the Federal Election Commission, it has made the annual payments.[24] The DSA emblem, a raised fist (also called the clenched fist) holding a rose, is the graphic against which the list of CPC's fifty-eight members and the CPC statement of purpose appears on the now-archived Internet files. Although no date appears on the Web page, the list of names and the statement formed an integral part of the DSA website.[25] Perhaps due to the local media exposure, the listing of CPC members on the DSA website was finally moved to one maintained by then representative Bernie Sanders.[26]

The raised or clenched fist with a rose is also used by the Socialist International. In full frontal display, showing all fingers, it has been employed historically as a persistent symbol of resistance and unity, solidarity, strength, or defiance. The red rose has a tradition dating back to the Middle Ages, but it was not until after World War II that the rose was adopted as a symbol by the European Socialist and Social Democratic parties.[27]

Those earlier CPC files, once part of the DSA website, can be accessed now only via the Internet Archive.[28] But it is instrumental to remember that perhaps the most powerful progressive caucus in Congress once proudly displayed its deep relationship with the DSA, which sought to infiltrate the U.S. establishment to push its socialist agenda.

After the passing of Michael Harrington in 1989, left-wing journalist E. J. Dionne writes, "If the organization he headed, Democratic

Socialists of America, had power in the United States, it was as a source of ideas for intellectuals, labor leaders and people in the Democratic Party's left wing."[29]

Harrington, when asked in an interview what differentiated DSA's brand of socialism from that practiced in the Soviet Union and Europe, responded: "Put it this way. Marx was a democrat with a small d. The Democratic Socialists envision a humane social order based on popular control of resources and production, economic planning, equitable distribution, feminism and racial equality. I share an immediate program with liberals in this country because the best liberalism leads toward socialism."[30]

Single-Payer, Income Redistribution

One of the archived CPC files is a document dated 1992 and called *A Progressive Agenda*, a lengthy list of progressive programs. Notable is the call for single-payer health care reform that would provide health care to all Americans with no deductibles, no copayments, no out-of-pocket expenses, and doctor choice. Additionally, the *Progressive Agenda* calls for a 50 percent reduction in military spending to pay for all its proposed programs.[31] It was a CPC member who officially introduced Obama's health care bill.

The Congressional Black Caucus—which included many CPC members—soon joined forces with the CPC to introduce an alternative federal budget for the 1993 fiscal year.[32] A series of similar blueprints followed. In January 1995, Sanders and the CPC introduced "The Progressive Promise: Fairness in Congress," an eleven-point counterproposal launched as part of CPC's Cancel the Contract campaign to challenge Newt Gingrich's Contract with America. It was a mirror of DSA's 1992 "Progressive Agenda."[33] The 1995 Progressive Promise compares closely, as well, to DSA's 1997 "Pledge for Economic Justice" and the launch of DSA's Campaign for Economic Justice (CEJ).[34]

Clearly, the CPC was the vehicle to carry out the DSA agenda. Success for the DSA's CEJ plan and other plans relied upon close coordination with the CPC.[35] Additionally, DSA had long-range plans for how the CEJ could be used. Ultimately it was seen as key to progressive election victories.[36]

The CPC *Progressive Agenda* failed to pass in 1995 and appeared again in 1998. The CPC continued to call for a 50 percent cut in defense spending and massive expenditures for government public works and fully funded single-payer health care.[37]

The CPC tried a new tactic in February 1999, a propaganda strategy to label conservatives as extremists.[38] Interestingly, the same thing happened again on March 28, 2011, when New York senator Charles E. Schumer, while on a conference call with reporters, instructed fellow Democrats to label Republicans and House Speaker John Boehner, and the spending cuts he wants, as extreme. "I always use the word extreme," Schumer said. "That is what the caucus instructed me to use this week."[39]

This is a decades-old Democratic tactic. California representative Henry Waxman has called Republicans extremists since 1991. The intensity of the attacks changed, however, in 1994 after the Republicans took control of the Congress. The most egregious offender, perhaps, was House Minority Whip David Bonior, who became the self-appointed tormenter of Speaker Newt Gingrich. Bonior filed more than seventy ethics violations against Gingrich.[40]

The CPC resorted to similar tactics in February 2001 when the George W. Bush administration was working to enact tax cuts. Although their tactics failed, progressive Democrats conceived outrageous arguments. The late senator Paul Wellstone (Minn.) said tax cuts would "hurt the children," while Representative Charles Rangel (D-N.Y.) said the Bush tax cuts would undermine national defense.

The CPC/CBC also came up with the now-famous deceptive *trigger* tactic, which surfaced a number of times during legislative debate in 2009–2010.[41] The devil, as they say, is in the details. The Democratic trigger—based on tax cuts—put no limits on spending. The formula allowed Congress to spend potential tax cuts before the trigger was activated.[42]

CPC's Sanders also came up with an ingenious income redistribution plan called *The American People's Dividend*. This would literally give three hundred dollars per year to every man, woman, and child in the United States, excluding any concern for whether they had earned any income or paid any taxes. The bill passed in the House with forty-eight cosponsors, mostly CPC members. The *tax cut* came with an estimated cost of $900 billion, about a third of an alleged $2.7 trillion surplus.

It was observed that, under Sanders's plan, the IRS would be converted to a welfare agency. It was an obvious wealth redistribution plan. Similar to the Democrats' 2009 so-called economic stimulus bill, it would do nothing to stimulate savings and investment. However, the CPC socialists were not in the majority in 1999. The plan to essentially remake America had to wait for a while.[43]

Progressive Democrats of America

The DSA was not interested in creating a third political party that would espouse socialist ideals. The group specifically aimed to infiltrate the Democratic Party. It even rejected the socialist New Party, which had occurred when the *fusion* of a third party and the majority party was allowed, such as the DSA-cosponsored Working Families Party in New York.

The New Party was a controversial 1990s political party that sought to elect members to public office with the aim of moving the Democratic Party far leftward to ultimately form a new political party with a socialist agenda. We cited evidence in our previous book, *The Manchurian President*, documenting that Obama was a member of the New Party and that many New Party leaders are currently associated with Obama. Print copies of the *New Party News*, the party's official newspaper, show Obama posing with New Party leaders, listing him as a New Party member, and publishing quotes from him as a member. Additionally, in an e-mail interview with Aaron Klein, Marxist activist Carl Davidson, a founder of the New Party, admitted Obama's participation with his party. The New Party endorsed Obama's 1995 run for the Illinois Senate.[44]

The DSA coalition building was evidenced in a July 1999 article that sounds familiar to coalitions formed by the Obama campaign for the 2008 presidential election. The CPC was operating out of the office of its chairman, Representative DeFazio. Assisted by the aides of his cochairs, from the Institute for Policy Studies, and friends from the unions, the caucus set up an e-mail network and a website. DeFazio was meeting with labor, environmental, and activist groups to put together a *shadow institute* similar to the Democratic Leadership Council's Progressive Policy Institute.[45]

The DSA and CPC are also closely allied with Progressive Democrats of America. PDA was launched in Roxbury, Massachusetts, at the end of the 2004 Democratic National Convention by delegates and activists from the campaigns of former Vermont governor Howard Dean and Ohio representative Dennis Kucinich. PDA worked to carve out a space for progressives in the Democratic Party.[46] The PDA is another organization created by progressives to counterbalance the Democratic Leadership Council, which was formed in 1985 following Ronald Reagan's sweeping win. Viewed as politically too far to the right and much too conservative, the DLC shut down in early February 2011.[47]

By July 2004 the PDA had already won the support of notorious leftist radical Tom Hayden and actors Ed Asner and Mimi Kennedy. Kennedy, a founding PDA board member, said the Democratic Party "needs our help to regain its soul. If this is to be the party of peace, of universal, single payer healthcare, of fair trade, then it needs people to speak out on those issues."[48]

Support groups met in July 2004 at Roxbury Community College for a parallel progressive convention that featured talks and panel discussions. Scheduled speakers included Dean, Kucinich, and Dr. James Zogby, founder and president of the Arab American Institute. Representative John Conyers (D-Mich.) also attended.[49] Attendees discussed an "Inside/ Outside" strategy whereby PDA would run candidates and lobby members inside the Democratic Party. At the same time, PDA would promote its goals of ending the war in Iraq and of ensuring universal health care, "fair and clean" elections, economic justice, and "environmental stability."[50]

Dean's influence on PDA is unmistakable. PDA hoped to follow Dean's *50 State Strategy* by setting up a chapter in all 435 congressional districts and organize in every voting precinct. By May 2007, PDA had only established 120 district chapters. PDA also carries on its fund-raising based on the 2004 Dean campaign fund-raising model, basically relying on sustainer donations averaging twenty-two dollars per month.

Bill Goold, CPC's former executive director, referred to PDA as CPC's *field operation*, providing members of Congress with grassroots support for their initiatives. This includes such things as Representative Conyers's investigation of the alleged 2004 Ohio voting fraud associated with Representative Jim McGovern's bill to end funding for the war in Iraq.[51]

The current PDA advisory board includes Hayden; Medea Benjamin and Jodie Evans, cofounders of CODEPINK; Steve Cobble, an associate fellow at the Institute for Policy Studies; and CPC members Representatives Conyers, Lee, Waters, and McGovern, as well as Donna Edwards (D-Md.), Raul Grijalva (D-Ariz.), and Lynn C. Woolsey (D-Calif.).[52]

Soros Group Advises Congressional Progressive Caucus

Another organization that forms a nexus with the DSA, CPC, and PDA is the George Soros–funded Institute for Policy Studies. In a

December 2008 *USA Today* article, Saul Landau, IPS senior fellow and vice chair, as well as professor emeritus at California State University, Pomona, admitted that the Institute for Policy Studies advises the Congressional Progressive Caucus.[53]

IPS was formed in 1963 by two veterans of the John F. Kennedy administration—Richard J. Barnet, formerly with the State Department, and Marcus G. Raskin, a former congressional staffer. IPS proclaims on its website that it has five decades of history intertwined with social movements and "turning ideas into action for peace, justice, and the environment."[54]

Raskin came out in his 1979 book, *The Politics of National Security*, for an "International Economic Order built on principles of equity, sovereign equality . . . and narrowing the gap between rich and poor nations."[55] Murray N. Rothbard responded to Raskin's socialist ideology in a July 1982 article in *Inquiry*: "it is scarcely noninterventionist to advocate a massive stripping of property from Americans and Western Europeans in order to subsidize Third World governments, a process that would kill the Western goose and lay virtually no golden eggs for Third World peoples, who will not find prosperity until they make it for themselves."

Saul Landau has been a friend of Fidel Castro for many years. Landau, who first visited Cuba in 1960 and 1961, announced in a September 2010 article he was again visiting Cuba.[56]

Another prominent IPS fellow, Arthur I. Waskow, served at one time as a legislative assistant to Representative Robert Kastenmeier, according to a 1977 Heritage Foundation study.[57] Kastenmeier's socialist ties were visible in December 1972 when he attended the Democratic midterm convention and was identified as a board member of the Democratic Socialist Organizing Committee's Democratic Agenda.[58]

Barnet, Raskin, and Waskow had all been active in radical movements dating to the anti–Vietnam War movement of the 1960s. During the same period, Barnet and Raskin both reportedly had contact with representatives of Hanoi's communist government in Paris.[59]

The IPS, described as an idea factory for the left, carried out projects in support of leftist dictators and revolutionary nationalists and various social movements. The current IPS board of trustees includes, among others: former New Left radical, IPS cofounder, and Campaign for America's Future/Institute for America's Future founder Robert L. Borosage; DSOC/DSAer Barbara Ehrenreich; Barack Obama bundler Jodie Evans; Landau; and the *Nation* editor and publisher Katrina vanden Heuvel.[60]

Obama and the DSA Are Old Pals

The stars aligned perfectly for the 2006 midterm elections for progressives when Democrats assumed control of both houses of Congress. This created a cadre-in-waiting for the second key event, the 2008 presidential election of Barack Obama. The cadre, more than half of the Democratic members of Congress, shared the new president's desire to *fundamentally transform* America. Many in this group of enablers inside the Obama government have long been allied overtly or covertly with the Democratic Socialists of America. Known collectively as the *Progressives in Congress*, they stood at the ready to introduce and enact wide-ranging transformative and controlling legislation.

Top DSA members have been closely linked to President Barack Obama for years. In early 1996 Obama spoke at a forum organized by DSA at the University of Chicago called "Employment and Survival in Urban America."[61] Dr. Quentin D. Young has long been active in Chicago socialist circles and is a longtime DSA activist. In 1992 he was the recipient of the Chicago DSA's Debs Award. He was once accused of membership in a communist group.[62]

Considered the father of the U.S. single-payer universal health care movement, Young advised Obama on health care in the 1990s. Young noted in a 2008 article in the official Communist Party USA magazine that while Obama had previously expressed support for single-payer, he later waffled when asked about his position.

Timuel D. Black Jr., a DSA member activist, was one of Obama's first Chicago advisers. In 1991 Obama turned to Black when he wanted to become a community organizer. Black mediated political disputes on behalf of Obama in the 1990s. He was reportedly involved in Obama's campaign committee during his successful 2004 state senatorial race.[63] A retired City Colleges of Chicago social science professor, Black and his wife, Zenobia, who are friends and neighbors of Obama (Black lives in Kenwood, Obama in nearby Hyde Park), were special guests of Senator Dick Durbin at Obama's inauguration.[64]

The late Rabbi Arnold Jacob Wolf, a longtime DSA member and antiwar and progressive activist, was a member of Rabbis for Obama. Wolf was a vocal supporter of Obama's presidential campaign; he was also one of his earliest supporters when Obama first ran for the Illinois Senate. Wolf held fund-raisers in his home for Obama, including a function in 1995 that was aimed at introducing Obama to the Hyde Park activist community.[65]

Eliseo Medina, international executive vice president of the Service Employees International Union, is a DSA honorary chair. During the 2008 presidential campaign, Medina served on Obama's National Latino Advisory Council.[66]

In its summer 2008 issue of *Democratic Left*, the DSA offered cautious support for Barack Obama's presidential campaign: "While recognizing the critical limitations of the Obama candidacy and the American political system, DSA believes that the possible election of Senator Obama to the presidency in November represents a potential opening for social and labor movements to generate the critical political momentum necessary to implement a progressive political agenda."[67]

Pelosi and the Socialist Agenda

Although her name is among those found on a 2001 list of Congressional Progressive Caucus members on the Democratic Socialists of

America website, no mention has been made about California representative Nancy Pelosi's political proximity to the DSA and the Socialist International.[68]

Representative Pelosi is a longtime member of the CPC executive committee. When she was elected in 2002 as House Minority Leader, this firmly established her link between the House Democratic Caucus and the Socialist International.[69]

This fact was reported in the *Washington Times* for all inside and outside the Beltway to read. It was only one of a number of times from 1998 forward that a warning was sounded that the Socialist International, by way of its connection with Democratic Socialists of America and, in turn, the Congressional Progressive Caucus, had a presence inside the American government.

Not mentioned is the fact that, until her party was defeated for control of the House of Representatives in the November 2, 2010, midterm elections—and until relieved of her duties on January 3, 2011, when the 112th Congress was sworn in—Speaker Pelosi was only two steps away from assuming the presidency. She was superseded in ascendancy to the Oval Office only by the vice president, Joe Biden.

Also not mentioned is the fact that neither the Speaker of the House, nor members of Congress, nor the president is required to undergo a background investigation before getting a security clearance. In a May 2009 *Accuracy in Media* article, Cliff Kincaid observes, "This loophole in the law enables the president and members of Congress to automatically qualify for security clearances, even if they have controversial backgrounds and associations, by virtue of the fact that they get elected to high office in Washington, D.C."[70]

Pelosi served as minority leader in the House 2003–2007. She became Speaker-elect in November 2006 and was sworn in on January 4, 2007, as the first female Speaker of the House.[71] After taking office as Speaker, Pelosi deftly managed three groups of Democrats: The CPC, expected to push the rhetoric of class warfare and work with a network of left-wing advocacy groups to coordinate attacks on corporations and *the rich;* the conservative Blue Dogs, who were expected to emphasize fiscal restraint and a balanced budget; and the New Democrat Coalition, which was expected to support trade deals and tax credits for business innovation, as well as government support for research and development.[72]

The November 2006 election had provided progressives with the opportunity to enact their vision of ending the war in Iraq. (It also provided them with the opportunity for unapologetic Bush-bashing, a strategy that not only helped Democrats to win that election, but also was unwisely continued through the 2010 midterm election.)

But it is always the CPC, of which Pelosi was a longtime member, pushing for the progressive agenda. Pelosi is said to be more progressive than Barack Obama. Her political skills were observed in November 2006 when the Pelosi-led sixty-three-member CPC formed the Progressive Majority Project. They pooled money, time, and staff to support progressive candidates running in twelve House races. Eight of the CPC-backed candidates won. Additionally, two CPC members, Representatives Sherrod Brown (D-Ohio) and Bernie Sanders, moved to the Senate.[73]

Missing from this sanitized version are details from a November 3, 2006, report by the Progressive Democrats of America, which had been instrumental in CPC's success. PDA had also been working with the CPC to support thirteen progressive candidates. A reported forty-one CPC members contributed $160,000 and many made personal appearances on the candidates' behalf.[74]

The Progressive Promise

On the heels of the 2006 election, a group of more than forty progressive activist groups met to devise a common strategy to support congressional Democrats. At the same time, the coalition planned to pressure both Speaker Pelosi and incoming Senate Majority Leader Harry Reid (D-Nev.) to move further to the left.[75]

Coalition members will be recognized in subsequent chapters as a cadre of usual suspects: progressive organizations, unions, and activist groups of many types. Chief among the members are USAction, Campaign for America's Future, ACORN, AFL-CIO, MoveOn.org, and the Sierra Club.[76]

Many of the same groups had come together in June 2005 to lend support to the CPC and its *Progressive Promise* agenda. In a November 2008 press release, the CPC wrote that it would be drawing on the agenda again in the soon-to-be-launched Barack Obama government.[77]

The CPC's new one-page document, titled "The Progressive Promise: Fairness for All," includes its four core principles. Key phrases would identify this as a socialist agenda even if it did not belong to the CPC. More specific items listed tell the rest of the tale: universal health care; moving toward a living wage, a longtime progressive goal; combating corporate media consolidation; environmental justice; cap and trade; and regulations for sustainable growth.[78]

More recently, on April 15, 2011, the House voted on two alternative budget continuing resolutions that originated within the CPC.

The Responsible Path Towards Investing in America plan was presented by CBC chair, Representative Emanuel Cleaver. It failed to pass in a 303–103 vote.[79]

The Progressive Caucus's alternative plan, the People's Budget—which would have raised taxes and gutted military spending—was introduced by CPC co-chair Representative Raul Grijalva. It also failed to pass. It is telling that in a 77–347 vote zero Republicans voted for it.[80]

Now that we have a clearer picture of how a socialist-founded caucus infiltrated Congress, we will next take a look at specific individuals and groups who are currently facilitating the DSA agenda from within our government, enacting legislation meant to fundamentally transform our country.

chapter two

RADICALS IN
THE HALLS

Imagine this. The Democratic chairman of the powerful House Judiciary Committee meeting with a U.S.-based, Marxist-oriented socialist organization to discuss how the group can cooperate to strengthen President Obama and advance their "one-world" plans. What about a congressional caucus openly funded by philanthropist George Soros while it coordinates clearly socialist legislative plans with full-fledged members of the radical network? How about congressmen who go on solidarity missions to socialize with communist leaders? Or lawmakers deeply associated with a stealth jihad group founded by the Muslim Brotherhood, which seeks to spread Islam around the world?

These activities form just the tip of the socialist iceberg for a large swath of lawmakers who take no great pains to hide their behavior or true ideology since they know the news media are largely uninterested in doing any real reporting on their radicalism—or may even approve of it.

It is time to take a closer look at some of the radicals in the halls, the socialist-oriented congressmen and congresswomen who make up one of the most important divisions of an army of laborers both inside and outside the government seeking to change the tenor of our country. These lawmakers routinely introduce legislation that has its origins in the crafty handiwork of the radical network, which aims to nudge our nation closer to a socialist entity.

The 111th Congress, which retired in January 2011, included 316 Democratic Party members. The Democratic Caucus's role is to assist members in achieving consensus and providing the tools necessary to push for and implement their goals. Amid speculation that the 2010 midterm elections had damaged the power of Democrats in the House, the eighty-two-member-strong CPC lost only a few members. The CPC actually increased its plurality within the Democratic Caucus. In comparison, the conservative Blue Dog Coalition lost half its members. In other words, in the election widely seen as repudiating Obama's progressive agenda, the most liberal bloc in Congress actually gained power.

The CPC made similar gains both before and after the 2006 midterm elections. In August 2006 the CPC gained nine new members and engaged in recruiting more. Additionally, the 2006 CPC held ranking minority positions on half of the House's twenty standing committees.[1]

Following the 2010 midterms, the Democratic Caucus voted in a 150 to 43 secret ballot to retain Representative Nancy Pelosi as their leader, the same position she held prior to the 2006 elections. Pelosi's only challenger was Representative Heath Shuler (D-N.C.), leader of the fiscally conservative Blue Dog Coalition, who argued that Pelosi needed to "go after presiding over the loss of the chamber."[2]

The existing Democratic leadership continues with Representative Steny Hoyer (Md.) as Democratic Whip and Representative Jim Clyburn (S.C.) serving in a newly created third-ranking position as assistant leader. Both were voted in by acclamation rather than by a recorded vote. Clyburn's position resulted from a compromise after he threatened to challenge Hoyer for the whip job.

Although the CPC is the largest caucus within the Democratic Caucus, several members of Congress belong to one or more of three smaller caucuses. Each is ethnologically and culturally based and leans mostly leftward. It is instructive to briefly take a closer look at these other caucuses.

The Congressional Black Caucus was founded in 1969 in the House of Representatives as the Democratic Select Committee and renamed in 1971. Representative Emanuel Cleaver (D-Mo.) was elected CBC chairman for the 112th Congress. Outgoing chairman Barbara Lee serves as vice chair. The CBC gained its third African-American Republican member in its forty-year history when Florida representative Allen West joined in the 112th Congress.[3]

The Congressional Hispanic Caucus, with twenty-four members, was founded in 1976. Representative Charles A. Gonzalez (D-Texas) was elected as CHC chairman. Representatives Rubén Hinojosa (D-Texas) will serve as first vice chair, Ben Ray Lujan (D-N.M.) as second vice chair, and Dennis Cardoza (D-Calif.) as whip.[4]

The Congressional Asian Pacific American Caucus, with fourteen members, was founded in 1994. The CAPAC executive board consists of Representatives Michael M. Honda (D-Calif.), chairman; Eni Faleomavaega (American Samoa), vice chairman; and Madeleine Z. Bordallo (D-Guam), secretary.[5]

Although part of the Democratic Caucus, two more caucuses would not generally be considered left-leaning. The Blue Dog Coalition, which leans fiscally toward center, lost half of its numbers in the 2010 midterms. Only twenty-four members remain in the 112th Congress. The other caucus is the New Democrat Coalition, founded in 1997, which is moderate and progrowth. Like the Blue Dogs, the numbers of the New Dems were seriously reduced.

A new postelection Populist Caucus was initiated early in December 2008 by the caucus's chairman, Representative Bruce Braley (D-Iowa). The Populist Caucus plank has been described as typically progressive, but with more of a rural farmer and union feel than the CPC, and with a heavily New Left and multi-ethnic approach. A revival of the caucus by the same name dating from the William Jennings Bryan era, the Populist Caucus comes most recently from the farm crisis of the early 1980s.

Braley sees his Populist Caucus from a different perspective. He wrote on his official House website that this is the "only caucus in

Congress devoted solely to addressing middle class economic issues."
The Populist Caucus's initial purpose was to influence legislation from
within the Democratic Caucus. Braley said his caucus would "give voice
to the populist anger created by the plummeting economy and opaque
bank bailout" of fall 2008. Membership in the Populist Caucus overlaps with that of the CPC, although there are several non-CPC members, including Braley.[6] In many ways, the Populist Caucus's agenda
resembles that of CPC's four-point "Progressive Promise."

The newest House caucus is the Sustainable Energy and Environment Coalition, founded in January 2009 by co-chairs Representatives
Jay Inslee (D-Wash.) and Steve Israel (D-N.Y.). SEEC's initiation is
concurrent with both Barack Obama's inauguration and his administration's stated goals of a *green economy*. It clearly leans toward the CPC
agenda. SEEC lists its accomplishments as playing a role in the passage
of the clean energy investments in the American Recovery and Reinvestment Act of 2009 and the American Clean Energy and Security
Act of 2009, as well as legislation intended to lower U.S. greenhouse
gas emissions and usher in a "new, prosperous American clean energy
economy."

The Progressive Congress

The Congressional Progressive Caucus has a number of auxiliary organizations.

The Progressive Congress was founded by CPC leadership and
staff, as well as key leaders of the progressive movement. The Progressive Congress includes two other arms: the Progressive Congress
Action Fund, an advocacy organization to engage the American public with progressives in Congress, and a research and education arm,
ProgressiveCongress.org.[7]

Each branch organization has a separate board of directors. Pro-
gressiveCongress.org board members include three *volunteer* members

of the CPC leadership: Representatives Keith Ellison (D-Minn.), Raul Grijalva, and Barbara Lee.

Remaining ProgressiveCongress.org board members include many of the usual suspects from the progressive movement: Robert L. Borosage, John Cavanagh (Institute for Policy Studies), Amy Isaacs (formerly with Americans for Democratic Action), Jeff Krehely (director of the LGBT Research and Communications Project at the Center for American Progress), Larry Mishel (executive director, Economic Policy Institute), and Katrina vanden Heuvel (the *Nation*).

Robert L. Borosage, whose name appears throughout this book, is president and codirector of Campaign for America's Future and its sister organization, Institute for America's Future. Among other affiliations, he is a former executive director and trustee of the Institute for Policy Studies, founder and chairman of Progressive Majority (PAC), founder of Campaign for New Priorities, and an associate editor of the Nation.

Borosage also serves on the board of directors of the Progressive Congress Action Fund. Here the similarity between the boards ends. In addition to a number of leading progressive bloggers, the board includes Celinda Lake, principal at Lake Research Partners; James Rucker, executive director and cofounder with Van Jones of Color of Change, formerly with MoveOn.org, and cofounder of the George Soros–funded Secretary of State Project; and Jim Dean, chair of Democracy for America and brother of Howard Dean.

The executive director for both organizations is Darcy Burner, who since 2009 has also run another CPC auxiliary organization, the Congressional Progressive Caucus PAC. The CPC PAC was established as a vehicle to support CPC members or candidates who believe, if elected, they will become CPC members. Burner ran unsuccessfully in 2006 and 2008 for U.S. representative in Washington state's 8th Congressional District. In April 2009 she replaced Bill Goold as executive director of the American Progressive Caucus Policy Foundation, which was set up in 2005. The APCPF is the ProgressiveCongress.org fore-

Committee, which looked into "possible links between nongovernmental organizations and terrorist financing networks." In June 2007,
ISNA was named as an unindicted co-conspirator in a U.S. Department of Justice legal case brought against Holy Land Foundation for
Relief and Development officials regarding the funding of millions of
dollars to the Hamas terrorist group.[14] The official court documents
named the ISNA as "entities who are and/or were members of the US
Muslim Brotherhood."[15]

In his October 2003 statement before the Senate Judiciary Committee's Subcommittee on Terrorism, Technology and Homeland Security, J. Michael Waller, the Annenberg Professor of International
Communication at the Institute of World Politics, testified: "The Islamic Society of North America is an influential front for the promotion of the Wahhabi political, ideological and theological infrastructure in the United States and Canada. . . . ISNA seeks to marginalize
leaders of the Muslim faith who do not support its ideological goals."[16]

This statement alone makes it clear that Representative Ellison—or
anyone else not in sync with ISNA's ideals—would not be associated
with the organization.

Waller expands on ISNA's range of influence, stating that the
group sponsors propaganda and doctrinal material for an estimated
1,500 to 2,500 mosques in North America in pursuit of its objective—dominating Islam in North America. ISNA's North American
Islamic Trust maintains physical control of a large percentage of U.S.
mosques. It not only owns and finances them, but also is subsidizing
construction of more mosques in the United States. ISNA also refers
Muslim clerics to the Federal Bureau of Prisons. Waller does not say,
but it is implied that this latter activity is for more than just providing
comfort to inmates.

Ellison has been openly proactive with ISNA and the Muslim
community for several years. In September 2007 he was the keynote
speaker at the Community Service Recognition Luncheon at ISNA's
annual convention, held in Chicago.[17] Ellison has also been advising

ISNA members how best to work inside American politics. He expounded on the topic at three more recent ISNA conventions.

At ISNA's annual convention held at the end of August 2008 in Columbus, Ohio, Representatives Ellison and André Carson (D-Ind.), the second Muslim elected to Congress, participated in a panel discussion titled "Mobilizing the Muslim Political Machine: Effective Strategies for Community-Based Political Advocacy." The panel focused on community organizing tools for and participation in the electoral process, as well as how to create political action committees.[18]

Ellison continued this theme ahead of the 2008 elections while speaking at a September 2008 "Rock the Muslim Vote" town hall. Emphasis is added below.[19]

> Getting engaged, getting involved, running for office, helping people run for office, organizing your community—these are the things that are going to make a change come about. *We have to build the kind of country that we want with the help of some people who are like-minded.* We cannot leave that responsibility to anybody else.

Ellison and Carson again participated at the July 2009 ISNA convention. The topic of discussion this time was "Effective Strategies for Muslim Political Advocacy."[20] Muslim Americans were involved in every level in the 2008 elections; "for the first time having a full-fledged seat at the table despite the negative rhetoric after 9/11." The panelists, including Ellison and Carson, shared ideas on how the Muslim community can effectively engage in political advocacy.

(At another ISNA session, panelists addressed the state of education in the Muslim community. The writer says this holds the key to the future of Islam and Muslims in America; it is necessary to "ensure that all American Muslims are provided the tools through education to be strong Muslims as well as productive and informed citizens." This ties in with our chapters on education, where we examine Obama administration funding for Muslim education efforts.)

At the most recent ISNA annual conference, held in July 2010 in Chicago, Ellison and ISNA's president, Ingrid Mattson, spoke on the topic "Understand the Need for Halal Accreditation."[21]

Halal, a Quranic word that means lawful or permitted, is at the center of Muslim life. One source states a Muslim "must earn income from Halal sources, be involved only in Halal transactions and consume Halal food and drink."[22] Ellison and Carson—and unnamed national leaders—spoke on the topic of "Muslim American Political Engagement: Next Steps & A Practical 'How-To.'"[23]

One of those national leaders perhaps was Rashad Hussain, Obama's envoy to the Organization of the Islamic Conference, which comprises fifty-seven Muslim nations. Hussain read a letter from Obama welcoming ISNA to the president's hometown of Chicago. "Outside of the hajj," or pilgrimage to Mecca, Obama said, "this convention constitutes one of the most diverse gatherings of Muslim people in the world, and that is a testament to the diversity and dynamism of Muslim communities right here in America."[24]

It is impossible not to believe at this point that Ellison is not only fully aware of his actions—or their possible consequences—but also a willing participant in the promotion of Islam in the United States. Another blatant example comes from December 2008, when Ellison was the first member of Congress to make a hajj to the Muslim holy city of Mecca in Saudi Arabia along with three million other Muslims.[25] The Muslim American Society of Minnesota paid $13,500 for Ellison's hajj. The MAS has been accused of serving as a U.S. branch of the Muslim Brotherhood while being established by Brotherhood activists.[26] While the MAS has denied it is a Brotherhood branch, its leaders have recognized that the group was founded by Muslim Brotherhood members. In 2004, then secretary general of MAS Shaker Elsayed stated to the *Chicago Tribune* that "Ikhwan [Brotherhood] members founded MAS." Elsayed even went so far as to admit that about 45 percent of MAS's active members belong to the Brotherhood, while claiming his group expanded beyond Brotherhood ideology.[27]

The final word comes from a May 1991 article on the strategic goal of the Muslim Brotherhood in North America. Mohamed Akram (aka Mohamed Adlouni) writes for the Shura Council of the Muslim Brotherhood that the brotherhood "must understand that their work in America is a kind of grand Jihad in eliminating and destroying the Western civilization from within and 'sabotaging' its miserable house by their hands and the hands of the believers so that it is eliminated and God's religion is made victorious over all other religions."[28]

Congress's Friends of Palestine

In 1988, CBC members Representatives Maxine Waters and John Conyers, Jr., and fellow DSA member Ron Dellums were founding advisory board members of the Middle East Children's Alliance.[29] MECA was founded in Berkeley, California, by Barbara Lubin and Howard Levine following Lubin's first trip to Palestine and Israel at the beginning of the so-called first intifada. Lubin allegedly "witnessed the grave injustice, poverty and violence of the Israeli occupation paid for with US tax dollars."[30] Lubin is allied with the Workers World Party, a Marxist-Leninist sect aligned with communist North Korea.[31] She is also a staunch supporter of Representative Barbara Lee and has appeared at numerous rallies to show her support. Lee holds the distinction of being the only member of the House to vote against the United States going to war against al-Qaeda following the events of 9/11.[32]

In June 2010, Representatives Lee and Ellison wrote a letter to Obama stating they were "deeply troubled by the military action aboard the [Palestinian] aid flotilla en route to Gaza . . . resulting in the death of nine civilians, including one American." Additionally, they requested that Obama "support a thorough investigation" and that he "call for a lifting of the blockade on Gaza."[33] The year before, in January 2009, only two CBC members, Representatives Waters and Gwen

Moore (D-Wis.), voted against H. Res. 34, which recognized Israel's right to defend itself against attacks.[34]

Representative Conyers is not a friend to Israel, either. In 2001, for example, he called for an investigation into Israel's "use of U.S.-made weapons against the Palestinians as a violation of the Arms Export Control Act, which limits the use of American-made weapons to legitimate defensive purposes." Conyers also cosponsored the Humanitarian Exports Leading to Peace Act (or HELP Act, HR 742), which "would allow U.S. farmers, humanitarian aid organizations and businesses to send food, medical supplies and agricultural goods directly to Iraq."[35]

MECA is a member organization on the steering committee for the WWP front group, International A.N.S.W.E.R.; the United For Peace and Justice antiwar coalition cochaired by the pro-Castro socialist Leslie Kagan; the anti-Israel coalition, the U.S. Campaign to End the Israeli Occupation; the Palestine Solidarity Movement, the student arm of the International Solidarity Movement, which supports the dissolution of Israel; the Justice in Palestine Coalition; and the Middle East Policy Advisory Committee.[36]

MECA is also the fiscal sponsor for the International Solidarity Movement, the radical, anti-Israel organization that "recruits westerners to travel to Israel to obstruct Israeli security operations" and "justifies Palestinian terrorism against Israeli civilians."[37]

Another founding advisory board member was the late Columbia University professor Edward Said. While a student at Columbia, Barack Obama took at least one class with Said, a well-known apologist for terrorism. Said is credited with changing the field of Middle East studies toward an anti-Western and anti-Israel bias.[38]

Ali Abunimah, who runs the Electronic Intifada website, reported he met Barack Obama at many pro-Palestinian events in Chicago. In May 1998 Abunimah took a photo of Barack and Michelle Obama seated at a table at an Arab community dinner with anti-Israeli professor Edward Said and his wife, Mariam. According to one news report,

Said called for "a nonviolent campaign 'against settlements, against Israeli apartheid.'"[39]

Red Friends

Many Congressional Progressive Caucus members count communist regimes and their leaders among their friends and causes. Cuba, for example, has held a particular fascination for the radical left for decades. Beginning in 1969, U.S. college students participated in the Venceremos Brigade, going to Cuba to show solidarity with Cuban workers by working side by side with them in the sugarcane fields, thus challenging U.S. policies toward the country.[40]

The country has been on the U.S. secretary of state's State Sponsors of Terrorism list since March 1, 1982. Only three other countries share the list with Cuba: Iran, since January 19, 1984; Sudan, since August 12, 1993; and Syria, since December 29, 1979.[41]

In the August 2010 State Department Country Report on State Sponsors of Terrorism, the section on Cuba paints the country as one wanting it both ways. While the Cuban government and "official media publicly condemn acts of terrorism by al-Qa'ida and its 'affiliates,' it is at the same time critical of how the U.S. combats international terrorism. While Cuba does not support 'armed struggle in Latin America and other parts of the world,' at the same time the Cuban government of Cuba provides a 'physical safe haven and ideological support' to members of three known terrorist organizations designated by the U.S. as Foreign Terrorist Organizations: the Revolutionary Armed Forces of Colombia (FARC), the National Liberation Army of Colombia (ELN), and Spain's Basque Homeland and Freedom Organization (ETA). Although Cuba does not appear to have lent financial support to these groups, the Report states that Cuba does provide them with 'living, logistical, and medical support.'"[42]

Cuba is a totalitarian communist state headed by General Raul

Castro, who replaced his brother Fidel Castro as chief of state, president of Cuba, and commander in chief of the armed forces on February 24, 2008. The current Cuban government, which assumed power by force on January 1, 1959, is ruled by the one permitted political party, the Cuban Communist Party.[43]

Nevertheless, radicals in Congress want to reverse U.S. policy with Cuba through two pieces of legislation still pending at the time of writing that would undo a U.S. policy that has remained unchanged for several decades. H.R. 4645, the Travel Restriction Reform and Export Enhancement Act, "seen as the best chance in years to put an end to the prohibition on U.S. citizens traveling to Cuba," was scheduled for review, or *markup*, by the House Foreign Relations Committee in September 2010. The House leadership decided at the last minute to postpone the bill until after the November midterm elections.[44]

The House bill was introduced in February 2010 by Collin Peterson (D-Minn.) with seventy-three cosponsors, the majority of which are Democrats and members of the CPC, CBC, and CHC. S.428, Freedom to Travel to Cuba Act, was also introduced in February 2010 in the Senate by Byron Dorgan (D-N.D.) with thirty-nine cosponsors, all Democrats.[45]

Not all members of Congress agree with the legislations' intent. The bills are opposed by five Cuban American politicians, three Republicans, and two Democrats, who state they are "deeply troubled that such changes would result in economic benefits to the Cuban regime and would significantly undermine U.S. foreign policy and security objectives."[46]

On the other hand, Representative Barbara Lee wants the Obama government to "loosen restrictions on travel by academic, religious, and cultural groups" imposed during the George W. Bush administration. Lee wants a return to "the 'people-to-people policies'" of the Clinton administration.[47]

Representative Lee is no stranger to Cuba. In a review of Lee's April 2009 book, *Renegade for Peace and Justice*, Mark Hemingway commented at National Review Online on Lee's numerous visits to Cuba and her fondness for Castro: "Lee's fondness for the brutal dictator probably stems from the fact that he helped her good friend, Black Panther leader Huey Newton. Accused of killing an underage prostitute, assault, and tax evasion, Newton went to Cuba for three years in the mid–1970s rather than stand trial."[48]

Lee's fondness for Cuba was exhibited in April 2009, when she led a congressional delegation to Havana and had a four-and-a-half-hour meeting with Raul Castro. Lee told reporters, "All of us are convinced that President Castro would like normal relations and would see normalization, ending the embargo, as beneficial to both countries."[49] The meeting by Lee and five other members of the CBC reportedly took place in secret, without the customary presence of U.S. State Department officials or reporters.

The Cuban Communist Party daily *Granma* reported that the lawmakers accompanying Lee were CBC members Emanuel Cleaver (D-Mo.), Marcia L. Fudge (D-Ohio), Laura Richardson (D-Calif.), Bobby L. Rush (D-Ill.), and Melvin L. Watt (D-Calif.).[50]

After the meeting with Castro and other Cuban government officials, Lee and CBC members praised Castro as "warm and hospitable during their visit." Reflecting on her moments with Castro, Lee said, "It was quite a moment to behold."[51] The Communist Party USA's *People's World* reported on the CBC trip. Representative Richardson said Castro "talked, like Obama, about 'turning the page' in U.S.-Cuba relations. She added that 'He looked right into my eyes and he said, How can we help? How can we help President Obama?'"[52]

Lee is the former chief of staff to Ronald Dellums. Lee, who won Dellums's seat when he retired in 1998, is a radical activist in her own right, with a long record of support for revolutionary causes.[53] Lee has been described as an ideological clone to Dellums. While serving as a member of the California State Assembly, in July 1992, Lee not only attended a conference of the Committees of Correspondence, a CPUSA spin-off, but also was elected to serve on its ruling body, the National

Coordinating Council, a fact Lee has both denied and finally admitted.[54] Lee and longtime avowed communist Angela Davis served together in the CoC. Additionally, while serving on Dellums's congressional staff, Lee attended a so-called "conference of 'non-aligned nations'" in Havana.[55]

Lee's connections to the CPUSA are long-standing. The online newsletter *People's Weekly World* reported in December 2006 that at its banquet in Oakland, honored guests "included anti-nuclear-weapons leader Jackie Cabasso, the Blue Diamond Workers Organizing Committee, and two Sacramento-based immigrant rights coalitions," all of which received certificates from Representative Lee and Friends of *People's Weekly World/Nuestro Mundo*.[56]

Another CPC member with ties to Cuba is Representative Jim McDermott (D-Wash.), described as closely allied with the DSA. In November 1999 the DSA was partly responsible for a flood of protesters expected to attend the World Trade Organization conference in Seattle. The DSA's pitch—that the WTO was "a disaster for democracy, workers and environment"—was echoed by national leaders such as the late Minnesota Democratic senator Paul Wellstone, Green Party activist Ralph Nader, late Teamster leader Jimmy Hoffa, and political consultant Patrick Buchanan.[57]

McDermott joined the Seattle City Council in extending a special invitation to Fidel Castro to visit Seattle during the WTO meeting. McDermott assured Castro he would be "respectfully, graciously and warmly" received. McDermott added: "I am also hopeful that your visit will give us an opportunity to educate the American public about Cuba."

A delegation of six CBC members had visited Cuba in February 1999 to evaluate the U.S.-imposed embargo ahead of an upcoming debate in Congress. The delegation included Representatives Sheila Jackson-Lee (D-Texas), Barbara Lee, Maxine Waters, Earl Hilliard (D-Ala.), the late Julia Carson (D-Ind.), and Gregory Meeks (D-N.Y.), as well as unnamed "legislative aides, community leaders, business people and journalists."[58] *La Habana* reported the visit was organized by U.S.-based Pastors for Peace, headed by Reverend Lucius Walker, who accompanied the delegation.[59] The group held a question-and-answer session with Cuban foreign minister Roberto Robaina and met with Fidel Castro for six hours.

This was followed in September 2000 with a Cuban Parliament delegation participating as special invited guests in the CBC's annual convention in Washington, D.C. Six Cuban deputies, including Cuban Parliament president Ricardo Alarcon, were granted travel permission by the U.S. State Department to participate in the CBC meeting.[60] Radio Habana Cuba reported the thirty-eight-member CBC took, "for the first time, a strong position against the blockade and in favor of radical changes in Washington's aggressive policy towards Cuba."

Nearly a year later, in July 2001, Representative Jackson-Lee joined the CPC majority voting in favor of an amendment halting enforcement of travel restrictions on U.S. citizens to Cuba—but only after President Bush certified Cuba had released all political prisoners, and extradited all individuals sought by the U.S. on charges of air piracy, drug trafficking, and murder.[61]

The most recent development regarding U.S.-Cuban relations came January 14, 2011, when President Obama eased restrictions to allow students "seeking academic credit and churches traveling for religious purposes" to travel to Cuba. Also, any American may "send as much as $500 every three months to Cuban citizens who are not part of the Castro administration and are not members of the Communist Party." Finally, more U.S. airports will be allowed to offer charter service to Cuba. Currently, only airports in Miami, Los Angeles, and New York City are allowed to offer authorized charters to Cuba.[62] These changes are in addition to ones Obama made the previous year, similar to travel policies under President Clinton. Critics, such as House Foreign Affairs Committee chair Representative Ileana Ros-Lehtinen (R-Fla.), said, "These changes undermine U.S. foreign policy and security objectives and will bring economic benefits to the Cuban regime."[63]

Similar views are shared by Representative Jackson-Lee on Venezuela.

In February 2007, although she met with members of Hugo Chavez's government and executives from the major oil companies, she did not meet with Chavez himself. In a telephone interview, Jackson-Lee said: "We've made a serious mistake in not engaging with President Chavez. . . . I came to break the tension, to warm up a chilled relationship." In a press conference following her trip, Lee said: "Venezuela has many friends in this new Congress." Jackson-Lee also urged the United States to lift its ban on selling F-16 fighter jets and spare parts to Chavez.[64] Her trip to Venezuela was paid for by the House Foreign Affairs Committee, on which she served. Representative Jackson-Lee's trip was the first by a member of Congress since the Democrats took control of both the House and Senate in the 2006 elections and after Chavez won reelection.

Her positions on Cuba and Venezuela are only the beginning of her progressive voting record and often outlandish behavior.

Unaccountably, in July 2009, Jackson-Lee turned up at the Michael Jackson funeral service and, with cameras rolling, expounded for a full eight minutes. As conservative pundit Michelle Malkin describes it, Representative Jackson-Lee took the opportunity to "pimp" a congressional resolution honoring Michael Jackson. She went so far as to hold up a big, framed copy of the resolution to "the King" and the crowd cheered. Inexplicably, Jackson-Lee also defended the dead singer against allegations of child molestation, saying members of Congress "understand the Constitution" . . . "we understand laws" . . . and "people are innocent until proven otherwise."[65]

A year later, in July 2010, Jackson-Lee, who once asked where she could find photos of the American flag Neil Armstrong planted on Mars—not the moon—insisted "we have two Vietnams, side by side, North and South, exchanging and working. We may not agree with all that North Vietnam is doing, but they are living in peace."[66]

The same month she did what has been characterized as the dumbest thing she has ever done—while talking to the NAACP, nonetheless. She attempted to link the Tea Party to the Ku Klux Klan. Jackson-Lee said: "All those who wore sheets a long time ago have now lifted them off and started wearing [applause], uh, clothing, uh, with a name, say, I am part of the tea party. Don't you be fooled."[67]

Ahead of the November 2010 midterm election, Jackson-Lee called on U.S. Attorney General Eric Holder to monitor the Tea Party to see whether they intimidated black and Hispanic voters in her district at the polls.[68]

More recently, in January 2011, Jackson-Lee, who holds a law degree from the University of Virginia Law School, stunningly said on the House floor that repealing the national health care law is unconstitutional. The passage of Republicans' H.R. 2 violates both the Fifth Amendment's right to due process and the Fourteenth Amendment's equal protection clause, she said:[69]

> The Fifth Amendment speaks specifically to denying someone his or her life and liberty without due process. That is what H.R. 2 does and I rise in opposition to it. And I rise in opposition because it is important that we preserve lives and we recognize that 40 million–plus are uninsured. . . .
>
> Can you tell me what's more unconstitutional than taking away from the people of America their Fifth Amendment rights, their Fourteenth Amendment rights, and the right to equal protection under the law?

After naming people who would be helped by Obamacare (and their diseases, for example, "a schizophrenic, a dialysis patient, and somebody whose mother cannot otherwise get dental care"), Jackson-Lee said: "I know they would question why we are taking away their rights."

Jackson-Lee declared Obamacare *was* constitutional, and had been vetted. Repealing the legislation, therefore, would take away the constitutional rights, she said, "of those who ask the question: 'Must I die? Must my child die, because I am now disallowed from getting insurance?'"

John Conyers, Jr.: Socialist

Another founding member of both the CPC and the CBC, and a friend to communists, is Representative John Conyers, Jr. Like Representative Barbara Lee, Conyers has called for reducing or ending U.S. economic sanctions and travel restrictions against Cuba.[70]

Conyers has a record of supporting Marxist movements, including the Soviet-front groups the World Peace Council and the United States Peace Council. In 1979, when he addressed the first national council of the USPC, Conyers said, "It's people like you who should be members of Congress" and "from you I can see the future of America." Conyers has also backed dictators such as Cuba's Fidel Castro and Venezuela's Hugo Chavez.[71]

In his 1987 book, *Covert Cadre: Inside the Institute for Policy Studies*, S. Steven Powell describes how the DSA-affiliated, pro-communist Institute for Policy Studies "sought to directly influence Washington policymakers by establishing its Washington School, whose seminars served to 'provide a forum at which the leftist community can meet on a regular basis' and 'influence government policy making.'"[72]

Conyers, whom Powell describes as one of IPS's strongest supporters in Congress, participated in IPS's Washington School programs, including teaching a class titled "American Politics: Who Gets What, When and How," with IPS fellow Michael Parenti. Also, in February 1983, Conyers moderated an IPS budget conference on Capitol Hill. Earlier, in a June 1, 1979, *New York Times* op-ed piece coauthored with IPS cofounder Marcus Raskin, Conyers claimed "government's responsibility is to revitalize the nation's economy through creative forms of public ownership," in other words, socialism.[73]

Another report comes from May 1974, during the opening convention rally of the Communist Party–front National Alliance Against Racism and Political Repression, where Conyers addressed an audience of five hundred at the Trinity Methodist Church in Detroit. Present were two NAARPR cofounders, Communist Party luminary Charlene Mitchell and admitted communist Angela Davis.[74] Conyers reportedly praised NAARPR for "'building a great coalition' as he had long proposed." The late labor columnist Victor Riesel berated Conyers for taking the time to fly into Detroit on May 10 to join a member of the Communist Party USA Central Committee and others to "whip up a typical radical rally." Two years later, in 1976, it was Conyers who was lauded in a message by Angela Davis, then NAARPR cochair, for being reliable, "at a time when corruption, immorality, and undisguised disdain for the people of the country are the distinguishing marks of those in government."[75]

Conyers is not bothered in the least when it comes to associating with, defending, or serving with fellow radicals and involvement with radical causes. He served on the national executive board of the Communist Party–front National Lawyers Guild. He was the only member of Congress in January 2003 to address and "lend his prestige" to an antiwar rally in Washington, D.C., that was organized by the International A.N.S.W.E.R. coalition.[76]

Former representative and former CPC/CBC member Cynthia McKinney and other prominent political figures, including Reverends Jesse Jackson and Al Sharpton, also spoke at the A.N.S.W.E.R. rally. Although he did not attend, Reverend Lucius Walker read an antiwar statement from CPC/CBC member Representative Rangel.[77]

Speaking on March 1, 2003, at the Rally to Reclaim Our Rights held in Chicago, Conyers reportedly blasted President George W. Bush for his "drive to war" with Iraq. Conyers also warned Attorney General John Ashcroft that his plans would "further weaken the Bill of Rights and other constitutional guarantees." The event was sponsored by the Chicago Committee to Defend the Bill of Rights (CCDBR), an organization founded in the 1950s allegedly to oppose constitutional infringements committed by the House Un-American Activities Committee. CCDBR's personnel were described as "virtually, all proven members or sympathizers of the Communist Party USA."[78]

Greetings and messages of support at the March 2003 gathering came from Representative Rush, Illinois state senator Barack Obama, and Alderman Dorothy Tillman, as well as from religious and community leaders.[79]

Conyers, former representative Bonior, and Canadian MP Joe Comartin of the New Democratic Party participated in plenary sessions at the November 2003 DSA National Convention held in Detroit. Another notable speaker was DSA honorary chair Cornel West.[80]

A petition—"The Call to Drive Out the Bush Regime"—initiated in July 2006 by the revolutionary direct action group, The World Can't Wait, bears the signatures of Representatives Conyers, Rush, and Maxine Waters and former representatives McKinney and Major Owens, all CPC/CBC members. This was followed on October 5 with Conyers speaking to a rally of The World Can't Wait in Detroit.[81]

In February 2010, Conyers and Sander Levin, brother of Senator Carl Levin, spoke to approximately 325 people at the Detroit Call for Action anti–Tea Party rally held in the United Food and Commercial Workers union hall in Madison Heights, Michigan. The event was sponsored by a wide spectrum of groups, from DSA on the left to Organizing for America, a political arm of the Democratic National Committee and the Obama administration, described as being on the "right."[82]

Conyers was the guest of honor at a reception held on October 2, 2010, by DSA and Young Democratic Socialists (YDS) members and friends at the Hunan Dynasty restaurant prior to the One Nation Working Together rally held in Washington, D.C. Conyers delivered a ten-minute speech before leaving to fly back to Detroit.[83] The One Nation event was endorsed by several unions—SEIU, United Auto Workers, AFL-CIO—and dozens of socialist, Marxist, and communist groups, including DSA.[84] Conyers was caught on tape calling for a one-world government. He asked for DSA to "organize against the war in Afghanistan and in support of Obama's policies."[85] "I see that us making him more cooperative with our plans is going to strengthen him and not weaken him," Conyers says to applause from the DSA activists. "Whose job do you think it is to get him straightened out and get him on the right track? Ours! Ours!" Conyers exclaimed to more applause. At the end of the video, Conyers states, "I look forward to our next meeting. I want us to schedule it."

Promoting the concept of a one-world government, Conyers told those assembled, "We know that when unions, political ideology, clergy, labor, civil rights come together and just people who are progressive enough to see in this one-world concept that we're all in this together, it makes certain things pretty easy to understand where we are coming from." The congressman called for picketing and protests to "make it clear to him [Obama] that there probably isn't anybody above the tenth grade who doesn't know that you cannot win a war in Afghanistan."

Nothing speaks more loudly of a congressman's (or congresswoman's) character than to be accused of ethical violations. Sadly, two CPC/CBC members have not only nurtured relationships with the Cuban regime, but also have gotten themselves into hot water with their fellow members.

Waters in Hot Water

On July 30, 2010, CPC/CBC member Representative Maxine Waters chose an ethics trial rather than accept charges on ethics violations, or even resignation from the House, to avoid further embarrassment to herself, Congress, or the Obama administration.[86]

As one journalist pointed out, this set up the unprecedented situation of back-to-back ethics trials for two members of Congress. Waters put herself in the same situation as fellow CPC/CBC member Representative Rangel, who was also facing charges from the House Ethics Subcommittee. Rangel was forced in March 2010 to give up the chairmanship of the powerful House Ways and Means Committee after being admonished by the House Standards of Official Conduct

Committee. Rangel was found guilty on November 16, 2010, on eleven of twelve ethics violations (two of the original thirteen were combined) based on evidence involving his "alleged use of a rent-stabilized apartment in Manhattan as a campaign office." Rangel had also violated his use of congressional stationery to enlist support for a City College of New York center named after him. Further allegations state Rangel's financial disclosure statements failed to "accurately reflect" his ownership of a vacation villa in the Dominican Republic.[87]

The Ethics Committee recommended censure, with the House required to approve the punishment. This fell far short of the severity of an expulsion. Once censured, a lawmaker is compelled to stand before Congress and listen while the House Speaker reads him the proverbial riot act.[88] Censure it was. On December 2, 2010, the House voted 333–79 to censure Rangel even though he had pled earlier in the day for a lesser penalty, a reprimand.[89]

Regarding Waters's ethics problem, at the end of November 2010, her hearing was postponed by the House Ethics Committee after new documents surfaced ten days prior to the originally scheduled date of November 29. This freed the committee from the specter of back-to-back proceedings against senior African-American lawmakers. The case was sent back to a four-member subcommittee that had investigated Waters and brought the charges.[90] The lengthy House investigation of Representative Waters that began in 2009 was derailed by infighting within the politically charged Ethics Committee over errors in building a case against her, according to congressional sources.[91]

The investigation came apart when both the Ethics Committee and staff members argued over whether documents should be subpoenaed and when the trial should be scheduled and for how long. Waters's refusal to agree to a negotiated settlement—to concede that she had made mistakes and to accept an admonishment, that is—caught everyone by surprise. The staff had to renew its search for evidence. The case inevitably moved forward to the Republican-controlled House in the 112th Congress.

Representative Waters's office was charged with "improperly" working in September 2008 to "press for aid to prevent the failure of Boston-based OneUnited Bank, which eventually stayed afloat with the help of money from the Troubled Assets Relief Program."[92]

Waters's husband, Sidney Williams, was not only a member of the OneUnited board, but also owned stock in the bank. OneUnited's stock value declined by half between June and August 2008, falling from $350,000 to $175,000. According to the Ethics Committee, had it not been for the influx of TARP funds, the stock would have been worthless.[93]

On August 13, 2010, Waters blasted both the Ethics Committee and the D.C. media, denying she had "violated anything." Her performance, however, failed to win anyone over.

This is only one in a long line of ethics problems for Representative Waters, who has been cited by Citizens for Responsibility and Ethics in Washington for "various ethical breaches that, like this one, involve her apparently using her station to benefit members of her family." Her children have worked as paid political consultants for politicians and causes backed by Waters. Both her husband and son benefited from a lease, reportedly worth hundreds of thousands of dollars, to run a golf course, from a politician who had benefited from Waters's backing. Her husband made money from consulting for a bond underwriting firm with connections to political backing by Waters. Her daughter also made thousands of dollars that "looks a lot like selling spots on her mother's sample ballots"—ranging from $250 to $171,000 each.[94]

This is the same Maxine Waters who, on May 22, 2008, when speaking on the floor of the House, nearly exposed herself as a socialist. Her words, while she was busy "grilling" oil executives on the House floor, say it all: "And guess what this liberal would be all about? This liberal would be all about socializing—er, uh [stutter, stammer] . . . would be about . . . basically . . . taking over, and the government running all of your companies."[95]

As much as she tried hard to not to say *nationalizing*, Waters's brain betrayed her and so the equally damaging *socializing* came out. One journalist remarked: "The oil industry reps were probably thinking, *'we've seen this movie before, it's called Hugo Chavez in Venezuela.'*"

Unfortunately, reading the excerpt from the transcript fails to provide the full impact of Waters's slip of the tongue. Waters's socialist tendencies are on full display and leave room for questions. She has praised Marxist dictator Fidel Castro, and called for an end to the U.S. trade embargo against the Castro government.

She has made international headlines for her frequent trips to Cuba to visit her convicted cop-assassin friend, Joanne Chesimard. Also known by her Black Liberation Army name, Assata Shakur, Chesimard murdered a New Jersey state trooper in May 1973 and was sentenced to life plus 26 to 33 years in prison following her jury conviction in 1977. However, in 1979, she escaped from jail with the help of *visitors* and fled to Cuba, where she was located in 1984 by the FBI—which has a $1 million bounty for information leading to her apprehension.[96]

On September 14, 1998, the House of Representatives, of which Waters was a member, passed a unanimous resolution requesting Castro extradite Chesimard to the United States. The name on the resolution, however, was Joanne Chesimard and not Assata Shakur. Waters realized Chesimard's identity after the vote and wrote a letter to Fidel Castro saying she, as chair of the Congressional Black Caucus, and other CBC members had "mistakenly voted" in favor of the resolution. She claimed the Republicans had "slipped" the bill into an accelerated calendar in order to look "tough on Cuba" for the November elections. Waters claims the Republicans had deliberately used Chesimard's given name in order to deceive. Had she known Chesimard's identity, she writes, she would have voted otherwise.[97]

Waters's letter to Castro was quoted on Radio Habana Cuba during an October 2, 1998, newscast. Waters told Castro he had a right to "grant political asylum for individuals from the U.S. fleeing political persecution."[98]

Rangel: Another Castro Admirer

Representative Charles Rangel is another admirer of both Cuba and Marxist dictator Fidel Castro. The CBC's point person on Cuba and Haiti and a frequent critic of the U.S. embargo against Cuba, Rangel introduced along with Representative Barbara Lee the Free Trade with Cuba Act in January 2007. The act would remove the trade embargo and repeal other economic, travel, and communications restrictions.[99]

This marked more than a decade of Rangel's working to repeal the Cuban Democracy Act of 1992, which was said to have ended U.S. assistance to the Castro government. In October 1995, when Castro toured Harlem, Rangel reportedly greeted him with a bear hug at an event in a local church, where, it was reported, the congressman joined in a prolonged standing ovation for the visiting dictator.

In 2002 Rangel took a privately funded trip to Cuba with his wife and son. There he met with Fidel Castro. After the watchdog group Center for Public Integrity began making inquiries in 2006, Rangel amended his travel disclosure form for the April 2002 trip. He reimbursed both the Cuban government and New York grocery store magnate John Catsimatidis, who had paid $1,922 in expenses incurred by the congressman's son, Steven.

The trip had allegedly been designed to raise awareness about endangered birds. In reality, it served as a cover for Rangel to meet with Cuban dictator Fidel Castro, allegedly to "discuss the uneasy U.S.-Cuba relationship."

Former Speaker Pelosi has more than a few communist and Marxist friends. One case in point is her relationship with left-wing Colombian senator Piedad Cordoba. Cordoba has worked closely with Pelosi on Colombian and Venezuelan issues. In the past, Cordoba has been linked to terrorists and Marxists and said to have been a key player in helping to undermine her own government.[100] Cordoba is a close friend of Venezuelan Marxist dictator Hugo Chavez and a frequent visitor to Chavez's presidential palace. Cordoba had become such a fixture in

Venezuela it was snidely said she's more at home in the corridors of the palace of President Hugo Chavez than she is in Colombia.[101]

She is also trusted by FARC, the Revolutionary Armed Forces of Colombia, and often photographed with them. Established in 1964 as the military wing of the Colombian Communist Party, FARC is Colombia's oldest, largest, most capable, and best-equipped Marxist insurgency.[102] In September 2009, Cordoba mediated the release of hostages in FARC captivity. However, in April 2010 it was reported that Colombia's inspector general had compiled a list of charges against Cordoba alleging she had collaborated with the FARC outside the parameters of her role as a hostage release negotiator. In June 2009, prior to her involvement negotiating for the release of the hostages, Cordoba said that the investigation was a "politically motivated 'farce.'"[103]

This all came after July 2008, when Pelosi illicitly stepped outside her role as Speaker and attempted to institute her own foreign policy by communicating with Cordoba. Pelosi exceeded the boundaries of a member of Congress, assuming a position traditionally ascribed to the State Department, and told Cordoba that she and Representative Jim McGovern (D-Mass.) were ready to help arrange swaps of captured terrorists for hostages held by FARC terrorists.[104]

John Lewis, "Marxist Revolutionary" Race Baiter

Georgia representative John Lewis is a member of both the CPC and the CBC. Although a distinguished civil rights leader of the 1960s, Lewis has been characterized as a Marxist revolutionary.[105] Lewis has a history or radical associations. A founder of the Student Nonviolent Coordinating Committee, one of the 1960s' most active black revolutionary groups, Lewis served from 1963 to 1966 as its chairman.[106]

By 1967, the Department of Defense stated the SNCC was no longer a civil rights group. According to the DoD report, SNCC had become a "racist organization with black supremacy ideals and an expressed hatred for whites." The same report on SNCC activities includes information on Lewis's travels and activities while he represented the organization. In his defense, it should be noted that Lewis had stepped down due to a conflict with SNCC's increased militancy.[107]

As of June 29, 1963, Lewis is identified as a member of the Communist Party USA in New York City and an "ardent supporter" of SNCC. Information from mid-December 1963 reveals Lewis as a member of the Fair Play for Cuba Committee, which called for an end to the U.S. economic boycott of Cuba. In 1964 Lewis and Donald Harris made a trip to Africa on what Lewis characterized as "a 'Mission of Learning' and to improve relations between the liberation movement of Africa and the civil rights struggle in this country."[108]

Lewis condemned U.S. policy in Vietnam in a January 1966 statement urging Americans to "use any method to avoid the draft."[109]

An example of SNCC activities under Lewis's leadership is a February 12, 1966, Lincoln Day for Peace and Freedom rally. While claiming it was to honor Abraham Lincoln's birthday, the event was staged by the Freedom Now Committee to demand "complete freedom for American Negro citizens now and immediate withdrawal of all U.S. troops from Vietnam."[110]

Nationwide events had been planned months earlier at an SNCC meeting in D.C. In Los Angeles, the demonstration began with speeches by Lewis and others in front of the Seventy-Seventh Street police precinct, followed by a walk to the Greater Tabernacle Baptist Church. It was reported that fewer than one hundred actual demonstrators participated and about 25 percent of them were either members of W.E.B. DuBois Clubs of America, the youth arms of the Communist Party USA, or Communist Party members, or former party members.[111] The W.E.B. DuBois Clubs were founded in June 1964 in California out of the radical upsurge on college campuses. DuBois, the storied champion of African-American liberation, joined the CPUSA in 1961.[112]

Lewis served as a vice chairman for the Southern Region of the National Committee Against Repressive Legislation, or NCARL, founded in 1960. He was also a member of the Southern Region of the NCARL's predecessor, the National Committee to Abolish HUAC (or the House Un-American Activities Committee), established in 1969.[113] NCARL was affirmed before HUAC as being a communist-front organization. An NCARL member organization in Chicago was called the Chicago Committee to Defend the Bill of Rights, which operated as NCARL's Midwest regional office.[114]

Now known as the Defending Dissent Foundation, NCARL continues as a sister organization to CCDBR. In October 2006, honorary cochairpersons for an event honoring Frank Wilkinson, CCDBR's founder and admitted communist, included four Obama political mentors: Representative Danny K. Davis (D-Ill.); Timuel Black, who is also a CCDBR director; the Honorable Abner Mikva; and Dr. Quentin D. Young.[115]

Lewis was one of several movement leaders in 1966 who defended the W.E.B. DuBois Clubs against the requirement by the attorney general of the United States to register with the federal government as a communist-front organization under the terms of the Internal Security Act of 1950.[116] Joining Lewis was David Dellinger, organizer of the 1967 protest march on the Pentagon. The following year, Dellinger was one of the radicals charged with conspiring to incite riots at the 1968 Democratic National Convention and was tried as one of the Chicago Seven with Black Panther leader Bobby Seale, Tom Hayden, Rennie Davis, Abbie Hoffman, and Jerry Rubin of the Youth International Party. Hayden, while in the South in the early 1960s, served as Students for a Democratic Society's first field secretary.[117]

More recently, during the 111th Congress, Representative Lewis served on the House Ways and Means Committee and chaired the Subcommittee on Oversight. Lewis has said his "voting record reflects his belief in religion and nonviolence, not leftwing ideology." However, Lewis's voting record shows that he "votes exactly the same way as do his openly socialist fellow members of the Progressive Caucus."[118]

Lewis also involved himself in the explosive events of March 20, 2010, the day members of the House of Representatives voted on the Obamacare bill. It was alleged that Tea Party demonstrators outside the U.S. Capitol had screamed "nigger" at a procession of CPC/CBC members that included Lewis.[119] *Politico* reported some less inflammatory, yet contradictory information. House Majority Whip Clyburn said he had heard from Representative Lewis that a Tea Party protester had "called him the N-word." A Lewis staffer "confirmed that Lewis had been the target of that slur."[120] However, Martin Knight writes in March 2010 on RedState.com, "Let's be blunt; John Lewis is a liar. He claimed the *N-word* was 'shouted' over and over at him and yet no camera among the many there has caught anything of the sort. In other words, there is no doubt about it; he was and is lying straight through his teeth."[121]

Representative Lewis has a long history of such behavior. In October 2008, for example, he compared Republican presidential candidate Senator John McCain (R-Ariz.) to the late segregationist Alabama governor George Wallace. Lewis accused McCain of fostering "an atmosphere of hate" and "hostility" like the one in 1963 that led to white supremacists bombing a church in Birmingham, Alabama. Lewis said the "negative tone" of the John McCain–Sarah Palin campaign was "sowing the seeds of hatred and division."[122] A few days later, Lewis walked back from his comments: "A careful review of my earlier statement would reveal that I did not compare Sen. John McCain or Gov. Sarah Palin to George Wallace. It was not my intention or desire to do so."

However, Lewis was not done. On October 11, 2008, Lewis went after McCain in harsh terms. "George Wallace never threw a bomb," Lewis noted. "He never fired a gun, but he created the climate and the conditions that encouraged vicious attacks against innocent Americans who were simply trying to exercise their constitutional rights. Because of this atmosphere of hate, four little girls were killed on Sunday morning when a church was bombed in Birmingham, Alabama."[123]

The Future: Circumventing Congress

Even though Democrats, particularly in the House, were seriously trounced in the 2010 midterm elections, the determination of progressives to continue pushing a socialist agenda is alive and well.

Unions immediately announced they were gearing up for major fights on Capitol Hill. They said they are also preparing for a potential clash with the White House if President Barack Obama compromises with Republicans.[124]

Additionally, a new *blueprint* immediately surfaced that lays out options President Obama has available to him to circumvent the Republican-controlled House. In these endeavors, most assuredly the CPC and unions will be able and willing supporters. Although it is possible the blueprint was a back-pocket Plan B all along, Obama's 2008 transition team chief, now Center for American Progress president and CEO John Podesta, possibly had such a plan in mind before the 2008 votes were counted. What is certain is that Podesta was preparing for any and all possibilities prior to Obama taking up residence in the Oval Office.

The *Washington Post* reported on November 9, 2008, that a transition team of "four dozen advisers, working for months in virtual solitude, set out to identify regulatory and policy changes Obama could implement soon after his inauguration." The team had reportedly compiled a "list of about 200 Bush administration actions and executive orders that could be swiftly undone to reverse White House policies on climate change, stem cell research, reproductive rights and other issues."[125]

Also on November 9, 2008, Podesta told *Fox News Sunday* host Chris Wallace, "We're looking at—again, in virtually every agency to see where we can move forward, whether that's on energy transformation, on improving health care, on stem cell research."[126] Podesta was specifically referring to methods by which Obama could circumvent Congress using his executive powers. Podesta continued to say the president could use his executive authority in the place of congressional action, if necessary.[127] Two years later, Podesta made the rounds again, this time proposing that Barack Obama should employ all the executive authority available to him and circumvent Congress by any and all means possible to push his radical agenda.

A Center for American Progress report, *The Power of the President*, released in November 2010 and compiled by CAP executive vice president Sarah Rosen Wartell, enumerates the types of executive authority available to Obama: executive orders, rulemaking, agency management, convening and creating public-private partnerships, commanding the armed forces, and diplomacy.[128]

Podesta writes in the rollout announcement to the report:

> The U.S. Constitution and the laws of our nation grant the president significant authority to make and implement policy. These authorities can be used to ensure positive progress on many of the key issues facing the country. . . .
>
> The upshot: Congressional gridlock does not mean the federal government stands still. This administration has a similar opportunity to use available executive authorities while also working with Congress where possible. At the Center for American Progress, we look forward to our nation continuing to make progress.

Podesta's CAP announcement also includes a list of ideas. Although he admits this is "by no means an exhaustive list of the important policy objectives President Obama can pursue over the next two years," Podesta says it "illustrates the range of important executive branch work beyond proposing and negotiating legislation."

Wartell's fifty-four-page CAP report details loopholes and workarounds Obama can use to accomplish progressive goals while bypassing the democratic process and Congress.[129]

What remains to be seen is whether President Obama pursues some, none, or any of these suggestions.

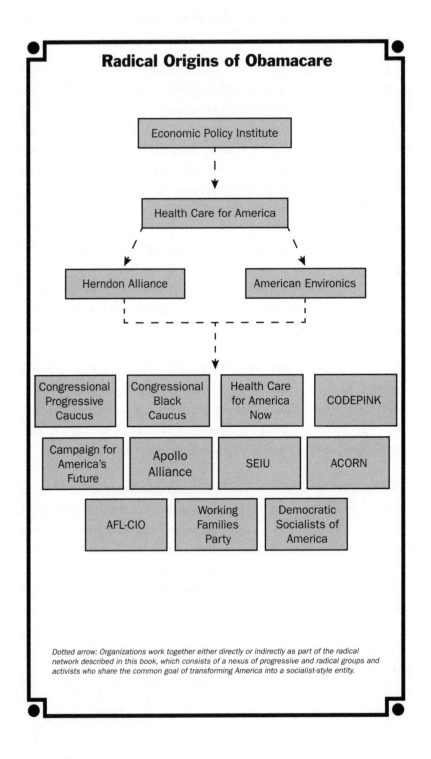

Radical Origins of Obamacare

Economic Policy Institute

Health Care for America

Herndon Alliance

American Environics

Congressional Progressive Caucus

Congressional Black Caucus

Health Care for America Now

CODEPINK

Campaign for America's Future

Apollo Alliance

SEIU

ACORN

AFL-CIO

Working Families Party

Democratic Socialists of America

Dotted arrow: Organizations work together either directly or indirectly as part of the radical network described in this book, which consists of a nexus of progressive and radical groups and activists who share the common goal of transforming America into a socialist-style entity.

chapter three

THE RADICAL ORIGINS
OF OBAMACARE

We have to pass the bill so that you can find out what is in it," then House Speaker Nancy Pelosi said on March 9, 2010.[1] This stunningly condescending remark typifies the kind of arrogant attitude taken by those in the legislative and executive branches, and their news media backers, who were responsible for pushing President Obama's historic health care bill on the American public. Amazingly, Pelosi did not try to disguise the possibility there could be stealthy, Trojan horse–like aspects to the complex, 2,700-plus-page Senate bill; she simply lectured us on how the legislation will be good for the country, and indicated we are not allowed to know any specifics.

What must be understood is that Obamacare, the most comprehensive health care initiative in our nation's history, did not write itself overnight, or even during the course of the first two years of Obama's presidency. You are about to learn how the legislation, deliberately masked by moderate, populist rhetoric, was carefully crafted and perfected over the course of decades and is a direct product of laborious work by the same radical network whose evolution we outlined in the previous chapters and whose influence and extremism we will expose throughout this work, a coalition of radical groups and activists with socialist designs who seek to "reform" our health care industries, which account for a significant portion of the U.S. capitalist enterprise. Few have endeavored to identify those responsible for the legislation. Here we lay bare the radical origins of Obamacare and the socialist-stained groups that helped repackage and rebrand the legislation as being good for all Americans.

Democratic Socialists of America Agenda

Less than two weeks after Pelosi's patronizing comment, on March 21, the House agreed to Senate amendments to the health care bill and passed the legislation by a margin of 219 to 212. The Patient Protection and Affordable Care Act became Public Law No. 111–148 when it was signed on March 23 by President Obama.[2]

The Democrats' health care bill was introduced on September 17, 2009, in the House by its sponsor, Representative Charles Rangel, chairman of the House Ways and Means Committee. Rangel and the majority of the bill's forty cosponsors are members of the CPC.

This should come as no surprise. At the end of April 2009 the leaders of the four major progressive groups in the 111th Congress—the Progressive, Black, Hispanic, and Asian Pacific American caucuses—sent a joint letter to President Obama and the Democratic leadership of the House and Senate stressing that "our support for enacting legislation this year to guarantee affordable health care for all firmly hinges on the inclusion of a robust public health insurance plan like Medicare."[3]

Representative Rangel has run on both the Democratic and the DSA-supported, ACORN-affiliated, New York fusion ticket of the Working Families Party. He has long pushed for expansion of government-funded health care. In 1999 and again in 2001, Rangel adopted the CPC's position paper that called for making "health care a right, not a privilege" and the expansion of other health care entitlement programs.[4]

The CPC has pushed since at least 1992 for "Cradle to Grave Health Care" that includes a "state-based single payer health care plan."

Likewise, many progressive and socialist groups, including the Communist Party USA, share the common quest.

Radicals Galore

Obamacare had its origins in an initiative openly associated with a slew of radicals. One is a group funded by philanthropist George Soros, a second, a terrorist-supporting, communist-hailing extremist; and, to top it off, another is a socialist activist who is the father of the U.S. single-payer movement.

Jacob S. Hacker, an expert on the politics of U.S. health and social policy, is now a professor of political science at Yale University. He is also a fellow at the New America Foundation in Washington, D.C., and a former junior fellow of the Harvard Society of Fellows.[5] Hacker is a third-generation progressive academic whose lineage was influenced by a famed socialist. For the past twenty years, his father, Andrew Hacker, has been professor emeritus in the political science department at the City University of New York's Queens College.[6] The titles of Andrew Hacker's books, of which there are seven, reveal the scope of his teachings: *Money: Who Has How Much and Why* (1999), *Two Nations: Black and White, Separate, Hostile, Unequal* (2003), *The Rich and Everyone Else* (2006).[7]

Andrew's father, Louis Morton Hacker, taught at Columbia from 1935 to 1967.[8] Louis, a professor of economics at Columbia, was a leading proponent of adult education, and from 1949 to 1958 was the first dean of the university's School of General Studies. He was the author of a dozen books on American history. He was also an active member of the American Civil Liberties Union. In the 1960s, he defended several Columbia faculty members who "refused to cooperate with Congressional committees investigating left-wing activities."[9]

Important to note is that Louis Hacker's mentor at Columbia was Charles A. Beard, a Fabian socialist and a leader in the Progressive school of American history. According to Beard, Hacker's early work was concerned with "social justice" and "class analysis." In the early 1930s, Hacker emerged as a leading Marxist scholar. He later denounced Marxism and embraced conservatism.[10]

Jacob Hacker not only advised both Hillary Clinton and Barack Obama on health care during the presidential campaign, but is also the author of *Health Care for America*, the centerpiece of the George Soros–funded Economic Policy Institute's Agenda for Shared Prosperity. Hacker's proposal for guaranteed, affordable health care for all Americans is the foundation for Barack Obama's health care plan.[11]

In other words, whoever the winning presidential candidate turned out to be, the underlying plan for the Democrat health care legislation would be the Hacker/Economic Policy Institute *Health Care for America* plan. It bears noting that the radical network perfected this legislation over the course of many years and was ready to introduce health care legislation regardless of who won the 2008 Democratic primaries. In other words, Obama was simply the vehicle through which this particular health care legislation would be presented.

In his *Health Care for America* briefing paper, posted on January 11, 2007, on the Economic Policy Institute website, Hacker states, "the most promising route forward is to build on the most popular elements of the present structure—Medicare and employment-based health insurance for well-compensated workers—through a series of large-scale changes that are straightforward, politically doable, self-reinforcing, and guaranteed to produce expanded health security."[12] Hacker adds that his proposal, *Ideas for Reform*, is built on an earlier plan he developed in 2003 for the Covering America project.

Hacker's 2003 plan proposes to create a public health insurance program called "Medicare Plus," which would offer coverage to all legal residents not otherwise covered by Medicare or employer-sponsored insurance. Employers would be required to either provide a minimum level of coverage to their workers or pay a payroll tax. Workers and their dependents in firms that choose to pay the tax would be covered under the Medicare Plus program. Individuals covered under the Medicare Plus program would also pay an income-related premium. Medicaid coverage would be folded into the Medicare Plus program.[13]

Legislation based on Hacker's "Medicare Plus" plan—H.R.676, Expanded and Improved Medicare for All Act (United States National Healthcare Insurance Act)—was introduced on February 2, 2005, in the House by Representative John Conyers. Presenting cosponsors were Dennis Kucinich, Jim McDermott, and Donna Christensen (D-U.S. Virgin Islands), all CPC members, as were the majority of additional cosponsors.[14]

A brief summary of *Medicare for All* posted on the Healthcare-NOW website says the act establishes a unique, publicly financed, privately delivered American health care system that uses and expands upon the existing Medicare program for all U.S. residents—not just citizens—and U.S. territories. Hacker claimed the plan would be of the highest quality while being cost-effective for all. Neither employment status, income, nor health care status would matter, while all those who are uninsured or underinsured would be guaranteed access—by law.[15]

Healthcare-NOW, not to be confused with the organization Health Care for America Now, was established in 2004 for one purpose—to lobby on behalf of single-payer health care. Healthcare-NOW's broad base includes socialist, labor, church, and community organizations and, most notably, Physicians for a National Health Program.[16]

A single-payer health system is defined as universal health care "provided for an entire population through a single insurance pool out of which costs are met." All medical fees are collected via single-payer health insurance, which then "pays for all services through a single government (or government-related) source."[17]

Healthcare-NOW cochairs include Dr. Quentin D. Young, PNHP's national coordinator, and Leo Gerard, president of the United Steelworkers union. Medea Benjamin is a member of the board of directors. The board also includes numerous PNHP members.[18]

It must immediately be asked why Benjamin, who leads CODE-

PINK, a group that concerns itself with radical antiwar activities, would serve on the board of a health care initiative. Benjamin lived for some time in Fidel Castro's communist Cuba, and has described her experiences there as feeling "like I died and went to heaven." She is known to have led solidarity missions against U.S. military adventures in the Middle East and sponsored flotillas attempting to aid Hamas in the Gaza Strip. She initiated a campaign to donate six hundred thousand dollars to the families of insurgents killed fighting American troops in Iraq.[19]

The inclusion of Benjamin, alongside other radicals, clearly illustrates the manner in which the radical left has hijacked such diverse causes as environmental activism, race relations, the economy, and health care as part of their multipronged assault of nudging a socialist agenda that has little to do with the actual subject at hand.

The Campaign for America's Future pushed Hacker's plan as well. CAF referred to it as *Health Care for All*. Roger Hickey wrote on February 17, 2008, that, while the Economic Policy Institute was publishing the plan, CAF had already been at work discussing it with both Democrat and Republican presidential candidates. Hickey also acknowledged that Hacker's plan was the health care template for both Obama and Clinton. Additionally, Hickey wrote that unions and community action groups were rallying behind it.[20]

There is also another, interesting side to this story. In 1997, while he was a graduate student at Yale, Jacob Hacker caused a stir by describing the failure of President Clinton's health care efforts. His criticism was broadened in his 1999 book, *The Road to Nowhere*.[21]

But this was not the end. Hacker next attacked the Democratic *overambition* on health policy, which led to Hacker's alternative, *Health Care for America*. In turn, his plan was bitterly debated in Washington. Former Speaker Pelosi declared his plan as "essential" for health care reform. Republican senator Mitch McConnell of Kentucky, not viewing Hacker's plan from the progressives' perspective, called the inclusion of universal health care a "deal-breaker."

Hacker, noted as a champion of universal health insurance, is also a "student of the Big Failure" of the collapse of Clintoncare. Hacker said that not only was it too complex, but also that Democrats would do well in the future to avoid a "politically unworkable" massive expansion of Medicare.

Medicare for All, in Hacker's opinion, was tantamount to a single-payer system, like Canada's, and inevitably unpopular with Americans.[22]

However, Hacker's plan, for lack of a better description, was a gentler, kinder version of many similar plans. It emphasized choice, empowerment, and incremental reform and avoided "radical transformation." This, it was observed, helped the plan gain influence with Democrats, particularly in 2007 with the three major Democratic presidential candidates.

One flaw in Hacker's plan was that he had failed to acknowledge that Medicare was already in trouble. Critics pointed out that the "true price" of Hacker's plan was concealed. The escalation of Medicare costs was proportionate to those in the private sector. There were no savings.

As predicted by critics in early 2009, we are now confronted with overwhelming and incomprehensible federal involvement in all aspects of health care as our nation faces a tsunami of debt that keeps on growing. Sold as measures to help "tame" private sector health inflation, in reality, Washington—meaning taxpayers—would end up paying for it. This is why we believe it is so significant that radicals who strive to collapse the U.S. capitalist system were deeply involved in the origins of Obamacare.

Public Option and Soros Funds

Hacker is credited with dreaming up the concept of the *public option*, as outlined in the previously cited papers while he was yet a graduate student.[23]

Medicare Plus comes from his 2001 *Cover America* project paper, subsequently published in October 2003 by the Economic and Social Research Institute. The second source is the *Health Care for America* plan sponsored and promoted by the Economic Policy Institute.

Until the Congressional Budget Office pointed out the public option in the House bill "might insure" 10 million people, and would leave an additional 16–17 million uninsured, Hacker and his proponents were all for a huge public health care program. The proposal was estimated as "unlikely to insure anyone" and assuredly would "leave 33 to 34 million uninsured."

This wildly differs from Hacker's original public option proposal with an estimated 129 million *enrollees* and only 2 million people left uninsured.

Even the progressive *American Prospect* heard the death knell of the public option as long ago as August 2009.[24]

While described as "carefully thought out" and "deliberately funded," the "brilliant experiment" of getting all the "pieces in place for health reform before the 2008 election" had soon turned out "badly," Mark Schmitt writes.

The whole push for Hacker's plan lay "at the feet" of Campaign for America's Future's Roger Hickey, Schmitt adds. Hickey pitched his case for a "limited 'public option'" while making the rounds of single-payer advocates. In Hickey's opinion, it was the "best they could hope for," while secretly hoping the public option would "someday magically turn into single-payer." Hickey also made the rounds to all the presidential candidates, offering them a win-win campaign strategy. He acknowledged that while they could not politically support the unpopular single-payer plan, they could still talk up the public option to "attract a real progressive constituency," Schmitt informs us.

Here, then, we have the unholy alliance of Hacker's health care policy wedded to the Hickey–Health Care for America Now political strategy.

The silence of Campaign for America's Future, HCAN, and others on the details in the Congressional Budget Office report was observed by PNHP blogger Kip Sullivan. HCAN, Sullivan writes, failed to inform the public that the public options they pushed in the health care bill were a "mere shadow" of the ones it had previously endorsed.[25]

Additionally, HCAN's steering committee members failed to inform readers of their websites on how "small and ineffective" the public options now proposed by the Democrats were when compared to the one originally proposed by Hacker, Sullivan continues. Regardless, he writes, HCAN urged its members and the public to "tell Congress to support a public option."

In a December 20, 2009, article in the *New Republic*, Hacker says he had been "the thinker most associated with the public option, which [he had] long argued is essential to ensuring accountability from private insurers and long-term cost control."[26]

Even though, he writes, "the core demand of progressives"—the "public option"—was removed from the Senate version of the health care bill, progressives should "continue to support the effort."

Although Hacker at first believed the health care reform legislation should be killed, he said that would be wrong. Even without the public option, he writes, the legislation "could move us substantially toward those goals."

Obama and Single-Payer

Without question, Barack Obama has failed to deliver for his single-payer health care supporters. At the top of the list of those he has disappointed is Dr. Quentin D. Young. Obama was first educated by Young in the concept of single-payer health care.[27]

Progressive John Nichols, who says he has known Obama since the early 1990s, relates candidate Obama's remarks from a July 8, 2008, town hall meeting at McEachern High School in Powder Springs, Georgia. Obama not only firmly avowed he was a progressive, but also clearly stated he believes in universal health care—progressive code language for *single-payer*:[28]

> I am somebody who is no doubt progressive. I believe in a tax code that we need to make more fair. I believe in universal health care. I believe in making college affordable. I believe in paying our teachers more money. I believe in early childhood education. I believe in a whole lot of things that make me progressive.

Obama spoke on the issue of single-payer again in August 2008 at a town hall–style meeting in Albuquerque, New Mexico.[29] "People don't have time to wait," Obama said. "They need relief now. So my attitude is let's build up the system we got, let's make it more efficient, we may over time—as we make the system more efficient and everybody's covered—decide that there are other ways for us to provide care more effectively."

Obama was for single-payer before he was against it, David Sirota wrote in May 2009 at the left-leaning *AlterNet*. In 2003 Obama said he "supports a single-payer health care system, and that the only reason we 'may not get there immediately' is 'because first we have to take back the White House, we have to take back the Senate, and we have to take back the House.'" Sirota writes, "we have." By "we" Sirota means the left. Conditions met.[30]

Speaking to the Illinois AFL-CIO on June 30, 2003, Obama said, "I happen to be a proponent of a single payer universal health care program. . . . I see no reason why the United States of America, the wealthiest country in the history of the world, spending 14 percent of its Gross National Product on health care cannot provide basic health insurance to everybody. . . . A single payer health care plan, a universal health care plan. And that's what I'd like to see."[31]

Sirota goes on to note that in 2006, while Obama was still in the Senate, he talked with him about single-payer. Obama began to walk back from his earlier position. Sirota writes: "Obama said that although he 'would not shy away from a debate about single-payer,' right now he is 'not convinced that it is the best way to achieve universal health-care.'"[32]

By May 2007 Obama had backed further away from this position. He told the *New Yorker* that if Congress were starting from scratch, then single-payer would make sense. However, unlike Canada, the United States doesn't have the "legacy systems" in place and trying to pull it off would be too disruptive.[33]

Sirota quotes from a May 5, 2009, Associated Press article that Senate Finance Committee chairman Max Baucus (D-Mont.) was also sounding retreat. Baucus said everything except for single-payer was on the table. Single-payer was neither practical nor politically feasible, he said.[34]

At the end of August 2009, David Shalleck-Klein of the *Hill* reported a definite shift away from inclusion of single-payer by House members who had previously backed it.[35]

Health Care for America Now, ACORN, and Unions

One significant group leading the charge to transform health care has been Campaign for America's Future. CAF was founded in 1990 by Robert L. Borosage. CAF officially launched in 1996. Roger Hickey, cofounder of the Economic Policy Institute, is credited as being a CAF cofounder as well.

In October 1999, CAF launched its *Issues 2000: Health Care* initiative. CAF's support for government-provided health care—and holding "the privileged" responsible—is clear in its inaugural statement:[36]

Citizens must have affordable, comprehensive health care that cannot be taken away. It is simply obscene that an estimated 43.4 million Americans have no health insurance, including 11 million children. America remains the only industrial country that denies this basic security to its people, even as more and more working families find they can't afford to buy health insurance and can't afford to go without it. The idea that nothing can be done to improve health care reflects the complacent sense of the privileged that nothing need be done. It is time to make access to quality health care a right for all Americans.

Nearly a decade later, on July 7, 2008, CAF unveiled the new lobby, Health Care for America Now, or HCAN, which deceptively maintains that it is a "national grassroots campaign."[37]

Do not be fooled. HCAN is the antithesis of a "grassroots movement." The term *grassroots* implies that the movement and the group supporting it are natural and spontaneous as opposed to movements that are orchestrated by traditional power structures. The word *orchestrated* would be more accurate in describing HCAN.

The credit for conceiving HCAN as an *all-out* assault goes to Jeffrey D. Blum, a former member of Students for a Democratic Society and director of USAction. The new national campaign was launched in July 2008 in fifty-two cities across the country, including thirty-eight state capitals by more than one hundred national and state-based groups that claim they represent labor, community organizations, doctors, nurses, women, small businesses, faith-based organizations, people of color, netroots activists, and think tanks with the stated aim of bringing together millions of Americans to demand quality, affordable health care for all.[38]

HCAN's lead member organizations include fellow K Street occupants and their funders. The northern K Street, one of two by that name in Washington, D.C., is known as the center for a number of think tanks, lobbyists, and advocacy groups—none of which would remotely be considered grassroots, and many of which form a who's who of radical groups: ACORN, AFSCME, Americans United for Change, Campaign for America's Future, Center for American Progress Action

Fund, Center for Community Change, MoveOn.org, National Education Association, National Women's Law Center, Planned Parenthood Federation of America, SEIU, United Food and Commercial Workers, and USAction.[39]

HCAN admitted in January 2010 that it anticipated spending $42 million in its final push for passage of Obamacare. Following the successful passage of the legislation, the Bermuda-based grant maker Atlantic Philanthropies admitted to pumping $26.5 million into HCAN. Other HCAN funders included the California Endowment, Open Society Institute, and unnamed individuals.[40]

HCAN member organizations are also funded by George Soros through his Open Society Institute and Open Society Foundations.[41]

From its state contact list it is pretty obvious to even the casual observer that HCAN is a front group. It is dominated by addresses and contacts for ACORN, SEIU, and USAction, as well as their state affiliates.[42]

HCAN boasts that both itself and its principles are supported by President Obama, Vice President Biden, and more than 190 members of Congress.[43]

However, Barack Obama did more than just support HCAN's principles. In early October 2008 Obama actually signed the Health Care for America Now statement in which he declared he is on the side of "quality, affordable health care for all and opposed to leaving Americans on their own with unregulated health insurance."[44]

Rebranding Radicalism

Once a comprehensive health care overhaul matured, the radical network went to work helping politicians sell the American public on Obamacare by crafting appealing, moderate language to sell a radical plan. Enter a little-known marketing outfit called the Herndon Alliance. An organization openly advocating for a universal, single-payer national health care system reveals the origins of the deceptive marketing of Health Care for America Now. Kip Sullivan, writing in late November 2008 at PNHP, accurately states that HCAN is a new incarnation of the Herndon Alliance, which, we shall see, specializes in crafting moderate language to sell radical principles.[45]

A comprehensive profile of the Herndon Alliance by *Politico* relates that when President Obama announces Americans can maintain their choice of doctors and insurance plans, "he is using a Herndon strategy for wringing fear out of a system overhaul. . . . Same goes for Senate Finance Chairman Max Baucus (D-Mont.), who says he wants a 'uniquely American solution,' another Herndon tactic for blunting attacks that Democrats favor a foreign brand of health care."[46]

According to its online history, the Herndon Alliance was founded in 2005 in Herndon, Virginia, as a coalition of national- and state-based advocacy, labor, faith, provider, and business groups with a common vision. The organization's declared goal is to reframe the health care reform discussion from one that has been policy driven to one that is *values-based* and would "help a larger portion of the population understand how health care reform could improve affordability and security in their own health care coverage."[47]

"We see ourselves as a service organization, arming the health care community with the best messaging information that is available out there, which had not been thought about until the last four years," stated Peter Van Vranken, who coordinates outreach for the Herndon Alliance from his home in rural Vermont.[48] Van Vranken is a longtime Democratic operative who consulted on health care for Senator John Kerry and Governor Howard Dean. He was a health program consultant at the Soros-funded Center for American Progress.[49]

The Herndon Alliance evolved following an early 2005 three-day meeting attended by about fifty people in Herndon, Virginia. The gathering was coordinated by Seattle family physician Bob Crittenden, now the Herndon Alliance executive director, and Philippe Villers, who serves on the current board of directors as secretary-treasurer.[50]

Philippe Villers and his wife cofounded Families USA, or FUSA, in 1981. FUSA's mission is to achieve "universal access to high quality, affordable health and long-term care for all Americans."[51] FUSA, one of the leading health care lobbying organizations in Washington, partnered with the White House to run a PR campaign to rehabilitate the image of the 2010 health care bill. The group has been a prominent supporter of universal, government-run health care. It spent tens of millions of dollars organizing and lobbying for health care coverage for children and the uninsured. After the Democrats abandoned their pursuit of government health care following public opposition, particularly during the heated debate about the issue in mid-2009, FUSA also dropped the aim but not without drawing harsh criticism from the left for abandoning its values.

Villers worked directly with the White House to lobby for Obama's health care bill. In June 2010, in an all-out effort by the White House to combat skepticism about the bill, progressive organizations, including Villers's FUSA, joined the battle for public opinion. Villers's group put on road shows in cities around the country, where officials from the U.S. Department of Health and Human Services and the agency that runs Medicare conducted presentations on important features of Obama's legislation.[52]

FUSA traces back to at least the Clinton administration. The group's executive director, Ron Pollack, was appointed in 1997 by President Clinton as the sole consumer representative on the Presidential Advisory Commission on Consumer Protection and Quality in the Health Care Industry, where he reportedly helped adapt a Patients' Bill of Rights that had been enacted by multiple state legislatures.[53]

The research component of the Herndon Alliance, meanwhile, is provided by Celinda Lake, who teamed up with a marketing research firm, American Environics. AE uses social-values surveys to gauge public opinion.[54] Celinda Lake describes herself as one of the Democratic Party's leading political strategists, serving as tactician and senior adviser to the national party committees, dozens of Democratic incumbents, and challengers at all levels of the electoral process. She has worked for a number of leftist institutions and unions, including the AFL-CIO and the socialist-led SEIU.[55] She also serves on the board of directors of the Progressive Congress Action Fund alongside Robert Borosage and James Rucker.[56] A partial list of the Herndon Alliance's "partners" is yet another who's who of progressive groups.[57]

Chavez Image Gurus

The public was rightly skeptical about Obamacare and the effects the U.S. president's legislation would have on the country's private insurance market, igniting a national debate on the issue that caused multiple immediate image problems for the White House. The health care bill prompted a backlash of concern from voters across the political spectrum, with many Americans fearing the proposed changes would affect their quality of care. And so the radical network went to work helping to carefully repackage Obamacare so the bill would be more palatable to the public.

Decision making was based on the theoretical work of American Environics, or AE, which was founded in 2004 by a team of American strategists and Canadian researchers.[58]

The group describes itself as a consulting firm that uses social-values surveys, cognitive linguistics, and political psychology to help foundations and nonprofits develop breakthrough social change initiatives. AE writes that since 2005 its research findings and strategic initiatives on health care, the economy, and the environment have been used by multiple members of Congress.[59]

In April 2005, current AE managing partners Ted Nordhaus and Michael Shellenberger started AE's American branch. They are the coauthors of the 2007 book *Break Through: From the Death of Environmentalism to the Politics of Possibility*, and the seminal 2004 essay "The Death of Environmentalism: Global Warming Politics in a Post-

Environmental World," which reportedly "took environmental interest groups to task for being out of touch."[60]

Before continuing, it is instructive to take a look at Shellenberger's background, which leftist-group watchdog Ron Arnold calls "hard left."[61]

Shellenberger previously worked for the anticorporate, antiglobalization Global Exchange in San Francisco before starting a spin-off public relations firm in 1996, Communication Works. By 2001 Shellenberger's firm had grown and he merged it with the ultraleft Washington-based Fenton Communications—Ira Arlook of Citizen Action fame (and cofounder of Campaign for America's Future) was a Fenton executive. Shellenberger split with Fenton before he created Americans for Energy Freedom.

In 2004 Shellenberger registered with the Department of Justice as a foreign agent. His prime client was none other than Venezuelan dictator Hugo Chavez. Shellenberger's private consulting firm, Lumina Strategies LLC, got a six-month, sixty-thousand-dollar subcontract to help build up Chavez's image, including by providing polling data.

The AE team of Nordhaus and Shellenberger put forth the argument that the best way to sell voters on progressive issues is to focus on *bridge values* and shared "fundamental beliefs, even if the targeted parties don't necessarily share progressives' every last goal."[62]

In the fall of 2005, AE presented its data on health care to key Democratic leaders and a who's who of Democratic interest groups, including Senator Hillary Rodham Clinton, Representative Pelosi, the Center for American Progress, Economic Policy Institute, and others.

Although viewers were sworn to silence, the *American Prospect* was given an early copy of AE's research.

The research contradicted polling data, Garance Franke-Ruta wrote in February 2006. Polls showed Americans as "strong supporters of Democratic issue positions, such as universal health care, despite voting habits that have made Republicans the dominant political actors," she claimed. Meanwhile, AE's "extensive plumbing of Americans' attitudes laid out a darker, more nuanced vision of what the nation actually believes," Franke-Ruta said. Remarkably, she also wrote: "They found a society at once more libertine and more puritanical than in the past, a society where solidarity among citizens was deteriorating, and, most worrisomely to them, a progressive clock that seemed to be unwinding backward on broad questions of social equity."

We write about Nordhaus, a pollster, and Shellenberger, a progressive public relations man, in *The Manchurian President*. The two men cofounded the Apollo Alliance sometime around 2002 and were two of its original national board members, as well as cofounders of the Breakthrough Institute.[63]

The Apollo Alliance helped draft not only the president's green jobs programs, but also the $787 billion economic stimulus bill and other proposed new energy legislation.[64] It is led by a slew of radicals, including Van Jones, Jeff Jones (no relation), who heads Apollo's New York branch and is a former top leader of the Weatherman terrorist organization, and Joel Rogers, a founder of the socialist New Party. We dedicate a large section of this book to the Apollo Alliance, including much new information on the group and its direct involvement in crafting Obama's legislation.

In May 2006 AE presented the *Road Map for a Health Justice Majority* to the Herndon Alliance, which then went to work on rebranding what became Obamacare. The paper includes information on what AE calls the Health Justice Base and the Anti–Health Justice Base. Developed from a *values perspective*, the *Road Map* provides a "long-term guide for how to build that Base into a true majority based on activating shared values."[65]

PNHP's Kip Sullivan criticizes the *Road Map* for what it did not do. Regarding the report's introduction, he writes, "the authors claim the report will answer the question, 'Who is more likely to support comprehensive health care coverage for all Americans?' But nowhere in the report are readers given the answer to that question."[66]

We agree with Sullivan, who also finds most of the *Road Map* to be a lot of meaningless gibberish. AE uses such descriptive terms as "brand apathy," "discount consumerism," "upscale consumerism," "more power for big business," "meaningful moments," "mysterious forces," "traditional gender identity," and "sexual permissiveness."

Sullivan attempts to comprehend the "cluster" AE calls the Health Justice Base. He writes: "It is not at all clear how this cluster differs from the other seven clusters, but one gathers from the name alone that these folks are the most enthusiastic advocates of 'health justice,' whatever that means." Unsurprisingly, AE reports that "100 percent of the members of the Health Justice Base are 'for comprehensive health care.'" "It is hard to imagine a more fundamental requirement for a 'health justice' advocate," Sullivan adds, "than someone who is willing to say health care is a right."

Logically, AE claims that more than 80 percent of every other cluster except one—the Anti–Health Justice Base—was "'for comprehensive health care' (only zero percent of the Anti-Base expressed support for 'comprehensive health care')," Sullivan continues. However, the Anti-Base "accounts for only 6 percent of the [tested] population."

The purpose of this research and testing is unclear, especially since, as Sullivan notes, AE does not provide the answer at the root of the work: "Who is more likely to support comprehensive health care coverage for all Americans?"

Although the whole *Road Map* is much more extensive, it is difficult to understand how the Herndon Alliance or Celinda Lake found it useful. Yet, somehow, the *Road Map* serves as a basis for the Herndon Alliance's plans to influence Americans into accepting the Obama government health care reform plans—for their own good, of course—whether it is the legislation passed and signed in March 2010 or another push for single-payer in the future.

HCAN's Richard Kirsch told Carrie Budoff Brown: "The research from 2006 to 2007 was fundamental to helping shape our view of how to talk about health care and, generally, how progressives and Democrats talk about health care."[67]

The Herndon Alliance says it conducted the research because it needed to hear what the public wants. It claims to need it to learn how to frame the issues of reform and access to health care to help those with insurance coverage understand that such reform was critical for them. Then, Herndon says, it could "move the population to create a majority of voters who, even when a policy was introduced, continued to favor healthcare reform."[68]

In other words, Hendon's new tactic appealed to the emotions of voters. Even Brown admits the group repositioned health care as part of the American dream.[69]

Caught Red-handed: New Messaging, Same Rejected Policy

Here it is worthwhile to look at the methods used by Herndon to re-brand Obamacare. It provides a case study of the modus operandi of the radical network—when it fails to achieve its transformative agenda, it takes a step back, repackages its policies, and tries again, careful to use the kind of language the public wants to hear to sell the same radical idea previously rejected by the populace.

One example is all that's necessary to make our case. The carefully crafted messaging for Obamacare can be observed from a publicly available section on the Herndon Alliance website called "Words We Use." HA says "it truly matters how we talk about health care reform."[70]

In focus groups, we could lose the issue 8:1 or win it 9:0 depending on what values, images, and feelings we evoked. Well-crafted progressive messages substantially outperform the strongest conservative counter messages, whereas weakly crafted messages fail to gain support. Now is the time to go on offense on health care reform, using language we know in advance works. We also know that simply changing our words is not enough. Reframing issues by using stories and narratives that bring up "kitchen table" issues are the strongest messages you can create.

The same page provides those pushing Obamacare with new words to use. Acceptable words include "quality affordable health care"; "American solutions"; "giving security and peace of mind"; "fair rules"; "government as watchdog"; "smart investments, investing in the future"; and "affordable health plans."

Unacceptable words include "universal health care"; "Canadian-style health care"; "Medicare for All"; "regulations"; "free"; "government or public health care"; and "wellness."

Taking the words to use or not use one step further, the Herndon Alliance suggests, for example, "We will never have 100% public support for health reform. We don't need to." Why? The Herndon Alliance writes: "to ensure that reform is implemented successfully, we do need to capture and keep the support of persuadable voters. We can't let radicals define the debate or allow us to lose sight of our audience."[71]

Persuadable voters? Depending on the issue, in this case the *individual mandate*, the Herndon Alliance identifies the *persuadable voters* as "women, Latinos, seniors, and under 40-year-olds" and "blue collar working women."[72]

Throughout 2005, 2007, and 2008 the Herndon Alliance "collaborated" with its partner organizations to "provide briefings to the staff members of presidential and congressional campaigns, coordinated with pro-reform organizations like AARP, SEIU, and many others, and trained advocates in messaging, always with the goal of ensuring that as many people as possible were talking about health care reform—together."[73]

Shock PowerPoint

In what might be characterized as the lemonade-from-lemons approach, Francesca Holme, project director for the Herndon Alliance, made a nine-frame PowerPoint presentation on May 4, 2010, to evaluate Obamacare. The first frame admits the bill's passage failed to "garner support for Democrats, the White House or anyone." It was the messaging's fault.

The second frame assesses blame—the "Current Climate Is Tough." Why? Because there is a lack of trust, knowledge/belief, and "openings to move people." The public is "exhausted" and frustrated with the economy.

Of course, these and other roadblocks—a movement toward "repeal and replace"; need better oversight, not a new law; government telling people what to do; reform is causing premiums to rise; and "paying for the undeserving"—can all be overcome with better messaging.

On June 21, 2010, the Herndon Alliance announced it was going to pursue a different mission—assuring "successful implementation" of the "public reaction to the legislation"—by helping Americans "put into context what the health care reform battle was about," for one thing. Additionally, of course, the Herndon Alliance will have to create a new persuasive message by conducting new rounds of research to identify communications strategies and messaging that best resonate with the public.[74]

The problem now for the Herndon Alliance and its partners is that, although the health care bill passed in March 2010, this is not the health care bill they really wanted—and they are afraid the bill that passed may not endure. Their work is far from over.

The messaging cycle recommenced in October 2010. On its resource page for *Opposing Repeal*, the Herndon Alliance recommends its partners use a particular type of language: "Use bridge language such as 'the law may not be perfect, but it does address real problems and provides help to people like me' and 'the law allows me some dignity and a chance to get the care I need (or the care my daughter needs, etc).'"[75]

Two months earlier, the Herndon Alliance had posted a "Post Passage Messaging Guide," based on research conducted in early August. It further reveals the growing level of concern—the opposition was successful in countering the Herndon Alliance's carefully crafted messaging—by defining the law as "increasing costs and a government takeover of the private sector, but it is clear that voters still do not have a clear idea of the law's status, content, or how it will be implemented."[76]

The Herndon Alliance advises: "It is helpful to use 'bridge' statements about the law, to give permission to people to relax their defensive reactions to the law. The strongest testing statement allows that 'the law isn't perfect, but we need to improve it, not repeal it.'"

This is how it works—and has been working for those partners pushing the health care reform agenda—against those who resist.

To keep everyone on message, Crittenden and Van Vranken convene weekly conference calls with between thirty and fifty organizations, including Health Care for America Now, FUSA, the AFL-CIO, and AARP, Brown revealed. "They trade notes and strategize. Like an air traffic controller, Van Vranken watches the health care traffic on the Internet all day, flagging developments that threaten the cause."[77]

Repealing Obamacare

Three Democrats—Representatives Dan Boren (Okla.), Mike McIntyre (N.C.), and Mike Ross (Ark.)—and all 242 House Republicans voted on January 19, 2011, to pass H.R. 2, the Repealing the Job-Killing Health Care Law Act.[78]

House Majority Leader Eric Cantor (R-Va.) and other members of the House Republican leadership challenged the Senate Democratic leadership to bring the legislation up for debate. "I think the American people deserve to see a vote in the Senate and the Senate ought not be a place that legislation goes into a dead end," Cantor said.[79]

On February 1, in an attempt to force a vote on repeal in the Senate, Republicans offered it as an amendment to S. 223, the FAA Air

Transportation Modernization and Safety Improvement Act, the FAA reauthorization bill being pushed on the Senate floor by Democrats.[80]

When all forty-seven Republican senators signed on to the repeal proposal, Senate Minority Leader Mitch McConnell said the Senate would vote despite objections by Senate Majority Leader Harry Reid. The Democrats held the 53 to 47 majority. "We pledged to the American people that we would seek to repeal this 2,700-page bill that seeks to restructure all of American health care and put the decisions in Washington," McConnell told reporters.

As anticipated, on February 2, Senate Democrats blocked the Republican effort. Senate Republican Whip Jon Kyl said, "Senate Republicans today made good on their promise to the American people to try to repeal the unconstitutional health spending bill known as Obamacare."[81]

It should be noted that Senate Republicans first attempted to repeal the Obamacare bill in March 2010, soon after its passage. Legislation was introduced on March 23—the day President Obama signed the Obamacare bill—by Senator Jim DeMint of South Carolina with a dozen Republican cosponsors.[82]

Republicans had been bolstered by the January 31, 2011, ruling by Judge Roger Vinson in a northern Florida federal district court that struck down the entire Obamacare bill as unconstitutional. Twenty-six states had brought a joint suit. Judge Vinson said that because the individual mandate is unconstitutional, the whole law is void. He agreed that the new law "violates people's rights by forcing them to buy health insurance by 2014 or face penalties."[83]

"Because the individual mandate is unconstitutional and not severable, the entire Act must be declared void," Judge Vinson writes. "This has been a difficult decision to reach, and I am aware that it will have indeterminable implications. At a time when there is virtually unanimous agreement that health care reform is needed in this country, it is hard to invalidate and strike down a statute titled 'The Patient Protection and Affordable Care Act.'"[84]

Radical Network Regroups

Ahead of its January 29, 2011, annual meeting, the Herndon Alliance released its *2011 Work Plan*. It is dated December 13, 2010, predating the Republicans' successful House repeal of Obamacare in January, the successful block by Democrats of Republican efforts in the Senate, and the Florida court ruling in February.[85]

The plan exhibits HA's ability to rework the narrative and shows that it is fully aware of the difficulty Obamacare faces to survive. "Unless we effectively flip the 'big government' narrative," HA writes, Obamacare remains "vulnerable." The alliance is prepared to help "the advocacy community, civic leaders, and elected officials in their work" to protect and implement Obamacare, as well as "push back on the oppositional frame of big government."

It seems HA has Fabian socialism tactics down pat. ACLU cofounder Roger Baldwin advised a socialist agitator early in the twentieth century to "steer away from making it look like a Socialist enterprise" and to employ subterfuge tactics. Convince people of your American values by flying lots of American flags; talk about the Constitution and what the Founding Fathers wanted America to become, Baldwin says.[86]

Here's the advice HA suggests in its plan: "We can and should take back words such as responsibility, fairness, freedom, and patriotism. For example, existing polls (CNN) showed the public voted primarily with the economy and jobs on their minds. But second to that issue, voters expressed wanting to return to the principles of the Constitution. We can't ignore the voices of Americans; we need to take control in how we relate to and respond to their concerns, their fears, and their desires."

With the wins and losses piling up, HA affiliates again swung into action. News emerged on February 4, 2011, that a new Democratic initiative was in the making to coordinate messaging in support of Obamacare. Controlling the message—messaging—is HA's specialty.[87]

According to unnamed sources, the initial leadership team includes

Paul Tewes, who was Obama's Iowa state campaign director during the Iowa caucuses. Other named team members are Tanya Bjork, who headed Obama's Wisconsin political campaign, and David Di Martino, who will serve as the initiative's communications consultant. The involvement in the initiative by Ron Pollack, executive director of FUSA, is a sure sign that HA is in the forefront. "It's designed to coordinate, increase cooperation and improve cohesiveness in messaging," Pollack says.

Their latest initiative is to push back against efforts at repeal—which it correctly says are coming from members of Congress, state legislatures, the courts, and public opinion—by "streamlining the pro-reform message," Jennifer Haberkorn writes in *Politico*.

It is clear that progressives are tone deaf—including HA messaging gurus—and still don't get it. Obamacare is not what the people want.

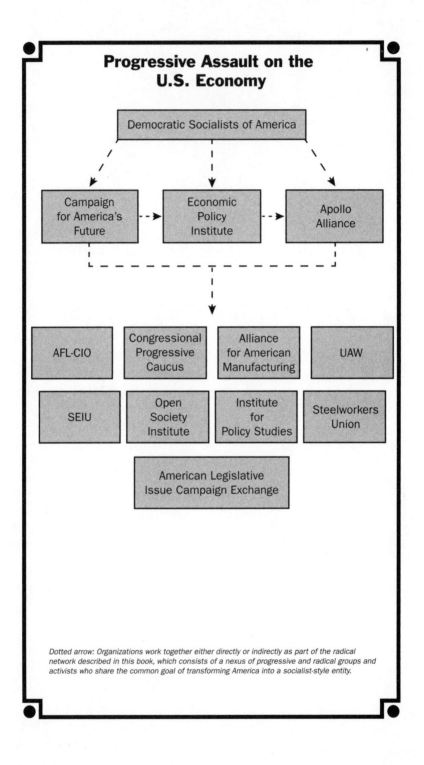

Progressive Assault on the U.S. Economy

Democratic Socialists of America

Campaign for America's Future

Economic Policy Institute

Apollo Alliance

AFL-CIO

Congressional Progressive Caucus

Alliance for American Manufacturing

UAW

SEIU

Open Society Institute

Institute for Policy Studies

Steelworkers Union

American Legislative Issue Campaign Exchange

Dotted arrow: Organizations work together either directly or indirectly as part of the radical network described in this book, which consists of a nexus of progressive and radical groups and activists who share the common goal of transforming America into a socialist-style entity.

chapter four

MAKING IT
IN AMERICA

Speaker Nancy Pelosi flashed a copy her *Making It in America* plan at a July 14, 2010, press conference after meeting with President Obama at the White House.[1] Pelosi told reporters it was a new strategy for U.S. manufacturing, but was still a work in progress. She said she was not going to share it with them, adding the plan was a positive initiative she had shared with the president. "We want everybody to make it in America," Pelosi said ten days later at a moderated forum at Netroots Nation 2010, a gathering of thousands of bloggers and progressive activists in Las Vegas.[2]

Pelosi talked about Making It in America, telling the audience the plan includes a series of bills that would be introduced after the summer recess. The strategy, she said, was to pass a succession of bills, one after the other, to support American manufacturing.[3]

Pelosi also told reporters that Congress—meaning the progressives in Congress—planned to take a look at the China currency problem, whether China is manipulating its currency to give goods made there a huge pricing advantage. She also pointed out that China imposes many other barriers to free trade, including not allowing American companies to bid on government procurement, even when the goods are made in China.[4]

"There is a strong interest in our caucus in holding China accountable for manipulation of currency. That would make a tremendous difference in our trade because currency manipulation is really a subsidy to their exports to America—an unfair advantage," Pelosi said.[5] The uncurious progressive media, bloggers, and activists did not dig deeper. Not only was Pelosi's *new* strategy not a work in progress, but little about it was *new*, period; indeed it is the culmination of the handiwork of a roster of leading radicals. Additionally, had the news media taken the time to check, they would have found not only that they had seen it before, in January 2009, but also that the plan to infuse the economy with huge amounts of stimulus money to create (and/or save) jobs had failed to work.

"President Obama and congressional Democrats—out of options for another quick shot of stimulus spending to revive the sluggish economy—are shifting toward a longer-term strategy that promises to tackle persistently high unemployment by engineering a renaissance in American manufacturing," Lori Montgomery and Brady Dennis wrote in August 2010 in the *Washington Post*.[6]

The seeds of the Make It in America campaign, Montgomery and Dennis reported, were planted in May 2010 when Representative Mark Critz (D-Pa.) defeated Republican businessman Tim Burns in a special election. Critz campaigned against allowing tax breaks for companies moving jobs offshore. In late June, House Democrats were briefed on a poll conducted for the Alliance for American Manufacturing that found voters were anxious about mounting U.S. debt owed to China.[7]

The Democrats' approach, Montgomery and Dennis wrote, was heralded by Obama when he visited Michigan twice at the end of July. The occasions of Obama's visits were the alleged comebacks of General Motors and Chrysler, as well as his helping to break ground at a new battery plant.[8]

The Alliance for American Manufacturing poll findings showed that likely voters saw job creation as more important than reducing the federal deficit and cutting government spending. The poll was also credited with helping to rebrand Obama administration policies, including government restructuring of the auto industry.[9]

The repackaging was described as including policies long pursued by the Obama government, such as *investing* in clean energy, infrastructure, and expanded broadband service. Additionally, more than two dozen pieces of Democratic legislation were aimed at creating a plan to promote manufacturing in the United States.[10]

Eric Cantor, then House Republican whip, called the Democrats' plan "more meaningless than harmful" after voting for the Democratic resolution encouraging packers to display the American flag on labels for domestic fruits and vegetables.[11]

Leo Gerard, president of the United Steelworkers, endorsed the plan, saying the AFL-CIO was backing the House Democrats' Make It in America strategy.[12]

With barely a whisper, in late July 2010, pieces of Make It in America legislation were passed in the House and the Senate:

★ H.R. 4380, the U.S. Manufacturing Enhancement Act, containing hundreds of tariff suspensions and reductions.[13]

★ H.R. 5874, the 2010 Supplemental Appropriations Bill for the U.S. Patent and Trademark Office, providing funds to help prevent new backlogs in processing of patent applications.[14]

★ H.R. 1855, the Strengthening Employment Clusters to Organize Regional Success (SECTORS) Act, to help address local skills shortages.[15]

★ H.R. 1875, the End the Trade Deficit Act, to establish a trade deficit reduction commission.[16]

★ H.R. 2039, the Congressional Made in America Act, to clarify application of the Buy American Act to products purchased for the use of the legislative branch.[17]

★ H.R. 3115, the Berry Amendment Extension Act, to direct the Department of Homeland Security to buy clothing, tents, and other products made in America.[18]

★ H.R. 4678, the Foreign Manufacturers Legal Accountability Act, to require foreign manufacturers of products
imported into the United States to establish registered
agents in the country.[19]
★ H.R. 4692, the National Manufacturing Strategy Act, to
require the president to prepare a quadrennial National
Manufacturing Strategy.[20]
★ H.R. 5156, the Clean Energy Technology Manufacturing
and Export Assistance Act of 2010, to establish a Clean
Energy Technology Manufacturing and Export Assistance Fund.[21]

Another piece of legislation did not make it beyond introduction
in the House. H.R. 5893, the Investing in American Jobs and Closing
Tax Loopholes Act, was intended to extend programs in the 2009
stimulus bill.[22]

In a September 9, 2010, press release, Representative Charles Rangel wrote that these bills were only the beginning, with more to come,
"as Democrats continue to bring forward ideas that can help spark a
manufacturing revival and level the playing field for American products." The Make It in America agenda, Rangel said, was an "essential
step toward economic recovery."[23]

When a progressive speaks about "economic recovery" it is time to
be concerned.

Democratic Socialists of America Origins

At first glance, the Democrats' push for a Make It in America jobs program appears to have originated from within the House of Representatives. Tracking the genesis of the program, however, leads directly to
a union-dominated organization and long-term plans by a socialist-led
organization.

In April 2010, the Populist Caucus, the House Trade Working Group, and the Congressional Progressive Caucus introduced a new American Jobs First platform. The four pieces of legislation that passed were described as "designed to put struggling Americans back to work and on a level playing field with workers in other countries."[24]

All four bills were read in the House and referred to committee, but were never passed on to the Senate.

On July 22, 2010, Democrat House spokesmen Majority Leader Steny Hoyer and Majority Whip Jim Clyburn proposed a new, preelection manufacturing plan, the Make It in America Agenda, a "manufacturing strategy based on the idea that when more products are made in America, more people will be able to make it in America." The agenda was to "create incentives for investment in industry, strengthen manufacturing infrastructure and innovation, and help to level the playing field for American companies that compete globally."[25]

Interestingly, in January 2011, remarking on the new book *Make It in America: The Case for Re-inventing the Economy*, published by the Dow Chemical Company Foundation, the Alliance for American Manufacturing not only said it was reminiscent of the Democrats' plan, but also commented that it "mirrors AAM's language."[26]

It soon becomes clear that the AAM, a union-dominated organization, had more than a passing influence on the Democrats' plan. AAM's reference above is to an August 2010 article posted on its website, "The Alliance for American Manufacturing is spurring a 'Make it in America' buzz."[27]

The article reports that after Congress was briefed in June on AAM's findings in a national economic poll, Democrats launched their own new "Make It in America" agenda.[28]

Shortly after Democrats lost control of the House in the midterm election, in a November private Oval Office meeting Hoyer urged Obama to "retool" his job creation message by adopting the slogan Make It in America.[29]

The House failed to get its bills out of committee and passed along to the Senate. In mid-February 2011, Senate Democratic leaders unveiled a new manufacturing legislative agenda that included specific trade- and manufacturing-oriented initiatives. Taking their cue from Obama's State of the Union address, the Democrats rolled out their Winning the Future agenda.[30]

Again, nothing within the legislation was new. AAM pointed out it was "continually calling for the adoption of a national manufacturing strategy to help revitalize the nation's industrial base," then remarked, "It's nice to see Capitol Hill listening to us."[31]

AAM's elation did not last long. Its attempts to nudge Congress along had not only failed, but also managed to draw criticism from AAM a month later. Executive director Scott Paul writes, "We've put forward a plan to keep it made in America that has broad support from the American people—right, left and center." Paul stresses that the new, 112th Congress, then in its third month, had not yet created a bill for American manufacturing jobs that could be sent to Obama for signing.[32]

After another month had passed, in early April 2011 when the federal government was facing a shutdown after failing to pass a budget for fiscal 2011 (which the Democrats had failed to pass while still in control of both houses of Congress), Democrats came up with yet another proposal. The Congressional Progressive Caucus's Budget Task Force devised a counterproposal to the fiscal reform plan submitted by Representative Paul Ryan (R-Wis.).

Calling it "Ryan's Roadmap to Ruin," Robert L. Borosage says the Republican's plan is "corrupt."[33]

"The People's Budget" plan was announced on April 5, 2011, by Congressional Progressive Caucus cochairmen Representatives Keith Ellison and Raul Grijalva.

The "Republican budget is not a blueprint for an economy that lifts up Americans who work for a living," they write. The Democrat talking points on this are clear, as they echo Borosage, calling Ryan's plan a "proven Roadmap to Ruin."[34]

Although the CPC plan would not be released for another week, it is clear in the CPC Task Force's letter to the CPC leadership that there's not a lot that's new in it.[35]

While the CPC leadership wanted the White House to adopt the phrase Make It in America, it was caught off-guard in May 2011, when President Obama inserted the new economic slogan, Win the Future, into the mix.[36]

After a year of promoting Make It in America, Representative Hoyer played it off expertly, telling Russell Berman of *The Hill*: "I'm not disappointed that he selected 'Win the Future,' I'm disappointed that he hasn't used 'Make It in America.' I think it's one and the same."

Hoyer "credited Obama with creating 1.75 million jobs over the last 15 months," Berman wrote. At the same time, Hoyer said the administration needed a "broader plan to make up for the much deeper job losses of the recession."

Berman also pointed out the obvious fact that the Democratic leadership's proposal included a "raft of legislation party lawmakers have proposed in recent years, some of which has drawn bipartisan support and the endorsement of the Obama administration."

The CPC has been coming up with nearly identical alternative budget plans since its founding in 1991. The CPC's plans are nearly identical to those of Democratic Socialists of America. The most recent CPC plan includes the recycled Make It in America jobs program.

Make no mistake, for progressives this is not about jobs. It's about electioneering and electing Democrats who will both control Congress and continue to push a progressive socialist agenda. In late January 2011, at a press conference following the House Democrats' annual retreat, Democratic leader Pelosi outlined the goals for Make It in America. Expectedly, it includes something called "Drive for 25," the Democrats' plan to gain twenty-five House seats in the 2012 elections and win back their majority.[37]

The Make It in America agenda will most likely appear on the campaign trail in 2012. It "is going to be an essential part of our campaign throughout the country," according to Representative Steve

Israel (D-N.Y.), chairman of the Democratic Congressional Campaign Committee.[38]

It is also not about jobs for *all* Americans. It's about union jobs, and union jobs mean union dues, which taken together mean campaign contributions for union-backed progressive candidates. Clear evidence for the latter comes again from the Alliance for American Manufacturing, which has sponsored an annual national Keep It Made in America town hall tour since its founding in 2007. Most recently, in 2010, AAM wrapped up its twelve-city, ten-state, seventeen-day tour just ahead of the midterm elections.[39]

The tour stops were attended by a few hundred individuals and featured a small galaxy of union superstars and political insiders. In 2009 at St. Louis, for example, three hundred people, including Steelworker, UAW, and SEIU members, attended. Speakers included Leo Gerard, Missouri senator Claire McCaskill, and Reverend Jesse Jackson. On the same tour, at Merrillville, Indiana, the crowd consisted of two hundred Steelworker activists.[40]

There is a good reason for the Steelworkers' predominating presence. The Alliance for American Manufacturing is led by none other than the United Steelworkers union.

Also included in all the Make It in America plans is a proposal to neutralize the alleged influence China holds over American manufacturing. As Speaker Pelosi promised in July 2010, H.R. 2378, the Currency Reform for Fair Trade Act, which had been introduced in May, passed on September 29 in the House and was forwarded to the Senate.[41] The House voted "to punish China for policies that unfairly favor its exports at the expense of the United States and other countries, the latest volley in what is developing as a global battle over jobs and commerce," Howard Schneider reported on September 29, 2010, in the *Washington Post*.[42] Schneider continued, "The vote, ahead of congressional elections in which economic issues will figure prominently, reflects growing international anxiety over China's policies—and particularly the management of its currency."

Prior to the bill's passage, in September 2010, the Fair Currency Coalition (which includes dozens of large and small trade union members), the Alliance for American Manufacturing, the American Manufacturing Trade Action Coalition, and the Citizens Trade Campaign (which includes Americans for Democratic Action and SEIU) sent letters of support to the House of Representatives.[43]

The Senate companion bill, S. 3134, the Currency Exchange Rate Oversight Reform Act of 2010, was introduced on March 17, 2010, and referred to committee. There has been no further action.[44]

"Buy American"?

The new Barack Obama campaign slogan Buy American, Vote Obama of late summer 2008 morphed into *Buy American* in the failed stimulus bill of February 2009, and was rebranded and repackaged as the Make It in America Democratic congressional strategy of midsummer 2010.

Buy American, Vote Obama came with its own logo, which was rolled out on stickers and flyers in select towns in Pennsylvania in August 2008.[45]

The logo is a circular emblem of solid red above solid blue, bisected by Harley-Davidson-like wings (which many found to resemble the Chrysler trademark and many others) and the Obama rainbowesque campaign logo in the center. Except for the shape—round instead of square—the Obama logo bears a strong resemblance to the red, white, and blue banded logo of the largest New Deal agency, the Works Progress Administration.

The Obama message was not new, either. In 1933 President Franklin D. Roosevelt signed the Buy American Act, which mandated a purchase preference for domestically produced goods in federal direct procurements. It is still in effect.[46]

Unnecessarily, the House Populist Caucus announced in early February 2009 that it would make its first major play by calling for the inclusion of a Buy American provision in the economic stimulus package.

There was an immediate Buy American pushback from America's friendly trading partner to the north, Canada. It caused sharp words between the two countries. WABC Radio's John Batchelor followed the exchanges closely: the Buy American mandate in "the hog farm of a stimulus package" passed in the House, he writes, was "now certain to grow fatter in the Senate."[47]

"The mandate was clear that the construction projects funded by the $820 billion must buy steel and iron products from American producers. Canada has gone to battle stations," Batchelor wrote on February 3, 2009.[48]

While President Obama made the rounds of the news talk shows to explain his plan, the Canadians were "at the battlements," with the "surprise of the day" being that the European Union also "went to battle stations." Batchelor writes: "EU officials asserted a direct threat at the Congress: 'We would look at all our options, including a WTO case, if "Buy American" passes.'"[49]

Buy American was a pander by the Democratic Party, Speaker Pelosi, and Harry Reid–led Senate to Obama's union backers—an "iPhoned up, networked, deep-benched, well-armed with cash and PACs" mob, as Batchelor describes them.[50]

While Canada mulled whether to adopt a Buy Canada campaign to counter Buy American, the *Times* of London reported on February 4 that Obama was getting ready to water down the Buy American plan after the EU issued a trade war threat in letters to U.S. political leaders in Congress, Secretary of the Treasury Timothy Geithner, and Secretary of State Hillary Clinton.[51]

By February 13, Buy American was out of the stimulus bill (or at least watered down). The day before Buy American went into effect, on February 16, Canada and the United States signed an agreement waiving the Buy American provisions, allowing Canada to participate in infrastructure projects funded under the economic stimulus bill.[52]

Radical Wizards Behind the Curtain

Barack Obama's and the Democratic Party's mighty allies include several radical progressive groups who not only supported Buy American—and more recently, the Make It in America—campaigns but also are key players in the drafting of the same legislation they promote. Additionally, most member organizations in these coalitions are often the same and the groups are overwhelmingly dominated by unions.

Added to this we have George Soros and his Open Society Institute funding of many of these same groups, including the Economic Policy Institute and the Democratic Socialists of America–connected Institute for Policy Studies. OSI has also coordinated on projects with the AFL-CIO, SEIU, the Steelworkers union, and other unions. Let's look at the groups.

Alliance for American Manufacturing

The Alliance for American Manufacturing, launched in April 2007, describes itself as a unique partnership between the United Steelworkers union and leading U.S. manufacturers. AAM sponsored what it calls successful Keep It Made in America tours and events, including an eleven-state bus tour with a focus on the auto sector. AAM conducted town hall meetings on manufacturing issues, as well as a nationally televised forum on manufacturing for presidential candidates.[53]

Leo W. Gerard, appointed by President Obama to the now-disbanded President's Advisory Committee on Trade Policy and Negotiations, is credited with helping create AAM.[54] Gerard's bio is lengthy. He is international president of the United Steelworkers union; a member of the AFL-CIO Executive Committee and chair of its Public Policy Committee; serves as cochairman of the BlueGreen Alliance; and serves on the boards of the now familiar, radical-led Apollo Alliance, Campaign for America's Future, and the Economic Policy Institute.

Gerard is not known to be a socialist outside of socialist circles. Two events connect Gerard with the Democratic Socialists of America. First, in 2001, Gerard became president of the United Steelworkers of America. Bob Roman, writing in *New Ground*, the online journal of the Chicago DSA, wrote that Gerard was a "Canadian export with ties to the Canadian New Democratic Party." CNDP, like DSA, is affiliated with the Socialist International.[55] Second, Gerard was one of two honorees on May 4, 2007, in Chicago at the DSA's Eugene V. Debs–Norman Thomas–Michael Harrington Dinner.[56] Additionally, Gerard serves on a number of boards—such as the Economic Policy Institute—that include a number of socialist members.

Although the authors found AAM's Web page naming its Project Partners inactive, a cache file for the same page, titled Who We Are, lists an obvious union-progressive, group-government agency coalition: AFL-CIO Industrial Union Council, Economic Policy Institute, International Trade Administration, American Economic Alert, U.S. Bureau of Labor Statistics, and U.S. Census Bureau Manufacturing, Mining and Construction Statistics.[57]

The inclusion of three federal government agencies is unexplained. To all intents and purposes, AAM appears to be just another union front group.

Founding AAM executive director Scott Paul was the principal lobbyist for the AFL-CIO Industrial Union Council and an AFL-CIO trade lobbyist. Paul interned from 1987 to 2001 with Senator Richard G. Lugar (R-Ind.), then served as the chief foreign policy and trade adviser to then House Democratic whip David Bonior.

In February 2010, AAM published a report titled *Buy America Works: Longstanding United States Policy Enhances the Job Creating Effect of Government Spending*, which makes a case for buying American to boost the American economy.[58] More than a year later, AAM's dissatisfaction with the inadequate growth in manufacturing jobs was expressed on April 1, 2011, by Scott Paul, who said, "We're still waiting for Congress to pass even a single measure that will substantially increase manufacturing jobs. With the economy at the top of the mind for most voters, Washington is still barking up the wrong tree."[59]

Making It in America failed to deliver.

Campaign for America's Future

The Campaign for America's Future, and its companion think tank, Institute for America's Future, were formed in July 1996 by a who's who of 130 labor leaders, academics, activists of all stripes, and others. Robert L. Borosage spearheaded the effort. He, Roger Hickey, and Robert Reich were CAF cofounders.[60]

Campaign for America's Future's fingerprints are all over the Make It in America campaign.

The executive summary for the report, *Where We're Going, How We'll Get There* by Eric Lotke and Armand Biroonak, was released on October 29, 2009, by Institute for America's Future. It concludes:[61]

> The next economy must be built on a solid platform. We need to rebuild our infrastructure, renew our manufacturing base and educate our people. America needs an industrial policy to help fit these pieces together. From workforce development to component manufacture, we need a strategic collaboration between the private sector and the government to reach our shared national goals. We need an opportunity for stakeholders to come together to remove obstacles, allocate resources, and create rules that work for everyone involved.

The Making It in America: Building the New Economy Conference was held on October 29, 2009, at the Washington Court Hotel in Washington, D.C. The event was hosted by the Institute for America's Future and the Alliance for American Manufacturing.[62]

CAF's website not only includes a section titled *Making It in America*, but also boasts, "Our Making It In America project is working to revive manufacturing as a key element in the new economy."[63]

Another section on the same Web page states: "The 'Making it in America' project exists to foster a broad public debate about this strategy, with an emphasis on reviving manufacturing as a key element of the new economy."

Borosage, in a July 2010 article titled "Making It in America," is critical of Barack Obama's accomplishments on American manufacturing. He writes on the IAF website:[64]

> Obama has suggested that America must lead in the green industries that surely will grow in the future—new energy, more efficient appliances, more sophisticated building efficiencies—and the supply chains associated with windmills, solar cells, batteries, fast trains, electric cars and more. Yet, Obama opposed the weak "buy America" provision put into the stimulus bill. His energy bill contained no serious effort at insuring that these products would be built here. Amendments designed to help manufacturers here were introduced into the bill in the dead of night because the administration needed the votes of industrial state Democrats to pass it. And because Ohio Senator Sherrod Brown and the Apollo Alliance had put together elements of a new energy industrial policy that House members could elbow into the legislation.

Here, again, we have a clear admission that the Apollo Alliance contributed to drafting the stimulus bill.

The progressive solution, Dave Johnson wrote on October 13, 2010, on the CAF blog, is "a national economic strategy that ensures the infrastructure, finance, supply chain, educational, legal, technical and regulatory elements are in place to enable American workers to compete." Johnson says the United States does not have something all our global competitors have, a "policy that promotes domestic manufacturing." Because of that lack of "an active and engaged industrial policy, we're handing business over to those that do," Johnson writes.[65]

Although the strategy clearly flopped in February 2009, Johnson suggests we should "Buy American."[66]

Economic Policy Institute

The progressive think tank the Economic Policy Institute was listed as a participant in the Alliance for American Manufacturing. Additionally, in August 2010, it was clearly supportive of the Make It in America initiative.[67]

The heads of eight major labor unions decided in 1986 that they would pool resources to create a think tank that would represent their interests.

In the "last few decades, organized labor has concentrated, with mixed success, on delivering unto the electoral process two basic commodities: bodies and money," Paul Taylor wrote in February 1987 in the *Washington Post*. "It now wants to add a third: ideas."[68]

EPI was described as to be "made up of some of the nation's most prominent liberal economists."

The eight unions—American Federation of State, County and Municipal Employees; United Auto Workers; United Steelworkers of America; United Mine Workers; International Association of Machinists and Allied Workers (IAM); Communications Workers of America; Service Employees International Union; and United Food and Commercial Workers International Union—made a five-year funding commitment to EPI, which included $460,000 for the first year, Taylor writes. EPI received an additional $340,000 first-year funding from foundations.

It was the view of John B. Judis, a member of the JournoList, writing in the spring 1992 issue of the *American Prospect*, that EPI "grew out of frustration with the failure of the AFL-CIO's Industrial Union Department to attract media interest in its studies. 'Union officials decided they would be better off following the corporations' example,'

noted one analyst, 'funding a group that was committed to their principles and ideas but not tainted directly by their label.'"[69]

Roger Hickey, a former EPI vice president, was quoted as having
said in 1993:[70]

> EPI had its start with money from the Stern Fund and a few small
> foundations, but several international unions soon came on board
> with major assistance. The basic idea was to revive the tradition of
> connection between the labor movement and academia, which had
> been so productive during the New Deal and the New Frontier.
> The economic issues we deal with are important to unions' survival.
> We convinced them of the need for an independent think tank, not
> connected with the AFL-CIO. Unions' own research departments
> are limited mainly to bread-and-butter matters.

EPI's five founding board members were Lester Thurow, former
dean of the Sloan School of Management, MIT; Robert Reich, then
at Harvard's Kennedy School of Government; Barry Bluestone, then
with the University of Massachusetts; Ray F. Marshall, secretary of
labor during the Carter administration; and Robert Kuttner, then an
economics writer for the *New Republic* and *BusinessWeek*.[71]

EPI's current board members include EPI's founding president, Jeff
Faux, and Bluestone, Kuttner, Marshall, and Reich. The names of several board members show the continued governance role of the original
founding and funding unions.[72]

R. Thomas Buffenbarger has served as president of IAM since 1997
and serves as a member of the Executive Council of the AFL-CIO. He
serves on the Executive Committee of the International Metalwork-
ers Federation, which represents 20 million workers in more than one
hundred countries, and as president of its Aerospace Department. He is
also a member of the U.S. Treasury Department's Advisory Committee to the International Monetary Fund.[73]

Anna Burger retired in August 2010 as chair of Change to Win, the five-union, 5.5 million worker federation formed in 2005 as an alternative to the AFL-CIO. Two of those five unions are the SEIU, of which Burger is secretary-treasurer, and the United Farm Workers.[74]

Larry Cohen has served as president of the CWA, the largest telecommunications union in the world, since 2005.[75]

Leo W. Gerard is international president of the United Steelworkers.[76]

Ron Gettelfinger served as president of the UAW from 2002 to 2010.

Gerald W. McEntee, president of the 1.6 million–member AFSCME (part of the AFL-CIO), is chairman of the EPI board and a founding member.[77]

Bruce S. Raynor is the former executive vice president of SEIU and former president of Workers United, the 150,000-member New York City–based garment workers union. He served as general president of UNITE HERE until suspended in April 2009 for misconduct and embezzling $15 million in union funds. At the end of March 2011, Raynor was accused of financial misconduct by SEIU in what Raynor characterizes as an effort by union leadership to push him out. On April 26, it was announced that Raynor had agreed to step down from both Workers United and SEIU.[78]

Andrew L. Stern, a former student radical in the 1960s, stepped down after thirteen years in office as SEIU president in April 2010.[79]

Richard L. Trumka has served as president of the AFL-CIO since September 2009. He had served as AFL secretary-treasurer since 1995. He was elected president of the United Mine Workers in 1982.

Randi Weingarten is president of the 1.4 million–member American Federation of Teachers, part of the AFL-CIO.

Board member Ernesto J. Cortes, Jr., although not a union leader, is a member of the National Executive Team of the Industrial Areas Foundation, which is much discussed in this book.[80]

EPI board members play key roles in a number of other organizations. For example, the July 2008 launch announcement of Health Care for America Now included a list of coalition members and representatives. Among those named are EPI board members Gerald McEntee and Anna Burger.[81]

As we detail in *The Manchurian President*, one of the key organizers behind the drafting of the Obamacare bill was EPI former vice president Roger Hickey.[82]

CAF's current board members include EPI's Jeff Faux and Leo W. Gerard. However, looking back to CAF's founding reveals a much expanded number of founders and advisers connected with EPI. On a list dating from 2003 are Bluestone, Buffenbarger, Faux, Kuttner, Marshall, McEntee, Reich, Stern, and Trumka. Also on the CAF list is EPI's current president, Lawrence Mishel.[83]

CAF/IAF has played what author Jarol B. Manheim calls a "second-tier role in bringing together on an infrequent but regular basis those with an interest in progressive social and political reform." Among these are the same union presidents that form EPI's board today.[84]

In February 2009, Obama announced members of the President's Economic Recovery Advisory Board, to be chaired by former Federal Reserve chairman Paul Volcker. Two EPI board members, union leaders Burger and Trumka, were named to the Advisory Board. (The Advisory Board was disbanded in late January 2011 and replaced with a new Council on Jobs and Competitiveness headed by General Electric CEO Jeffrey Immelt.)[85]

In a June 1, 2011, Bloomberg news interview, Trumka said that union enthusiasm for President Obama's reelection was waning. It was going to be more challenging to motivate union members.[86]

Trumka added the United States should become more like a European nation, providing pensions and health care for all citizens. "He said he is accustomed to criticism and doesn't mind if conservatives call that socialism," Bloomberg reported. "'Being called a socialist is a step up for me,' he said."

EPI board members Buffenbarger, Burger, and Gerard have served on at least one board of the Apollo Alliance. Burger, a signatory to the

2008 radical group Progressives for Obama, served on the Apollo Alliance steering committee in 2006. Gerard continues to serve on the Apollo Alliance's current board of directors.[87]

Gerard, according to an October 2007 article in the *American Prospect* by Jim Grossfeld, was the Apollo Alliance's key union backer.[88]

The Alliance bragged in a February 2009 news release of having influenced "specific content of many of the [stimulus] bill's provisions." The Alliance also claims policy proposals originated in 2008 in its New Apollo Program and the Apollo Economic Recovery Act.[89]

Faux said in 1987 that the "goal of this collaboration of academicians and labor" is "to 'create an intellectual climate that gives politicians more courage' to advocate greater government management of the economy." This was once known as *industrial policy.*

Dani Rodrik, professor of political economy at Harvard University's John F. Kennedy School of Government, writes that *industrial policy* is back. Actually, he says, it never went out of fashion. Although some may have written it off, he says, "successful economies have always relied on government policies that promote growth by accelerating structural transformation."[90]

Rodrik continues: "But when it comes to industrial policy, it is the United States that takes the cake. This is ironic, because the term 'industrial policy' is anathema in American political discourse. It is used almost exclusively to browbeat political opponents with accusations of Stalinist economic designs."

Ilya Podolyako, then a third-year student at the Yale Law School and an executive editor of the *Yale Journal on Regulation*, writes in April 2009:[91]

In the abstract sense, this system is the opposite of *laissez-faire* capitalism—the government owns enterprises and dictates both the nature and quantity of their output. This description naturally evokes images of the USSR, Cuba, or the People's Republic of China (before 1992), all countries with "command" economies.

The distinctive characteristic of these nations, however, was not the presence of state-owned enterprises (SOEs) per se, but the absence of a legal, noticeable private sector.

By February 1987 EPI had produced two studies. The first, a study of new job creation in 1979 through 1985 by economists Bluestone and Bennett Harrison, was commissioned by the Joint Economic Committee of Congress.[92]

The second, a study comparing United States economic performance for the past twenty-five years to that of Japan, West Germany, and Sweden, by economist Lucy Gorham, found the United States lagging behind. The study also found that "government spending in the other countries took a greater percentage of gross domestic product than did U.S. government spending."

The EPI's flagship publication is its annual *State of Working America*. It's claimed that its first issue in 1988 "galvanized a debate about the decline of real wages and income."[93]

It's Keynes, Again

It seems that the United States has come full circle. In March 1988, Faux, then EPI's chief economist, said: "The United States is like a business on the verge of bankruptcy. . . . It needs a financial plan. We've got to pay off our creditors, and at the same time, we've got to reinvest."[94]

Without a doubt, Faux subscribes to the grand economic theories of celebrated British economist John Maynard Keynes. Faux of 1988 sounds a lot like the Obama government of 2010. He writes:

The problem with the current dialogue is the implicit argument that first we have to get rid of the deficit, and then reinvest. But you can't put off that reinvestment without really hurting yourself in the long-term. . . .

My plan would be to increase taxes for the upper-income group, say the top 20 percent. It's like, send the bill to those who went to the party. Then we should cut excesses in the military sector. Then do something to discourage financial speculation—say a 1 percent turnover tax on every transaction. Finally, cut agriculture subsidies.

You can't cut this all in a snap because we're too close to a recession. And we have to raise revenues for new investment in education and training. My way would be a dime on the gas tax, and dedicate it for education and training. My reading of the polls is that people would be willing to pay it if they knew exactly what it would be going for.

As Zygmund Dobbs explains in his 1969 *Keynes at Harvard*, the answer to any economic dilemma is always Keynes.

A somewhat snarky but spot-on description of Keynes comes from William F. Shughart II, writing in September 2010 in Mississippi's *Bellingham Herald*:

During the Great Depression, economist John Maynard Keynes recommended increasing federal government spending, financed by borrowing, to boost the U.S. economy. It didn't matter how the new money was spent. If no better use could be found, Keynes suggested building pyramids or burying currency in bottles for people to dig up.

Keynes's theory that increased public spending would offset declines in consumer and business spending proved wrong. The unemployment rate remained in double digits until the "Greatest Generation" was called upon to sacrifice its blood and treasure to defeat the Axis powers.

The failure of Keynesian pump-priming seems to be lost on recent White House occupants.

EPI doggedly follows the Keynesian path. In 1988 several liberal think tanks were drafting blueprints for a possible incoming Democratic president to follow, with EPI among them.[95]

Bailey Morris wrote in July 1988 in the *Times* of London that Democrats wondered how they could capture the economic issue. Morris, who describes EPI as Democratic ideologues, continues: "The Democrats have their own supply-siders, a powerful bloc of liberals who believe that deficits do not really matter. They fear the growing obsession with deficit reduction will lead to a period of austerity and social unrest."[96]

Faux told the *New York Times* the main priority is to "encourage a Democratic administration not to respond to budget deficits with austerity measures in social programs." Faux added: "such moves had proved a trap both for President Jimmy Carter and for Walter F. Mondale, the Democrats' 1984 Presidential nominee." Carter, he continues, "responded to inflation by cutting the real incomes of working people. Mondale said he was going to tax Americans for the debts that Reagan ran up, and what happened is that Ronald Reagan became the candidate of full employment."[97]

This mind-set continued unabated in January 1990, when Roger Hickey, as EPI vice president, told the *Christian Science Monitor* that it was time for "more government spending on education, infrastructure (roads, bridges, airports, etc.), and industrial policy, such as helping business research the next generation of telecommunications."[98]

Exploratory Project for Economic Alternatives

EPI's thinkers did not exactly reinvent the wheel in 1986. One only needs to look at EPI president Jeff Faux's ideology from a decade prior. Faux had advocated a clearly collectivist anticapitalist economic remedy.

In 1977 Faux and Gar Alperovitz—also a founding adviser for the Campaign for America's Future—were economists for the foundation-supported think tank, Exploratory Project for Economic Alternatives.

An EPEA report recommended private and public owners of resources should become "'public trustees' with legal responsibility to manage them in the interests of the 'beneficiaries,' the American people." EPEA's literature said its goal was to "develop economic alternatives which move us away from a future dominated by the values of giant corporate and bureaucratic institutions."[99]

The appearance of the word *public* is a calculated misdirection. Although *public* refers to the people, what it really means is that control is totally in the hands of government.

The evolution of EPEA begins with the Democratic Socialists of America–affiliated Institute for Policy Studies. In 1968, two IPS fellows, Harvard historian and political economist Gar Alperovitz and sociologist Christopher Jenks, established an IPS spin-off, the Cambridge Institute in Massachusetts. The institute received funding from IPS. Largely staffed with Harvard and MIT members, the institute claims to have "avoided fashionable socialist and Marxist views, preferring a free-thinking approach in search of new social solutions." Alperovitz, in turn, spun off EPEA from the Cambridge Institute.[100]

EPEA worked closely with leftist consumer advocate Ralph Nader. Together, Alperovitz and Nader established COIN, Consumers to Fight Inflation in the Necessities.[101]

EPEA was all for economic democracy. EPEA argued for public ownership of large corporations and for "confronting public control over major economic decisions now in the hands of the private sector." Described as a "necessary extension of democracy," this sounds a lot like the Obama government's takeover of the banking and automotive industries.

It was Derek Shearer, now a faculty member at Occidental College, but once a member of IPS's National Conference on State and Local Public Policies, who coined the term *economic democracy*. Similar to the warnings of the Fabian socialists, Shearer famously said you can't use the word *socialism* but *economic democracy* "sells."

ALICE (American Legislative Issue Campaign Exchange)

ALICE, the American Legislative Issue Campaign Exchange, is perhaps the mother organization to progressive legislation-writing efforts.

Self-described as a "pro-labor, pro-environment, pro-good-government educational organization," ALICE launched in early 2003 as a collaborative project of the Economic Analysis and Research Network (EARN), the Center on Wisconsin Strategy (COWS), labor groups, and several other progressive organizations.[102]

EARN is coordinated by the Economic Policy Institute. A network of state and regional multi-issue research, policy, and advocacy organizations, EARN currently includes fifty-six organizations in forty-two states. It states its mission is to "improve the lives of Americans through state and local policy, and change the nature of the national policy debate—state by state."[103]

EARN national member groups include, among others, ACORN, Campaign for America's Future, Center for Community Change, Demos, Economic Policy Institute, and USAction. EARN also includes a number of state member groups.[104]

COWS at the University of Wisconsin–Madison is headed by Joel Rogers, a cofounder of the Apollo Alliance. Rogers, who works with EPI, professes to monitor labor-market trends in Wisconsin.[105]

The ALICE website provides a clearinghouse and hub for "activists, organizations, experts and elected officials who want a map to take the High Road."[106]

The ALICE home page provides an interactive feature called its Best Practices Policy Package, which includes sample legislation, issue analysis, strategy background information, a message center, media kit, and "Expert Advice from Alice."

By April 2004, ALICE claimed it was providing weekly updates to more than 7,400 elected officials and activists. Until the prior month, ALICE had been supported by Rogers and COWS. A fund-raising appeal gleaned support from several organizations, including the AFL-CIO.[107]

ALICE was intended to be the left's answer to ALEC, the American Legislative Exchange Council. ALEC was founded in 1973 by conservative Christian activist Paul Weyrich. Described in January 2005 by progressive writer Ruth Conniff, ALEC was used to draft model bills and fly state legislators to "posh, corporate-financed conferences to teach them how to push its agenda in statehouses across the nation."[108]

Conniff's article reveals a mega-case of leftist envy over perceived Republican monopoly of corporate sponsors, campaign funds, public policy, and winning congressional elections.

The ALICE website is no longer active and the last archived ALICE Web page dates from the end of May 2008.[109]

Apollo Alliance

The Apollo Alliance's fingerprints are also all over *Make It in America*. Can there be any doubt that H.R. 5156, the Clean Energy Technology Manufacturing and Export Assistance Act of 2010, which passed in the House in July 2010, is an Apollo Alliance product?[110]

The Apollo Alliance's *Make It in America: The Apollo Clean Transportation Manufacturing Action Plan* was released ahead of the 2010 midterm elections, in October.[111]

At an October 26, 2010, press conference, Senator Sherrod Brown, Leo Gerard, Chandra Brown, president of United Streetcar, and Cathy Calfo, executive director of Apollo Alliance, announced the new transportation manufacturing plan to reporters.[112]

> TMAP details how smart policies will leverage these infrastructure investments to create middle class jobs for Americans. New data from the Economic Policy Institute reveals that the $40 billion

TMAP investment scenario will create 3.7 million direct and indirect jobs—600,000 alone in the manufacturing sector over the next six years, the likely duration of a reauthorized transportation bill.

Several months earlier, in March 2010, the Apollo Alliance convened a task force from industry, labor unions, and policy experts—the Transportation Manufacturing Action Plan, or TMAP, task force—to "examine options for expanding the domestic production of advanced transit systems, vehicles, clean trucks, and their component parts."[113]

TMAP task force members, divided into five groups (transportation, labor, business, and environment leaders, and policy experts and academics), come from a long list of now-familiar names. Labor leaders include Gerard. Business leaders include AAM's Scott Paul. Policy experts and academics include Borosage, Kate Gordon, John Irons, research and policy director at the EPI, and Claudia Preparata, research director of Green For All.[114]

Among TMAP endorsers are the Ella Baker Center for Human Rights and Green For All, two Oakland, California–based organizations cofounded by former Apollo Alliance board member Van Jones.[115]

The report references the September 2008 release of the *New Apollo Program*, described as a "comprehensive economic investment strategy to build America's 21st-century clean energy economy, create more than 5 million high-quality green-collar jobs, and establish America as the global leader of the new clean energy economy."[116]

The Apollo Alliance released a second report in March 2009, the *Make It in America: Green Manufacturing Action Plan*. GreenMAP, part of the *New Apollo Program*, Apollo's "comprehensive national strategy for building a clean energy, good jobs economy," was developed by many of the same groups and representatives who were later involved with TMAP.[117]

GreenMAP included federal policy recommendations to "spur domestic clean energy manufacturing and increase the energy efficiency of our existing plants."[118]

Recommendations from GreenMAP were incorporated into Senator Sherrod Brown's proposed Investments for Manufacturing Progress and Clean Technology, or IMPACT, Act. They were also included in the American Clean Energy and Security Act, or ACES, which passed in the House in June 2009.

Several recommendations from TMAP are significant to monitor moving forward in the second half of the Obama administration. Such items as billions of dollars invested in transportation: public transit and intercity rail; a national freight plan, expansion of America's freight vehicle fleet, and so-called port cleanup and "clean freight"; and competitive financing for public and private transportation, reduced energy consumption, and funding U.S. manufacturing.[119]

In his January 2011 State of the Union address, President Obama consistently called for *investment* (government spending) for such budget-busting projects as providing 80 percent of America's electricity from clean energy sources by 2035 (natural gas and "clean coal") and providing high-speed rail for 80 percent of Americans within twenty-five years.[120]

Obama was cheered on by a coalition calling itself Transportation For America. Serving on the executive committee is none other than the Apollo Alliance and one of its member organizations, the Natural Resources Defense Council.[121]

Transportation For America's Equity Caucus clearly reveals its progressive agenda. The Equity Caucus, it states, was "formed by the nation's leading civil rights, community development, racial justice, economic justice, faith-based, health, housing, labor, environmental justice, tribal, and transportation organizations [to drive] transportation policies that advance economic and social equity in America." Signatories to the Equity Caucus's statement of principles include the Apollo Alliance, Center for Community Change, Change to Win, Gamaliel Foundation, NAACP, and SEIU, among others.[122]

However, as soon as the 2010 midterm elections were past, the Make It in America call for action outlined in the Apollo Alliance's

TMAP was "operating in a nearly mythical political universe that bears little resemblance to the changing political realities," Art Levin writes at *In These Times*.[123]

And so we have another major piece of legislation exposed to be the crafty handiwork of the radical network and its socialist designs.

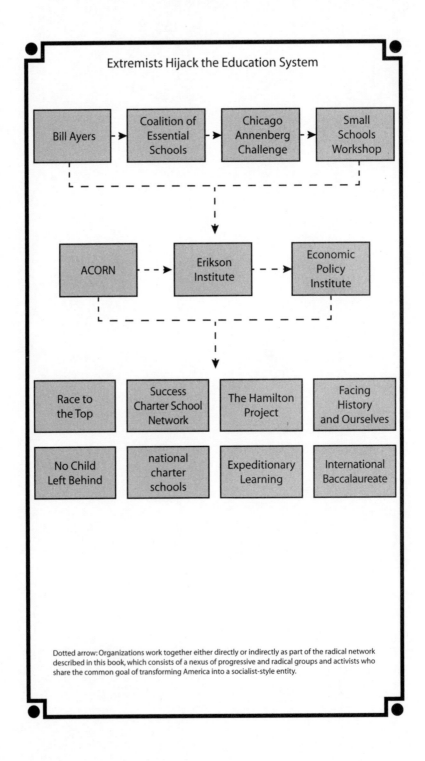

Extremists Hijack the Education System

Bill Ayers → Coalition of Essential Schools → Chicago Annenberg Challenge → Small Schools Workshop

ACORN → Erikson Institute → Economic Policy Institute

Race to the Top

Success Charter School Network

The Hamilton Project

Facing History and Ourselves

No Child Left Behind

national charter schools

Expeditionary Learning

International Baccalaureate

Dotted arrow: Organizations work together either directly or indirectly as part of the radical network described in this book, which consists of a nexus of progressive and radical groups and activists who share the common goal of transforming America into a socialist-style entity.

chapter five

BILL AYERS— EDUCATION CZAR?

We must ask what motivated Weatherman founder and Barack Obama associate Bill Ayers to "reinvent" himself as a leading education reformist after he reemerged from living underground as a wanted domestic American terrorist whose organization sought the downfall of the U.S. capitalist system while carrying out bombings of U.S. government buildings. We know Ayers did not suddenly moderate his views. As late as September 11, 2001, he gave an interview in which he declared he did not regret setting bombs and that he felt he "didn't do enough." When asked if he would "do it all again," Ayers replied, "I don't want to discount the possibility."[1] So what is motivating this radical to involve himself in reforming our school system?

Ayers is just one of several top 1960s anti-American radicals who currently toil full-time in education reform, alongside other major progressive education groups and even openly socialist activists with questionable intentions who form an arm of the radical network we have been exposing in this work. Here we will reveal how that radical network has been hard at work reforming our education system and how it views education as key to their ideological assault against our country by indoctrinating generations of our children. We will document how the network's educational agenda received a major boost with the election of Barack Obama, and how, shockingly, Obama has been using government money, including stimulus grants, to fund a slew of radical education initiatives, some even associated with Ayers and his Weatherman comrades, as well as with the disgraced Association of Community Organizations for Reform Now, or ACORN.

Before that, we must briefly review the history of the socialist infiltration of the American education system, and Obama's own early involvement in working to transform our school system.

Fabian Infiltration

The so-called socialist permeation began slowly near the end of the nineteenth century, when Fabian Society leaders came from England to the United States to train groups in the "art of socialism." The first converts were students on Ivy League and other major college campuses. One Ivy League school of special interest to us is Brown University in Rhode Island. It is the home of the Annenberg Challenge and the Coalition of Essential Schools, which we will discuss shortly. Brown University provides a good example of an early incubator for socialist indoctrination. A class on socialism offered before World War I had only managed to draw fifteen students; after the war, in 1918, the same class attracted fifty-five.[2]

Significantly, the class was taught by a true Fabian socialist, Alvin H. Hansen. Known as the American Keynes, Hansen later taught economics at Harvard Graduate School, where he, Seymour E. Harris, and J. Kenneth Galbraith indoctrinated hundreds of future instructors to "infect educational institutions" throughout the United States. Hansen was also an associate of Socialist Party leader Norman Thomas.[3]

The Annenberg Challenge

Fast forward to December 17, 1993. In a White House ceremony, President Bill Clinton announced the largest gift ever made to American public education: a $500 million, five-year "challenge to the nation designed to energize and support promising efforts at school reform throughout the country." Funds came from the late Honorable Walter H. Annenberg, former U.S. ambassador to Great Britain during the Richard Nixon administration.[4]

Brown University's president, Vartan Gregorian, a longtime Annenberg friend, served as adviser to the Annenberg Foundation and coordinated the Annenberg Challenge's programs and initiatives.

Beginning in early 1995 the Annenberg Challenge was to commit $15 million to the Education Commission of the States. The ECS was created in 1965 as a nonprofit, nationwide agency by the governments of all fifty states and four U.S. territories.

The first of two organizations already engaged in education reform to benefit is the New American Schools Development Corporation (NASDC), a nonprofit, nonpartisan organization formed in July 1991 and endorsed by both the George H. W. Bush and Clinton administrations. NASDC received $50 million in honor of its chairman, David T. Kearns, a former deputy secretary of education. The funds, as required by the terms of the Challenge, were met by another $50 million from private sources and put to use within eighteen months.

A second $50 million endowment went to the National Institute for School Reform at Brown University, established in October 1993 and renamed the Annenberg Institute for School Reform on the same day the Challenge was announced. The institute would support the seven-hundred-school Coalition of Essential Schools (CES).

The renamed institute was governed by a Board of Overseers and Theodore R. "Ted" Sizer. The Walter H. Annenberg Distinguished Professor at Brown University, Sizer founded the Coalition of Essential Schools in 1984. He was to continue as its chairman and serve as the institute's executive director.

The institute was to encourage "expansion of like-minded schools," most particularly Sizer's Coalition of Essential Schools. Another goal was to establish new alliances and extend existing relationships with such groups as the seven hundred CES schools, ECS, the Education Development Center in NASDC's ATLAS Communities project, teachers' colleges, and other CES-related regional organizations in several states.

The Challenge, Ayers, and Obama

Alexander Russo, a former Senate education staffer and journalist, provides a firsthand account of the chain of events connecting Ayers and Obama to the Chicago Annenberg Challenge. Russo wrote on April 1, 2000:[5]

> When three of Chicago's most prominent education reform leaders met for lunch at a Thai restaurant six years ago to discuss the just-announced $500 million Annenberg Challenge, their main goal was to figure out how to ensure that any Annenberg money awarded to Chicago "didn't go down the drain," said William Ayers, a professor of education at the University of Illinois in Chicago. Ayers, who was at that lunch table in late 1993, helped write the successful Chicago grant application.

Barack Obama was appointed as CAC's first chairman in 1995, the same year Bill Ayers reportedly held an Illinois state senatorial campaign event for Obama in Ayers's Hyde Park residence. It is the opinion of Stanley Kurtz, a senior fellow at the Ethics and Public Policy Center who has researched the Obama-Ayers relationship in depth, that no one would have appointed Obama as CAC chairman without Ayers's approval.[6]

After diligently reviewing the CAC archives, Kurtz found that the CAC foundation granted money to radical leftist activist causes. This includes ACORN.[7] We will soon document how, as president, Obama continues to push government funds to ACORN-affiliated schools.

The CAC archives document how Obama and Ayers worked as a team to further the foundation's agenda. Obama was in charge of fiscal matters, while Ayers was more concerned with shaping educational policy.

The documents show Ayers served as an ex officio board member while Obama chaired the CAC during the first year. Ayers also served on the board's governance committee with Obama, and worked with him to craft CAC bylaws. According to the documents, Ayers made presentations to board meetings chaired by Obama. Ayers also spoke for the Chicago School Reform Collaborative before Obama's board, while Obama periodically spoke on CAC's behalf at meetings of the Collaborative.

Obama stepped down as CAC board president in 1999 when he ran for the U.S. House of Representatives. He remained on the board after serving as president for the CAC's first four and a half years.[8]

The CAC granted more than $600,000 to the Small Schools Workshop, an organization cofounded by Ayers and now operated by Mike Klonsky, a former member of Students for a Democratic Society, a top communist activist, and the founder of a communist organization.[9]

Klonsky commented in September 2008 on his *Small Talk* blog:[10]

> The Small Schools Workshop was at that time, the main provider of research, training and support for teachers and principals in Chicago who were trying to redesign and restructure their large, overcrowded high schools into smaller learning communities.
>
> Whatever grant money that the Workshop received (not Ayers or me) over a 5-year period, was a relatively small amount compared with other university-based initiatives, and was used exclusively to fulfill the requirements of the grant.

The unwillingness by those involved to acknowledge the closeness of the CAC and SSW, as well as CAC-SSW conflicts of interest, is astounding. The role played by Patricia Ford is usually ignored. In 1991,

Bill Ayers was the founder and Ayers and Ford were the founding co-directors of the Small Schools Workshop; Mike Klonsky was founding executive director.[11] During the five years of CAC operations, Ford served as CAC's program director. She is now with the Stearns Family Foundation.[12]

The close working relationship between Ford, Klonsky, and Ayers is unmistakable. In May 1994, Klonsky and Ford coauthored "One Urban Solution: Small Schools," a journal article published in *Educational Leadership*. Two years later, in 1996, Ayers and Ford co-edited the book *City Kids, City Teachers: Reports from the Front Row*.[13]

It is significant to note that in 2002, while head of Chicago's public schools, Arne Duncan joined the small schools bandwagon. The Chicago High School Redesign Initiative, four new small high schools, was described at the time as Duncan's school reform centerpiece. Patricia Ford, by the way, served as executive director for Duncan's initiative.[14]

Bill Ayers has inaccurately been credited as the founder of the small schools movement. By Ayers's own account, after teaching preschool and kindergarten in New York City, in 1987 he returned to Chicago and brought the small schools concept with him and began promoting it for Chicago's public schools.[15]

By 1988, five years prior to the announcement of the Annenberg Challenge grant, according to Mike Klonsky, small schools—called charter schools—existed in Philadelphia's twenty-two high schools. The Small Schools Workshop launched in 1992; Klonsky estimated in 1994 that small schools had been established in fifty Chicago public schools, with between thirty and forty of them in elementary schools.[16]

Individual schools were "built around specific political themes [to] push students to 'confront issues of inequity, war, and violence,'" Kurtz writes. Ayers, he says, "believes teacher education programs should serve as 'sites of resistance' to an oppressive system." Ayers, he says, writes in his *Teaching Toward Freedom* that the point is "to 'teach against oppression,' against America's history of evil and racism, thereby forcing social transformation."[17]

Ayers's publicly stated version sounds harmless, however. In a November 1994 interview with the *Chicago Tribune*, Ayers stated the Small Schools Workshop is "dedicated to helping 'school people who are interested in following a strategy of creating smaller, more personal learning environments.'" Ayers added that SSW provides a "step-by-step program for setting up small schools in the Chicago public schools."[18]

Using CAC funds, in collaboration with Cross City Campaign for Urban School Reform and Chicago ACORN, the Small Schools Workshop worked with parent leaders and Chicago Public Schools to "recruit qualified teachers to their communities' understaffed schools." As a result, parents and members of low-income communities were trained and obtained teacher certificates to teach in local schools.[19]

The Erikson Institute, led by radical educator Barbara Taylor Bowman, received CAC funds for early childhood education. The institute trained both teachers and staff to "develop comprehensive curriculum for early childhood education in a network of Chicago public schools."[20]

The CAC supported both nationally known initiatives, such as the Comer Model, Success for All, and the Coalition of Essential Schools, as well as "locally-developed reforms," Alexander Russo reported in 2000. Most of these programs, Russo adds, were already under way before the CAC grant funds were received. Instead of using the funds for new projects, or to expand existing ones, they were used to strengthen and intensify ongoing programs.[21]

There were anecdotal reports of the CAC's success, but little evidence of impact. Bill Ayers, for example, painted a positive picture. Ayers said the CAC had done an "'astonishingly good job' in several key areas." It had "raised for public debate system wide the issues of school size, professionalizing teaching, and the relationships between communities and their schools." Ayers also believed CAC had "demonstrated the power of networks to create a sense of community among schools grappling with similar issues."

Other than such self-serving testimonials from people like Ayers, the true impact of the CAC funds is unclear, Russo relates. He was unable to find any signs of effectiveness outside of those espoused anecdotally by CAC principals. Additionally, Russo writes that "none of the networks contacted could supply research that attributes student-achievement gains to Annenberg funding."

Ayers's Brother, Father

Russo identified another major problem in late 1997: "only about half of the city leaders were familiar enough with the Chicago Challenge even to speculate on what its main activities had been." John Ayers, executive director of Leadership for Quality Education, and brother of Bill Ayers, told Russo the "tough work" being done by the CAC was unlikely to be noticed, or gain positive press, because the "hard work" was being done at the schools.

John Ayers, also a key player in Chicago's school reform movement, is now vice president and treasurer of the Carnegie Foundation for the Advancement of Teaching. The Ayers brothers' late father, Thomas Ayers, the longtime CEO of Commonwealth Edison, represented the city's business community interests via the Commercial Club of Chicago.[22]

In spring 1987, John Ayers and Barack Obama made contact through the Developing Communities Project, which Obama headed, and Obama's youth counseling efforts. Archived papers for former Chicago mayor Harold Washington show that not only Ayers but also Reverend Jeremiah Wright and Father Michael Pfleger—Obama religious advisers who were controversial during the 2008 presidential campaign for their inflammatory remarks—were on Obama's DCP youth counseling advisory committee.

More than a decade after the CAC funding ended, in 2008 John Ayers launched the school management organization Union Park High Schools, Inc. Plans are to create four charter high schools in Chicago in partnership with three labor unions—Service Employees International Union Local 73, the Illinois Federation of Teachers, and the Chicago Teachers Union—and Johns Hopkins University.[23]

Regarding the CAC, Russo said no major effort was made to break away from favoring the awarding of CAC grants to school reform and community activist groups. He points out that the amounts increased over time. In 1995, 25 percent of implementation grant funds went to these groups, and that grew to more than 50 percent in 1996, when eight out of fourteen grant awards went to these groups. And in 1997 an additional eight grants went to community organizations and reform groups.[24]

Some of the programs funded by the Chicago Annenberg Challenge will be covered in the sections that follow.

Coalition of Essential Schools

The Coalition of Essential Schools, founded by Ted Sizer, was one of the big winners, with a $50 million endowment in the Annenberg Challenge sweepstakes.

A champion of the progressive education philosophy of John Dewey, Sizer was persuaded that education "must be rooted in a kind of democratic pluralism." Educational policy should be determined from the "bottom up, at the level of the school, rather than as a result of state or federal directives." Schools, Sizer argued, "should abandon one-size-fits-all educational methods like standardized tests, grading and even the grouping of students into classes by age."[25]

Sizer held degrees from Yale and Harvard universities. Between 1972 and 1981, he served as headmaster at Phillips Academy in Andover, Massachusetts, and left to lead a five-year study of American high schools sponsored by the National Association of Secondary School Principals and the National Association of Independent Schools. As a result, in 1984 he founded the Coalition of Essential Schools while working at

Brown University from 1983 to 1997 as a professor. During the 1998–99 school year, Sizer and his wife, Nancy Sizer, were co-principals of Francis W. Parker Charter Essential School in Devens, Massachusetts.[26]

By 1993 there were approximately 700 K–12 member schools. The number of CES schools has grown to more than 1,000 with twenty regional centers in the United States. CES's two-tiered system of services includes support services to its regional centers. CES's regional centers may vary in program offerings, but all are guided by the Common Principles and share similar strategies.[27]

Although harmless-sounding, the Common Principles are by no means insignificant. Since CES's founding in 1984, literally hundreds of thousands of students have been influenced by them. The principles now number ten, with the last one added in 1998.[28]

Two of these principles bear closer examination. Number 4 says the choice of teaching materials is reserved for a school's principal and staff. This is not necessarily a good idea, as we discuss in the CES curriculum below.

The second principle that sets off an alert is Number 5, the very socialist-sounding "student-as-worker." This is reminiscent of the Red Sunday Schools of the 1910s and 1920s, when classes operated by the Socialist Party were used to indoctrinate children in class consciousness and how to become good workers. Bill Ayers called the Red Sunday Schools a "remarkable counterinstitution."[29]

There were twelve original CES schools, including such highly visible schools as Central Park East Secondary School in East Harlem, New York. It was designed and launched by CES cofounder Deborah Meier, now vice chair emeritus, senior scholar, Steinhardt School of Culture, Education, and Human Development, New York University.

The current CES executive board includes two progressive education luminaries, Meier and George H. Wood, principal of Federal Hocking High School, Stewart, Ohio, and executive director of the Forum for Education and Democracy.[30]

The CES national office administers professional development institutes through its CES University, which operates an annual Fall Forum for teachers and administrators. The CES national website is the fount of all CES information. CES also publishes an informational journal, *Horace*.[31]

Horace is named for the fictional character Horace Smith, the "beloved teacher (and later principal) of the archetypal Franklin High," whom Sizer used to "convey the reality of everyday school life" in the United States. This Horace lives on in the pages of Sizer's trilogy, *Horace's Compromise* (1984), *Horace's School* (1992), and *Horace's Hope* (1996).[32]

CES Curriculum

The CES curriculum is based on the concept of essentialism, which "strives to teach students the accumulated knowledge of our civilization through core courses in the traditional academic disciplines. It aims to instill students with the 'essentials' of academic knowledge, patriotism, and character development," David Miller Sadker and Karen R. Zittleman write in their text *Teachers, Schools, and Society*.[33]

Although Sadker and Zittleman see this as a "traditional or back-to-basics" approach, it is anything but. It is nearly impossible to pin down a single approach to CES curriculum development even though the CES website and *Horace* publications are loaded with suggestions. A 1996 article on developing the curriculum in CES schools by Kathleen Cushman provides a brief overview of the CES approach.[34]

The first example Cushman relates features the CES school, the Francis W. Parker Charter School at which Ted and Nancy Sizer were co-principals. She describes a group of teachers sitting around the table discussing how they will create a curriculum that fulfills the CES promise of "a project-based curriculum that integrates mathematics, science, and technology around Essential Questions." The *Essential Questions* is a complex outline described as the starting point for curriculum development. It includes such items as "Curriculum and courses should be organized not around answers but around big ideas—questions and problems to which content represents answers." *Benchmark Descriptors* include such concepts as "Transforming: student and adult work reflect depth and higher-order thinking prompted by essential questions." *Related Principles* are "Learning to use one's mind well" and "Less is more, depth over coverage."[35]

These indefinite, sweeping guidelines can be interpreted in just about any way imaginable.

In a second example, Cushman writes that a group like Foxfire, an approved CES curriculum, "gives student interest a larger role in shaping curriculum." The Foxfire Approach to Teaching and Learning emerged from an experiential education program originally devised to teach basic English skills to high school freshmen in Appalachian Georgia. The *Foxfire* magazine and series of books are the popularly known products of the program. The Foxfire Approach is defined by the *Core Practices*, described as the "decision-making framework the approach provides for teachers, and the ways the framework fits with John Dewey's notion of experiential education."[36]

Cushman states that although "few schools would risk going into a year without lesson plans in hand, many educators argue that involving students in developing curriculum is crucial." Meier, Jay Featherstone, and Bill Ayers agreed at a 1991 meeting of their North Dakota Study Group that the "question of what should be at the center of the curriculum should be at the center of the curriculum."[37]

Featherstone is professor emeritus at the Center for the Scholarship of Teaching, College of Education, Michigan State University, and a longtime leader in progressive education.[38]

Indoctrination

We begin our topical discussion of the CES curriculum with something called Radical Math.

Radical Math:

A recommended math curriculum is Radical Math, which describes itself as an "organization for educators working to integrate issues of political, economic, and social justice into math education." Radical Math was founded in 2006 by Jonathan Osler, "Math and Community Organizing" teacher at El Puente Academy for Peace and Justice, a public CES high school in Brooklyn, New York. The Radical Math website (www.radicalmath.org) provides what is described as "an evolving exploration of teaching and learning focused on both math skills and social justice issues."[39]

The 2005 Rethinking Schools publication, *Rethinking Mathematics: Teaching Social Justice by the Numbers*, by Eric Gutstein and Bob Peterson, for example, provides a "unique collection of more than 30 articles [that] shows teachers how to weave social-justice principles throughout the math curriculum, and how to integrate social-justice math into other curricular areas as well."[40]

Described as *real-world math*, the collection provides "teaching ideas, lesson plans and reflections by practicing classroom teachers and distinguished mathematics educators." *Rethinking Mathematics* is promoted as an aid to "help teachers develop students' understanding of society and prepare them to be critical, active participants in a democracy."

It is unmistakable that the emphasis is on social justice, not learning math.

Radical History:

Social Justice High School in Chicago is one of four smaller schools inside Little Village Lawndale High School, an experimental public school. LVLHS opened in 2005 following a nineteen-day hunger strike by Mexican immigrants.[41]

Students at SJHS are taught what has been generously described as a "very different version" of U.S. history. It includes material on the "near-genocide of the Native Americans by European colonizers and the murder of union leaders by the U.S. government in the early 1900s." The text is nothing more than a youth edition of the Marxist version of American history found in *A People's History of the United States* by the late Howard Zinn.

The impact and influence of Zinn's book cannot be overstated. The nonyouth version of the book is required reading for courses taught nationwide on college campuses. The book is said to be "so popular that it can be found on the class syllabus in such fields as economics, political science, literature, and women's studies, in addition to its more understandable inclusion in history."[42]

In a spring 2004 article in *Dissent* magazine, Daniel J. Flynn, then executive director of Accuracy in Academia, writes, "With all its limitations, [Zinn's] history [is] disrespectful of governments and respectful of people's movements of resistance."[43]

Zinn was much more than just a progressive's favorite historian. An FBI file on Zinn was released in July 2010 that blew all progressive preconceptions about him completely away. After more than two decades of teaching in the political science department at Boston University, exerting his influence on the progressive movement all the while, it was discovered Zinn had been a member of the Moscow-controlled and Soviet-funded Communist Party USA.[44]

Zinn was also found to be a pro-Castro activist and supporter of such radical groups as the Students for a Democratic Society, Progressive Labor Party, Socialist Workers Party, and the Black Panther Party. Zinn's support for communist military victory in Vietnam, and the communist regime, included a visit to Hanoi.

Cliff Kincaid of Accuracy in Media observes: "But in the same way that he tried to deceive the FBI agents who interviewed him about his CPUSA membership, it is now obvious that Zinn had been deceiving his 'progressive' and 'liberal' fellow-travelers for decades."

In a February 2009 telephone conference with high school students, Zinn warned them about becoming complacent with the status quo. Zinn said: "It has never been enough to elect a liberal. It's not enough to say, 'We have a good guy in office, we can relax.' If you relax, Obama becomes another politician."[45]

What's even more interesting is the report of another item Zinn told the students. Zinn said that for change to happen, "there needs to be 'movements from below.'" He reportedly said the United States will need "social movements from labor unions and black people and a movement to demand free health care to turn things around."

Following Zinn's death in January 2010, John Perazzo remarked at FrontPageMag.com: "few academicians did more than the late Boston University professor to poison the minds of so many young Americans with a vulgar narrative of history in which the United States was forever cast as the villain."[46]

Zinn's school of history is a "history of often unsubstantiated ephemera in the service of a grand theory—in Zinn's case that the U.S. is rotten to the core because it is built on the murderous greed of capitalism," writes Mary Grabar, a conservative professor of English.[47]

Grabar quotes from a passage about the Cold War from Zinn's *History*:[48]

> When, right after [World War II], the American public, war-weary, seemed to favor demobilization and disarmament, the Truman administration . . . worked to create an atmosphere of crisis and cold war. . . . The Truman administration . . . presented the Soviet Union as not just a rival but an immediate threat.
>
> In a series of moves abroad and at home, it established a climate of fear—a hysteria about Communism—which would steeply escalate the military budget and stimulate the economy with war-related orders.

Zinn continues the paragraph: "This combination of policies would permit more aggressive actions abroad, more repressive actions at home."[49]

Grabar observes: "The denial of over 100 million deaths by communist regimes is a deliberate rewriting of history that has implications today. The people writing such histories ignore, deny, or minimize deaths of very real people."

Ron Radosh, the author of *Commies: A Journey Through the Old Left, the New Left and the Leftover Left*, adds:[50]

> From Zinn's perspective, history should not be told from the standpoints of generals or presidents, but through that of people who struggle for their rights, who engage in strikes, boycotts, slave rebellions and the like. Its purpose should be to encourage similar behavior today. Indeed, Zinn candidly said that history was not about "understanding the past," but rather, about "changing the future." That statement alone should have disqualified anyone from referring to him as a historian.

Zinn's book sold more than 2 million copies after the first printing of a mere 5,000 copies in 1980. More than 100,000 new copies are printed and sold every year. This should be a great cause for concern since we know that a large number of these copies are a mandatory part of the curriculum for so many schools—including CES schools.[51]

The most recent paperback version of Zinn's *History* was published in November 2010. At Amazon.com, for example, in mid-January 2011 the nonfiction book ranked at #381 of the millions of books in the seller's inventory; #2 in Government-Democracy; #6 in Social Sciences–Political Science–Political Doctrines; and #30 in History-Americas.

Radical Science:

The global warming hoax is kept alive by competitive government grants to conduct research, Chuck Rogér writes in *American Thinker*. To keep the hoax alive, he writes, "politicians must generate a steady supply of believers to conduct 'research' as well as vote for said politicians, who keep the grants flowing. . . . Enter the public education machine."[52]

Evidence comes by way of Representative John Sarbanes (D-Md.), who told Nicholas Ballasy of CNSNews.com at the September 2010 Sustainability Education Summit: Citizenship and Pathways for a Green Economy—hosted by Secretary of Education Arne Duncan—that "environmental education in schools can 'promote the agenda' of climate change and population growth through the influence it has on children."[53]

This produces an "agenda of junk science alarmism," Rogér states, adding, "until now, Americans were unaware that public schools are supposed to breed fanatics for ruling class politics." Sarbanes, he continues, confirms "something that any informed clear thinker already knows: Corrupt, power-intoxicated politicians regularly team with 'scientists' to promote agendas for personal gain."[54]

Rogér raises the highly controversial book by Paul Ehrlich, *The Population Bomb*. Journalist Ross Douthat provides a thought-provoking observation about it:[55]

> When you kick off your argument by predicting that "the battle to feed all of humanity is over," and that "in the 1970s and 1980s hundreds of millions of people will starve to death in spite of any crash programs embarked upon now," and then proceed to argue for mass sterilization programs, the quarantine and abandonment of countries too overpopulated to save from total collapse, and various other "triage" methods (honestly, *The Population Bomb* has to be read to be believed), you pretty much forfeit the right to be praised for your prescience forty years down the line.

Then Douthat adds one caveat: "Unless, that is, one of your friends goes on to become the science advisor to the President of the United States."

Douthat is referring to mutual literary endeavors by Ehrlich and John P. Holdren, who now serves as Obama's science czar.

In the 1970s Paul Ehrlich and his wife, Anne H. Ehrlich, coauthored two books with Holdren: *Human Ecology: Problems and Solutions* in 1973 and *Ecoscience: Population, Resources, Environment* in 1978. In the former, the authors called for "a stable, low-consumption economy," saying that "global redistribution of wealth" is "absolutely essential, if a decent life is to be provided to every human being."[56]

Rogér adds that none of the Holdren-Ehrlich dire predictions have come true, nor are they likely to.

Holdren also previously served as president of the American Association for the Advancement of Science (AAAS). Founded in 1848, AAAS describes itself as an international nonprofit organization "dedicated to advancing science around the world by serving as an educator, leader, spokesperson and professional association."[57]

AAAS provides programs for all grades, kindergarten through high school, and from "academic to corporate laboratories." The tip-off that it is promoting a socialist agenda comes from its claim that it "promotes diversity." In the progressive lexicon, *diversity* is another word signaling social justice and plurality: race, nationality, gender, religion, and sexuality.[58]

As part of its Project 2061 Curriculum, AAAS produces textbooks for high school biology, middle grades science and mathematics, as well as algebra.[59]

Project 2061 has been on the CES list of top math and science *forces for change* since 1992. Kathleen Cushman writes at CES that the project's *manifesto* is the privately and government-funded hundred-page book *Science for All Americans*. The AAAS Project 2061 text has grown into the two-volume *Atlas of Science Literacy*.[60]

AAAS and Holdren are climate change true believers. In February 2007 the AAAS board released a statement approved the previous December: "The scientific evidence is clear: global climate change caused by human activities is occurring now, and it is a growing threat to society."[61]

Climate change, Holdren said, is "extremely interdisciplinary, making it not only really important but concretely woven into many subjects, from science to technology, economics, public policy, and politics."[62]

Learning about Islam:

A CES article, "Framing Discussions of Terrible Events," which offered questions that teachers could "use to frame dialogue about events surrounding September 11th," is no longer available on the CES website or elsewhere on the Internet Archive.

International Baccalaureate Program:

CES says the five-year curriculum framework for students ages eleven through sixteen of International Baccalaureate (IB) Middle Years Program "has much in common with Essential School ideas, and can be adapted to different school contexts."[63]

Next we turn to another Annenberg Challenge grant recipient, ACORN, which also uses some of the same curriculum just discussed.

ACORN Education

To date, the Annenberg Challenge grant funds awarded to Chicago in 1995 to improve public education are the most well known of the awards granted because of the connection to Bill Ayers and Barack Obama.[64]

Annenberg Challenge grant funds were also awarded indirectly to another controversial group, namely ACORN.

The $25 million, 2:1 matching challenge grant to New York Networks for School Renewal (NYNSR) helped to support four organizations in the development of small schools: New Visions for Public Schools, Center for Collaborative Education, Center for Educational Innovation, and New York ACORN.[65]

The five-year (1996–2001) Final Evaluation Report for the Annenberg Foundation Challenge for New York City was submitted in December 2001. It provides information on ACORN's educational activities.[66]

New York ACORN is described as a grassroots organization that began campaigns to improve specific, small autonomous public schools and to wage citywide campaigns around "equity and access issues" as documented in ACORN's *Secret Apartheid I, II,* and *III* reports.[67]

In 1995, ACORN's current CEO and chief organizer, Bertha Lewis, became ACORN's head organizer in Brooklyn. Lewis "led the fight for parent access to school choice" with ACORN's *Secret Apartheid* studies.[68]

ACORN's *Secret Apartheid I* report dating from 1995 is based on nearly one hundred test visits to schools within sixteen community districts and allegedly details evidence of institutional racism in New York City public schools and attempts to prevent "parents of color from making informed decisions about their children's education."[69]

The NY ACORN schools, although not so identified, are possibly included in the report as New Visions for Public Schools. ACORN's New Visions Schools were created around this time.

No further direct mention of either the ACORN or New Visions schools is found in the report. The schools were evaluated and quantified with the other participating schools collectively as NYNSR schools.

It Began in Little Rock

ACORN's foray into education reform dates from 1973, when ACORN supported organizing efforts of a Little Rock, Arkansas, high school student to "force his/her school to stop serving sour milk." ACORN members subsequently fought and won so-called quality of school life issues such as securing textbooks, construction of sidewalks around the Southwest Little Rock high school neighborhood, and "opposing the misuse of corporal punishment in rural communities."[70]

A circa 1996 report prepared for the Catholic Bishops of the United States by the Wanderer Forum Foundation includes landmarks in ACORN's history, political activities, and involvement with education reform.[71]

Through the Campaign for Human Development, in the funding period 1992–95, the Catholic Bishops awarded grants to community organizing efforts based on organizational techniques recommended by Saul Alinsky. ACORN, which recruits individual members, and four other organizations accounted for approximately 33 percent of the CHD annual expenditures. Individually, ACORN had received approximately 5 percent of the national CHD annual budget for 1992 through 1995, receiving $1,493,000 in national CHD grants.

The report cites ACORN's People's Platform, written in 1978, ratified in 1979 at ACORN's national convention in St. Louis, and revised and reapproved in 1990. The report states the platform specifies ACORN demands that the United States must "develop schools that are 'available for community needs, like adult education' and 'job training that is linked to specific employment,' and which 'can provide all support and services that a child cannot receive at home.'"

ACORN developed an alliance with Democratic Socialists of America to accomplish the goals outlined in the platform. ACORN, DSA, and unspecified others formed a political party, the New Party. NP supporters included Maude Hurd, national ACORN president, and Dr. Cornel West, an honorary DSA chair. The New Party operated out of the Bronx ACORN headquarters.

A New Party alliance, including ACORN, the Saul Alinsky–founded Industrial Areas Foundation, Sustainable America, and other groups, worked to promote nationwide "living wage" campaigns.

ACORN political activities went beyond get-out-the-vote drives. During the 1980 presidential campaign, for example, ACORN applied pressure to presidential candidates during the nomination campaign when they, the candidates, were most in need of ACORN's specialty, grassroots support.

In 1988, when ACORN backed Jesse Jackson's Rainbow Coalition, for example, ACORN had thirty of Jackson's delegates on the Democratic convention floor. Clearly, electoral politics, the 1996 report states, "became a powerful weapon in the ACORN arsenal."

Additionally, in the 1990s ACORN became openly active in congressional lobbying, with ACORN leadership following in the footsteps of its ally, Democratic Socialists of America, "operating 'from inside positions of power.'"

ACORN Charter Schools—New York

In 1995 New York ACORN began to establish its alternative New Visions Schools within the New York public school system. The schools emulated the Debbie Meier experimental public school model, Networks for School Renewal, which claims both small teacher-pupil ratios and small student bodies.

The Campaign for Human Development report specifically states that parents and educators must be reeducated to the Debbie Meier academic model for "substantive restructuring" with a "clear public commitment to an alternative understanding of educational purposes themselves."

In addition, each ACORN New Visions School had one full-time, paid ACORN "organizer associated with it, whose duties include organizing parents, class by class." ACORN also sought to ensure that "progressively-minded" teachers and principals were hired in the New Visions Schools.

The New Visions School plan was blatantly intended to create pro-union community activists. The report states, "These 'educational purposes' can facilitate the training of new community organizers. . . . Students are involved in hands-on activities in order to relate classroom learning to community service. These activities range from participation in labor and community organization movements to service as interns at local health care facilities."

The ACORN Community High School (K499) in Brooklyn was founded in 1996 as a partnership between the New York City Board of Education and ACORN.[72]

By 1997, ACORN not only had two partner schools in New York

City but also was involved in collaborative efforts in Chicago, St. Paul, Boston, and Seattle.[73]

The following year, ACORN organizations in Boston, Albuquerque, St. Paul, and New Jersey had developed charter school proposals. Additionally, in Chicago and Washington, D.C., ACORN members were developing what are called "schools-within-schools" inside several public schools, as well as charter school proposals.[74]

ACORN was also involved in a number of community organizing activities related to its schools. This included training low-income parents in political leadership skills, developing a broad-based civic organization to cut across class and ethnic lines, and connecting school to the larger issues of community development.[75]

ACORN Charter School—Chicago

ACORN and its charter schools in Chicago have a direct connection to the Chicago Annenberg Challenge, Bill Ayers, and Barack Obama. In 1993 Ayers was a consultant to Chicago ACORN on what is called his "signature issue: creating miniature 'schools-within-schools' built around themes, such as peace and Afro-centrism."[76]

Ayers and ACORN planned to set up a "series of ACORN-controlled mini schools in Chicago," Stanley Kurtz writes. Through the CAC, Ayers and Obama channeled money into ACORN education projects.[77]

The head of both Chicago ACORN and ACORN's national educational campaign is Madeline Talbott, who worked closely with Bill Ayers. Ayers's ethnically themed schools-within-schools plan provided ACORN with a "model for carving a mini-empire out of the Chicago public school system," Kurtz says.[78]

Obama served on the Woods Fund of Chicago board of directors, 1997–2001. Chicago ACORN received grants totaling $120,000 for 2000–2001. Also serving on the board in 2000 and 2001 was Bill Ayers. It has been stated that Obama and Talbott served together on the board; Illinois state records do not support that contention.[79]

Regarding Chicago's ACORN schools, the ACORN Charter School, a dual-language college preparatory school, opened for school year 1998–99 in Little Village, a largely Hispanic neighborhood.[80]

The Grassroots School Improvement Campaign received $150,000 in 1997 and again in 1998 from the Chicago Annenberg Challenge to "help develop leadership among parents and community members at several schools," including schools in Little Village. The ACORN Charter School is specifically named in 1998. GSIC received another $50,000 in CAC funds in 2001.[81]

In fall 2000, ACORN Charter School changed its name to Nuestra America (Our America) Charter School. A report released in December 2000 by the Illinois State Board of Education found that, although "the vast majority of charter schools—13 out of 17—exercised their option to have classes taught by college graduates with five years of experience in their fields, rather than certified teachers," the former Chicago ACORN Charter School had not used any certified teachers the previous school year.[82]

This was not the only problem ACORN faced with its charter school. In 1997 ACORN failed to locate a large enough facility for a full four-year program in Little Village and Pilsen. Two years later, in 1999, ACORN moved the school to West Humboldt Park, a mostly African-American neighborhood.[83]

William Campillo, who previously worked with the Small Schools Workshop, had been principal at the school for two years. Campillo charged that, since the school moved, ACORN had "abdicated" responsibility for the school and its 190 mostly Latino students. Campillo changed the school's name to reflect ACORN's absence.

Campillo also charged that ACORN had only wanted to use the school to recruit parents "for its political causes and to raise money," while not bothering to attend board meetings in over six months.

Another group of charter schools, the United Neighborhood Organization of Chicago schools (UNO), is likewise connected to Barack Obama and the Chicago Annenberg Challenge.

Alinskyite and Charter Schools

In 1980 Gregory A. Galluzzo and his wife, Mary Gonzales, created UNO. They write that in 1982, they "needed some expertise from someone who had done faith based community organizing." They hired Jerry Kellman, who had experience organizing in Pennsylvania and Illinois.[84]

When Barack Obama came to Chicago in 1985 to work as director of the Developing Communities Project, the man who hired him was Kellman. A year earlier, Kellman was still working for UNO when he left to join the Calumet Community Religious Conference, which operated both on the South Side, in the south suburbs of Chicago, and in Indiana. CCRC became Obama's employer; DCP was described as CCRC's inner-city operation.[85]

Galluzzo was a Saul Alinsky disciple and UNO was modeled on the Alinsky style of community organizing. UNO's mission was to build grassroots leadership in Chicago's Hispanic neighborhoods, "organize for power," and address such local issues as street violence, the Hispanic dropout rate, and overcrowding in schools.[86]

In February 2008, when Arne Duncan proposed closing the highly successful De La Cruz Middle School, the closing was delayed for one year after a hearing where teachers, parents, and students protested. As soon as De La Cruz shut down at the end of the school year, in June 2009, the Board of Education gave the recently repaired building to the UNO Charter School Network for a dollar-per-year rental fee. The plan all along had been to move UNO's Octavio Paz Charter School into the De La Cruz building.[87]

In September 2010, UNO and Teach For America announced a new partnership to provide twenty-five Teach For America corps members and two school principals for school year 2010–2011. Alexander Russo writes: "This agreement marks the first formal human capital agreement by Teach For America–Chicago with a charter school authorizer, making Teach For America the largest single-source supplier of teachers and school leaders for UNO charter schools."[88]

Teach For America is funded by a significant number of multimillionaire donors and numerous corporate, private, and public funders, including federal funding from the Department of Education, AmeriCorps, and NASA.[89]

In January 2011, it was learned that UNO's network of nine schools would add three new elementary schools. It would also expand by turning an existing middle school in Gage Park into a high school.[90]

Next we look at the educational program Facing History and Ourselves, which not only has connections with Barack and Michelle Obama and the Chicago Annenberg Challenge, but also has expanded into operating its own charter schools.

Facing History and Ourselves

Facing History and Ourselves was founded and designed in 1976 by Margot Stern Strom and Bill Parsons using Department of Education funds. Since 1981, the department has cited FHAO as an "exemplary model teacher training program."[91]

FHAO claims it has participated in major school reform efforts in Boston, Chicago, and Memphis as well as in smaller cities.[92]

Today FHAO is an international organization providing professional development services and curricular resources to educators. FHAO's stated focus is on "bringing ethical and moral philosophy to history and social studies classes, particularly regarding issues of racism, civic responsibility and tolerance."

FHAO offices can be found all over the United States and abroad, with 150 staff members in Chicago, Cleveland, Denver, London, Los Angeles, Memphis, New England, New York, the San Francisco Bay area, and Toronto, as well as working with other U.S. educators. The FHAO headquarters is in Brookline, Massachusetts. FHAO writes that its "ever-expanding global network" of educators reaches an estimated 1.9 million students annually, with teachers in more than eighty countries.[93]

Among several others, FHAO partners include Harvard Law School, New Visions for Public Schools, and PBS. FHAO supporters include Chicago's Crown family and the Department of State's Bureau of Educational and Cultural Affairs.[94]

An FHAO Faux Pas

A gross error in judgment was discovered in May 2010, when educators took students on a Wellesley Middle School field trip to the Islamic Society of Boston Cultural Center in Boston's Roxbury section. The center is New England's largest mosque. The furor began after it was learned that several sixth-grade pupils were videotaped kneeling during a prayer service at the mosque. The visit was described as part of a required introductory world religions social studies course, "Enduring Beliefs and the World Today." It was explained the students had also visited a synagogue, attended a gospel music performance, and met with Hindus.[95]

How these students came to participate in Muslim prayer activities is less concerning, perhaps, than the location where they did so and those who operate the cultural center itself.

The Muslim American Society holds classes at the Islamic center through its educational subsidiary, the Islamic American University.[96] The IAU is chaired by two controversial clerics, Yusuf Qaradawi and Jamal Badawi, former and current trustees of the Roxbury mosque, respectively. Qaradawi is said to preach to Muslims that "Jews should be exterminated, homosexuals should be executed, and Muslim men may beat their wives." If that is not enough, Badawi "tells his students that they must work to establish Islamic theocracies wherever they live and that all those who don't judge in accordance with Islamic law are wicked."[97]

Wellesley Middle School is on the list of Facing History and Ourselves' participating schools in New England. The FHAO coursework for all Wellesley public schools is officially assigned to a single eighth-grade social studies unit. No mention is made, however, that the curriculum stretches to sixth graders.[98]

This is not guilt by association—meaning we are not saying that, because the Wellesley Middle School's eighth graders are in the FHAO program, and it was sixth graders who visited and were praying at the mosque, the FHAO program is at fault. What this does suggest is that schools participating in the FHAO program may not be strictly adhering to their own guidelines; in this case, a program included in the eighth-grade curriculum may have found its way into a sixth-grade classroom.

FHAO and the Obamas

Facing History and Ourselves, meanwhile, received Chicago Annenberg Challenge grant funds for programs with the Chicago Public Schools. FHAO received $240,000 in 1998, $237,000 in 1999, $85,500 in 2000, and $50,000 in 2001.[99]

FHAO also received grant funds from the Joyce Foundation, upon whose board Barack Obama also sat: $100,000 in 1997 (for a two-year project) and $50,000 in 1999 (for a one-year project).[100]

Bill Ayers presented the paper "The Educator as Moral Leader" at an FHAO gathering in Chicago on March 13, 2001.[101]

Michelle Obama served on the Chicago Advisory Board for Facing History and Ourselves in 2006 and 2007. Senator Barack Obama, as keynote speaker in May 2006 at FHAO's "largest-ever Chicago Benefit Dinner," spoke to more than one thousand guests "about the importance of combating indifference with empathy and action." Penny Pritzker, long associated with Obama, was an event cochair.[102]

At the May 2007 16th Annual Facing History and Ourselves Benefit Dinner in Chicago, Michelle Obama spoke of the "need to develop greater understanding through global education" and "expressed her appreciation for Facing History and Ourselves' work to help children develop a 'moral compass' and become part of the 'global community.'"[103]

Three of the many *amazing* people who have worked with FHAO over the decades have connections to Barack Obama.[104]

Martha Minow has served as chair of FHAO's International Board of Scholars since October 2009, but has been a friend and adviser to Facing History for almost two decades.

Eboo Patel, one of Barack Obama's faith advisers, is the founder and executive director of Interfaith Youth Core, a Chicago-based international nonprofit "working to build mutual respect and pluralism among religiously diverse young people by empowering them to work together to serve others."[105]

Samantha Power is a special assistant to President Barack Obama and senior director of multilateral affairs on the staff of the National Security Council.[106]

In a 2008 article, "Choosing to Participate," a twelfth-grade CES student explains the meaning of "Upstander" and "including others in your Universe of Obligation." These terms come from the FHAO classroom—as defined by journalist and academic Samantha Power.[107]

FHAO Schools

FHAO's North America Project promises to travel anywhere professional development for teachers is required.[108]

The FHAO curricula are used either in part or in full in the social studies program of Coalition of Essential Schools member schools.

There are clearly CES-FHAO partnerships. A CES article informs: "New York City's Facing History School (FHS), a small public CES high school created with FHAO as a lead partner, uses a curriculum that is rooted in history and choice making."[109]

In October 2008, FHAO began operating its own Small Schools Network with a collection of just twelve schools. There are now more than twenty-five schools and over ten thousand students receiving classroom materials, support, and professional development services. Start-up funds came from the Einhorn Family Charitable Trust.[110]

FHAO Critique

No better or more accurate criticism of FHAO can be provided than those already written. Jeff Jacoby provides commentary on a 1995 critique written by the late Lucy S. Dawidowicz, whom Jacoby describes as a "towering scholar of the Holocaust" and author of *The War Against the Jews: 1933–1945*.[111]

After examining twenty-five Holocaust curricula used in schools, Dawidowicz was asked to prepare an article defending FHAO from critics in the Department of Education. She later commented: "I never did so. . . . Putatively a curriculum to teach the Holocaust, Facing History was also a vehicle for instructing 13-year-olds in civil disobedience and indoctrinating them with propaganda."[112]

Jacoby writes that Dawidowicz "rebuked Facing History for twisting the Holocaust into a case study of ethical ambiguities. Its 'message of moral relativism,' she noted in 1990, 'has reached the students using the curriculum.'"[113]

The 1994 curriculum manual and its seminars, Jacoby writes, "use the Holocaust as an analogy or a key to dealing with every social ill from battered women to homelessness to the 'stereotyping' of Asian-Americans." FHAO continuously "pushes students to see contemporary America as a latter-day Weimar Republic, slipping down the slope that leads to Dachau."[114]

The new curriculum, he tells us, "opens by quoting welfare lobbyist" Marian Wright Edelman, who wrote in 1993:[115]

Ironically, as Communism is collapsing all around the world, the American Dream is collapsing all around America for millions of children, youths, and families in all racial and income groups. American is pitted against American as economic uncertainty and downturn increase our fears, our business failures, our poverty rates, our racial divisions, and the dangers of political demagoguery.

American children, according to FHAO, have been "taught to hate and fear." FHAO "attributes 'much of the violence that threatens our society' to 'bigotry and hate.'"[116]

This is a "grim, bitter portrait," Jacoby says, and an "apt introduction to a manual that constantly associates America with prewar Germany." FHAO makes the Holocaust "stand for everything," he adds, "hastening the day when it will stand for nothing. Least of all anti-Semitism."

Incomprehensible, as well, is the inclusion of Nation of Islam leader Louis Farrakhan in FHAO materials. Farrakhan, Jacoby writes, is the "most poisonous source of Jew-hatred in America today." FHAO students, he continues, are taught that "Farrakhan 'has attracted African-Americans by speaking directly to the pain and pride' they feel, and that this is why Farrakhan's 'message has been so warmly received even though parts of it stereotype and demean other groups.'"

FHAO is accused of giving a "false account of anti-Semitism and related events in Nazi-era Germany carefully designed to drive home the lesson that most people are prone to bigotry and are a dangerous force."[117]

Sandra Stotsky writes in her 2004 paper, "The Stealth Curriculum: Manipulating America's History Teachers," that FHAO is "[p]ossibly the most malevolent of the organizations professing to address citizenship education."[118]

Regarding FHAO's 2002 supplementary resource book, *Race and Membership in American History: The Eugenics Movement*, Stotsky calls it "even more poisonous" with its "causal connection between the American eugenics movement and the Holocaust." In the end, she writes, "Americans appear almost directly responsible for the Final Solution. The net effect is the discrediting of American society."

The danger here, as Stotsky correctly assesses, is that social studies teachers will use FHAO's "implicit thesis about who was responsible for the Holocaust because its resource books are likely to be their only source of information on the topic."

An even greater concern is that outsiders cannot find out what takes place in FHAO workshops as they are restricted to teachers whose schools arranged and paid for them to attend. Details on FHAO's website are password-protected.

chapter six

RED-UCATION

We have seen how radicals have long pushed education reform and how Obama himself has been involved in this process from almost the start of his professional life. What follows is our exposé of the Obama administration's education initiatives, specifically how Obama, ever since he became president, has been pushing public funding in the direction of radical education initiatives, including, shockingly, those led by extremist names and groups that you are starting to become familiar with by reading this book.

Obama's funding of radical educational initiatives has happened often enough during the first half of his presidency to have created a discernable pattern. A careful examination by the authors of several education grant lists found a healthy presence of radical educators and program organizers, organizations, schools, and educational programs. Several of these have previous and current ties to Obama and his administration that must be exposed.

From the start, Obama has not been very forthcoming in his public declarations regarding education. At the onset of Obama's presidency, the White House unveiled Obama's educational plan for change, the 2008 *Blueprint for Change*, which was exceptionally long on rhetoric and short on policy.[1] The plan devotes four pages to education, while its content is general and lacking in specifics.

Likewise, when Obama expounded on his education plans in a September 2008 speech in Dayton, Ohio, it too was heavy on voter-pleasing promises while devoid of hints as to how any of them would be accomplished.[2]

Some goals are verifiable, such as programs that have been created and funded. Others are not. For example, Obama said he would "close the achievement gap by investing in early childhood education." This is a hot topic among educators.

Obama said he would fight to ensure the United States is the world leader in high school graduation rates. This falls into the wishful thinking category. The Organisation for Economic Co-Operation and Development reported in January 2008 that, of the top ten countries in student performance, the United States stood next to last. It is bested by China, Korea, Singapore, Hong Kong, Japan, Hungary, England, and the Russian Federation.[3]

Goals such as increasing the number of high school students taking college-level or AP courses by 50 percent have a feel-good ring to them. They are, however, nonspecific. Equally vague is Obama saying his administration would raise expectations for our kids and give schools the resources necessary to meet them. This, he claims, would ensure more kids have access to quality after-school programs and summer school and extended school days for students who need them.

The Obama plan includes bringing technology into the classroom: the addition of digital touchscreens and laptops, students designing PowerPoint presentations, building websites, and e-mailing experts in the field, as well as providing less informed teachers with the necessary training. These are admirable goals; how such a massive and expensive project for all the nation's schools would be accomplished is not explained. Nor is how it will be funded.

There are some more realistic programs. These include Obama's plans for an Innovative Schools Fund to invest in schools, a Teacher Service Scholarship program to recruit and train top talent into the teaching profession, and New Teacher Quality Grants directed to improving student academic success and to train thirty thousand high-quality teachers a year, with an emphasis in the fields of math and science.

Some promises have been fulfilled. A February 17, 2009, White House fact sheet outlines some of the intentions stated in the American Recovery and Reinvestment Act of 2009, or ARRA. Funds were to be used on the local level to prevent teacher layoffs, make improvements in education, and help make college affordable. On the one hand, the fact sheet provides some specifics regarding how the funds would be spent; on the other, it includes more nonspecific, broad-sweeping statements. The results—or lack of results—cannot be measured.[4]

The lines between the actual ARRA and U.S. Department of Education funding and programs are blurred, adding to the difficulty in tracking the gains—and the losses.

Significant ARRA funds were committed to the Investing in Innovation Fund, or i3, as it is called. In March 2010 Secretary of Education Arne Duncan announced the final priorities and the grant application for $650 million in i3 funds. The funding for i3 was to come from the $5 billion in ARRA funds marked for education reform. Either individual school districts or groups of districts could apply. Additionally, consortiums of schools and entrepreneurial nonprofits were also allowed to submit applications.[5]

The Department of Education was criticized because rural school districts competed at a significant disadvantage due to their size and the location of their remote districts. It was noted that hundreds of remote districts have only one school.[6]

The winning i3 grantees include a radical educational organization with ties to the Obama administration.

The Erikson Institute in Chicago rated at number 34. The institute requested just shy of $5 million for its project, "Achieving High Standards for Pre-K–Grade 3 Mathematics: A Whole Teacher Approach to Professional Development." One of the three faculty founders, and president of the institute from 1994 to 2001, is Barbara Taylor Bowman, the Irving B. Harris Professor of Child Development. Bowman is the mother of White House adviser and longtime Barack and Michelle Robinson Obama friend Valerie Jarrett.[7]

Bowman is also chief early childhood education officer for Chicago Public Schools.[8]

In December 2009, Arne Duncan honored Bowman at a luncheon. Bowman served as Duncan's consultant on early learning for the first six months after he was named secretary of education.[9]

The Erikson Institute was among the first thirty-five school partnerships awarded Chicago Annenberg Challenge funds in December 1995. The institute was partnered with a program called Building Early Childhood Centers of Excellence to develop and improve curriculum and assessment in preschool through third grade in six Chicago schools.[10]

Others in the Barack Obama orbit associated with the Erikson Institute include one of its former trustees and members of the executive committee, the late Thomas Ayers; Bernardine Dohrn also served on the board. In his 1998 book, *A Kind and Just Parent: The Children of Juvenile Court*, Bill Ayers calls Bowman a "neighbor and a friend."[11]

Dohrn's position on the teaching staff at Northwestern University was a matter of controversy in November 2001. In a *Chicago Tribune* interview, Daniel D. Polsby, formerly with NU and now dean and professor of law at George Mason University, said that what NU was doing was "participating in the laundering of evil."[12]

The Erikson Institute also has a direct link to communist influence through *Life Trustee* Bernice Targ Weissbourd, an early childhood educator and a well-known initiator and leader of the family support movement. She has numerous links to Barack Obama and people associated with him and the Obama administration.

Without question, Bernice Weissbourd exemplifies far-left progressives. Then known as Bernice Targ, her name was entered into the *Congressional Record* as part of the July 1947 testimony before the House Un-American Activities Committee by Walter S. Steele. A catalog for the "openly Communist influenced" Abraham Lincoln School for Social Sciences, located on the campus of Northwestern University in Chicago, includes the names of Bernice Targ, a teacher, and Frank

Marshall Davis. (During the 1940s, after becoming a member of the board of directors at the Abraham Lincoln School—often called the *Little Red Schoolhouse*—Davis taught the school's first courses on the history of jazz. Davis is well known as having been Barack Obama's mentor in Hawaii during the 1970s.)[13]

Weissbourd's Marxist views connect with those of Dr. Quentin D. Young, whom she has known since he entered Chicago's Hyde Park High School at the early age of thirteen. Young and Weissbourd met when they both joined the political group the American Student Union.

The ASU was formed when the Communist Party–influenced National Student League joined with the Student League for Industrial Democracy, the campus branch of the socialist League for Industrial Democracy.[14]

Bernice Targ married Bernard Weissbourd, a pioneer of radium analysis for the Manhattan Project. He also served on the board of directors for the *Bulletin of the Atomic Scientists*.[15]

According to his son, Robert M. Weissbourd, his father held Student Non-Violent Coordinating Committee meetings in the family backyard. Weissbourd founded the Center for Psycho-Social Studies, which became the Center for Transcultural Studies.[16]

Race to the Top

Equally controversial is Race to the Top (RTTT). Former Chicago mayor Richard M. Daley, Jr., remarked in September 2010: "You leave no child left behind. You race to the top. Next year, you race to the bottom. Next year, you race to the side. Everybody's racing to something. . . . Why can't you send us money to build our schools. . . . All the teachers know that these are just political slogans. We should end it."[17]

There have been two rounds of RTTT awards to date, with forty-seven total applicants. Round one produced two winners. Delaware,

Vice President Joe Biden's home state, received $119 million; Tennessee received $500.5 million. Round two produced ten grantees receiving awards between $75 million and $700 million.[18]

After the first two rounds of awards, some assessments are anything but encouraging. An April 2010 headline, "Stimulating the Status Quo," by Lindsey Burke of the Heritage Foundation, for example, speaks volumes.[19]

While ARRA is full of good intentions—to prevent job losses and spur education reform—Burke, for one, doubts that will be the case. Instead of providing long-term solutions, she writes, the spending will "prevent states from addressing fiscal problems, rethinking existing programs, and increasing efficiency."[20]

Conservative think tanks are monitoring the Obama administration education reform programs closely. An April 2010 report from the National Center for Education Statistics at the Department of Education reveals creating and/or saving jobs in public education is not the solution. Cato Institute's Andrew J. Coulson stated the situation is this: beginning in 1970, student enrollment in elementary and secondary schools increased by 7 percent while data shows staff in public elementary and secondary schools increased by 83 percent.[21]

A Heritage Foundation report reemphasizes the financial aspect. While it is suggested increased spending will translate into academic achievement, the increases have resulted in one thing only—increased federal spending per student without measurable results.[22]

In Burke's opinion, ARRA funds may well create far more problems in the future than they fix now. Instead of budgetary shortfalls being addressed by rethinking priorities and finding ways of increasing efficiency, ARRA funds will, in the end, make future reforms more difficult.[23]

Also at the Cato Institute, Neal McCluskey discovers another problem. He writes in April 2010 that round one produced just two winning states. It appears those states won because they managed to convince teachers' unions to endorse their reform proposals.[24]

The New Mexico *Independent* noted a week earlier that states had decided that applying for round two of Race to the Top just wasn't worth it.[25]

Even the clearly progressive Economic Policy Institute had little good to say about the Race to the Top selection process.[26]

In an April 2010 briefing paper, EPI's William Peterson and Richard Rothstein write that Delaware and Tennessee won because they scored the highest points (454.6 and 444.2, respectively) out of a possible 500. The precise numerical scores determined the winners, a process presented as objective and scientific.

However, they disagree, saying the selection process was subjective and arbitrary, even leaning toward bias or chance, with evaluations based on each state's ability to comply with reform policies. In these days of stressed state budgets, they write, every state was entitled to a fair share of ARRA funding.

A perhaps unexpected complicating factor in the application process is *union buy-in*. In RTTT's round one, winners Tennessee and Delaware appear to have had applications slanted more toward union buy-in than education reform. Burke writes that the winners had nearly 100 percent union support for their grant applications. Additionally, the head of the teachers' union in Delaware made the trip to Washington, D.C., to pitch its state's proposal. Meanwhile, Florida's application was said to include a robust reform plan, but not as much union support. Burke writes: "One of the reviewers for Florida's application stated, 'The fact that only 8% of union leaders . . . endorsed the state's application raises a concern about barriers. . . . The application does not address how the state will move forward assertively to generate union buy in.'"[27]

Diane Ravitch, a progressive research professor of education at New York University and a historian of education, calls the whole exercise a *Race to Nowhere*. In December 2009, Ravitch posed some deeply disturbing questions. She asks: "Does anyone believe that this sorry game of musical chairs will improve education? Does anyone in Washington or at central headquarters grasp the pointlessness of the disruption needlessly inflicted on students, families, teachers, principals, and communities in the name of *reform*? Do these people have no shame?"[28]

Drawing on her education history expertise, she writes that RTTT takes her back to the nineteenth century, when free schooling meant "wealthy men decided that it was their civic duty to help civilize the children of the poor." Although the wealthy may have seen themselves as "doing good deeds . . . their schools were stigmatized as charity schools for children of paupers and were avoided by children of the middle class."[29]

Addressing charter schools in particular—many of which do qualify directly or indirectly for this publicly funded *do-goodery*—Ravitch opines that this historic pattern of privatized public schools run by rich men and women who "see themselves as saviors of the children of the poor" may be making a comeback. This "repellent portrait," she writes, "undermines the democratic foundations of public education." If this is the case, she believes, society will allow the wealthy to become the "patrons to educate children of color." Education will be "seen as a private charity rather than as a public responsibility," she concludes.

Ravitch directs attention to another issue. Race to the Top is counterintuitive to equal education opportunity and twentieth-century goals of affirmative action. With RTTT, she writes, it has become a race of who can get where or achieve what goal first. Who can privatize the most schools or close the most public schools or replace the most public schools with charter schools? Who, she asks, "seriously believes that this combination of policies will produce better education?"

As someone well acquainted with New York City schools, Ravitch writes that, even though New York City was not only *not* a faithful representation of No Child Left Behind, it is now "outfitting itself to be a faithful representation" of the Race to the Top. NCLB and the RTTT are really the same, she says, except the Obama-Duncan Race has "nearly $5 billion as a lure to persuade states to climb aboard the express train to privatization."

Lawmakers in New York state, for example, agreed in 2010 to double the number of charter schools as a way to compete for RTTT money. There are already more than one hundred charter schools in New York City alone.[30]

Coincidentally, the Obama administration's fiscal 2011 budget includes a request for a $54 million increase in the Charter School Grants Program. This will bring the total to around $310 million and closer to the goal of doubling the previous amount.[31]

Charter School Network

On September 29, 2010, Secretary Arne Duncan announced that the Success Charter School Network was one of twelve charter school management grantees awarded a total of $50 million.

The SCS Network, launched in 2006, was granted $2 million to establish thirteen new schools and to expand another three schools to serve an additional 4,200 students in New York City.

With millions more federal taxpayer dollars at stake in upcoming years, SCS Network head and former City Council member Eva S. Moskowitz is in hot pursuit of both funds and establishing new charter schools.

In January 2011, for example, Moskowitz made a sales pitch to middle-class families for a new charter school, the Upper West Side Academy. Her plan raised opposition from District 3's Community Education Council, which contends the charter school would "siphon middle- and upper-middle-class families from schools that desperately need them for stability," the teachers' union, and New York Communities for Change, the newest incarnation of New York ACORN.

Moskowitz was colorfully described in April 2010 as "feared, revered, and reviled in like proportions. As the face of the social-Darwinist wing of the local charter movement, she's been cast as the grim reaper of moribund neighborhood schools, a witting tool of privatizing billionaires, and a Machiavellian schemer with her sights set on the mayoralty."[32]

Noah Gotbaum, president of District 3's Community Education Council, says Moskowitz is the "spokesperson in demonizing the public schools." Her philosophy is "that you've got to burn the village to save it."[33]

The actions of Obama and Duncan outraged Glen Ford of the *Black Agenda Report*, who wrote in June 2010: They "spent their first year and a half in office coercing states to expand charters or lose out on more than $4 billion in federal education moneys. Obama's allies on Wall Street invest heavily in charter schools, tapping into the public money stream to build their own vision of corporate education."[34]

Indeed, the SCS Network board of directors reads like a who's who of hedge fund bigwigs. Board chair Joel Greenblatt and board member Robert Goldstein are both of Gotham Capital. The remaining board members are all hedge funders.[35]

At a late October 2009 New York City cocktail party, Greenblatt and John Petry, then partners in the hedge fund Gotham Capital (Petry is still a board member, but now with Columbus Hill Capital Management), worked the room to "identify new candidates" for investment in the SCS Network.[36]

Hedge fund executives have been identified as the "first significant political counterweight to the powerful teachers unions." The teachers' unions oppose the expansion of the charter school movement for cause—the charter schools, funded by taxpayer dollars, but run as a private enterprise, do not have to hire unionized teachers.[37]

Glen Ford views the hedge funders as profiteers looking to turn charter schools into cash cows. The formula is simple: taxpayers finance the private contracts, the public has no control, and the investors reap the rewards. "Charter schools are a low-risk, fast buck dream, tailor-made for corporate exploitation and political manipulation," Ford writes.[38]

Going forward, there will be a steady flow of funds for charter schools made available by the Department of Education. In fiscal 2011 alone, the department plans to make between $45 million and $62 million available to state educational agencies (SEAs) for its Charter Schools Program, dependent upon congressional appropriations. It may also make additional awards available later in fiscal 2011 and 2012 for the list of unfunded applicants. Between seven and twelve SEA applicants will receive an estimated range of individual awards of $1 million to $15 million per year, with the estimated average award at $5 million. In turn, SEAs will make subgrants to eligible charter school applicants in their states.[39]

The department's plans are simple: expand the number of charter schools by spending money to help plan and implement them.

Consistent with Duncan's track record with Chicago Public Schools, there will be a focus on projects designed to turn around "persistently low performing schools," either by creating new charter schools in the vicinity of one or more schools closed due to restructuring, or by creating a new charter school under the restart model of intervention.

The restart model of intervention is when an existing school is converted into a charter school or is closed and reopened under a charter school operator. Herein is the opportunity for CSOs like the Success Charter School Network, Moskowitz, and the hedge funders to profit handsomely.

Another RTTT issue, the use of student achievement data to evaluate, reward, and fire teachers, was criticized in an April 2006 report produced by the Hamilton Project, a Democratic economic research and policy group at the Brookings Institution.[40]

In a January 2010 editorial, Aaron Collier wrote that RTTT's areas of reform are in line with those of the Hamilton Project.[41]

Secretary Duncan has been speaking out since July 2010 against state laws that prevent the use of student data to evaluate teachers, as well as encouraging union leaders to accept changes to tenure.[42]

The fact that Secretary Duncan and the Hamilton Project are in agreement is not surprising. The connection provides an excellent

example of how Obama administration policies are incestuously intertwined with the agenda of interest groups outside the D.C. Beltway.

Early in June 2008, presidential candidate Barack Obama named
Jason Furman, who worked closely with former Treasury secretary Robert Rubin, as his economic policy director. Furman had been serving as
executive director for the Hamilton Project. Rubin, who cofounded the
Project in 2006, then chaired Citigroup Inc.'s executive committee.[43]

But the Obama administration's relationship with the Goldman
Sachs–funded Hamilton Project is much closer than this.[44]

It was learned in April 2006 that Obama was one of a group of
"Democratic luminaries who unveiled the latest entry in the effort to
help Democrats define just what they do stand for."[45]

The Hamilton Project's executive director in April 2006 was Peter
Orszag, who headed Obama's Office of Management and Budget until
July 2010, when he resigned. He serves on the Project's board.[46]

RTTT was also endorsed by a long list of progressive educators
and progressive groups calling itself the Education Equality Project
(EEP).[47]

In August 2009, EEP announced it was joining its partners, the
Education Trust, Democrats for Education Reform, and the Center for
American Progress, in signing a letter of support for RTTT guidelines
to Secretary Duncan.[48]

EEP's core set of principles calls for "the swift, decisive, nontradi-
tional action required to finally bring equity to our education system."[49]
The inclusion in the principles of the phrase "a country divided for too
many years by racial discrimination and injustice" should have been a
tip-off to alleged conservatives of the organization's intent.

Universal Health Care in the NCLB

The Obama administration reauthorized No Child Left Behind in
March 2010 as the Elementary and Secondary Education Act.[50]

A quick assessment of the NCLB/ESEA legislation finds that the call for health insurance for all children and their parents is a barely disguised call for universal health care. Since the original wish list was formalized in early 2001, and it is now 2010, it appears that NCLB's goal of lifting all children out of poverty has failed in spite of the fact that the Democratic Party served as the majority in Congress from 2006 until the end of 2010.

The first NCLB casualty was the elimination of school choice, which, although limited, would have provided opportunity for children to escape persistently low-performing public schools.[51]

It was noted in March 2010 that Secretary Duncan disliked the school choice or supplemental services (SES) provisions in NCLB.[52]

Under the Obama administration, the removal of the SES provision left low-income parents in underperforming public schools with few options.[53]

As Diane Ravitch pointed out, the Obama-Duncan RTTT program promoted a race to see who could replace the most public schools—primarily underperforming schools—with charter schools.

ARRA reward opportunities were plentiful for charter schools and the creation of new charter school programs.

In a March 2009 online town hall meeting, Obama was clear on his definition of a charter school. Charter schools are not private schools; they are public schools funded by public dollars with a state-mandated curriculum. Occasionally they are paired up with nonprofit groups. The flexibility is in the design. For example, in Chicago, Obama said, charter schools are paired with a museum and an arts program, or it may be a science-oriented charter school or a language academy.[54]

Obama also claimed the charter schools were nonselective, meaning students are not cherry-picked. The schools, he said, are required to admit anybody. Due to demand, the charter schools often have long waiting lists and may use a lottery system for admission.

The major flaws in Obama's description of charter schools are the important facts he left out. Charter schools don't have to keep any

students. Students who don't excel or who cause problems can be ex-
pelled, Clay Burell points out at Change.org.

There are many ways to say *no*. Enrollment caps, for example; public
schools can't claim them. Public schools must provide for all students
with special needs and those who are not English-speaking. Most significantly, as Burell writes, public schools "don't get the supplemental
funds from the billionaires, so they spend less per student than charters."

Regardless, in a February 2010 press release, the Obama administration firmly stated charter schools were the focus in its rewrite of
NCLB.[55]

The administration backed this up with considerable funding. The
fiscal 2010 budget included charter school grants totaling $268 million,
an increase of $52 million over funding in 2009. The Department of
Education identified this as the first step in the Obama administration's overall strategy to meet its commitment. Plans include doubling
financial support for charter schools in the next four fiscal years.[56]

Obama's fiscal 2011 budget includes a $54 million increase, which
will bring the annual amount to more than $320 million.[57]

Radicals on Obama Pet Project

Another of Barack Obama's long-term pet projects and campaign
promises is replicating the Harlem Children's Zone, or HCZ, as the
first part of his plan to combat urban poverty. The nonprofit organization funds and operates a neighborhood-based system of education and
social services for the children of low-income families in a hundred-
block area of Harlem in New York.[58]

At a June 2009 White House gathering, President Obama again
highlighted HCZ as one of the innovative nonprofit programs "making
a difference in communities across the country."[59]

Using the HCZ as its blueprint, in April 2010 the Department of
Education launched its Promise Neighborhood program as the first

federal initiative to put education at the center of comprehensive efforts to fight poverty in urban and rural areas. In fiscal 2010, $10 million was made available to provide one year of funding to support as many as twenty organizations, which would allow for implementation of "cradle-to-career services designed to improve educational outcomes for students in distressed neighborhoods."[60]

The program, Secretary Duncan said, "brings all the Department's strategies together—high-quality early learning programs, high-quality schools, and comprehensive supports to ensure that students are safe, healthy and successful."[61]

When Obama added that this would be an all-hands-on-deck operation, he did not mention that the Promise Neighborhoods program is aligned with a progressive think tank program, that of the Economic Policy Institute's Broader, Bolder Approach to Education, or BBA.

The BBA was founded in June 2008 as a task force of national policy experts convened by EPI president Lawrence Mishel to "consider the broader context" of NCLB in the "nation's approach to education and youth development policy." BBA views public investment as necessary to education reform.[62] BBA's initial signatories include Barbara Taylor Bowman and other familiar names, again affiliated with Barack Obama or organizations associated with him and/or the Obama administration. Interestingly, at its founding, the task force also included Arne Duncan, then chief executive officer of Chicago Public Schools.

The application deadline for the first twenty one-year planning Promise Neighborhood grants, ranging between $400,000 and $500,000, was in June 2010. A total of 339 communities applied for the planning grants. (The Obama administration has asked Congress for an additional $210 million in new funding for fiscal 2011 to move from planning to implementation.)[63]

The first Promise Neighborhoods grantees were announced in September 2010, with the number of recipients expanded to twenty-one.[64]

Again, some of the grantees are controversial.

At the top of the list is the Abyssinian Development Corporation

(ADC) in New York. Funds will not be used to start charter schools; rather, they will be used for a new project to "emphasize a partnership with the traditional schools in the area," including Bread & Roses High School, identified as a failing school by the state.[65]

The name of Bread & Roses High School goes directly to its socialist roots. Founded in 1997, it was inspired by a 1912 protest song created by James Oppenheim for workers involved in the Lawrence, Massachusetts, mill strikes. The song's lyrics are said to encapsulate the workers' beliefs that "all people have an inherent right to life's basic necessities like food, money, and shelter (bread) and they also need a chance to appreciate beauty and be creative (roses)."[66]

Bread & Roses was founded in collaboration with the community-based organization ACORN, one of the school's partners, as a New Visions school.

In its 2009–2010 School Comprehensive Educational Plan, Bread & Roses states the school collaborates with ACORN to provide free English as a Second Language classes to parents and families. The school will collaborate with its partners, including ACORN, to "bring meaningful workshops and experiences to families: Healthcare, immigration issues, housing issues."

ACORN had been using foundation grants for more than a decade to launch its own New York public schools. Sol Stern wrote in the spring 2003 issue of *City Journal* that ACORN used such "warm-sounding names" as Bread & Roses High School as "political-indoctrination centers with mediocre academic records." The curriculum is filled with "'social justice' themes that wouldn't be out of place at an ACORN community organizers' training school," Stern adds. In the past, ACORN's schools have bused students to Washington, D.C., to "demonstrate against 'tax cuts for the rich.'"[67]

We saw in the previous chapter the involvement of ACORN schools with the Facing History and Ourselves program, which Bread & Roses incorporates into its curriculum.[68]

Near the bottom of the list is Universal Community Homes in

Philadelphia, a not-for-profit community development company. Universal's grant award sounds innocuous enough. The company has "partnered with the School District of Philadelphia to target nine (9) public schools for this initiative." Time and resources committed to the project include "leveraging their current facility plan for all schools, which will involve making fundamental policy decisions about the outcomes of all schools, including those that will be consolidated or closed."[69]

According to a summary of its application, the Universal Institute Charter School is included.[70]

Damaging information is inadvertently divulged in the Department of Education data. Universal was formed in 1993 under the direction of Kenneth Gamble, described as "one of Philadelphia's greatest talents, world-renowned lyricist, composer, producer." Gamble serves as Universal's chairman.[71]

During the 2008 presidential campaign Barack Obama set his field office, the Pennsylvania Campaign for Change, at 1501 Christian Street. Gamble even cut the ribbon. Signage on the building identifies it as home to Universal Educational Management, part of Gamble's Universal Companies.[72]

What Universal's grant application does not explain is that Gamble is the property owner of Philadelphia's first mosque, the United Muslim Masjid, a predominantly African-American mosque that opened in October 1994. Gamble—aka Luqman Abdul Haqq—is also the face behind the United Muslim Movement (UMM), incorporated in Philadelphia in June 1994. UMM's goal is to create a "central mosque in the city along with an organization that would be able to 'respond to the social, economical, political, educational, and religious needs'" facing the UMM communities.[73]

No longer listed on the UMM website is a list of member organizations that have been accused in court documents of terror ties—ICNA (Islamic Circle of North America), ISNA (Islamic Society of North America), which is tightly connected with the Muslim Brotherhood, and the American Muslim Council (AMC).[74]

Gamble is also a member of the Board of Directors (Majlis ash-Shura) of the Muslim Alliance in North America (MANA), headed by Siraj Wahhaj, an unindicted co-conspirator of the 1993 World Trade Center bombing. Gamble is reported to have been involved with MANA's leadership since April 2001, when the group was initially established as a national organization at the UMM mosque. The formation of MANA, which focuses its efforts on African-American converts to Islam, was inspired by Jamil Al-Amin, the onetime Black Panther "justice minister," H. Rap Brown. MANA's enthusiasm for Al-Amin is said to remain "untainted in the wake of his conviction for the 2000 murder of a sheriff's deputy."[75]

UMM is connected with the Jawala Scouts, or the Jawala Scout Youth Leadership Program, described as an Islamic paramilitary boys group, with children as young as seven involved. The Jawala Scouts were incorporated in Philadelphia in August 2005. The e-mail contact associated with the Jawala website is haqqone@hotmail.com, once identified as the e-mail address of Kenneth Gamble.[76]

According to the Jawala Scouts website—which describes the Scouts as a scouting program for young men from ages seven to seventeen—the program is designed to teach, train, and impart to Muslim youth the virtues of *taqwa*, discipline, responsibility, courage, leadership, self-defense, survival, and sportsmanship. In the Quranic verses, *taqwa* is the state of "being conscious of Allah." Activities include military drilling and firearms safety—for seven- to seventeen-year-olds.[77]

By no means are the Jawala Scouts like Boy Scouts in the traditional sense.[78]

Some people feared as recently as 2007 that Gamble wants "to build a black Muslim enclave" in Philadelphia. The Universal website would suggest this is not unrealistic.[79]

The Universal Plan: Universal Companies, Philadelphia, Penn., page on the MANA website informs that, for more than ten years, Universal's successful community revitalization efforts in the city of Philadelphia have been "one of the best-kept secrets in Muslim America."[80]

An April 2002 article in the *Philadelphia City Paper* describes the neighborhood as clearly Muslim, with residents in traditional Muslim garb, conducting prayers on the sidewalks. The author remarked, "Neighbors don't seem to mind the Muslim presence. They're just happy to see the drug dealers gone and the streets cleaner and safer, and they don't care who does it, as long as it gets done."[81]

In April 2008, it was reported that the Philadelphia office of CAIR (the controversial Council on American-Islamic Relations) was convening a workshop at Gamble's mosque. It was remarked, "That certainly helps understand Gamble's political-religious orientation."[82]

Even more telling is a message Gamble posts on Universal's MANA web page: "We are not just here for Universal, we are down here for Islam."[83]

Another grantee is the Cesar Chavez Public Policy Charter High School. In September 2005, Irasema Salcido, founder of the Cesar Chavez Public Charter Schools for Public Policy, received an envelope announcing a grant award for more than $1.5 million from progressive funder the Bill and Melinda Gates Foundation.[84]

In October 2008, Salcido began development of a Promise Neighborhood initiative in the neighborhoods adjacent to the Chavez Ward 7 campus in Parkside-Kenilworth.[85]

The Promise Neighborhood initiative gained several influential partners. The steering committee includes America's Promise Alliance, the Chavez Schools, DC Appleseed, and the Urban Institute.[86]

The Urban Institute first called for socialized health care in the United States in 1980. In a May 2006 report, UI concluded "public insurance appears to offer the best financial protection from high out-of-pocket expenses and financial burden for low-income families."[87]

Another ACORN-affiliated grantee is the Dudley Street Neighborhood Initiative (DSNI), a member of the Boston Green Justice Coalition Steering Committee. ACORN is also a member.[88] We find ACORN connected with DSNI in August 2001 when they and the Industrial Areas Foundation were members of the National Advisory

Group for the Institute for Education and Social Policy at New York University.[89]

Expeditionary Learning and International Baccalaureate Schools

In his September 2008 speech on school reform in Dayton, Ohio, Barack Obama advocated funding that would enable states and school districts to create a "'portfolio' of successful public school types, including charters, nonprofit schools, Montessori schools, career academies, and theme-focused schools."[90]

In particular, Obama singled out Mapleton Expeditionary School of the Arts in Thornton, Colorado, one of six smaller schools created after the school district closed down a large, low-performing high school. MESA and four other new schools were set up as education lab rats, with each using a different education model. MESA was based on a model that grew out of Outward Bound.[91]

In May 2008, Barack Obama chose MESA as the site for his second presidential campaign stop in Colorado. Obama lavished praise on MESA, which serves a high-poverty, urban and recent-immigration population, as Colorado's first district public high school to get all its seniors, forty-four, into four-year colleges.[92]

He likewise praised MESA's principal, social entrepreneur Michael Johnston. Johnston is not only a cofounder of New Leaders for New Schools, a national principal training program, and an advisory board member for Democrats for Education Reform–Colorado, but also serves as one of Obama's top advisers. Obama singled out MESA and Johnston again for praise in late October 2008 in a $4 million campaign ad buy.[93]

In February 2009, Barack and Michelle Obama and Arne Duncan visited Capital City Public Charter School, the first public school the president visited after he was sworn in. Like MESA, it is an Expeditionary Learning school.[94]

Remarking that his administration would reward "successful" schools, Obama said: "This kind of innovative school . . . is an example of how all our schools should be. . . . We're very proud of what's been accomplished at this school, and we want to make sure that we're duplicating that success all across the country."[95]

Obama has an established pattern of politically connected visits to schools belonging to the Coalition of Essential Schools, as well. In October 2009, after visiting New Orleans for the first time as president, Obama visited Dr. King Charter School, which was flooded during Hurricane Katrina and was the first public school rebuilt in New Orleans's Lower Ninth Ward. (It was here that nine-year-old Tyren Scott asked Obama, "Why do people hate you?")[96]

The Roots of Expeditionary Learning

The Expeditionary Learning (EL) model of education is built on the work of Kurt Hahn, the founder of Outward Bound. Additionally, it incorporates the work of educational leaders John Dewey, Ted Sizer, and Howard Gardner. The nonprofit group Expeditionary Learning partners with schools and/or school districts to "implement and assess the best curriculum and practices."[97]

The EL School network claims to serve 150 schools in twenty-eight states and the District of Columbia and to support 50,000 students and 4,000 teachers. As with most progressive education programs, other than schools and school districts, EL is supported by grants from the Bill and Melinda Gates Foundation, the Stuart Foundation, the Barr Foundation, and others.[98]

EL curriculum includes "purposeful, rigorous 'learning expeditions' that have intellectual, service, and physical dimensions." EL's expeditions contain several projects and performances—and form the core curriculum—that are theme- or topic-based, each lasting between six and nine weeks. Students' fieldwork is described as "central to learning expeditions, draws students out of the school building and engages them in real-world investigations, such as interviewing community members concerning neighborhood development or collecting samples of local water to assess its quality."[99]

EL also emphasizes intellectual and character development. The EL school design is highly organized, although tracking is eliminated, with extended blocks of time figured into the schedule. Students may even stay with the same teacher for two years or longer. EL has a whole-school focus with faculty work teaching and learning centered.[100]

International Baccalaureate

The Obama administration's fiscal 2011 budget includes $100 million for College Pathways and Accelerated Learning, described as a "new authority under the Administration's ESEA reauthorization proposal designed to increase graduation rates and preparation for college matriculation and success by providing college-level and other accelerated courses and instruction in high-poverty middle and high schools." This includes funding for Advanced Placement/International Baccalaureate (AP/IB) courses, dual-enrollment programs, and early college high schools.[101]

Barack Obama has an old connection to the International Baccalaureate Organization. The Chicago Annenberg Challenge expenditure files show funds were provided to the Beverly/Morgan Park International Baccalaureate School in 1997–99, during the time Obama and Bill Ayers served on the CAC board.[102]

"This irrefutable evidence of funding of the IB program by an unrepentant domestic terrorist and IBO's willingness to accept the money, speaks volumes about the organization's integrity and ideology," Lisa McLoughlin writes at her Truth About IB website.[103]

IB Chicago
An IB case study shows Chicago Public Schools implemented its first IB program, a Diploma Programme, in 1981 at the then-

underperforming Lincoln Park High School. This was part of Chicago's federally mandated desegregation efforts.[104]

In 1996, under its new superintendent, Paul G. Vallas, CPS added fourteen more IB high schools. Three years later, CPS added the IB Middle Years Programme, beginning with 669 students in neighborhood schools. By 2004 there were more than 2,800 students participating in the program (50.9 percent African-American, 36.4 percent Latino, 9.2 percent Caucasian).[105]

A March 2005 Chicago Public Schools press release uncovered by McLoughlin states that Chicago has "THE highest concentration of IB schools in the country."[106]

Chicago's DePaul University website currently states CPS has the "largest concentration of IB programs of any urban school district in the world."[107]

The policy manual for school year 2010–2011 announces that CPS's IB curriculum has been rolled into its Gifted and Enriched Academic Programs (GEAP). The IB preparatory programs were renamed International Gifted Programs, "designed for intellectually able 6th, 7th and 8th grade students."[108]

This is only one in a long line of changes for CPS schools. Between 1996 and 2004 there were seven reorganizations of Chicago's high schools. These were all after the Daley administration took over in 1995. All "failed," George N. Schmidt writes in October 2005 at *Substance News*.[109]

CPS, under Paul G. Vallas and Arne Duncan, "maintained 'a variety of differentiated programs, schools, and instructional approaches' that reflect and deepen sharp divisions of race and class," Paul Street wrote in December 2008 in the *Black Agenda Report*. He added that Chicago's labor market has changed; postindustrial Chicago has become globalized Chicago. CPS has provided two different educational experiences for the children it serves: one for the "disproportionately white first group and another for children from the disproportionately black and Latino second group."[110]

By March 2008, Duncan and Mayor Daley had shifted emphasis to serving "underserved communities." Magnet schools were established in wealthy Chicago north side communities. The Lincoln Park school, previously deemed as "under-performing," was now identified as "underutilized" and was "crashed into 'underserved,'" *Substance News* reports.[111]

That led to Daley and Duncan announcing that the Oscar Mayer Elementary School would no longer be a neighborhood elementary school. It would be "morphed" into Oscar Mayer Montessori for the lower grades and Oscar Mayer International Baccalaureate for the upper grades.

It naturally follows that Arne Duncan is well schooled in IB's programs. He has also attended and participated in plenary sessions of world conferences for heads of IB schools.[112]

IB Curriculum

The IB program was originally designed to provide a certified education for children of diplomats. As of February 2006, IB was part of the curriculum for more than 1,700 schools worldwide, with more than six hundred programs operating in America.[113]

But the IB curriculum—now grown to nearly one thousand U.S. campuses and in 139 countries—is so much more—and less.[114] IB is not a curriculum at all, McLoughlin writes. IB provides a framework. "IB's claim to fame is that its programs are the same, everywhere in the world," she adds.[115] McLoughlin calls IB the "biggest educational scam perpetrated on American schools today." While IB students "learn diversity, multiculturalism, and international-mindedness, can they do math? Do they learn grammar? Can they write a paper?" she asks.[116]

Another criticism is that IB not only is anti-American, but that it also undermines national sovereignty and promotes radical environmentalism. Also, until recently, IB endorsed the Earth Charter, which supports the equal distribution of wealth within and among nations.[117]

Another cause for concern is Carol Bellamy, a radical feminist who has served as chairman of the IB board of directors since April 2009. Bellamy formerly led the United Nations Children's Fund. During her ten years at UNICEF, the organization promoted abortion rights, sex education for children, and a radical feminist agenda.[118] Bellamy was described "as doctrinaire a feminist as you will find" by Carey Roberts in 2004. "While serving as a state senator in New York [from 1973 to 1977], Bellamy had voted against a bill that would have granted legal rights to an infant who managed to survive a botched abortion."[119]

Roberts reports that, in August 2003, the Catholic Family and Human Rights Institute issued the report "Women or Children First?" It documented that UNICEF was "involved in back-door support for abortion programs around the world." The report concluded that under Bellamy's leadership, "radical feminism has come to define the current UNICEF, even to the possible detriment of UNICEF's original mandate to help children."[120]

IB Funding

IB's early funds came from the United Nations. Funding now comes from the IB Foundation, the 20th Century Fund, the Ford Foundation, UNESCO, and the Bill and Melinda Gates Foundation.[121]

Since 2005, Bellamy has served as president and CEO of World Learning, described as a "global leader in international education, training, exchange and development, with programmes in over 75 countries." Based on Bellamy's funding sources for World Learning, McLoughlin deduces that another IB funding source is most likely the Tides Foundation.[122]

However, local, state, and federal tax dollars—estimated in the multimillions—pay for IB programs nationwide, IB investigator Debra K. Niwa reported in March 2010.[123] While nearly 93 percent of IB's 1,095 school sites are in U.S. public schools, it is unknown how many of the IB programs have been adopted with public knowledge or approval, Niwa adds.

Niwa also points out how the use of IB programs in public schools is a "cash cow" for the organization. For example, as of February 2010, Arizona's Tucson Unified School District (TUSD) had spent $939,000 on IB programs. One school offers the IB Diploma Program for the second year at a magnet high school. The program began with forty-two juniors, no seniors; in school year 2009–2010 there were thirty-two seniors. This does not mean that all participating students are diploma candidates. Some, Niwa writes, are only taking one or more IB classes. Yet, in spite of the expense—and necessary TUSD budget cuts and proposed school closures—the school district plans to add IB programs to more schools. Niwa observes that the IB's "budget-busting programs . . . will require multi-millions of extra revenue dollars."

This is a prime example of where the $100 million in funding in the Obama administration's fiscal 2011 budget for Advanced Placement/International Baccalaureate (AP/IB) courses will come in real handy.[124] IB published a twenty-nine-page online booklet on how to capitalize on ARRA funds for IB schools. It really is nothing more than a twenty-nine-page sales pitch for schools to "partner" with IB.[125]

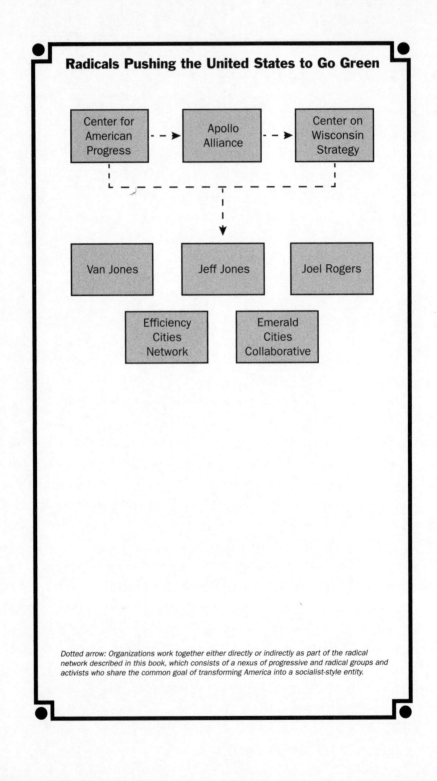

Radicals Pushing the United States to Go Green

Center for American Progress → Apollo Alliance → Center on Wisconsin Strategy

Van Jones

Jeff Jones

Joel Rogers

Efficiency Cities Network

Emerald Cities Collaborative

Dotted arrow: Organizations work together either directly or indirectly as part of the radical network described in this book, which consists of a nexus of progressive and radical groups and activists who share the common goal of transforming America into a socialist-style entity.

chapter seven

REDS TURNING AMERICA GREEN?

Like so many other causes, the radical "progressive" network has hijacked the issue of environmental activism to push its own socialist aims. It has formed an army of front groups that have had a direct hand in helping to craft environmental legislation and policy sold to the public as no less than helping to save the planet. These groups, allied with "progressive" politicians, and aided, wittingly or not, by a sympathetic news media, have used everything from misinformation to scare tactics to intimidation to advocate the questionable science of "global warming," while literally conspiring to minimize any data that does not fit the now embattled theory. The radical network has been a champion of "green" activism as part of its multipronged assault on our nation, in this case in large part to achieve redistribution of American and Western wealth and power.

In a pertinent case study of these radical progressives' influence on environmental policy, let's go back to September 2008, when the University of Colorado–based Presidential Climate Action Project, or PCAP, released a lengthy proposal to guide the environmental policies during the first hundred days of the forty-fourth U.S. president, regardless of whether Barack Obama or Senator John McCain won that year's election.[1]

After Obama was victorious, the PCAP began working with John

Podesta's Center for American Progress. CAP was founded in 2003 with seed money from George Soros, who also donated $3 million to its sister organization, the Project Action Fund.[2] Podesta and CAP are heavily influential in helping the Obama White House. A *Time* magazine article profiles Podesta's group's influence in the formation of the Obama administration, stating, "Not since the Heritage Foundation helped guide Ronald Reagan's transition in 1981 has a single outside group held so much sway."[3]

In November 2010, following GOP electoral victories in the House, CAP released a fifty-four-page road map for President Obama to bypass the new Republican Congress and rule until 2012 via executive order. The plan calls for Obama to push a "progressive agenda" on issues of health care, economy, environment, education, federal government, and foreign policy.[4]

Podesta argued that "the U.S. Constitution and the laws of our nation grant the president significant authority to make and implement policy," including in executive orders, diplomacy, rulemaking, and commanding the armed forces. "The ability of President Obama to accomplish important change through these powers should not be underestimated," he wrote in the plan's introduction.[5] The PCAP has a cozy relationship with Podesta's CAP and some of its radicals. The PCAP has proposed a sweeping new plan that, among other radical aims, astonishingly calls for Obama to use the military and Department of Defense to combat so-called global warming.

William S. Becker, the PCAP's executive director, told Aaron Klein in November 2009 that his group's initial proposals received a "very positive reception from the moment we delivered (the 100-day proposal) last November to John Podesta. We continue to work with some colleagues inside the (Obama) administration, as well as continuing to push for bold action from the outside." Becker at the time confirmed his group is "about to propose a new and more assertive strategy for President Obama to raise the bar on the U.S. climate goal, with or without Congress."[6]

Becker said the White House "adopted quite a few of our recommendations or variations of them." He cited a few examples of the influence of the PCAP's 2008 plan on Obama's initial presidential policies:[7]

★ The PCAP recommended that the United States reach a bilateral climate deal with China prior to the upcoming U.N. Climate Change Conference in Copenhagen. The United States has since signed several agreements with China to share technology that reduces greenhouse-gas emissions.

★ The PCAP recommended an executive order that removed the gags from federal climate scientists. This became one of Obama's first actions on environmental policy.

★ The PCAP recommended an overhaul of federal energy management to beef up efficiency requirements for federal agencies and to restore absolute carbon reduction targets that had been rescinded by the Bush administration. The Obama administration issued a new federal energy management order in October, including a requirement that agencies develop absolute targets for greenhouse-gas reductions.

★ The PCAP recommended (as did many others) that the Environmental Protection Agency embrace California's vehicle emission standards and begin the process of regulating greenhouse gases under the Clean Air Act. The EPA is doing both.

★ The PCAP recommended major budget increases for states and communities to engage in energy and climate actions and to weatherize the homes of low-income families. This was part of Obama's stimulus package.

True to his word, Becker and his PCAP have prepared an entirely new blueprint, titled *Plan B: Near-Term Presidential Actions for Energy and Environmental Leadership.*[8]

The plan, to be implemented beginning January 2011, recommends Obama use the U.S. military and Department of Defense "for technology innovation and its procurement of energy-related goods and services to accelerate energy efficiency gains in the U.S. economy." It directs the White House to "make clear to the Secretary of the Navy that long-term objectives in the Gulf Coast restoration plan should include the restoration of vital ecosystems that were degraded prior to the [2010 BP] oil spill and would enhance the economy of the region while protecting Gulf Coast communities from the anticipated impacts of climate change."

The plan seeks to direct the Department of Defense and the White House Council on Environmental Quality to assess the past performance and the potential role of the U.S. Army Corps of Engineers in nonstructural disaster prevention projects that involve ecosystem restoration.

On other fronts, the PCAP's plan aims for a presidential proclamation to "strengthen national energy and climate goals to meet or exceed the President's commitment in the Copenhagen Accord to hold global warming to no more than 20 Celsius above pre-industrial levels."

The PCAP plan seeks to create new federal incentives in grant and loan programs to "reward" states that adopt "progressive climate and energy policies." The new plan directs Obama to create a National Low Carbon Fuel Standard that requires fuel refiners to reduce the life cycle greenhouse gas emissions of transportation fuels sold in the United States by 5 percent in five years and 10 percent in ten years.

Obama introduced a plan for a National Low Carbon Fuel Standard (NLCFS)—which likewise required that "all transportation fuels sold domestically contain 5 percent less carbon by 2015 and 10 percent less by 2020"—in April 2007, on the eve of Earth Day, at the University of New Hampshire.[9]

Obama and Senator Tom Harkin (D-Iowa) introduced the National Low Carbon Fuel Standard Act of 2007 on May 7 of that year. The bill was referred to the Committee on Environment and Public Works, where it remained. It never became law.[10]

The NLCFS proposal would "nationalize" a similar plan signed into law by California's Republican governor Arnold Schwarzenegger in January 2007. The then governor "issued an executive order establishing a low carbon fuel standard for transportation fuels sold in his state."[11]

In February 2007, Schwarzenegger and presidential candidate Senator John McCain (R-Ariz.) "called for the U.S. to implement a National Low Carbon Fuel Standard." The following month, Senators Dianne Feinstein (D-Calif.), Susan Collins (R-Me.), and Olympia Snowe (R-Me.) "introduced a measure that would require fuel suppliers to increase the percentage of low-carbon fuels—biodiesel, E-85 (made with cellulosic ethanol), hydrogen, electricity, and others—in the transportation fuel supply by 2015."[12]

Similar legislation was approved in British Columbia in April 2008.[13] The European Union also proposed legislation in January 2007, which was adopted in December 2008.[14]

The PCAP plan calls on Obama to push Congress and the G-20 nations to be more aggressive in phasing out fossil energy subsidies, including producer and consumer subsidies, as well as to reduce or eliminate carbon subsidies under the administration's control.[15]

The PCAP plan seeks to ask Congress to give Obama sweeping power to authorize the creation of a "Carbon Subsidy Reduction Commission" that identifies subsidies that are not critical to economic stability or national security, and develops an "all or nothing" list of subsidies to be eliminated upon the president's approval.[16]

A review of the PCAP's relatively modest-sized advisory committee and list of signatories yields interesting finds. Kit Batten, managing director for energy and environmental policy at Podesta's CAP, is a signatory.[17] The PCAP leadership consists of a chairman emeritus, a cochair, and a list of twenty board members and technical advisers.

One of those advisers is Van Jones, a Center for American Progress fellow and President Obama's former "green jobs" czar.[18]

Until his resignation, Jones had filled the post of Special Adviser to Obama for Green Jobs, Enterprise and Innovation at the White House Council on Environmental Quality. In April 2009, Aaron Klein reported that Jones was a founder and leader of the communist revolutionary organization STORM—Standing Together to Organize a Revolutionary Movement. That organization had its roots in a grouping of black activists protesting the Persian Gulf War in 1991. STORM was formally founded in 1994, eventually becoming one of the most influential and active radical groups in the San Francisco Bay area.[19]

Jones told the *East Bay Express* in 2005 that he first became radicalized in the wake of the 1992 Rodney King riots in Los Angeles, during which time he was arrested. "I was a rowdy nationalist on April 28th, and then the verdicts came down on April 29th," he said. "By August, I was a communist. I met all these young radical people of color—I mean really radical: communists and anarchists. And it was, like, 'This is what I need to be a part of.' I spent the next 10 years of my life working with a lot of those people I met in jail, trying to be a revolutionary," he said.

Jones boasted to the *East Bay Express* that his current environmental activism was really a means to fight for racial and class "justice." This is a crucial admission. A member of the radical network actually stated he is championing a cause, in this case the "green" movement, for something that is not related to the actual movement, but instead is about class "justice," a key socialist policy aim. Jones's involvement in any environmental cause, in this case the PCAP, needs to be immediately questioned.

Jones, meanwhile, went on to found the Ella Baker Center for Human Rights in 1996, named after a little-known civil rights firebrand and socialist activist.

Jones's STORM organization worked with known communist leaders. Its official manifesto, *Reclaiming Revolution*, had been published on the Internet until Klein and others wrote articles and blog entries linking to the online publication.

The ninety-seven-page manual describes Jones's organization as having a "commitment to the fundamental ideas of Marxism-Leninism." "We agreed with Lenin's analysis of the state and the party," reads the manifesto. "And we found inspiration in the revolutionary strategies developed by Third World revolutionaries like Mao Zedong and Amilcar Cabral."

Cabral was a neo-Marxist revolutionary theoretician and leader of Guinea-Bissau and the Cape Verde Islands in their independence movement from Portugal, serving afterward as prime minister. Jones named his son after Cabral and reportedly concludes every e-mail with a quote from the African leader.

One section of the official STORM manifesto describes a vigil that Jones's group held on September 12, 2001, at Snow Park in Oakland. That event drew hundreds and articulated "an anti-imperialist line," according to STORM's own description. The radical group's manual boasted that its 9/11 vigil was held to express solidarity with Arab and Muslim Americans and to mourn the civilians killed in the terrorist attacks "as well as the victims of U.S. imperialism around the world."

Jones's routine involvement in antigovernment activism included a 2002 keynote speech at a rally at People's Park in Berkeley to mark the national launch of a Maoist, terrorist-supporting, antiwar group, Not in Our Name, founded by Revolutionary Communist Party member C. Clark Kissinger. The antiwar rally urged "resistance" against the U.S. government.

Subsequent revelations about Jones include that he signed a statement for 911Truth.org in 2004 demanding an investigation into what the Bush administration may have done that "deliberately allowed 9/11 to happen, perhaps as a pretext for war." In a 2005 conference, Jones characterized the United States as an "apartheid regime" that civil rights workers helped turn into a "struggling, fledgling democracy." Jones signed a petition calling for nationwide "resistance" against police, accusing them of using the 9/11 attacks to carry out policies of torture. Amazingly, just days before his White House appointment, Jones used a forum at a major youth convention to push for a radical agenda that included "spreading the wealth" and "changing the whole system."

Radical Groups Craft Legislation

Jones and other radicals are leaders of multiple important "green" groups with strong influence over White House policy. One of the most influential of those groups is the Apollo Alliance, a project of the Tides Center, which is a spin-off of the Tides Foundation, a George Soros–funded organization founded in 1976 by antiwar activist Drummond Pike.[20]

The Tides Center's board chairman is Wade Rathke, who is best known as the founder and chief organizer of the Association of Community Organizations for Reform Now, or ACORN. Rathke is also president of the New Orleans–based Local 100 of the Service Employees International Union.

The Tides Foundation makes very clear its openly leftist agenda: "We strengthen community-based organizations and the progressive movement by providing an innovative and cost-effective framework for your philanthropy."[21]

Immediately after the September 11, 2001, terrorist attacks, for example, Tides established a "9/11 Fund" to advocate for a "peaceful national response" to the terrorist attacks. *Discover the Networks* notes that Tides later replaced the 9/11 Fund with the "Democratic Justice Fund," which was financed in large part by Soros's Open Society Institute. Soros has donated more than $7 million to Tides over the years.[22]

The Apollo Alliance claims it was founded in the aftermath of the 9/11 attacks "to catalyze a clean energy revolution in America." Apollo Alliance cofounders Bracken Hendricks and Representative Jay Inslee, in their 2007 book, *Apollo's Fire: Igniting America's Clean-Energy Economy*, spelled out Apollo's aims:[23]

Apollo co-founder Dan Carol deserves credit for having the "vision" to "[broaden] the coalition on climate and energy solutions through a focus on economic transformation . . . at the heart of a political movement that is finally emerging as a new politics for the country, linking concern over climate change, national security, and energy to hope for good jobs, stronger communities, and a more robust democracy."

Among Apollo Alliance board members are a grouping of radicals, including Van Jones, Joel Rogers, and Jeff Jones.[24]

Jeff Jones joined Students for a Democratic Society, or SDS, from which the Weatherman organization splintered in the fall of 1965. Two years later, he became SDS's New York City regional director, a position in which he participated in nearly all the group's major protests until 1969, including the 1968 Columbia University protests and the violent riots that same year at the Democratic National Convention.

In 1969 Jones cofounded Weatherman, later known as the Weather Underground Organization, with Bill Ayers and Mark Rudd, who had led the Columbia University protests. The three signed an infamous statement calling for a revolution against the American government inside and outside the country to fight and defeat what the group called U.S. imperialism. President Obama came under fire during the 2008 presidential campaign for his longtime, extensive association with Ayers.

Jones was a main leader and orchestrator of what became known as the Days of Rage, a series of violent riots in Chicago organized in October 1969 by the Weatherman. The culmination of the riots came when he gave a signal for rowdy protesters to target a hotel that was the home of a local judge presiding over a trial of antiwar activists.

Jones went underground after he failed to appear for a March 1970 court date to face charges of "crossing state lines to foment a riot and conspiring to do so." He moved to San Francisco with Ayers's wife, Bernardine Dohrn. That year, at least one bombing claimed by the Weatherman went off in Jones's locale at the Presidio army base.

Jones's Weatherman took credit for multiple bombings of U.S. government buildings, including attacks against the U.S. Capitol on March 1, 1971, the Pentagon on May 19, 1972, and the State Department in 1975.

As we have seen with scores of other members of the Radical Network, the Apollo Alliance in May 2011 rebranded itself following an onslaught of negative publicity about its radicalism. It joined forces with BlueGreen Alliance and took on the group's namesake starting July 1, 2011.[25] Apollo is now known as the BlueGreen Alliance, although for the sake of clarity we will continue to refer to the group as the Apollo Alliance.

The Apollo Alliance, meanwhile, boasts in its own promotional material that it helped to craft portions of the $787 billion "stimulus" legislation (officially called the American Recovery and Reinvestment Act, or ARRA) that President Obama signed into law in early 2009. The Alliance was involved in writing the "clean energy and green-collar jobs provisions" of the bill, for which $86 billion in funds were earmarked, including public money "to build new transit and high speed rail lines, weatherize homes, develop next generation batteries for clean vehicles, scale up wind and solar power, build a modern electric grid, and train a new generation of green-collar workers."[26]

Apollo also recommended the stimulus bill allocate $11 billion for the development of a so-called "Smart Grid," which would use digital technology to deliver electricity from suppliers to consumers. Ultimately, the bill allocated precisely that amount to Smart Grid–related projects, including a $100 million provision for job training related to Smart Grid technology.[27]

In addition to its influence over "stimulus" funds, the Apollo Alliance was also instrumental in helping draft a "clean technology" bill.

The Investments for Manufacturing Progress and Clean Technology Act of 2009, or IMPACT, was sponsored by Senator Sherrod Brown (D-Ohio) and is also being promoted by Senator Debbie Stabenow (D-Mich.). The act seeks to establish a $30 billion revolving loan fund to help small and midsized manufacturers retool their factories to produce so-called clean technologies and become more energy efficient.[28]

The Apollo Alliance has boasted in promotional material the act was based on the group's recently published "GreenMAP" or Green Manufacturing Action Plan, which laid out aggressive steps to scale up production of American-made clean energy systems and components while making U.S. factories more energy efficient.[29]

When Senator Brown formally introduced the act in June 2010, he was reportedly joined by Apollo Alliance chairman Phil Angelides and other notable business, labor, and "clean energy" leaders. "Without a program to support our own domestic manufacturers, policies that create new demand for clean energy will just lead to more imports," Angelides told reporters alongside Brown. "It is critical that Congress enact legislation that provides direct and substantial investment in clean energy component manufacturing to ensure that jobs are created in the U.S.," Angelides said.[30]

Brown commented, "We can revive American manufacturing through investment in clean energy. This bill will help our manufacturers retool, put our auto suppliers back to work and produce clean energy technologies."[31]

The Green Collar Association, a clearinghouse that supports green-collar job growth through education and training, reported that shortly after Apollo's GreenMAP report was released in April 2009, Brown and Stabenow asked the Apollo Alliance to help them draft model clean energy manufacturing policies based on the report's recommendations.[32]

According to the Apollo Alliance, this is also how Senator Brown's Investments for Manufacturing Progress and Clean Technology Act was "born."

> The IMPACT Act would expand domestic clean energy manufacturing by establishing a $30 billion revolving loan fund to help small and mid-sized manufacturers restructure their facilities to become more energy efficient while producing what the act calls clean technologies. The bill would also increase support for Manufactur-

ing Extension Partnerships (MEP's) that link smaller manufacturers to clean energy supply chains and markets.

The Apollo Alliance states that some of its other proposals, such
as "investing in home weatherization, transmission grid upgrades and
public transit projects," were included in the American Recovery and
Reinvestment Act. "But to achieve the kind of green-collar job growth
needed to lift the U.S. out of the current recession—and put us on a
path to a clean energy future—we need a federal clean energy and climate bill that puts a cap on greenhouse gas emissions and establishes a
strong federal renewable energy standard."

Another piece of legislation that bears Apollo's fingerprints is the
Consolidated Land, Energy, Aquatic Restoration Act of 2009, or the
CLEAR Act, which was passed 209–193 on July 30, 2010. It now requires Senate confirmation. The bill is somewhat ambiguous, so federal
agencies will need to determine how it is implemented. It is being sold
as a government response to the Gulf oil spill crisis, but the bill itself
stretches far beyond addressing that tragedy to include page after page
of provisions that are unrelated to the oil spill.[33]

The latest version of the CLEAR Act:[34]

★ Imposes changes and higher taxes for onshore natural
gas and oil production. It fundamentally changes leasing onshore by the Forest Service and Bureau of Land
Management, which affects not just leasing for natural
gas and oil, but also for renewable energy including wind
and solar.

★ Creates over $30 billion in new mandatory spending for
the Land and Water Conservation Fund and the Historic
Preservation Fund.

★ Raises direct taxes on natural gas and oil by over $22 bil-
lion in ten years—with the taxes eventually climbing to
nearly $3 billion per year. This tax only applies to U.S. oil
and gas production on federal leases.

★ Requires the federal takeover of state authority to permit drilling in state waters, which reverses sixty years of precedent.

★ Allows 10 percent of all offshore revenues—an amount possibly as high as $500 million per year—to be spent on a new fund controlled by the Interior secretary to issue ocean research grants (ORCA fund).

★ Establishes a "marine spatial planning" regulatory authority—which allows for ocean zoning that could lead to restrictions on fishing, energy production, and even onshore activities such as farming.

The Senate version of the bill was introduced by Senators Maria Cantwell (D-Wash.) and Susan Collins. Cantwell was a founding board member of the Apollo Alliance and in 2006 a member of the Alliance's National Advisory Board.[35]

Discover the Networks notes that in July 2009, Senate Majority Leader Reid and House Speaker Pelosi appointed Apollo Alliance chairman Angelides to serve as chairman of the newly created Financial Crisis Inquiry Commission.[36]

Apollo Alliance personalities are involved in a consortium of "green" groups tied to the White House and President Obama. It is instructive to take a closer look at one charitable foundation, the Center for Neighborhood Technology.

Writing on March 14, 2008, in her *Chicago Sun-Times* blog, Lynn Sweet commented:[37]

Sen. Barack Obama, who had been declining to reveal earmarks he requested in 2005 and 2006, finally did so [. . .] Obama also sought money for the Center for Neighborhood Technology, where his neighbor Jacky Grimshaw is a honcho.

We'll get back to "honcho" Jacky Grimshaw shortly, but first let's look at those 2005 and 2006 earmarks. In 2005 Obama requested

$1 million and secured $400,000 for the Center for Neighborhood Technology's I-Go Car Sharing Program. In 2006, Obama requested $2.2 million for the Center for Neighborhood Technology's Information for Communities Project.[38]

Also, while Obama sat as a paid director on the board of the Chicago Woods Fund from 1999 to 2002, the nonprofit donated $150,000 to the Neighborhood Technology Fund.[39]

As Aaron Klein first reported in February 2008, Obama sat on the Woods Fund board alongside Bill Ayers.[40] Executives and board members of the Center for Neighborhood Technology, meanwhile, contributed $20,688 to Obama's campaigns.[41]

Vice President of the center is Jacquelyne (Jacky) Grimshaw, who has been a part of the Chicago political machine for quite some time. She served as "director of intergovernmental affairs" under Mayor Harold Washington, and had previously been described as Washington's "chief lobbyist," "top aide," as well as a "political analyst" and a "longtime political activist."[42]

On December 3, 2002, when Illinois governor-elect Rod Blagojevich named his transition committees, Obama was listed on the Health Committee and Grimshaw on the Transportation Committee.[43]

Grimshaw was named in May 2008 to represent Obama on the Credentials Committee for the Illinois Democratic delegation to the Democratic National Convention held in August 2008 in Denver.[44]

The Center for Neighborhood Technology, together with the Apollo Alliance, endorsed the Livable Communities Act of 2010, which seeks to create an Office of Sustainable Housing and Communities to encourage comprehensive regional planning and sustainable development by breaking down federal agency and department barriers.[45] The Center for Neighborhood Technology summarizes the act thus:[46]

> The Livable Communities Act would strengthen communities and increase housing affordability for families by encouraging sustainable development. Grant money made available through the leg-

islation, for instance, would fund projects that prioritize vibrant downtown business districts within walking distance of homes and transit stops, brownfield redevelopment in struggling industrial areas, and public transit options to reduce household transportation costs—the second highest expense for Americans after housing.

The Office of Sustainable Housing and Communities would oversee two grant programs established by the Livable Communities Act. One grant program would make $2.2 billion available for communities to build and improve affordable housing, strengthen public transportation, promote transit-oriented development, and redevelop brownfield sites. A second grant program would provide $500 million to support comprehensive regional planning that recognizes the interconnectedness of transportation, housing, community and economic development, and environmental sustainability.[47]

Representative Earl Blumenauer (D-Ore.) was instrumental in establishing a Congressional Livable Communities Taskforce in addition to an already existing White House Livable Communities Task Force. A personality whose name pops up continuously in the promotion of "Livable Communities" is Apollo Alliance cofounder Bracken Hendricks, now with, yes, you guessed it, the Center for American Progress.[48]

Hendricks addressed the White House Task Force on Livable Communities on issues of public safety, electronic government, oceans policy, trade and the environment, and smart growth.[49] His own bio at the Center for American Progress boasts he "served as an advisor to the campaign and transition team of President Barack Obama, and was an architect of clean-energy portions of the American Recovery and Reinvestment Act."[50]

Look Who's Educating Government

Meanwhile, a "green" energy coalition has been working to educate the government on issues of the environment. The Efficiency Cities

Network (ECN) describes itself as an "informal policy learning network of government staff, researchers and technical assistance providers, and NGOs currently active in or committed to making scaled efforts at high-road (i.e., concerned with equity and democracy, not just sustainability) energy retrofits (seeking increased energy efficiency, conservation, and clean generation) of urban building stock."[51]

The group holds regular sessions on energy and environmental policy issues with officials from Congress, the Department of Energy, and local governmental agencies.[52] Hendricks has been a presenter, as has Joel Rogers.[53] The Efficiency Cities Network is hosted in collaboration with Green for All, their Retrofit America's Cities Community of Practice project, and the Center on Wisconsin Strategy, or COWS.[54]

Rogers is also on the board of the Emerald Cities Collaborative, a "consortium of diverse organizations—businesses, unions, community organizations, development intermediaries, social justice advocates, research and technical assistance providers—united around the goal of 'greening' our metropolitan areas in high-road ways that advance equal opportunity, shared wealth, and democracy within them."[55] The group's board council includes Green for All and the Apollo Alliance.[56]

"Global Warming," "Clean Coal"

In the analysis of President Obama's ongoing environmental policy, the one elephant in the room is the remarkable discovery that much of the science behind so-called global warming is now in question following the illegal release in November 2009 of thousands of e-mails and other documents from the University of East Anglia's Climatic Research Unit (CRU). The e-mails show that some climate researchers declined to share their data with fellow scientists, conspired to rig data crucial to the global warming consensus of international bodies, and sought to keep researchers with dissenting views from publishing in leading scientific journals.

A review of the CRU's records found the organization dumped much of the raw temperature information on which the body's predictions of global warming are based. In other words, other experts are not able to check basic calculations said to show a long-term rise in temperature over the past 150 years.[57] In a statement on its website, the CRU said: "We do not hold the original raw data, but only the value-added (quality controlled and homogenised) data."

Dr. Harrison "Jack" Schmitt is a former United States senator from New Mexico as well as a geologist and former Apollo astronaut who currently is an aerospace consultant. In an article published by the Science and Environmental Policy Project, Schmitt relates:[58]

> There has been an absolute natural increase in global surface temperature of half a degree Centigrade per 100 years (0.9 degrees Fahrenheit) over the last three and a half centuries. Observational climate data and objective interpretations of those data strongly indicate that nature, not human activity, exerts the primary influence on this current long term warming and on all global climate variations. Human influence through use of fossil fuels has been and remains minor if even detectable. Claims to the contrary only find support in highly questionable climate models that fail repeatedly against the reality of nature.

CRU director Professor Philip Jones was in charge of the two key sets of data used to draw up the reports of the UN's Intergovernmental Panel on Climate Change, the enormously influential panel that sets worldwide climate policies. Amazingly, after the scandal hit, Jones told the BBC the past fifteen years there has been no "statistically significant" warming, although he argued this was a blip rather than the long-term trend.[59]

One after the other, an avalanche of news stories broke that global warming "catastrophes" were really anything but. Central to the alarmist theory espoused by global warming proponents such as Al Gore is that the oceans are rising due to the melting of ice caps and that soon the seas could flood land. However, in April 2009 a study concluded ice is actually expanding in much of Antarctica.[60] The results of ice-core drilling and sea ice monitoring indicated there was no large-scale melting of ice over most of Antarctica, although experts stated they were concerned at ice losses on the continent's western coast. Antarctica has 90 percent of the earth's ice and 80 percent of its fresh water.

Then scientific papers were released finding sea levels worldwide were not rising. In one new scientific paper presented at the fourth International Conference on Climate Change, Nils-Axel Morner, former emeritus head of the paleogeophysics and geodynamics department at Stockholm University, revealed that observational records from around the world—locations like the Maldives, Bangladesh, India, Tuvalu, and Vanuatu—show the sea level isn't rising at all. Morner concluded there is no "alarming sea level rise" across the globe. His paper says a UN report warning of coastal cities being deluged by rising waters from melting polar ice caps "is utterly wrong." Manfred Wenzel and Jens Schroter, writing in the *Journal of Geophysical Research*, came to similar conclusions.[61]

Meanwhile, "green" champions in the United States cannot even agree on the existence of their own claimed programs. Case in point— board members and endorsers of the Apollo Alliance, which successfully promoted "clean coal" funding as part of President Obama's $787 billion "stimulus" bill, also have endorsed a group led by Al Gore that opposes the White House's "clean coal" efforts, going so far as to claim "clean coal" doesn't exist.

The Alliance helped draft "clean energy and green-collar jobs provisions" of the bill, for which $3.4 billion was earmarked to "work toward making coal part of the solution and reducing the amount of carbon dioxide emitted from industrial facilities and fossil fuel power plants." The Alliance has long pushed "clean coal." In 2007 Senate testimony, Apollo Alliance president Jerome Ringo talked about a blueprint his group drew up, claiming "hundreds of thousands of additional jobs will be created in the clean energy technology sector, including renewables, clean coal and bio-fuels."[62]

A slew of groups that support the Apollo Alliance as well as individuals on Apollo's board endorsed what was known as the "New Apollo Program and the Apollo Economic Recovery Act," a mock recovery act on which sections of Obama's "stimulus" bill were partly based. That act also called for funding for "clean coal."[63]

However, many of those same Apollo endorsers and board members also are members of Gore's lobby group that opposes "clean coal" initiatives. In 2008, Gore launched the Reality Coalition, a national grassroots and advertising effort with a simple message: in reality, there is no such thing as clean coal.[64] Coal, Reality Coalition argues, cannot be considered clean until its carbon dioxide emissions are captured and stored. Gore's group has backed a multimillion-dollar ad campaign, running in print, broadcast, and online media, opposing Obama's "clean coal" initiatives.[65]

At the launch of Reality Coalition, Gore wrote a *New York Times* op-ed arguing that until coal is truly clean, there should be no new coal-fired power plants built in America.[66] Gore's group is backed by the Natural Resources Defense Council, the United Steelworkers union, and the Sierra Club.[67] Leaders of all three groups also are board members of Apollo Alliance, which promotes "clean coal."[68] The Sierra Club's chairman and executive director, Carl Pope, is an Apollo board member as well.

Larry Schweiger, president and CEO of the National Wildlife Federation, stated, "We need to clean up coal, not spend billions on a scheme to market coal as clean."[69] However, the National Wildlife Federation is an Apollo Alliance endorser.

Gene Karpinski, president of the League of Conservation Voters, previously declared of Gore's group that "the coal industry is running a cynical and dishonest campaign to mislead the American people, while they stand in the way of real solutions. The 'Reality' Coalition is aimed at holding them accountable for their outlandish claims."[70] However, the League is an Apollo Alliance endorser.

Obama himself forges ahead with "green" initiatives as if the science behind global warming is concrete. Just days after the hacked e-mail scandal first broke, Obama and his team attended a global summit in Copenhagen where global warming was discussed and the White House worked with the leaders of China, India, Brazil, South Africa, and about twenty other countries to commit to emission cuts that will be open to international review.[71]

The Obama administration has been urging government agencies to prepare for the "inevitable effects" of global warming. Channeling Van Jones, the White House interagency task force on adapting to climate change even recommended the government should develop a strategy to help poor countries contend with the climate change.[72]

"Rule one: *Never* allow a *crisis* to go to waste," Obama's former chief of staff Rahm Emanuel said in a television interview just after the November 2008 elections. "They are opportunities to do big things."[73]

Fast-forward to June 15, 2010, with the nation roiling from a massive oil spill in the Gulf of Mexico. Obama addressed the nation and used the BP oil crisis to call for a radical new environmental agenda.[74]

He demanded "better regulations, better safety standards, and better enforcement" when it comes to offshore drilling.[75] He lamented that "countries like China are investing in clean energy jobs and industries that should be right here in America." Obama demanded the United States "accelerate" the transition to clean energy, implying government funding programs for that agenda.

He said progress had been blocked time and time again by "oil industry lobbyists," and suggested that achieving energy independence was an issue of national security. The time has come, he said, for the United States to "seize control of our own destiny." But, he warned: "The one approach I will not accept is inaction. The one answer I will not settle for is the idea that this challenge is too big and too difficult to meet."[76]

Climate Treaty and
Communist Group Founder

The White House proceeded to push Obama's Climate Change Initiative, which would make available $30 billion to reduce greenhouse gas emissions. In addition, $100 billion a year will be provided through taxpayer and private resources to deal with the so-called threat of global climate change.[77] This in addition to the billions already spent on "green" initiatives as part of Obama's stimulus bill, crafted and perfected by a slew of radicals.

At Copenhagen, Obama "took note" of an accord, which is not legally binding, but which endorses the continuation of the Kyoto Protocol, under which thirty-nine industrialized countries and the European Union commit themselves to a reduction of four greenhouse gases.[78] The accord claims that "climate change" is "one of the greatest challenges of our time" and emphasizes a "strong political will to urgently combat climate change in accordance with the principle of common but differentiated responsibilities and respective capabilities." It also recognizes that "deep cuts in global emissions are required according to science." The accord agrees that developed countries would raise funds of $30 billion from 2010 to 2012 of new and additional resources and that the world will raise $100 billion per year by 2020, from "a wide variety of sources," to help developing countries cut carbon emissions.

The accord was cut down from a 160-page "Climate Treaty," which had been distributed to negotiators from 192 countries. That treaty reportedly took some of the world's most experienced climate NGOs almost a year to write and contains a full legal text covering all the main elements needed to provide the world with a "fair and ambitious agreement" that keeps "climate change" impacts below the "unacceptable" risk levels supposedly identified by scientists.[79]

"This is the first time in history that a coalition of civil society groups has taken such a step. Together we have produced the most coherent legal document to date showing balanced and credible climate solutions based on equity and science," said Kim Carstensen of WWF International, one of the groups that helped craft the treaty.[80]

The treaty was also drafted by "Greenpeace, WWF, IndyACT—the League of Independent Activists, Germanwatch, David Suzuki Foundation, National Ecological Centre of Ukraine, and expert individuals from around the world."[81]

IndyAct.org appeared as a drafter on the actual proposed treaty reviewed by these authors.[82] That group lists offices in Beirut, Lebanon, and states on its website that it is "made up of different groups, each with a crucial role and function. The team is comprised of a league of members, a governing board, an advisory council, management staff and volunteers."[83]

As of this writing, the IndyACT home page website prominently states the group is "part of 350.org." 350.org describes itself as "an international campaign that's building a movement to unite the world around solutions to the climate crisis—the solutions that science and justice demand. Our mission is to inspire the world to rise to the challenge of the climate crisis—to create a new sense of urgency and of possibility for our planet." 350.org lists a board of twenty of its leaders, referred to as "messengers." One of those "messengers" is, drum roll please . . . Van Jones![84]

The Radical Media Circle

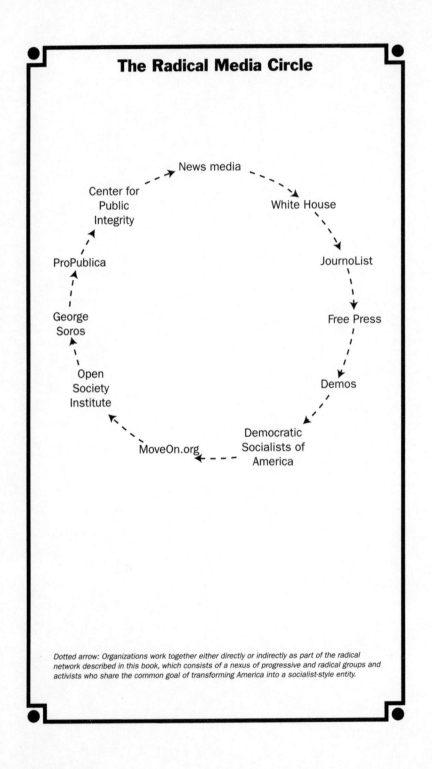

Dotted arrow: Organizations work together either directly or indirectly as part of the radical network described in this book, which consists of a nexus of progressive and radical groups and activists who share the common goal of transforming America into a socialist-style entity.

chapter eight

RED MEDIA ARMY

Central to advancing the agenda of President Obama and the progressives who helped to craft White House policy has been the U.S. news media, which has largely failed to report on the glaring radicalism of the president and the company he has sought to keep. Worse still, the news media, whose job should be to serve as a watchdog on government waste and fraud, instead has been used to rubber-stamp socialist policy aims. Some have been wondering what drives this almost unprecedented media bias. We will show how many in the news media are connected to the same radical network instrumental in helping to craft White House policy. Indeed, the news media serve almost as a battalion of the radical network, helping to rebrand and sell radical policies cloaked in moderation, hiding the real intentions of the policy or issue at hand.

In one of countless examples, in 2009 then *CBS Evening News* anchor Katie Couric posted one of her regular "Notebook" videos at CBSNews.com in which she read a poem outright campaigning for Obamacare. Just before a Senate vote on the bill, Couric waxed poetic about her wish that Senator Olympia Snowe would "save Harry Reid's Christmas with a deal she brought forth."[1]

In another one of her "Notebook" clips, Couric denounced "fear and frankly ignorance" that is driving people to town hall forums opposing health care. She expressed alarm the Obamacare debate "uncovered disturbing attitudes and emotions that have nothing to do with policy. Are we really still debating healthcare when a man brings a handgun to a church where the President is speaking?"[2]

An October 2010 report by the Business and Media Institute at the Media Research Center, meanwhile, likewise documents how the three big networks—ABC, NBC, and CBS—repeatedly portrayed Obama as a leader who is cutting taxes, while they ignored the potential $4.2 trillion in taxes—that's about $14,000 apiece or $56,000 for a family of four—that could hit Americans as a result of Obama's fiscal policies. "Those potential tax increases are almost 20 times the size of the $214 billion temporary tax cuts Obama included in the stimulus bill. Tax cutter? Hardly," read a summary of the new report.[3]

The study looked at all 171 network evening news reports containing the terms "tax cut" or "tax cuts" from September 1, 2008, to August 31, 2010. The study revealed that:

★   Obama was portrayed as a tax cutter by ABC, CBS, and the NBC evening news programs four times as often as his tax increases were mentioned—66 stories to 16.

★   Not one of the 171 reports pointed out that Obama's potential tax hikes are nearly twenty times the size of his cuts.

★   Three-quarters of the evening reports failed to include economists to comment on taxes.

★   Among the remaining one-quarter of the reports, liberal or left-wing groups were allowed airtime to talk about taxes 75 percent of the time—38 reports to 9.

★   NBC's *Nightly News* portrayed Obama as a tax cutter fourteen times more than as someone who wants tax increases.

This network brand of kid-glove treatment toward Obama mirrors much of the news media coverage throughout the president's tenure and even before. In early 2008, after it became clear that Obama, at the time a little-known junior senator from Illinois, was positioned to upset the well-financed and popular Hillary Clinton for the nomination, major questions immediately should have loomed large about this young senator. What were his background and personal history? What were his politics, and who and what had shaped his views? What was his record as a politician? And what was he promising to do as president? Much of Obama's already known past, as well as that of some of his closest associates, was remarkably radical for so prominent a politician. Still, the news media remained mysteriously uninterested in investigating those radical ties.

Coauthor Brenda Elliott and I personally experienced the disdain and the sting of the pro-Obama news media immediately following the release of our book *The Manchurian President* on May 3, 2010.

Multiple reporters, including from such publications as *Time* and *Newsweek*, sent expletive-laden e-mails to our publicist saying they did not want to receive a copy of the number one nonfiction book, which had skyrocketed to the top at Amazon.com.

As is customary in the run-up to the release of a new title, Maria Sliwa, who has represented dozens of bestselling books, cultivated a list of reporters to whom she regularly sends releases. After sending out a press release to key media contacts announcing our forthcoming book, Sliwa was stunned by what she described as "unprecedented" e-mail replies she received regarding the *Manchurian President* announcement.[4]

"Ridiculous crap," retorted John Oswald, news editor for the New York *Daily News*.

"Never, ever contact me again," wrote *Time* senior writer Jeffrey Kluger.

Newsweek deputy editor Rana Foroohar quipped, "This is sensational rubbish that is of no interest to any legitimate publication."

"Absolute crap," replied Evelyn Leopold, a *Huffington Post* contributor who served for seventeen years as UN bureau chief for Reuters until recently.

Nancy Gibbs, editor-at-large for *Newsweek*, fired, "Remove me from your list."

David Knowles, AOL's political writer, responded, "seriously, get a life."

Ben Wyskida, publicity director for the *Nation*, claimed *Manchurian* is "so offensive" and "so far afield."

The reporters rejected our thoroughly documented book before receiving review copies of the title.

Sliwa, who identifies herself as liberal and teaches journalism at New York University, noted that when reporters are not interested in her releases, they normally do not reply. Sliwa said that in her ten years of working in public relations, she has never received the kind of response from reporters provoked by publicizing *The Manchurian President*.

The media bias toward Obama was shockingly revealed again in July 2010 after *The Daily Caller* website drew attention to the controversial JournoList—an e-mail Listserv comprising several hundred journalists and activists who used the online group to discuss minimizing negative publicity surrounding Obama's radical ties.[5] The list was founded by *Washington Post* blogger Ezra Klein, formerly an associate editor for the *American Prospect* political magazine, who worked on Howard Dean's primary campaign in Vermont in 2003.

Daily Caller reporter Jonathan Strong documents how JournoList members fumed when ABC News anchors Charles Gibson and George Stephanopoulos dared to ask Obama during a mid-April 2008 debate about his relationship with his controversial pastor for nearly twenty years, Reverend Jeremiah Wright, Jr. Numerous industrious bloggers and some reporters had highlighted some of Wright's seemingly anti-American, anti-white, anti-Semitic remarks, but the controversy did not really become a national theme in the 2008 race until the ABC News debate. Gibson asked Obama why it had taken him so long— nearly a year since Wright's remarks became public—to dissociate himself from the rhetoric of his spiritual guide. Stephanopoulos asked, "Do you think Reverend Wright loves America as much as you do?"[6]

That softball question was enough to set off JournoList members.

Richard Kim, of the *Nation* magazine, quipped that Stephanopoulos was "being a disgusting little rat snake."[7]

Spencer Ackerman of the *Washington Independent* urged his news media colleagues to deflect attention from Obama's relationship with Wright by instead attacking Obama's conservative critics. Ackerman wrote, "Fred Barnes, Karl Rove, who cares—and call them racists."[8]

Michael Tomasky, a writer for the *Guardian*, took things a step further, telling members of JournoList: "Listen folks—in my opinion, we all have to do what we can to kill ABC and this idiocy in whatever venues we have. This isn't about defending Obama. This is about how the [mainstream media] kills any chance of discourse that actually serves the people." Tomasky demanded, "We need to throw chairs now, try as hard as we can to get the call next time. Otherwise the questions in October will be exactly like this. This is just a disease."[9]

Baltimore Sun columnist Thomas Schaller suggested members of JournoList conspire to minimize publicity into Obama's ties to Wright. "Why don't we use the power of this list to do something about the debate?" Schaller proposed coordinating a "smart statement expressing disgust" at the questions Gibson and Stephanopoulos had posed to Obama. "It would create quite a stir, I bet, and be a warning against future behavior of the sort," wrote Schaller. Tomasky replied. "YES. A thousand times yes."

When Senator John McCain picked Alaska governor Sarah Palin as his running mate, JournoList members conspired to attack her within hours. Daniel Levy of the Century Foundation noted that Obama's "non-official campaign" would need to work hard to discredit Palin. "This seems to me like an occasion when the non-official campaign has a big role to play in defining Palin, shaping the terms of the conversation and saying things that the official [Obama] campaign shouldn't say—very hard-hitting stuff, including some of the things that people have been noting here—scare people about having this woefully inexperienced, no foreign policy/national security/right-wing Christian wing-nut a heartbeat away . . . bang away at McCain's age making this unusually significant. . . . I think people should be replicating some of the not-so-pleasant viral e-mail campaigns that were used against [Obama]."

Ed Kilgore, managing editor of the *Democratic Strategist* blog, argued that journalists and others trying to help the Obama campaign should focus on Palin's beliefs. "The criticism of her really, really needs to be ideological, not just about experience. If we concede she's a 'maverick,' we will have done John McCain an enormous service. And let's don't concede the claim that [Hillary Clinton] supporters are likely to be very attracted to her," Kilgore said.

Other reporters conspired to attack Palin based on her decision not to abort her baby when she became pregnant at age forty-four. Ryan Donmoyer, a reporter for Bloomberg News who was covering the campaign, noted, "Her decision to keep the Down's baby is going to be a hugely emotional story that appeals to a vast swath of America, I think." *Politico* reporter Ben Adler, now an editor at *Newsweek*, replied, "but doesn't leaving said baby without its mother while she campaigns weaken that family values argument? Or will everyone be too afraid to make that point?"

Suzanne Nossel, chief of operations for Human Rights Watch, added: "I think it is and can be spun as a profoundly sexist pick. Women should feel umbrage at the idea that their votes can be attracted just by putting a woman, any woman, on the ticket no matter her qualifications or views." *Mother Jones*'s Stein approved of Nossel's idea. "That's excellent! If enough people—people on this list?—write that the pick is sexist, you'll have the networks debating it for days. And that negates the SINGLE thing Palin brings to the ticket," he wrote. Another writer from *Mother Jones*, Nick Baumann, chimed in: "Say it with me: 'Classic GOP Tokenism.'"

Kilgore recommended another focus: "I STRONGLY think the immediate task is to challenge the 'maverick' bullshit about Palin, which everybody on the tube is echoing. I'll say it one more time: Palin

is a hard-core conservative ideologue in every measurable way." Avi Ze-
nilman of *Politico* advised: "The experience attack is a stupid one. It's
absolutely the wrong tack—the tack that McCain took when he was
losing, and that Hillary and Biden took all primaries." Joe Klein of
Time entered the debate by giving the other JournoListers a sneak peek
at the next edition of his magazine: "We're reporting that she actually
supported the bridge to nowhere. First flub?"

After Obama was victorious in the presidential elections, Journo-
List members rejoiced in such a way that their reactions are best captured by reprinting some of their e-mails word for word:[10]

DAVID ROBERTS, *GRIST*: It's all I can do not to start bawling.

LUKE MITCHELL, *HARPER'S*: I'm picturing something like VJ Day
in Times Square. Seriously!

JOHN BLEVINS, SOUTH TEXAS COLLEGE OF LAW: It's all I can do
to hold it together.

MOIRA WHELAN, NATIONAL SECURITY NETWORK: I'm looking
across the street at my polling place, and the line is wrapped
around the block. I nearly burst into tears when I saw it. I'm feeling
like today is closing the door on a terrible era, and opening another.
I'm glad you started this thread because I was feeling kind of like I
was the only one who is deeply emotional today.

This is only the beginning. The JournoListers could hardly hold
back their tears:

HENRY FARRELL, GEORGE WASHINGTON UNIVERSITY: I had to
close my office door yesterday because I was watching YouTube
videos of elderly African Americans saying what this meant to
them and tearing up.

JOSH BEARMAN, *LA WEEKLY*: 11 months ago I burst into tears by myself on a plane while watching Hardball when my mind wandered to the image of President Obama being sworn in. I've been fighting it ever since.

EZRA KLEIN, *AMERICAN PROSPECT*: OHIO!

ALEC MACGILLIS, *WASHINGTON POST*: If you need further proof that VA is looking to go blue, check out what's going on in VA—5 in deepest Southside Virginia, where Tom Perriello, my college roommate and a very good guy, is now up .06 percentage points—2,000 votes—against Virgil Goode with 88 percent reporting.

GREG ANRIG, CENTURY FOUNDATION: This is really happening.

ADELE STAN, MEDIA CONSORTIUM: At last I can breathe.

SPENCER ACKERMAN, *WASHINGTON INDEPENDENT*: YES WE DID!

STEVEN TELES, YALE UNIVERSITY: I'm not sure why, but this part of the Battle Hymn of the Republic came to me. . . . Glory! Glory! Hallelujah! Glory! Glory! Hallelujah! Glory! Glory! Hallelujah! Since God is marching on.

Obama's win clearly served as a collective victory for the Journo-Listers. These activists recognized the United States was finally on the fast track toward the transformation they had been nudging all along.

SPENCER ACKERMAN: [*QUOTING OBAMA*]: " . . . we may not get there in one year or in one term, but America I promise you, we as a people will get there."

HOLY. F*CKING. SHIT.

MICHAEL TOMASKY, *GUARDIAN*: I'm just jelly. Lord!

HAROLD POLLACK, UNIVERSITY OF CHICAGO: I am awed by the responsibility we have taken on. Tomorrow a desperately ill African-American woman will present at my university hospital for care, and she will be turned away. She will expect us to live up to what we feel tonight. So we've got a lot to live up to.

ADAM SERWER, *AMERICAN PROSPECT*: My take.

SPENCER ACKERMAN: Goddamn, did an Obama speechwriter ghost that post? That's pitch-perfect, Adam. Take a bow.

RYAN DONMOYER, BLOOMBERG NEWS: Best quip I heard today, courtesy of a Facebook friend: "I wonder if Sarah Palin is still unclear about what a community organizer does."

SETH MICHAELS, MYDD.COM: there are flag-waving whooping crowds around the white house. afl-cio hq is insane here.

The AFL-CIO, of course, was heavily instrumental in the election of Obama.

KATE STEADMAN, KAISER HEALTH NEWS: i can't imagine anything like it except a world series/superbowl win, and several of my co-workers told me it never gets the entire city so riled. i think what makes it even more amazing is the incredible diversity in this city and how we all came together for this, especially in victory.

MOIRA WHELAN, NATIONAL SECURITY NETWORK: I've never felt anything like U Street tonight. Hugging, kissing strangers . . . everything.

ALYSSA ROSENBERG, *GOVERNMENT EXECUTIVE*: I've gotta be all non-partisan on GovExec, so I hope you'll all indulge me a minute here. On Monday night in Manassas, the band warming up the crowd before Obama arrived played "I Need You to Survive." I think the core lyrics are pretty good statement of principles for progressives, especially going forward from a victory like this one:

> *It is his will, that every need be supplied.*
> *You are important to me, I need you to survive.*

A lot of horribly ugly stuff got repudiated tonight. But it doesn't end here. We need to keep making the case to the folks who disagreed with us, the folks who booed McCain during his concession speech tonight.

Yes, that's right, JournoList members broke into song. It only got worse, with these activists suggesting violence and internment for their political opponents.

MATT DUSS, CENTER FOR AMERICAN PROGRESS: [McCain aide] Randy Scheunemann Fired [last week]

LAURA ROZEN, *MOTHER JONES* (NOW OF *POLITICO*): Can you imagine if these bozos had won?

November 7

LAURA ROZEN: People we no longer have to listen to: would it be unwise to start a thread of people we are grateful we no longer have to listen to? If not, I'll start off: Michael Rubin.

MICHAEL COHEN, NEW AMERICA FOUNDATION: Mark Penn and Bob Shrum. Anyone who uses the expression "Real America." We should send their ass to Gitmo!

JESSE TAYLOR, PANDAGON.NET: Michael Barone? Please?

LAURA ROZEN: Karl Rove, Newt Gingrich (afraid it's not true), Drill Here Drill Now, And David Addington, John Yoo, we'll see you in court?

JEFFREY TOOBIN, THE *NEW YORKER*: As a side note, does anyone know what prompted Michael Barone to go insane?

MATT DUSS: LEDEEN.

SPENCER ACKERMAN: Let's just throw Ledeen against a wall. Or, pace Dr. Alterman, throw him through a plate glass window. I'll bet a little spot of violence would shut him right the fuck up, as with most bullies.

JOE KLEIN, *TIME*: Pete Wehner . . . these sort of things always end badly.

ERIC ALTERMAN, AUTHOR, *WHAT LIBERAL MEDIA*: F*cking NASCAR retards. . .

November 12

MICHAEL HIRSH, *NEWSWEEK*: so many of you still seem tied down to your old ideological moorings. on the early evidence Obama is not similarly tied down on any level, whether diplomatically or economically (or politically: note his big-tent approach to Joe Lieberman). a post-ideological presidency—what a novelty, and what a relief! but this new Obamian world view, i fear, also puts many of you who are part of this group in danger of imminent irrelevance. cheers, Mike Hirsh

The *Daily Caller*'s Jonathan Strong reports that JListers wanted the government to shut down Fox News.[11]

The very existence of Fox News, meanwhile, sends JournoListers into paroxysms of rage. When Howell Raines charged that the network had a conservative bias, the members of JournoList discussed whether the federal government should shut the channel down.

"I am genuinely scared" of Fox, wrote *Guardian* columnist Daniel Davies, because it "shows you that a genuinely shameless and unethical media organisation *cannot* be controlled by any form of peer pressure or self-regulation, and nor can it be successfully cold-shouldered or os-tracised. In order to have even a semblance of control, you need a tough legal framework." Davies, a Brit, frequently argued the United States needed stricter libel laws.

"I agree," said Michael Scherer of *Time*. "Roger Ailes understands that his job is to build a tribal identity, not a news organization. You can't hurt Fox by saying it gets it wrong, if Ailes just uses the criticism to deepen the tribal identity."

Jonathan Zasloff, a law professor at UCLA, suggested that the federal government simply yank Fox off the air. "I hate to open this can of worms," he wrote, "but is there any reason why the FCC couldn't simply pull their broadcasting permit once it expires?"

Jonathan Strong relates more from the JList missives:[12]

On JournoList, there was rarely such a thing as an honorable political disagreement between the left and right, though there were many disagreements on the left. In the view of many who've posted to the listserv, conservatives aren't simply wrong, they are evil. And while journalists are trained never to presume motive, JournoList members tend to assume that the other side is acting out of the darkest and most dishonorable motives.

When the writer Victor Davis Hanson wrote an article about immigration for *National Review*, for example, blogger Ed Kilgore didn't even bother to grapple with Hanson's arguments. Instead Kilgore dismissed Hanson's piece out of hand as "the kind of Old White Guy cultural reaction that is at the heart of the Tea Party Movement. It's very close in spirit to the classic 1970s racist tome, The Camp of the Saints, where White Guys struggle to make up their minds whether to go out and murder brown people or just give up."

One hundred and seven names have been confirmed as part of the JournoList e-mail group of about four hundred reporters and activists. Known members of JournoList included such notables as Nobel Prize–winning columnist Paul Krugman; staffers from *Newsweek, Politico, Huffington Post, Time,* the *New Republic,* the *Nation,* and the *New Yorker*; contributors to CNN, *Washington Post,* MSNBC, the *Washington Independent, American Prospect,* the *Atlantic,* the *Washingtonian, Harpers, AlterNet, Slate,* the *Chicago Tribune,* Bloomberg, the *New York Observer,* the *Economist,* and others.[13]

Uncovering the Radical Network

The *Daily Caller* and others hit on a big story—members of the news media conspired to aid Obama. The bigger story, however, largely overlooked but investigated by Brenda Elliott and myself, is exactly who these so-called reporters were conspiring with.

It turns out among the individuals who were part of the controversial JournoList e-mail group were activists with ties to the White House and a socialist group closely linked for years to President

Obama. Further, we have found some JournoList members served on an editorial board alongside Bill Ayers and Bernardine Dohrn, while other members were activists from a far-left think tank with close ties to a Marxist-founded, George Soros–funded group that petitions for more government control of the Internet.

The known JournoList names include John B. Judis, senior editor at the *New Republic* and a contributing editor to the *American Prospect*. Judis started reporting from Washington in 1982, when he became Washington correspondent for the Chicago-based socialist journal *In These Times*.[14]

Also a confirmed JournoList member is Frida Berrigan, contributing editor and a member of the editorial board for *In These Times*. As of 2009, both Ayers and Dohrn were on the publication's editorial board.[15]

Eight members of JournoList currently or previously worked for the New America Foundation, a left-leaning nonprofit public policy institute and think tank with offices in Washington, D.C., and Sacramento, California.[16] The chairman of the New America Foundation board of directors is Eric Schmidt, chairman and CEO of Google. Schmidt is a member of President Obama's Council of Advisers on Science and Technology.[17]

A New America Foundation fellow is Timothy Wu, a professor at Columbia Law School and the chairman of Free Press, a George Soros–funded, Marxist-founded organization with close ties to the White House. Free Press published petitions for more government control of the news media. It recently published a study advocating the development of a "world class" government-run media system in the United States.[18]

The New America Foundation is funded by what are now familiar usual suspects: the Soros-funded Open Society Institute, which appears in the wide-ranging $250,000–$999,999 category, and Free Press and the Tides Foundation, listed in the $10,000–$24,999 category.[19]

Another JournoList member is Robert Kuttner, cofounder and co-editor of the *American Prospect*, one of five founders of the Economic Policy Institute, and a distinguished senior fellow of Demos.[20]

The far-left think tank Demos originally recommended that the Obama administration hire Van Jones, who is also a Demos personality.[21] According to Demos's own website, while Obama was a state senator in 1999 he served on the working group that founded Demos.[22] Months before Obama hired Jones in March 2009, Chuck Collins, an associate of Soros and a longtime leftist activist linked to socialist causes, penned a piece recommending the White House hire Jones.[23]

Collins is director of the Tax Program for Shared Prosperity at Demos and also serves as a staffer at the Institute for Policy Studies.[24] The IPS website proudly lists Demos as a "partner" organization.[25]

Obama may be more closely linked to Collins. Official newspapers of the socialist-oriented New Party list Collins as among the party's founding builders in their fall 1994 editions. As we write in our previous book, *The Manchurian President*, newspaper evidence shows Obama as a member of the New Party.[26]

Kuttner and other members of the JournoList are linked to Democratic Socialists of America.[27] Kuttner himself addressed the group's November 1989 national convention in Maryland. In 1990 the group was selling a list of pamphlets, including *Democratic Promise: Ideas for Turning America in a Progressive Direction*, by both Kuttner and Democratic Socialists of America founder Michael Harrington. In 1998, DSA's official publication described Kuttner as a "socialist."

Kuttner, meanwhile, seems to have cooled to Obama, writing in a November 2010 *AlterNet* editorial, "I cannot recall a president who generated so much excitement as a candidate, but who turned out to be such a political dud as chief executive. Nor do his actions since the election inspire confidence that he will be reborn as a fighter."[28]

Kuttner's problem? Obama was not progressive enough! "Had Obama made clear that the real obstacle to comprehensive health reform and cost savings is the private insurance industry, not our one island of socialized medicine—Medicare—he might have clarified who is really on the side of America's seniors," states Kuttner. But Kuttner holds out hope for Obama. "My audacious hope is that progressives can move from disillusion to action and offer the kind of political movement and counter-narrative that the President should have been leading," he writes. "Even Barack Obama might embrace us, if only as a last resort."

Three other Campaign for America's Future founders—James Galbraith, Todd Gitlin, and Michael Kazin—were members of the JournoList group.[29]

Several Obama administration officials were on JournoList. The *Daily Caller* identified as JournoList members two of the administration's chief economic advisers, Jared Bernstein, the vice president's top economist, and Jason Furman, deputy director of the National Economic Council. Also Ilan Goldenberg, a Middle East policy adviser at the Pentagon. Another member identified by the *Daily Caller* was Ben Brandzel, "now a top staffer at Organizing for America, the political arm of the Obama White House."[30]

By peeling back the layers of the onion, we easily discover the radical network. Let's take a closer look at Brandzel. He's served as advocacy director at the Soros-funded MoveOn.org, where he founded the MoveOn Student Action organization. He also served as director of new media campaigns and fund-raising at Organizing for America.[31]

Brandzel was a speaker at the Social Democratic Movement of Netroots Nation, a group whose agenda seeks to amplify "progressive voices by providing an online and in-person campus for exchanging ideas and learning how to be more effective in using technology to influence the public debate."[32] Sound like the JournoList agenda? Well, speaking alongside Brandzel was none other than JournoList founder Ezra Klein.[33]

Brandzel is an online progressive operator. He served as the director of online engagement for the John Edwards campaign.[34] He worked with various manifestations of the MoveOn model, including the Australian Getup.org.au and the global Avaaz.org.[35] Avaaz, cofounded by Res Publica, a global civic advocacy group, and MoveOn.org, is a "global web movement to bring people-powered politics to decision-making everywhere."[36] Avaaz sponsored a petition calling for Israel to lift its naval blockade of the Hamas-controlled Gaza Strip.[37] Israel maintains the blockade is necessary to ensure Hamas cannot rearm.

Another bona fide member of JournoList was the publication *Mother Jones*, which includes on its board reported Democratic Socialists of America member Adam Hochschild. Also, the Economic Policy Institute, part of JournoList, is led by Democratic Socialists of America member Larry Mishel. Unsurprisingly at this point, EPI members have joined the Obama administration, including William Spriggs, a senior adviser in the Department of Labor, and Rebecca Blank, undersecretary for economic affairs in the Department of Commerce. EPI staffer and JournoList member Jared Bernstein is now Vice President Biden's economic adviser.

Also on JournoList was the editor of the *Nation* magazine, Katrina vanden Heuvel, an EPI trustee who presides over an editorial board that includes Democratic Socialists of America members Norman Birnbaum, Barbara Ehrenreich, and Deborah Meier.[38]

Even before the JournoList story broke, progressives had hinted at the existence of such a list. In little-noticed comments, a member of the controversial JournoList e-mail group first publicly exposed that news media reporters "threw their support" to Barack Obama, then a presidential candidate. John B. Judis, senior editor at the *New Republic* and a contributing editor to the *American Prospect*, described in a May 2008 article for the *New Republic* that has been strangely scrubbed from the magazine's website how members of the news media openly backed Obama.[39]

At first, reporters backed Obama's chief rival for the Democratic nomination, Hillary Clinton. But Clinton alienated reporters by her attacks on Obama instead of recognizing him as a "historic" candidate, conceded Judis.

Wrote Judis: "Race is the deepest and oldest and most bitter conflict in American history—the cause of our great Civil War and of the upheavals of the 1950s and '60s. And if some voters didn't appreciate the potential breakthrough that Obama's candidacy represented, many in the Democratic primaries and caucuses did—and so did the members of the media and Obama's fellow politicians."

Judis added that as Clinton "began treating Obama as just another politician, they recoiled and threw their support to him." He wrote that Clinton's negative ads attacking Obama resulted in her losing "the opinion-making class's vote during those fateful early weeks of the primary season."

"This included her fellow politicians, who would serve as superdelegates, and the media," he wrote. Judis quoted from an anti-Clinton editorial in the *St. Louis Post-Dispatch* that slammed Hillary Clinton's campaign as recalling "the worst of the Clinton years; the divisiveness and the bickering; the too-casual, if artful, blend of truth and half-truth." "I heard the same refrain from journalists and bloggers who had been either pro-Hillary or on the fence," wrote Judis.

Marxist-Led, Soros-Funded Free Press and More Governmental Control

It is instrumental to take a closer look at Free Press, whose activists were conspiring with JournoList members. The group has close ties to the Obama administration. It was founded by Robert W. McChesney, professor at the University of Illinois, and former editor of the Marxist journal *Monthly Review*. In February 2009, McChesney wrote in a column, "In the end, there is no real answer but to remove brick-by-brick the capitalist system itself, rebuilding the entire society on socialist principles."

The board of Free Press has included a slew of radicals, such as Obama's former "Green Jobs" czar Van Jones.[40]

In May 2010, Free Press released a forty-eight-page document, *New Public Media: A Plan for Action*, in which it advocated the development of a "world class" government-run media system in the United

States.[41] "The need has never been greater for a world-class public media system in America," begins the document. "Commercial media's economic tailspin has pushed public media to the center of the debate over the future of journalism and the media, presenting the greatest opportunity yet to reinvigorate and re-envision the modern U.S. public media system," argued the Free Press document.

The Free Press study urges the creation of a trust fund—largely supported by new fees and taxes on advertising and the private media—to jump-start the founding of a massive government-run public media system that will ultimately become self-sufficient. "We believe local news reporting should become one of public media's top priorities," said Free Press managing director Craig Aaron, one of the paper's co-authors.

"We should redeploy and redouble our resources to keep a watchful eye on the powerful and to reliably examine the vital issues that most Americans can't follow closely on their own," Aaron stated.

Free Press, meanwhile, also has urged the Federal Communications Commission to investigate talk radio and cable news for "hate speech." The organization claims media companies are engaging in "hate speech" because a disproportionate number of radio and cable news networks are owned by nonminorities.[42]

Free Press was one of thirty-three organizations that drafted a twenty-five-page petition asking the FCC to "initiate an inquiry into the extent and effects of hate speech in media and to explore non-regulatory means by which to mitigate its negative impacts."[43]

"Hate speech thrives, as hate has developed as a profit-model for syndicated radio and cable-television programs masquerading as 'News,'" claims the petition. The petition contends "traditional media" have "largely failed" to "provide the accurate information needed for an informed democracy."

"These failures often damage communities of color at disproportionate rates," the petition states. The paper singles out talk radio as "particularly problematic."

"Hate has seemingly emerged as a profit-model for many radio programs syndicated throughout the country, because only a few companies own the majority of the radio stations nationally." The paper claims a disproportionate number of media companies are owned by nonminorities, causing "hate speech" to fester. "The media has a history of unequal representation of and discrimination against people of color, and rapid media consolidation has exacerbated the situation. In this climate of inaccurate and apathetic reporting and under-representation of people of color in traditional media, hate has festered and grown."

The petition states it is not asking the FCC to impose any sort of content regulations pertaining to so-called hate speech in the media. "Rather [we] respectfully request that the Commission initiate an inquiry into the extent and effects of hate speech in media and to explore non-regulatory means by which to mitigate its negative impacts."

Obama Administration Ties

On June 29, 2009, President Obama appointed Julius Genachowski, his longtime friend and top fund-raiser (who personally raised over five hundred thousand dollars for the presidential campaign), as chairman of the FCC. It was Genachowski's third stint at the agency.[44]

Genachowski was a classmate of Barack Obama's at both Columbia University and Harvard Law School. Since early July 2009, Genachowski's press secretary has been Jen Howard, former press director at the liberal/left media think tank Free Press.[45]

Obama's "Internet Czar," Susan P. Crawford, spoke at a Free Press May 14, 2009, "Changing Media" summit in Washington, D.C., as revealed in our book *The Manchurian President*. Crawford's pet project, OneWebDay, which she founded, lists as "participating organizations" Free Press and the controversial Association of Community Organizations for Reform Now, or ACORN. OneWebDay seeks to "[deepen] a culture of participation in building a Web that works for everyone."[46]

Crawford and Kevin Werbach, who codirected the Obama transition team's Federal Communications Commission Review team, are advisory board members at Public Knowledge, a George Soros–funded public interest group. A Public Knowledge advisory board member is Timothy Wu, who is also chairman of the board for Free Press. Like Public Knowledge, Free Press also has received funds from Soros's Open Society Institute.

In May 2010, Free Press policy director Ben Scott was named a policy adviser for innovation at the State Department. "We will miss Ben's leadership, wise counsel, and strategic brilliance—for Free Press and the overall movement for media and technology policy in the public interest," said Free Press president Josh Silver.[47] Scott authored a book, *The Future of Media*, which was edited by the founder of Free Press, Robert W. McChesney.[48]

Many of the themes of Free Press can be seen throughout the Obama administration.

Crawford was chosen to head up the Obama transition's FCC Review team. After the inauguration, Obama named her Special Assistant to the President for Science, Technology, and Innovation Policy—or Internet Czar.

Wired magazine calls Crawford "the most powerful geek close to the president," and notes that prior to her work for the administration, she was a "prolific" writer on net neutrality. Crawford teaches cyber and telecommunications law at the University of Michigan, is a member of the National Economic Council, and served from 2005 to 2008 as a member of the board of ICANN (Internet Corporation for Assigned Names and Numbers), which assigns domain names on the Internet.

Meanwhile, speaking at the May 14, 2009, "Free Press Summit: Changing Media" held at the Newseum in Washington, Crawford advocated for newspaper subsidies.[49]

Completing the radical network circle, Crawford is controversial as well for her connection to ACORN. It was discovered in September 2009 that Crawford's OneWebNow project lists both ACORN and

Free Press as "participating organizations."[50] Crawford also has a board member, Mitchell Kapor, who is an ACORN apologist.[51]

Crawford and Kevin Werbach are advisory board members at Public Knowledge.[52]

Public Knowledge claims to be bipartisan, working with groups from both sides of the aisle, including Free Press and the Open Society Institute.[53]

Public Knowledge advisory board member Timothy Wu writes on his blog that in his "spare time" he is the chair of the "media reform organization Free Press." According to his Columbia University faculty profile, Wu is chairman of the board for Free Press, as well as a fellow at the New America Foundation.[54]

Wu is credited with "popularizing the concept" *net neutrality* in his 2003 paper "Network Neutrality, Broadband Discrimination," presented at the Silicon Flatirons conference in Boulder, Colorado (February 3, 2003). Wu's paper is "believed to be the first use of the term."[55]

In June 2008, Wu held that the U.S. Constitution is "flawed because the founders did not anticipate the problem of 'the abuse of private power.'" The Bill of Rights, Wu says, "was merely designed to protect people against government and the founders were concerned about the exercise of 'public power.'"[56]

Also tied to Free Press is Stanford law professor and net neutrality advocate Lawrence Lessig, who served as a technology adviser to Obama during the 2008 presidential campaign and then was mentioned as a potential candidate to head the FCC. Lessig has been described as a "guru" to Free Press founder McChesney.[57]

In June 2006 Lessig wrote on his blog: "The Dems Get Net Neutrality."[58]

Lots happening with Net Neutrality, most significantly that the Democrats seem to have decided that this is their issue. The extraordinary tie created in the Senate Commerce Committee (11–11) on party lines (plus the amazing Senator Snowe) seems to signal a decision by leaders of the party that this is a fight they want to lead. The slogan does have a nice right to it—"Republicans: They sold the environment to Exxon, and sold the war to Halliburton. Now they want to sell the Internet to at&t." (yea, the new logo is no-caps. a kinder, gentler . . .)

In my view, this is good news and bad. Good for the Dems that they got it. Bad that the issue is now within the grips of party politics. I guess it was just a matter of time, given how much money the cable and telcos have put on the table.

Lessig memorably drew some controversy during the 2008 campaign after he circulated a video depicting Jesus lip-syncing to Gloria Gaynor's late-1970s disco hit "I Will Survive." In the video, a mock Jesus is seen stripping down to just a diaper while he effeminately struts along a city street and finally gets run over by a speeding bus.[59] Lessig is the founder of Stanford's Center for Internet and Society. Prior to joining the Stanford faculty, he was the Berkman Professor of Law at Harvard Law School. Lessig was also a fellow at the Wissenschaftskolleg zu Berlin and a professor at the University of Chicago Law School.[60] In 2001 Lessig founded Creative Commons, a nonprofit organization devoted to expanding the range of creative works available for others to build upon legally and to share.[61]

In January 2009, Creative Commons launched a massive repository of broadcast-quality video footage, working with Al Jazeera to make the Arab network's video footage available for free downloading.[62]

Lessig's Creative Commons website announced on March 20, 2009, that the Obama administration was utilizing his group's licensing:[63]

Recovery.gov is the website that provides US citizens with the ability to monitor the progress of the country's recovery via The American Recovery and Reinvestment Act. As with Whitehouse.gov, the Obama administration is presciently using our Attribution license 3.0 for all third party content on the website while all the original

content website created by the federal government remains unre-
stricted by copyright and therefore in the public domain.

National Public (Soros) Radio?
Associated Soros?

Several radical groups, meanwhile, need to be carefully observed for
their influence on the news media, most prominently the Soros-funded
Center for Public Integrity and the Knight Foundation.

In October 2010, the publicly funded NPR News terminated the
contract of its longtime news analyst, Juan Williams, after remarks he
made to Bill O'Reilly on Fox News Channel concerning Muslims at
airports.[64]

"Look, Bill, I'm not a bigot. You know the kind of books I've written about the civil rights movement in this country. But when I get
on the plane, I got to tell you, if I see people who are in Muslim garb
and I think, you know, they are identifying themselves first and foremost as Muslims, I get worried. I get nervous." Williams also warned
O'Reilly against blaming all Muslims for the actions of "extremists."
After his termination from NPR, Fox News was quick to offer Williams a $2 million contract for a full-time analyst gig.[65]

NPR and progressive media groups receive a slew of donations
that originate in part with Soros-funded organizations. On October
2, 2009, NPR announced a $1 million grant from the Knight Founda-
tion.[66] The Center for Public Integrity, or CPI, which has been accused
of promoting the progressive agenda, announced on October 10, 2010,
that it was receiving a $1.7 million grant from the Knight Founda-
tion.[67] CPI, which maintains it is objective, has received millions in
funding from Soros's Open Society Institute.[68] Ten days later, NPR
announced a $1.8 million grant from OSI.[69]

The next day, on October 18, NPR and the openly progressive
Huffington Post merged their nonprofit "reporting" arm into the Soros-

funded CPI, with the Knight Foundation providing $250,000 to help with the merger.[70] Two days later, the progressive Media Matters for America, which has long tried to minimize its funding from Soros, announced a $1 million grant from OSI.[71]

Let's take a closer look at the Center for Public Integrity, which is an "investigative journalism group" founded by Charles Lewis, a former producer at CBS and ABC television networks.[72] This arm will tie directly into the Associated Press.

Soros provided at least four grants to CPI, including: a $72,400 one-year grant in 2000 supporting "an investigative journalism series on prosecutorial misconduct"; a $75,000 one-year grant in 2001 supporting "an examination of wrongful convictions resulting from prosecutorial misconduct"; a $100,000 one-year grant in 2002 "to investigate the political spending of the telecommunications industry on the federal, state and local levels"; and a $1 million three-year grant in 2002 "to support the Global Access Project."[73]

The CPI board includes Charles Ogletree, a Harvard University professor closely linked to Obama as well as to the Black Panthers during Ogletree's student years and to radical black ideology.[74] Ogletree was a mentor to both Barack and Michelle Obama and served on the President's Black Advisory Council. "I met Barack when he arrived at Harvard Law School in fall of 1988. He was quiet and unassuming, but had an incredibly sharp mind and a thirst for knowledge," Ogletree said in an interview in 2008 with *Essence* magazine. "Even then I saw his ability to quickly grasp the most complicated legal issues and sort them out in a clear, concise fashion," said Ogletree.[75]

Ogletree explained that Obama was a regular participant in an after-class activity the Harvard professor created called the Saturday School Program—a series of workshops and meetings held Saturday mornings to expose minority students to issues in the study of law. During Obama's senatorial career, Ogletree advised the politician on reforming the criminal justice system as well on constitutional issues.[76]

Ogletree is closely linked to radical black activism.[77] As a student in 1970 at Stanford University near San Francisco, a center of black radicalism at the time, Ogletree organized an Afrocentric dormitory.[78] He edited a campus Black Panther newspaper called the *Real News* and traveled to Africa and Cuba as part of student activist groups.[79]

Ogletree attended nearly every day of the trial of Black Power activist and communist Angela Davis. He moved on to Harvard Law School, where he continued his political activism, becoming national president of the Black Law Students Association. Ogletree gained national prominence in 1991 when he represented Anita Hill during the controversial Senate confirmation hearings at which she accused Supreme Court justice nominee Clarence Thomas of sexual harassment. In 2000, Ogletree joined the Reparations Coordinating Committee, serving as the group's cochair. The committee pursued a lawsuit to win reparations for descendants of African slaves. The committee was convened by the TransAfrica Forum, a partner organization of the leftist Institute for Policy Studies.[80]

Ogletree represented Henry Louis Gates, Jr., the Harvard professor who found himself at the center of a race controversy after he was handcuffed in his Cambridge, Massachusetts, home by police following a burglary report.[81] Obama mentioned the incident in a prime-time news conference, stating the police "acted stupidly" in dealing with Gates.[82]

How influential is the CPI? The AP announced in July 2010 it will allow its subscribers to publish free of charge work by four nonprofit groups, the CPI and also the Investigative Reporting Workshop at American University, the Center for Investigative Reporting, and ProPublica.[83]

Henry Louis Gates, Jr., sits on the board of ProPublica. The group defines itself as "an independent, non-profit newsroom that produces investigative journalism in the public interest."[84] ProPublica was founded with a $10 million annual grant from Herbert and Marion Sandler.[85]

In 2008, the Sandlers were behind two controversial California political action committees, Vote Hope and PowerPac.org, which spent about $5 million in pro-Obama ads in that state. The two groups were run by the Sandlers' son-in-law, Steve Phillips, the former president of the San Francisco School Board.[86]

The journalistic integrity of the Sandler-backed ProPublica has been repeatedly called into question. A report by the Capital Research Center concluded ProPublica "churns out little more than left-wing hit pieces about Sarah Palin and blames the U.S. government for giving out too little foreign aid."[87]

Slate reporter Jack Shafer raised questions about ProPublica's ability to provide independent nonpartisan journalism in light of the nature of the Sandlers' political donations, which include "giving hundreds of thousands of dollars to Democratic Party campaigns."[88]

The watchdog website UndueInfluence.com slammed ProPublica's claim of independence, stating the site is "as independent as a lapdog on a leash with allegiances sworn in advance to left-wing causes."[89]

The Soros-funded CPI's journalism has been called into question. One widely debunked CPI study from 2008—covered extensively by the AP—claimed it had found President Bush and top administration officials had issued hundreds of false statements about the national security threat from Iraq as "part of an orchestrated campaign that effectively galvanized public opinion and, in the process, led the nation to war under decidedly false pretenses."[90]

Writing on FrontPageMag.com, Richard Poe, a writer for the Center for the Study of Popular Culture, concluded that CPI and other Soros-funded so-called watchdogs "have a long history of coordination with Soros and his Shadow Party. They are beholden to Soros personally for his financial support. His influence often shows in their choice of targets."[91]

The AP itself has called the arrangement to distribute pieces from the Soros- and Sandler-funded nonprofits a six-month experiment that could be broadened to include other investigative nonprofits and to serve its nonmember clients, which include broadcast and Internet outlets. "It's something we've talked about for a long time, since part of our mission is to enable our members to share material with each other," said Sue Cross, a senior vice president at the AP. She added the development in 2006 of an Internet-based system for members to receive AP material made it easier to do this kind of sharing and to offer new products like the investigative service.[92]

Cliff Kincaid of Accuracy in Media succinctly points out:[93]

Soros' media influence extends to other news organizations and media outlets. The Nation magazine and its Nation Institute have been supported by the Open Society.

In 1994 Soros received the Burton Benjamin Memorial Award at an International Press Freedom Awards dinner, sponsored by the Committee to Protect Journalists. Five years earlier, OSI gave four grants, totaling $220,000, to the Committee to Protect Journalists. Benjamin was senior executive producer at CBS News and served briefly as chair of the Committee to Protect Journalists before his death in 1988.

Other Soros media connections include:

★   As an investor in the Times Mirror Company, Soros funded the Project on Media Ownership, headed by Professor Mark Crispin Miller at New York University, whose purpose was to expose "media concentration." A total of $300,000 over several years came from George Soros's Open Society Institute (OSI). In 1999, a survey commissioned by the Project on Media Ownership and the Benton Foundation and paid for by OSI found that 79 percent of adults would favor a law requiring commercial broadcasters to pay 5 percent of their revenues into a fund for public broadcasting.

★   OSI gave $60,000 to the Independent Media Institute, whose executive director, Don Hazen, is a former publisher of *Mother Jones*. Hazen has called Soros a "progressive philanthropist." A story carried by the Independent Media Institute on its *AlterNet* project says Soros "believes in democracy, positive international relations and effective strategies to reduce poverty, among other things."

★ OSI gave a $75,000 grant to the Center for Investigative Reporting. The group's board of advisers includes prominent journalists.

★ OSI gave $200,000 to the Fund for Investigative Journalism. This group features prominent journalists on its board.

★ OSI's "Network Media Program" gave $22,157 to Investigative Reporters and Editors.

★ Soros Foundations have provided $160,000 to MediaChannel.org, a so-called "media issues supersite, featuring criticism, breaking news, and investigative reporting from hundreds of organizations worldwide." The executive editor is Danny Schecter, a former news program producer and investigative reporter at CNN and ABC. It was created by Globalvision News Network, whose board includes "Senior executives from the world's leading media firms."

★ OSI has contributed $70,000 toward the far-left Independent Media Center, or Indymedia, known as an "independent newsgathering collective," whose servers were seized by a federal law enforcement agency on October 7, 2004. The action was apparently related to an investigation into international terrorism, kidnapping, or money laundering.

★ OSI provided $600,000 to the Media Access Project, a so-called telecommunications public interest law firm critical of conservative influence in the major media.

★ OSI provided $30,000 to the Media Awareness Project,

a "worldwide network dedicated to drug policy reform" and promoting "balanced media coverage" of the drug issue.

★   OSI provided $200,000 to the Association for Progressive Communications, "an international network working for peace, human rights, development and protection of the environment."

From Soros to the White House

Some personalities from these and other Soros-funded groups ended up with positions in the Obama administration. Case in point is President Obama's "Diversity Czar" at the Federal Communications Commission, who was officially designated the FCC's associate general counsel and chief diversity officer in July 2009. Mark Lloyd is a senior fellow at the Center for American Progress. At CAP, Lloyd "focus[es] on communications policy issues, including universal service, advanced telecommunications deployment, media concentration and diversity." Lloyd is also a consultant to Soros's Open Society Institute.[94] In 2007 Lloyd wrote an article for CAP called "Forget the Fairness Doctrine," in which he instructed liberals to file complaints with the FCC against conservative radio stations. "What [his article] lays out is a battle plan to use the FCC to threaten stations' licenses with whom they do not agree politically," said Seton Motley, director of communications at the Media Research Center, in an August 14, 2009, interview on the *Glenn Beck Show*. "And now he's at the FCC waiting to take their calls. This is not about serving the local interest, it's about political opposition," Motley said.[95]

For his part, Lloyd attributes the "rise and influence of Rush Limbaugh and other conservative radio hosts" to "'relaxed ownership rules' and other pro-business regulation that destroyed localism," Motley told Glenn Beck.[96]

Lloyd says he is not interested in reinstating the Fairness Doctrine, an FCC decree that at one time required broadcast stations to demonstrate "balance" to the FCC in the presentation of public issues. The doctrine was a legacy of the early days of television broadcasting when there were only three or four stations in each major market. Ronald Reagan, whose career before politics had been in the mass media, effectively abolished the doctrine in 1983, which allowed talk radio to emerge as a largely conservative medium, though this was not foreseen at the time. But the doctrine's abolition also occurred when cable, satellite TV, and later, the Internet, were dramatically expanding the diversity of information outlets. So even its advocates had trouble sustaining the original justification for the Fairness Doctrine, which was the argument in 1949, that electronic mass media were "a limited public resource."[97]

Instead of pushing to reinstate the Fairness Doctrine, Lloyd calls for "equal opportunity employment practices," "local engagement," and "license challenges" to "rectify" that "perceived imbalance," Fox reported. According to Lloyd, there is "nothing in there about the Fairness Doctrine."

In an intent clearly to provoke, Lloyd wrote: "The other part of our proposal that gets the 'dittoheads' upset is our suggestion that the commercial radio station owners either play by the rules or pay. In other words, if they don't want to be subject to local criticism of how they are meeting their license obligations, they should pay to support public broadcasters who will operate on behalf of the local community."

Lloyd "concluded that 91% of talk radio programming is conservative and 9% is 'progressive,'" Matt Cover reported in August 2009 at CNSNews.com. Lloyd's report "argued that large corporate broadcasting networks had driven liberals off the radio, and that diversity of ownership would increase diversity of broadcasting voices," Cover adds.[98]

Lloyd's prescriptions for media reform are more fully described in a book he wrote while still full-time with the Center for American

Progress: *Prologue to a Farce: Communications and Democracy in America* (2007). In the book, among other things, he "presents the idea that private broadcasters (private business) should pay a licensing [fee] which equals their total operating costs so that public broadcasting [stations] can spend the same on their operations as the private companies do," according to George Fallon at RightPundits.com (August 14, 2009). Lloyd's intent was to use the funds to "improve the Corporation for Public Broadcasting"—whose budget was already $400 million for 2009.[99]

Additionally, Lloyd writes that he did not want only to "redistribute private profits" but also to "regulate much of the programming on these stations to make sure they focus on 'diverse views' and government activities." Lloyd contends that large corporate broadcasting networks have "driven liberals off of radio" based on a belief that "diversity ownership will reflect in diversity programming," Cover says.[100]

Elsewhere in *Prologue to a Farce*, Lloyd states:[101]

> The Corporation for Public Broadcasting (CPB) must be reformed along democratic lines and funded on a substantial level. Federal and regional broadcast operations and local stations should be funded at levels commensurate with or above those spending levels at which commercial operations are funded. This funding should come from license fees charged to commercial broadcasters. Funding should not come from congressional appropriations. Sponsorship should be prohibited at all public broadcasters.

The appointment of Lloyd coincided with Obama's designation of longtime personal friend, top campaign fund-raiser, and Free Press–linked Julius Genachowski as chief commissioner of the FCC. On December 1, 2010, Genachowski announced he was going to push for net neutrality, a plan that would prohibit Internet service providers (such as Verizon, Comcast, and AT&T) from blocking or serving up some websites faster and at better quality than others.[102] In other words, the government would interfere in the content of private service companies.

Genachowski told reporters in a statement that he thinks he has "a sound legal basis" to pursue net neutrality rules.

The "Public Value Test"

In early December 2010, Michael J. Copps, one of the five commissioners on the FCC, came up with a "new" television and radio licensing plan that is ripped from the pages of a 1997 European Union treaty agreement. Yet, once again, the creativity demonstrated by progressives in finding new and radical approaches to force diversity in broadcast media upon the unaware public is boundless.

As we conclude in *Manchurian President*, FCC diversity czar Mark Lloyd commingles his anticorporatist, anticapitalist stance—portraying private industry as not only owning, but also in full editorial control of television, radio, the Internet, even long-distance telephone service—with his media justice, civil rights agenda.

In a December 2007 article in the *Nation*, Katrina vanden Heuvel, the publication's editor, reports Obama slammed the decision by FCC chairman Kevin Martin to ram through a "vote to remove a long-standing newspaper/broadcast cross-ownership ban." Martin ignored the "public will, undermining democratic diversity and bowing to the corrupting campaign contributions and high-powered lobbyists of the largest media companies," vanden Heuvel adds.[103] "Today the FCC failed to further the important goal of promoting diversity in the media and instead chose to put big corporate interests ahead of the people's interests," Obama said.[104]

A week earlier vanden Heuvel had written: "Obama has been a stalwart supporter of encouraging diversity in the ownership of broadcast media. An Obama presidency, he has pledged, will promote greater coverage of local issues and better responsiveness by broadcasters to the communities they serve; it would also push for better opportunities for minority, small business and women-owned media firms."[105]

Blogger Ben Compaine commented in November 2007 that both Democrats and Republicans in Congress "insist on the quaint notion of 'locally-owned' media, when there is no sustained body of research that demonstrates that locally owned newspapers, radio or TV stations provide more, better, or more diverse information than corporately owned media entities."[106] "Thanks to the efforts of the advocacy group, the Free Press, and the unexamined assumptions of many journalists," Compaine continues, "there is an overwhelming misperception that the mass media are becoming more concentrated, when the numbers show they are not."[107]

This brings us to Michael J. Copps and his *new test* strategy for government regulation of the airwaves—and more. *Washington Times* associate editor Peter Suderman wrote in May 2010 at Reason.com that Copps, who has "pushed to involve the FCC in everything from journalism to satellite TV service" and "been the Commission's chief proponent of strong net neutrality regulation, wants an FCC with few or no limits on its power."[108] Upon Obama's ascension to the Oval Office in January 2009, Copps's *Washington Post* profile at WhoRunsGov? states that, after eight years of not getting his voice heard, Copps now had a chance to "sit in the majority."[109] "The former Hill staffer now has more influence sitting here in Washington," the article states. Copps is an advocate of punishing indecent and offensive material on radio and television and an ardent adversary of media consolidation.

Copps is quoted as saying, "I'm not trying to establish a national nanny here, but we only have to send one case to [license] hearings and the message would go forth to broadcasters all over the U.S. that this is a new era. Right now, [broadcasters] not only don't fear us, they don't respect us, either."[110] This is a strongly worded warning. One might deduce that if one approach by the FCC to exert its heavy hand fails, the agency—with a three-Democrat majority—will simply change tack.

A prime example of such a change in strategy comes from the April 6, 2010, ruling by the U.S. Court of Appeals for the District of Columbia, which states the FCC has "limited power over Web traffic under current law."[111] Undeterred, Susan Crawford, Obama's Internet czar, stated in an April 10, 2010, *New York Times* op-ed that the FCC could "regain its authority to pursue both network neutrality and widespread access to broadband by formally relabeling Internet access services as 'telecommunications services,' rather than 'information services,' as they are called now."[112]

Relabeling is the name of the game. The Fairness Doctrine, diversity, and media justice have been rebranded as the *public value test*. In his December 2, 2010, speech, "Getting Media Right: A Call to Action," at the Columbia University School of Journalism in New York, Copps proposed replacing the current licensing process for television and radio stations with a public value test.[113] Copps said the test "would get us back to the original licensing bargain between broadcasters and the people: in return for free use of airwaves that belong exclusively to the people, licensees agree to serve the public interest as good stewards of a precious national resource."[114] Copps proposed the test "would be 'meaningful commitments' to news and public affairs programming. 'These would be quantifiable and not involve issues of content interference,'" Copps said.

"Increasing the human and financial resources going into news would be one way to benchmark progress. Producing more local civic affairs programming would be another. Our current children's programming requirements—the one remnant of public interest requirements still on the books—helped enhance kids' programming. Now it is time to put news and information front-and-center," he said.

The test would include "enhanced disclosure about each station's performance; meaningful increases in local programming; and evidence of a detailed plan for news coverage in the event of an emergency or disaster." The "goal here is a more localism in our program diet, more local news and information, and a lot less streamed-in homogenization and monotonous nationalized music at the expense of local and regional talent," Copps added, suggesting that 25 percent of prime-time programming should be locally or independently produced.

Additionally, Copps proposed the FCC "should 'determine the extent of its current authority' to compel stations to disclose who pays for anonymous political ads." Copps suggests that if the FCC should "lack the tools we need to compel disclosure," it would "go ask for them." Copps does not say whom the FCC should ask.

Under the public value test rules, Copps also wants to increase the frequency for television and radio station licensing. Instead of every eight years, licensees would have to apply every four years. We could find no precedent in the United States for a public value test, or the use of the phrase before December 2, 2010, by Copps. However, what we did discover is that, beginning in April 2004, there was an issue over the public value test in the United Kingdom, particularly as it applied to the BBC as a "public service provider."

In the BBC situation, however, it is the commercial broadcasters who were so incensed. Additionally, the BBC story, which follows, is a cautionary tale. "The wolves are circling like never before," Steven Vass wrote on June 27, 2004, in the *Sunday Herald*.[115]

> Commercial broadcasters have long argued the BBC's licence fee is an anachronism that gives it an unfair competitive advantage, which it abuses by producing mass-market programmes that go head to head with the other channels. They jealously eye the swathes of BBC viewers and listeners they could be selling to advertisers, and they dislike the whole idea of public service broadcasting, arguing that the market should decide what programmes fill our screens.

The BBC director general, Mark Thompson, repeatedly used the phrase *public value*. He said, "We believe that over the next decade the BBC will have a bigger role than ever in building public value."[116] In October 2006, the public value test was put to the test regarding the BBC's online on-demand service. Even though the BBC charter would not come into full effect until 2007, the BBC had conducted a four-month online trial of the service, the "prototype integrated Media

Player (iMP)." The BBC governors agreed to commit to some of the charter's policies, including the public value test.[117]

On January 2, 2007, the BBC Royal Charter and Agreement came into effect. The charter required the BBC Trust "to subject all new BBC services to a Public Value Test (PVT) to assess whether they would be in the wider public interest." A Public Value Assessment was required to be carried out by the trust and a "separate, independent Market Impact Assessment" was to be conducted by the Office of Communications.[118]

The BBC's plan to offer the service was slammed by the British communications regulatory agency Ofcom, which determined BBC's "rivals would be affected." The BBC's plans, it said, "would hit DVD sales and rentals." The BBC's charter, however, still required "all new services to be put to a Public Value Test." If the BBC's plans were found to not be in the public interest, "they would be scrapped."[119]

If not in the public interest, then scrapped!

However, the public value test is not exclusive to the BBC and the United Kingdom. A July 14, 2009, *European Report* article informs that the public value test model was also being used by Germany, Belgium (Flanders, VRT), and Ireland, which had "also taken the plunge."[120] The origination comes from the European Union's Amsterdam Protocol of 1997, which is explained by Wolfgang Kleinwæchter, of the Department of Media and Information Studies at the University of Aarhus in Denmark and the NETCOM Institute, Leipzig:[121]

> With the growth of private broadcasting and the dramatic rise of prices for film and sports rights in the 1990s, the competition for advertising money became harder. Private broadcasters started to argue that the financing system of public broadcasters is a violation of European competition law. The license fee would give public broadcasters an unfair privilege and would undermine the capacity of private broadcasters to compete under equal conditions. . . .
>
> As a result of this debate the European Council discussed the

issue and adopted as part of the "Amsterdam Treaty" (2nd of October 1997) a special "Protocol on Public Broadcasting Services," which both reflects the unanimously political will of the European governments to keep the system of public broadcasting services alive, and also takes note of the special interests of private broadcasters.

Kleinwæchter provides the socialist context for the EU protocol, which says that a financing system based on license fees is legal and justified because public broadcasting is "directly related to the 'democratic, social and cultural needs of each society' and it is an important element to safeguard 'pluralism.'"[122] The key word here is *pluralism*, which is a fancy way of saying *diversity*.

Diana L. Eck of the Pluralism Project at Harvard University takes the definition one step further. It is not just diversity, but an "energetic engagement with diversity." It is not just tolerance, but an "active seeking of understanding across lines of difference." It is not just relativism, but "the encounter of commitments." Finally, pluralism is based on dialogue. "Pluralism involves the commitment to being at the table—with one's commitments," she writes.[123]

"On the other hand," Kleinwæchter continues, the protocol "says that funding of public broadcasting should not 'affect trading conditions and competition.'" There "should be a 'fair balance,' which should allow private broadcasters to compete under 'fair conditions' whatever this is," he adds. "At the same time, the protocol says, that, according to the principle of subsidiarity, the concrete practice is a sovereign decision of the member state."[124]

Taken a step further, Kleinwæchter writes, this "European issue became a global issue when 'trade in services' became a part of the mandate of the World Trade Organization's (WTO) negotiations on global trade liberalization." Interestingly, Kleinwæchter points out, "according to the WTO rules, there should be no national subsidies for the production of goods and services which would distort competition."

Without question, adoption of the *public value test* would take the

United States down the same path that Britain has traveled for more than a decade and the countries of the EU since 1997 and bring it into alignment with the dictates of the WTO.

Obama's Media, Social Army

Another group of individuals with whom Barack Obama networked, and which has helped nudge along the Obama agenda, stems from an interesting social working group with whom he participated during the 1997–2000 time frame. The Saguaro meetings are "an overlooked chapter in Obama's well-thumbed biography," Daniel Burke points out in June 2009 for Religion News Service. Obama, he adds, both used and built on these political connections, including hiring Saguaro alumni to work in the White House.[125] The Saguaro Seminar is a series of meetings with the obscure goal of determining what "we know about our levels of trust and community engagement" while "developing strategies and efforts to increase this engagement." A signature effort was the multiyear dialogue (1995–2000) "on how we can increasingly build bonds of civic trust among Americans and their communities."[126]

Following the Obama inauguration, Thomas Sander, executive director of the Saguaro Seminar on Civic Engagement in America at Harvard University, wondered, "Now that Obama is elected, how will the Obama administration rate in the care and feeding of this tremendous network?"[127] Sander writes that it was clear to him that, when Barack Obama participated in the seminar, although it was clear politicians "have much more of a natural interest in stoking grassroots networks before elections and tend to neglect them after election victories, when it is often less clear both how to use these networks and 'what's in it for them–the politicians?'"[128]

One of those networks is clearly the Saguaro Seminar itself, which ended with a final report, *Better Together*, released in December 2000, which provides us with a window to view and evaluate this group, including a number of people who went on to prominent media positions or who have used their positions of influence to support Obama either directly or indirectly in the media.[129]

The idea for the Saguaro Seminars begins with Robert D. Putnam, who is attributed with charting the "decline of civil engagement in the USA over the last 30 years or so." His 1995 book, *Bowling Alone: America's Declining Social Capital*, which is a follow-up to his 1993 collaborative work concerning community and social capital, *Making Democracy Work*, set the stage, and was followed in January 1995 by an article also titled "Bowling Alone: America's Declining Social Capital."[130] In 2000 there was a follow-up version by Putnam, *Bowling Alone: The Collapse and Revival of American Community*, in which Putnam used new data to show how disconnected we are from our "democratic structures" and how we may reconnect.[131]

In a January 2001 review of *Bowling Alone*, David Moberg explains at *In These Times* that Putnam defines *social capital* as connections among individuals and "'community' adapted to a large-scale capitalist society." Social capital, Moberg explains, is "more abundant in small communities than in big cities, but networks that constitute social capital develop in churches, unions, PTAs, neighborhood clubs, fraternal organizations and even bowling leagues (which have declined in the United States, thus 'bowling alone')."[132]

The Participants

Barack Obama, according to Putnam, was "one of the few black men in the group." Obama's entrée to the group was his community organizer background and the fact that "they wanted a diversity of ages, races, regions and occupations."[133] Another black man in the group was the Reverend Kirbyjon Caldwell, a megachurch pastor from Houston who served as a spiritual adviser to President George W. Bush and is said to play a similar role with Obama. "Oddly, Caldwell said through a spokesman that he doesn't recall meeting Obama at the seminar," Burke writes.[134]

Burke described Obama as "young and unknown." As you will see, that is not an entirely true statement. At least four other Saguaro participants were known by Obama prior to 1997. Additionally, as Burke indicates, within this grouping we find a number of people who have either been instrumental in promoting Obama's agenda or have used their positions of influence on his behalf.

As we wrote in *The Manchurian President*, in 1992 Barack Obama served on the founding board of Public Allies, an organization dedicated to training a cadre of community organizers. Public Allies cofounders Vanessa Kirsch and Katrina Browne, at Obama's suggestion, interviewed his wife, Michelle Obama, to head a new Chicago office. She served as executive director from spring 1993 until fall 1996. Barack Obama left the Public Allies board when Michelle was hired, although he served on the Public Allies national board from 1997, when both he and Vanessa Kirsch participated in the Saguaro Seminars, until 2001, the approximate time when the seminars ended.[135] Clearly, Barack Obama and Vanessa Kirsch were well known to each other prior to their attendance at Saguaro.

A second Saguaro Seminar member Obama knew prior to 1997 is the Reverend Bliss W. Browne. In December 1995, Browne's United Imagination Network (Imagine Chicago), a collective of five elementary schools and one high school, was one of the first thirty-five school networks and their partners to receive school improvement funds from the Chicago Annenberg Challenge. Imagine Chicago received a $25,000 planning grant.[136] Barack Obama served as president of the newly formed CAC board of directors from 1995 to 1999. He continued as a member of the board until 2002. Bliss Browne writes in 1999 that Imagine Chicago was "designed [in 1992] as a partnership between community builders, educators, and the city's young people." Young people for the pilot program came from Chicago groups. This included Public Allies, which was then headed by Michelle Obama.[137] The Chicago Annenberg Challenge funded the Urban Imagination Network from 1996 through June 2002. The Urban Imagination Network Teacher Formation was funded from 1998 to 1999 by the Fetzer Institute and the Chicago Annenberg Challenge.[138] However, Obama quite likely knew Katrina Browne prior to the CAC award. She served as one of the Public Allies' teachers under Michelle Obama's management.[139]

The third Saguaro Seminar member with whom Obama was familiar is William Julius Wilson, who participated in the February 25, 1996, town hall meeting on "Economic Insecurity" at the Ida Noyes Hall at the University of Chicago. The meeting, titled "Employment and Survival in Urban America," was sponsored by the Chicago Democratic Socialists of America (DSA), University of Chicago DSA Youth Section, and University Democrats.[140] Panelists for the meeting included Barack Obama, then running for the 13th Illinois Senate District, and Professor William Julius Wilson, of the Center for the Study of Urban Inequality at the University of Chicago.

Wilson based his presentation on his forthcoming book, *When Work Disappears: The World of the New Urban Poor.* Wilson demanded "the left not be intimidated by the Contract on America and how it has limited the terms of the debate. What we need, he asserted, was a jobs policy based roughly on the New Deal's WPA. The work would concentrate on badly needed infrastructure maintenance and improvement. It would be a universal program; [these new] jobs would be available to everyone." Wilson's socialist ties are unmistakable. In July 1988, when Michael Harrington, the founder of Democratic Socialists of America, was discussing his recent autobiography, *The Long Distance Runner,* with Richard D. Heffner, host of the television program *Open Mind,* he told Heffner, "Wilson's a Socialist. He's a member of Democratic Socialists of America." At the same time, in 1989, Wilson was a member of the National Advisory Council of the Social Democrats USA (SD/USA). Like the DSA, the SD/USA is a member of the Socialist International.[141] Wilson was still a member of the SD/USA National Advisory Council in April 2008.[142]

If fall 1991, Henry Louis Gates, Jr., joined the faculty at Harvard University as the W.E.B. Du Bois Professor of the Humanities, chair of Afro-American studies, and director of the W.E.B. Du Bois Institute for Afro-American Research at Harvard, after having taught at Yale, Cornell, and Duke universities. Between fall 1991 and fall 2001, Gates is said to have exploded the senior faculty ranks in Afro-American studies by raiding top scholars from other schools. There were ten professorships at the start of the fall 2001 term, including Gates himself (English), Kwame Anthony Appiah (philosophy), Cornel West (religious studies), and William Julius Wilson (Kennedy School of Government). Wilson serves on the Executive Committee of the W.E.B. DuBois Institute for African and African American Research and as a member of the board of directors at the Center on Budget and Policy Priorities. He was also a founding member of the Campaign for America's Future in July 1996.[143]

The next Saguaro Seminar alum Barack Obama knew prior to 1997 is Martha Minow. The dean of Harvard Law School, Minow is the daughter of Newton Minow, the former chair of the FCC, who serves as senior counsel at Chicago's firm Sidley Austin. It was Martha Minow who recommended Sidley hire Obama for a summer job in 1989, after his first year of law school.[144] Martha Minow told *Politico*'s Carrie Budoff Brown in late August 2008, "So we were in the midst of one of our intensive discussions about civic engagement. . . . And after one of these ranging discussions, across the political sectors, he did this tour de force summary. We just said, 'When are you running for president?' It became a joke. We started to nickname him 'governor.'"[145] Barack Obama chose Martha Minow in August 2009 to serve on the board of the Legal Services Corporation.[146] The prior relationship suggests that Minow was acting as one of the many godmothers and godfathers who shepherded Barack Obama's career.

Obama named another fellow Saguaro Seminar classmate, Xavier de Souza Briggs, in January 2009 to serve as associate director of the White House Office of Management and Budget. Briggs took a two-year professional leave from MIT effective Inauguration Day.[147] Briggs was placed in charge of the cabinet departments of Housing and Urban Development, Treasury, Transportation, Justice, Commerce, and Homeland Security. Earlier, he served as a senior policy official during the Clinton administration, 1998–1999, and an adviser to the World Bank and the Rockefeller Foundation. He was also a community planner in the South Bronx, Chicago, and other cities.

In particular, Briggs, perhaps as a result of the Saguaro Seminars, is reputed for his work on social capital and the *geography of opportunity*, which is described as a "policy and research field concerned with the consequences of segregation by race and income and with efforts to respond, such as through 'housing mobility' programs that help families exit high-poverty, high-risk neighborhoods in search of better places to raise their children." Briggs served as a team leader on the Obama-Biden transition team for the Department of Health and Human Services, Federal Housing Finance Board, and Interagency Council on Homelessness Review.[148] In July 2005, the Brookings Institution Press published Briggs's *The Geography of Opportunity: Race and Housing Choice in Metropolitan America.* The foreword was written by William Julius Wilson.

Two other Saguaro Seminar alums are members of the so-called mainstream media. The first of these is left-liberal journalist E. J. Dionne, whom Roger Kimball described in July 2008 at *Pajamas Media.* Dionne, Kimball writes, had issued a "valentine to the return to socialism." The subtlety is there. Dionne writes: "In the campaign so far, John McCain has been clinging to the old economic orthodoxy while Barack Obama has proposed a modestly more active role for government."[149] Note the trademark Obama reference to *clinging* and Dionne's approval for an Obama prescription for a "more active role for government," in other words, socialism. Kimball comments: "when you stop laughing at the distinctly immodest, er, fib, start totting up the ways Obama wants to run your life and take your money."[150] This is not Dionne's first ode to socialism. In April 1999 he penned the *Washington Post* editorial "A

World Safe for Socialism."[151] Writing about a Democratic Leadership Council forum attended by President Bill Clinton, British prime minister Tony Blair, German chancellor Gerhard Schroeder, Dutch prime minister Wim Kok, and Italian prime minister Massimo D'Alema, Dionne said they "represent anything but old-style state socialism. All subscribe to versions of the 'Third Way' approach to politics that Blair and Clinton have been marketing and that the DLC was celebrating."[152] Dionne praised the Third Way, saying it "gave liberals and, yes, socialists presentable new clothes to wear. The Third Wayers' real challenge comes now that they hold power in so many places."

The other member of the legacy media, George Stephanopoulos, has had a number of exclusive interviews with Obama. In May 2007, thirteen weeks after Obama announced his candidacy in Springfield, Illinois, Stephanopoulos conducted Obama's first Sunday morning interview. On January 27, 2008, a second interview centered on Obama's primary win in South Carolina.[153] Four months later, on April 17, 2008, Stephanopoulos defended his questions asked of Obama about Bill Ayers, during the recent Democratic presidential debate:[154]

> "We have been researching this for a while," Stephanopoulos said in a phone interview from New York. ABC News political correspondent Jake Tapper, he said, had blogged about the issue April 10, after it was first reported by *Politico*, the political news website. "Part of what we discovered is that Sen. Obama had never been asked directly about it, even though it's being written about and talked about and Republicans are signaling that this is gonna be an issue in the general election."

This, of course, was the debate during which Obama delivered his most-untruthful response:[155]

> This is a guy who lives in my neighborhood, who's a professor of English in Chicago who I know and who I have not received some

official endorsement from. He's not somebody who I exchange ideas from on a regular basis. And the notion that somehow as a consequence of me knowing somebody who engaged in detestable acts 40 years ago, when I was 8 years old, somehow reflects on me and my values doesn't make much sense, George.

It is not beyond the realm of possibilities that Stephanopoulos was providing Obama with cover on the Ayers matter.

However, in his September 8, 2008, interview with Stephanopoulos, things did not go so well for Obama. This is the interview in which Obama famously suffered a slip of the tongue and made the reference to "my Muslim faith." (Obama's hometown apologist, Lynn Sweet of the *Chicago Sun-Times*, writes that Obama "was discussing false rumors [that he is a Muslim] when he slipped up.")[156]

On January 10, 2010, Obama gave Stephanopoulos an exclusive retrospective on his first year in office. In his second interview of the year with Stephanopoulos, on April 9 on *Good Morning America*, after he had signed the START treaty, Obama slammed Sarah Palin—after Stephanopoulos set up a question for Obama to tee off:[157]

> STEPHANOPOULOS: I want to get to some of those broader issues. Because you're also facing criticism on that. Sarah Palin, taking aim at your decision to restrict the use of nuclear weapons. Your pledge not to strike nations, non-nuclear nations, who abide by the nonproliferation treaty. Here's what she said. She said,
>
> "It's unbelievable, no other administration would do it." And then she likened it to kids on the playground. She said you're like a kid who says, "Punch me in the face, and I'm not going to retaliate." Your response?
>
> OBAMA: I really have no response. Because last I checked, Sarah Palin's not much of an expert on nuclear issues.

Clearly, Stephanopoulos was spinning for Obama on July 19, 2010, on *GMA* when, Scott Whitlock writes at the Media Research Center, he "lobbied that if one were to 'set aside' the Fort Hood terror attack and the botched Christmas bombing, there haven't been successful attacks on America in the last few years."[158]

Stephanopoulos came to Obama's defense again after *Washington Post* journalist William Arkin brought up the problems leading up to the Fort Hood slaughter: "That's been conceded by the administration. But, the President came out, ordered a review and they've now addressed those problems, haven't they?"[159]

And let's not forget that *Politico* reported in January 2009 that former Clinton administration spokesman George Stephanopoulos "has daily strategy and message chats with former Clinton administration alumni: Rahm Emanuel—Obama's White House chief of staff—and CNN pundits Paul Begala and James Carville."[160]

The Media Research Center's Brent Bozell asks, "What's worse than the liberal media's sycophantic coverage of President Barack Obama? ABC's George Stephanopoulos actively helping design and deliver the Administration's strategy and message—which he is then charged with reporting."

Although not a member of the traditional media, Obama named far-left radical the Reverend Jim Wallis, publisher of *Sojourners* magazine, as a member of his Advisory Council for Faith-Based and Neighborhood Partnerships in an executive order dated February 5, 2009.[161] Obama and Wallis became close at the Saguaro Seminars, Eli Saslow wrote in January 2009 in the *Washington Post*. Wallis told Saslow: "We hit it off. We had very similar ideas about how faith could contribute to public life. He wanted that to be a major part of his career going forward."[162]

Three years earlier, on April 5, 2006, then U.S. senator Obama and Wallis participated in the launch of the newly founded think tank the Hamilton Project, at the Brookings Institution. Obama and Wallis discussed the white paper "An Economic Strategy to Advance

Opportunity, Prosperity and Growth," which "calls on the nation to address the two most significant risks to economic growth and opportunity: the country's large fiscal imbalances and inadequate investment in key growth enhancing areas."[163] At the inaugural event, Obama and Wallis also delivered twin speeches titled "Restoring America's Promise of Opportunity, Prosperity and Growth."[164]

In the 1960s, Wallis joined the civil rights movement and the anti–Vietnam War movement, and he participated in peace protests at Trinity Evangelical Divinity School in Illinois, a "conservative Christian seminary where he was then enrolled," *Discover the Networks* informs. Wallis "railed against American foreign policy and joined the radical Students for a Democratic Society."[165] While at Trinity, Wallis "founded an anti-capitalism magazine called the *Post-American*, which identified wealth redistribution and government-managed economies as the keys to achieving 'social justice,'" *DTN* writes. In 1971, Wallis "and his *Post-American* colleagues changed the name of their publication to *Sojourners*."[166] Wallis "championed the cause of communism" and demanded greater levels of social justice in the United States, *DTN* continues.[167]

Wallis and his organization have been well documented, including challenging Israel's right to exist. Joan Harris, writing for Accuracy in Media, writes: "*Sojourners* never criticizes a Marxist state. The US and the West are the only violators of human rights to them because they are capitalist. Marxists, by Sojourners' own definition, cannot violate human rights."[168] "In many interviews, [Wallis] has stressed his belief that capitalism has proven to be an unmitigated failure," *DTN* adds.[169]

In his 1976 book, *Agenda for Biblical People*, Wallis called the United States "the great power, the great seducer, the great captor and destroyer of human life, the great master of humanity and history in its totalitarian claims and designs."[170] In April 2010, Wallis stated that "social justice" is at the heart of the Bible. "The God of the Bible is the God of justice," he said. "Though the poor are in the center of God's concern. . . . Poverty breaks the heart of God. And it breaks the heart of the church. So, this is about Christians who may disagree on politics. Republicans, Democrats, it doesn't matter. Left or right. We have different views on the role of government. Doesn't matter, but justice is integral to the gospel."[171]

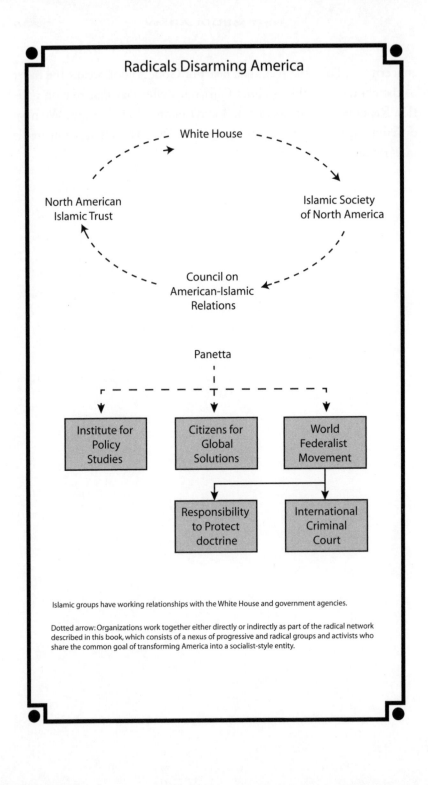

Radicals Disarming America

White House

North American
Islamic Trust

Islamic Society
of North America

Council on
American-Islamic
Relations

Panetta

Institute for
Policy
Studies

Citizens for
Global
Solutions

World
Federalist
Movement

Responsibility
to Protect
doctrine

International
Criminal
Court

Islamic groups have working relationships with the White House and government agencies.

Dotted arrow: Organizations work together either directly or indirectly as part of the radical network described in this book, which consists of a nexus of progressive and radical groups and activists who share the common goal of transforming America into a socialist-style entity.

chapter nine

DISARMING AMERICA

Since assuming office, President Obama and his administration have been minimizing the threat of Islamic fundamentalism while maintaining close associations with Islamic groups of questionable character. At the same time, a network of radical left-wing organizations, working with like-minded administration officials—many with deep ties to those same radical groups—have been engaged in a multipronged assault that seems aimed at disarming America as a superpower by emboldening our enemies, spurning our allies, and dismantling the greatest military the world has ever known.

"We cannot fully know what leads a man to do such a thing," President Obama stated in a Rose Garden appearance one day after a Muslim Army psychiatrist, Major Nidal Malik Hasan, was accused of being the lone gunman in a shooting massacre at the Fort Hood, Texas, military base in which Hasan murdered thirteen in cold blood, wounding thirty others.[1] Obama urged Americans not to "jump to conclusions" about the motives behind the shooting, a theme the president echoed in a speech the next day in which he downplayed religion as a motive in the deadly attack.

"They are Americans of every race, faith and station," Obama said, speaking of the broad diversity of those who serve in the armed forces. "They are Christians and Muslims, Jews and Hindus and nonbelievers. They are descendants of immigrants, and immigrants themselves. They reflect the diversity that makes this America. But what they share is a patriotism like no other. What they share is a commitment to country that has been tested and proved worthy."[2]

Hasan's Islamic motivations were immediately clear. According to eyewitnesses, Hasan reportedly jumped onto a desk and, like scores of other Muslim terrorist attackers, shouted "Allahu Akbar!" before firing more than one hundred rounds at soldiers processing through cubicles in the Soldier Readiness Center, where personnel receive routine medical treatment immediately prior to and on return from deployment, and on a crowd gathered for a college graduation ceremony.[3]

It would quickly emerge that Hasan attended the Dar Al-Hijrah mosque in Falls Church, Virginia, in 2001, at the same time as Nawaf al-Hazmi and Hani Hanjour, two of the hijackers in the September 11 attacks.[4] The mosque at the time was led by Anwar al-Awlaki, an Islamic cleric who, according to U.S. government officials, had become "operational" as a senior talent recruiter, motivator, and participant in planning and training for al-Qaeda operations.[5] Hasan expressed admiration for al-Awlaki's teachings, with U.S. intelligence agencies intercepting e-mails between the two in which Hasan wrote to al-Awlaki, then living in Yemen, that "I can't wait to join you" in the afterlife. Hasan also asked al-Awlaki when jihad is appropriate, and whether it is permissible if innocents are killed in a suicide attack.[6]

In an emerging scandal, it would be made public that officers within the Army were aware of Hasan's tendencies toward radical Islam since at least 2005. According to an internal Army investigation leaked to the media, in one incident in August 2007, Hasan gave a classroom slide show presentation titled "Is the War on Terrorism a War on Islam: An Islamic Perspective."[7]

"It's getting harder and harder for Muslims in the service to morally justify being in a military that seems constantly engaged against fellow Muslims," he was quoted as saying in the presentation.[8] On one of the slides, Hasan wrote: "If Muslim groups can convince Muslims that they are fighting for God against injustices of the 'infidels'; ie: enemies of Islam, then Muslims can become a potent adversary ie: suicide bombing, etc." [sic]. The last bullet point on that page read simply: "We love death more then [sic] you love life!" Hasan's presentation was "shut down" by the instructor because Hasan appeared to be defending terrorism.[9]

Even though Hasan's Islamic motivations were apparent, Obama and the U.S. government persisted in raising other questions. The Army called for a formal inquiry into whether Hasan was mentally sane.[10]

The theme of seemingly minimizing Islamic terrorism inside the United States would continue on December 25, 2009, when Umar Farouk Abdulmutallab, a Muslim Nigerian citizen, attempted to detonate plastic explosives hidden in his underwear while on board Northwest Airlines Flight 253, en route from Amsterdam to Detroit, Michigan.[11] In a knee-jerk reaction, Obama immediately referred to Abdulmutallab as an "isolated extremist," while Secretary of Homeland Security Janet Napolitano claimed there was "no indication" the attack was "part of anything larger."[12] However, it emerged Abdulmutallab traveled to the mountainous Shabwah Province of Yemen to meet with "al-Qaeda elements."[13] Al-Qaeda in Yemen released a video, with its logo in the corner of the screen, of Abdulmutallab and others training in a desert camp, firing weapons at such targets as the Jewish star, the British Union Jack, and the letters UN. The tape included an apparent martyrdom statement in which Abdulmutallab justified his actions against "the Jews and the Christians and their agents."[14]

With Abdulmutallab's terrorist training exposed, Obama quickly changed his tune, declaring one week later the United States is at war with al-Qaeda and will do "whatever it takes" to overcome the terrorist organization. Still, he qualified those statements by distancing mainstream Muslim ideology from the terrorist group, explaining that al-Qaeda offered "nothing but a bankrupt vision of misery and death including for fellow Muslims."[15]

Those statements fit with the theme of the Obama administration's repeated attempts to remove Islam as a motivation in Islamic terrorist attacks. In multiple speeches, Obama has referred to the phenomenon of Islamic terrorism as "violent extremism."[16] In April 2010, the reference became official policy when counterterrorism officials announced Obama's advisers will remove religious terms such as "Islamic extremism" from the central document outlining the U.S. national security strategy and will use the rewritten document to emphasize that the United States does not view Muslim nations through the lens of terror.[17] The change is a significant shift in the National Security Strategy, a document that previously outlined the Bush Doctrine of preventative war and stated: "The struggle against militant Islamic radicalism is the great ideological conflict of the early years of the 21st century."[18]

The change seems to not take into account that terrorists themselves openly define their attacks as religious Islamic jihad. In just one recent example, when Faisal Shahzad, a Pakistan-born U.S. citizen, pleaded guilty to carrying out the failed May 1, 2010, Times Square car bombing, he called himself a "Muslim soldier."[19] In an in-person interview with Aaron Klein in the West Bank city of Jenin, a twenty-three-year old Palestinian man who has volunteered to become a suicide bomber described his motivation.[20] Asked by Klein whether he is compelled to carry out a suicide attack in response to U.S. or Israeli policies, the man replied, "The will to scarify myself for Allah is the first and most major reason. It is true that the Zionists are occupying our lands and that it is our religious duty to fight them, including through suicide attacks. The goal is not the killing of the Jews, but that this is the way to reach Allah." He continued, "The goal is satisfying Allah and his instructions. No money interests, nothing. No brainwash, no pressure; it is my decision. All the other lies are pathetic Israeli propaganda. I pray that Allah gives me the honor to be dead in an operation. This is the supreme and the noblest way to ascend to Allah. These martyrs have special status in the next world and have bigger chances to watch Allah's face and enjoy the magnificent pleasures he offers us."

Al-Qaeda's own defining statement urges jihad in the name of Allah. On February 23, 1998, Osama bin Laden and Ayman al-Zawahiri, a leader of Egyptian Islamic Jihad, along with three other Islamist leaders, cosigned and issued a fatwa, or binding religious edict, that defined the Islamic goals of al-Qaeda, calling on Muslims to kill Americans and their allies where they can, when they can. "This is in accordance with the words of Almighty Allah, 'and fight the pagans all together as they fight you all together,' and 'fight them until there is no more tumult or oppression, and there prevail justice and faith in Allah,'" read the statement, which was written under the banner of the World Islamic Front for Combat Against the Jews and Crusaders.[21]

The Obama administration's shift away from associating terrorism with Islam is typified in statements from John Brennan, the White House's top counterterrorism adviser. "Our enemy is not terror because terror is a state of mind and, as Americans, we refuse to live in fear," Brennan told an audience at the prestigious Center for Strategic and International Studies. "Nor do we describe our enemy as jihadists or Islamists because jihad is holy struggle, a legitimate tenet of Islam meaning to purify oneself or one's community."[22]

Brennan stated that Obama's strategy "is absolutely clear about the threat we face. Our enemy is not terrorism because terrorism is but a tactic. Moreover, describing our enemy in religious terms would lend credence to the lie propagated by al-Qaeda and its affiliates to justify terrorism, that the United States is somehow at war against Islam. The reality, of course, is that we have never been and will never be at war with Islam. After all, Islam, like so many faiths, is part of America."

Then he listed an Obama national security priority: "This includes addressing the political, economic and social forces that can make some people fall victim to the cancer of violent extremism. . . . And I think there's more work we need to do to understand the psychology behind terrorism. But a lot of times, the psychology is affected by the environment that has those political, social, economic factors that contribute to that." Here Brennan is insisting it is our country's policies that drive terrorism, as opposed to Islamic terrorist groups' openly stated mission of spreading Islam around the world. By minimizing Islamic motivation, Brennan, like the Obama administration as a whole, is making it more difficult to defeat terrorism since its root cause—Islamic fundamentalism—is being obscured.

Brennan also cleanses Muslim cleric Anwar al-Awlaki, who encourages murder in the name of Islam, of any tie to Islam.[23] "Individuals like Anwar Awlaki, who recently released a video, demonstrated that his rhetoric is anything but peaceful," Brennan said. "It's anything but Islamic. It is dedicated to murder and lashing out."[24]

Hamas Co-Conspirator Has Close Ties to Obama Administration

Brennan believes that by encouraging the assimilation of terrorist organizations into Middle Eastern governments and by fostering so-called moderate elements of such organizations, those groups may moderate their doctrine. In a July 2008 article in the *Annals*, a publication of the American Academy of Political and Social Science, Brennan argued it "would not be foolhardy, however, for the United States to tolerate, and even to encourage, greater assimilation of Hezbollah into Lebanon's political system, a process that is subject to Iranian influence."[25] Outside of al-Qaeda, the Iranian-backed Hezbollah has the distinction of having killed the most Americans in terror attacks, including the 1983 Beirut barracks bombing that killed 241 American servicemen.[26] It is also responsible for scores of terrorist actions targeting Israelis, including rocket launchings against civilian population centers. Hezbollah's attacks against the Israeli north in 2006 killed forty-three Israeli civilians and wounded more than four thousand.[27]

Continued Brennan: "Hezbollah is already represented in the Lebanese parliament and its members have previously served in the Lebanese cabinet, reflections of Hezbollah's interest in shaping Lebanon's political future from within government institutions.

This political involvement is a far cry from Hezbollah's genesis as solely a terrorist organization dedicated to murder, kidnapping and violence."[28]

At a press conference in August 2008 at the Center for Strategic and International Studies in Washington, D.C., Brennan declared, "Hezbollah started out as purely a terrorist organization back in the early '80s and has evolved significantly over time. And now it has members of parliament, in the cabinet; there are lawyers, doctors, others who are part of the Hezbollah organization."[29] Maintenance of a civilian unit of doctors and lawyers by terrorist groups is not uncommon in the Middle East. Hamas has long brandished a civilian wing that provides medical care and education to the Palestinian population. According to Israeli security officials, Hezbollah and Hamas emphasize this outreach to endear their terror groups to the local population.[30]

Speaking in February 2010 at what became a controversial question-and-answer session for Muslim law students at New York University, Brennan announced the Obama administration is working to calibrate policies in the fight against terrorism that ensure Americans are "never" profiled. "We need to be looking at ourselves as individuals. Not the way we look or the creed we have or our ethnic background. I consider myself a citizen of the world," he said. Brennan told the audience the Obama administration is trying to "make sure that we as Americans can interact in a safe way, balance policies in a way that optimizes national security but also optimizes the opportunity in this country never to be profiled, never to be discriminated against."[31] Profiling has long been a controversial issue. Many counterterrorism officials believe profiling is necessary to ensure U.S. security, but liberal and human rights groups largely oppose the practice.[32]

Brennan came under fire by conservative pundits after a video of his NYU session surfaced on the Internet, although his remarks about profiling went largely unnoticed. At the session, Brennan stated that having a percentage of terrorists released by the United States return to terrorist attacks "isn't that bad," since the recidivism rate for inmates in the U.S. prison system is higher. He also criticized parts of the Bush administration's response to 9/11 as a "reaction some people might say was over the top in some areas" that "in an overabundance of caution [we] implemented a number of security measures and activities that upon reflection now we look back after the heat of the battle has died down a bit we say they were excessive, okay."[33]

Brennan's NYU session was organized by the Islamic Society of North America, or ISNA, a radical Muslim group that was an unindicted co-conspirator in a scheme to raise money for Hamas.[34] The ISNA boasted on its website that it facilitated the meeting at NYU with Brennan.[35] ISNA, whose members asked Brennan scores of questions during the event, stated the meeting was intended to initiate a "dialogue between government officials and Muslim American leaders to explore issues of national security."[36]

The Justice Department named ISNA an unindicted co-conspirator in its case against the Holy Land Foundation in Texas, which was found guilty of raising money for the Hamas terrorist organization.[37] In 2009, founders were given life sentences for "funneling $12 million to Hamas."[38]

ISNA is reportedly known for its promotion of Saudi-style Islam in mosques throughout the United States, notes *Discover the Networks*.[39] *DTN* notes that through its affiliate, the North American Islamic Trust—a Saudi government–backed organization—ISNA reportedly holds the mortgages on 50 to 80 percent of all mosques in the United States and Canada. "Thus the organization can freely exercise ultimate authority over these houses of worship and their teachings," states *DTN*.

ISNA was founded in 1981 by the Saudi-funded Muslim Students' Association.[40] The two groups are still partners. Aaron Klein previously attended an MSA event at which violence against the United States was urged by speakers.[41] "We are not Americans," shouted one speaker, Muhammad Faheed, at the MSA event in New York's Queensborough Community College in 2003. "We are Muslims. [The United States] is going to deport and attack us! It is us versus them! Truth against falsehood! The colonizers and masters against the oppressed, and we will burn down the master's house!"

Islam scholar Stephen Schwartz describes ISNA as "one of the chief conduits through which the radical Saudi form of Islam passes into the United States."[42] According to terrorism expert Steven Emerson, ISNA "is a radical group hiding under a false veneer of moderation" that publishes a bimonthly magazine, *Islamic Horizons*, that "often champions militant Islamist doctrine."[43] The group also "convenes annual conferences where Islamist militants have been given a platform to incite violence and promote hatred," states Emerson. Emerson cites an event in which al-Qaeda supporter and PLO official Yusuf Qaradawi was invited to speak at an ISNA conference. Also, ISNA has held fund-raisers for terrorists, notes *Discover the Networks*. After Hamas leader Mousa Marzook was arrested and eventually deported in 1997, ISNA raised money for his defense. The group also has condemned the U.S. government's post–9/11 seizure of Hamas's and Palestinian Islamic Jihad's financial assets.[44]

The ISNA, meanwhile, has an extensive relationship with the Obama administration, one that started even before Obama took office in 2009. One week before Obama's presidential inauguration, Sayyid Syeed, national director of the ISNA Office for Interfaith and Community Alliances, was part of a delegation that met with the directors of Obama's transition team. The delegation discussed a request for an executive order ending "torture."[45]

ISNA president Ingrid Mattson represented American Muslims at Obama's inauguration, where she offered a prayer during the televised event.[46] Mattson also represented ISNA at Obama's Ramadan dinner at the White House.[47] In June 2009, Obama's top aide, Valerie Jarrett, invited Mattson to work on the White House Council on Women and Girls, which Jarrett leads.[48] That July, the Justice Department sponsored an information booth at an ISNA bazaar in Washington, D.C.[49] Also that month, Jarrett addressed ISNA's forty-sixth annual convention.[50] According to the White House, Jarrett attended as part of Obama's outreach to Muslims.

Obama Religion Adviser Plots with Ground Zero Imam: America "Ideal Place" to Renew Islam

The ISNA's Mattson was present at Obama's August 14, 2010, White House dinner that marked the start of the Islamic Ramadan month of fasting.[51] It was at that dinner that Obama famously expressed support for the rights of an Islamic organization, the Cordoba Initiative, to build an Islamic cultural center and mosque two blocks from the area known as Ground Zero.[52] After recognizing the sensitivities of the area and referring to Ground Zero as "hallowed ground," Obama continued, "But let me be clear. As a citizen, and as President, I believe that Muslims have the same right to practice their religion as everyone else in this country. And that includes the right to build a place of worship and a community center on private property in Lower Manhattan, in accordance with local laws and ordinances."

Obama's remarks ignited a political firestorm in a country where polls indicated the vast majority of Americans opposed the Ground Zero mosque. Within twenty-four hours, Obama was insisting that he had not meant to indicate that he supported the building of the Islamic center, but was simply making a legal point. "I was not commenting and I will not comment on the wisdom of making the decision to put a mosque there," he said. "I was commenting very specifically on the right people have that dates back to our founding."[53]

A religion adviser to Obama, meanwhile, has close ties to the imam behind the Islamic cultural center near Ground Zero. The two have been documented together discussing America as "the ideal place for a renewal of Islam."[54]

In February 2009, Obama named Chicago Muslim Eboo Patel to his Advisory Council on Faith-Based and Neighborhood Partnerships.[55] Patel is the founder and executive director of Chicago-based Interfaith Youth Core, which says it promotes pluralism by teaming people of different faiths on service projects.[56]

Imam Feisal Abdul Rauf, the controversial Muslim leader behind the plan to build the Islamic center and mosque two blocks from Ground Zero, wrote the afterword to Patel's 2006 book, *Building the Interfaith Youth Movement: Beyond Dialogue to Action*.[57]

Patel is listed as one of fifteen "Muslim Leaders of Tomorrow" on the website for the American Society for Muslim Advancement, which is led by Rauf.[58] In Patel's 2007 book, *Saving Each Other, Saving Ourselves*, he recounts discussing with Rauf the future of Islam in the United States.[59]

Rauf "understood the vision immediately and suggested that I visit him and his wife, Daisy Khan, at their home the following evening," Patel recalled. Khan founded the society with her husband and has aided him in his plans for the mosque near Ground Zero.[60]

"The living room of their apartment on the Upper West Side was set up like a mosque, with prayer rugs stretched from wall to wall," wrote Patel in his book. "I arrived at dusk, prayed the maghrib prayer with Daisy and Imam Feisal and then talked with them about how America, with its unique combination of religious devotion and religious diversity, was the ideal place for a renewal of Islam.

"In the twentieth century, Catholicism and Judaism underwent profound transformations in America," Rauf observed. "I think, this century, in America, Islam will do the same."

Patel boasts of a "critical mass" of Muslims in the United States. "Islam is a religion that has always been revitalized by its migration," he wrote. "America is a nation that has been constantly rejuvenated by immigrants. There is now a critical mass of Muslims in America."

Patel in March 2010 wrote a *Huffington Post* piece referring to Obama's former "green jobs" czar Van Jones as a "faith hero."[61] "In my last post on Van, I called him an American patriot," wrote Patel. "That is high praise in my book. But watching Van's speech at the NAACP, I have another title for him, one that I reserve for the true giants of history. Van Jones is a faith hero."

Rauf, meanwhile, caused a stir with his proposed $100 million, thirteen-story Islamic cultural center and mosque near the corner of Park Place and West Broadway. Rauf sparked controversy in July 2010 when he refused during a live radio interview with Aaron Klein to condemn violent jihad groups as terrorists.[62] Rauf repeatedly refused on the air to affirm the U.S. designation of Hamas as a terrorist organization or call the Muslim Brotherhood extremists. The Brotherhood openly seeks to spread Islam around the world, while Hamas is committed to Israel's destruction and is responsible for scores of suicide bombings, shootings, and rocket attacks aimed at Jewish civilian population centers.

During the interview, Rauf was also asked by Klein who he believes was responsible for the September 11 attacks. "There's no doubt," stated Rauf. "The general perception all over the world was it was created by people who were sympathetic to Osama bin Laden. Whether they were part of the killer group or not, these are details that need to be left to the law-enforcement experts."[63]

Rauf has been on record several times blaming U.S. policies for the September 11 attacks.[64] He has been quoted refusing to admit Muslims carried out the attacks. Referring to the 9/11 attacks, Rauf told CNN, "U.S. policies were an accessory to the crime that happened. We [the U.S.] have been an accessory to a lot of innocent lives dying in the world. Osama bin Laden was made in the USA."[65]

Madeline Brooks, a reporter who attended a May 7, 2010, sermon by Rauf, quoted the Islamic leader as stating "some people say it was Muslims who attacked on September 11."[66] Rauf's 2004 book had two different titles, one in English and the second in Arabic. In the United States his book was called *What's Right with America Is What's Right with Islam*. The same book, published in Arabic, bore the name *The Call from the WTC Rubble: Islamic Da'wah from the Heart of America Post–Sept. 11.*[67]

Meanwhile, in April 2009, Homeland Security Secretary Janet Napolitano swore in a member of her agency's Advisory Council who is a strong supporter of the radical Islamist theologian who calls for "war" with the non-Muslim world and whose teachings inspired and continues to govern al-Qaeda and Islamic terrorist organizations worldwide.[68] Mohamed Elibiary, president and CEO of the Freedom and Justice Foundation of Carrollton, Texas, also spoke at a conference that honored the anti-U.S. founder of the Iranian Islamic revolution, Ayatollah Khomeini. Elibiary has strongly criticized the government's persecution of fund-raisers for Hamas and is a defender of the Council on American Islamic Relations, or CAIR.[69]

Elibiary fervently endorses the teachings of Egyptian writer Sayyid Qutb, who is widely considered the father of the modern Islamic terrorist revolution.[70] Osama bin Laden and terror groups worldwide rely on Qutb for their fatwas and ideology.[71]

Elibiary has criticized the U.S. government's prosecution and conviction of the Holy Land Foundation and five former officials for providing more than $12 million to Hamas; they depict the case as a defeat for the United States.[72]

He wrote an op-ed in the *Dallas Morning News* suggesting the convictions were part of a U.S. government policy of "denying our civil liberties and privacy at home" while pursuing antiterror policies that have "left thousands of Americans dead, tens of thousands maimed, trillions of taxpayer dollars squandered and our homeland more vulnerable than ever."[73]

The Homeland Security Advisory Council, part of the executive office of the president, was formed by an executive order by President George W. Bush in 2002.[74]

Qutb, executed in 1966 on charges of attempting to overthrow the Egyptian government, called for the creation of a worldwide Islamic state. Qutb declared, "There is only one place on earth which can be called the home of Islam (Dar-ul-Islam), and it is that place where the Islamic state is established and the Shariah is the authority and God's limits are observed."[75]

Qutb labeled the non-Muslim world the Dar-ul-Harb—the house of war. "A Muslim can have only two possible relations with Dar-ul-Harb: peace with a contractual agreement, or war," wrote Qutb. "A country with which there is a treaty will not be considered the home of Islam," he said.[76]

Elibiary has regularly upheld the teachings of Qutb. He writes that he sees in Qutb "the potential for a strong spiritual rebirth that's truly ecumenical allowing all faiths practiced in America to enrich us and motivate us to serve God better by serving our fellow man more."[77]

After *Dallas Morning News* editorial page editor Rod Dreher criticized Qutb's writings, Elibiary engaged in a lengthy, published e-mail feud in which he repeatedly defended Qutb. In one exchange, Elibiary wrote, "I'd recommend everyone read Qutb, but read him with an eye to improving America not just to be jealous with malice in our hearts."[78]

In 2004, Elibiary was one of seven advertised speakers at an Irving, Texas, conference titled "A Tribute to a Great Islamic Visionary," celebrating the sixteenth anniversary of Khomeini's death. Under a heading "Selected Sayings of the Holy Prophet," one advertisement read: "Allah has made Islam to prevail over all other religions."[79]

The main ad for the event, listing Elibiary, declares, "Neither east nor west is the main principal [sic] of an Islamic revolution . . . and outlines the true policy of non-alliance for the Islamic countries and countries that in the near future, with the help of Allah SWT, will accept Islam as the only school for liberating humanity."[80]

The local CBS-11 News in Texas reported on the event. CBS reporters Todd Bensman and Robert Riggs reported that one speaker at the conference was a Washington, D.C., imam, Mohammad Asi, known for his radical views.[81] At the event, CBS-11 reported, Asi issued a strongly worded anti-American, anti-Jewish speech in which he said American imperialism and pro-Israel Zionism are "diabolical, aggressive, bloodthirsty ideologies that are trying to take over the world and destroy Islam."

Another speaker at the conference, a ten-year-old boy, opened the tribute by praising Khomeini for reviving "pure" Islamic thinking and saving the religion from being conquered by the West, reported

CBS-11. The boy called President Bush "the greatest enemy of the Muslim Ummah."

Elibiary claimed to CBS-11 he did not know the event at which he was an advertised speaker was a tribute to Khomeini until after he arrived. He claimed he arrived at the event before hearing the first speakers, which included the boy, and also before Asi spoke. "I didn't attend the whole thing," he said, while calling Asi an "extremist."

Obama's important policy goal of Muslim outreach culminated in the president's historic address to the Islamic world from Cairo, Egypt, on June 4, 2009. The speech, in which Obama referenced his Islamic experiences as a child in Indonesia and the Muslim faith of his paternal family, was a major departure from the tone of his presidential campaign, when those who factually reported on the candidate's Muslim background, including these authors, were denounced as fearmongers and leaders of smear campaigns. In the address, Obama referred to the Quran as "holy" four times and quoted several verses from the Islamic text.[82] He also used Muslim terminology, such as the Quranic obligation of *zakat*, or charity. Obama used his speech to tackle what he said were seven major issues of import that "we must finally confront together."

First, he pointed to "violent extremism in all its forms." He vowed "America is not—and never will be—at war with Islam. We will, however, relentlessly confront violent extremists who pose a grave threat to our security. Islam is not part of the problem in combating violent extremism—it is an important part of promoting peace," Obama declared. The U.S. president did not once use the word *terrorism*.

Obama went on to claim that "violent extremists have exploited these tensions in a small but potent minority of Muslims." However, poll data in America, the Middle East, and Europe suggests Obama's "potent minority of Muslims" who support "violent extremists" actually consists of a widespread plurality. A Pew Research Center poll of Muslims in America, released in May 2007, found 26 percent of Muslims between the ages of eighteen and twenty-nine affirmed that there could be justification in some (unspecified) circumstances for suicide bombing, and 5 percent of all the Muslims surveyed said that they had a favorable view of al-Qaeda.[83] Given the Pew Center's estimate of 2.35 million Muslims in America, and the total of 13 percent that avowed a belief that suicide bombings could ever be justified, that's over 180,000 supporters of suicide attacks (subtracting the number of children), notes terrorism researcher Robert Spencer.[84]

In January 2007, *Jerusalem Post* columnist Michael Freund pointed to worrying survey results from other polls: 25 percent of Muslims in Britain approved of the July 7, 2005, jihad terror bombings in London; 30 percent said they would rather live under Islamic law, or Shariah, than in a Western pluralistic society. Forty-four percent of Muslims in Nigeria thought suicide attacks were "often" or "sometimes" justified, with only 28 percent rejecting them in all cases. Roughly 14 percent of Muslims in France, Britain, and Spain approved of suicide attacks against civilian targets, and only 45 percent of Muslims in Egypt considered terror never justified.[85]

A July 2006 global Pew survey found that among Muslims in Lebanon, 39 percent regard acts of terrorism as often or sometimes justified. In Jordan, a majority—57 percent—say suicide bombings and other violent actions are justifiable in defense of Islam while in Turkey, Morocco, and Indonesia the support for terrorism is at 15 percent or fewer. In Pakistan, 1 in 4 supports suicide bombing. When it comes to suicide bombings in Iraq, however, Muslims in the surveyed countries are divided. Nearly half of Muslims in Lebanon and Jordan, and 56 percent in Morocco, say suicide bombings against Americans and other Westerners in Iraq are justifiable.[86]

Other surveys found that upwards of 50 percent of the general public supports suicide terror in such "moderate" Arab countries as Egypt and Jordan. A Jerusalem Media and Communications Centre poll revealed that 77.2 percent of Palestinians supported terrorist kidnappings, while 6 out of 10 Palestinians also said they were in favor of firing Qassam rockets at Israeli towns and cities.[87]

Startlingly, when referring to Palestinian terrorism in his Cairo address, Obama used the term *resistance*, signifying legitimate means of opposition. "Palestinians must abandon violence. Resistance through violence and killing is wrong and does not succeed," he said.[88]

The Obama administration's outreach efforts to the Muslim world took a strange turn when NASA administrator Charles Bolden in June 2010 told Al Jazeera that Obama informed him before he took the NASA job that the president wanted him to do three things: inspire children to learn math and science, expand international relationships, and "perhaps foremost, he wanted me to find a way to reach out to the Muslim world and engage much more with dominantly Muslim nations to help them feel good about their historic contribution to science . . . and math and engineering."[89]

The NASA administrator spoke to Al Jazeera as part of a Middle East tour marking the one-year anniversary of Obama's address to the Muslim world. In the interview with Al Jazeera, Bolden described space travel as an international collaboration of which Muslim nations must be a part. "It is a matter of trying to reach out and get the best of all worlds, if you will, and there is much to be gained by drawing in the contributions that are possible from the Muslim (nations)," he said.[90]

When Bolden's remarks stirred controversy in the media, White House spokesman Robert Gibbs at first tried to downplay the comments. "That was not his task, and that's not the task of NASA," Gibbs said of Bolden's described Muslim outreach efforts.[91] But in a subsequent statement to Fox News, White House spokesman Nick Shapiro said that Obama indeed "wants NASA to engage with the world's best scientists and engineers as we work together to push the boundaries of exploration."[92]

Also, Representative Pete Olson, ranking Republican on the House Space and Aeronautics Subcommittee, told FoxNews.com that he spoke to Bolden and the NASA administrator described the outreach program as part of the administration's space plan during a conversation they had in June 2010.[93] "He confirmed it to me," Olson said. The

Texas Republican said he thinks the program existed until the "uproar" compelled the administration to put the brakes on the outreach project.

NASA has long been one of the crown jewels of American exceptionalism, leading the world in space exploration, scientific discovery, and aeronautics research. NASA's achievements are groundbreaking—from its Apollo program, which landed the first humans on the moon, to its Voyager 1, currently the farthest human-made object from earth, to its Skylab space station, or its shuttle program, or the Hubble Space Telescope, and various probes, pathfinders, and rovers that encompass the Mars Exploration Program.[94]

For many, NASA evokes the self-confidence of President John F. Kennedy's 1961 pledge that America would land on the moon within the decade.[95] "There was no finer expression of belief in American exceptionalism than Kennedy's," states prominent political pundit Charles Krauthammer, who contrasts Kennedy's attitude with that of Obama. Krauthammer points to a 2009 press conference in which Obama told a French reporter: "I believe in American exceptionalism, just as I suspect that the Brits believe in British exceptionalism and the Greeks believe in Greek exceptionalism."[96] "Which of course means: If we're all exceptional, no one is," noted Krauthammer.

Indeed, Obama's new budget for NASA takes a stab at the space agency's lunar program—a program that has long represented American exceptionalism and that was seeking to return humans to the moon by 2020 in line with President George W. Bush's "vision for space exploration" developed in the aftermath of the loss of the space shuttle *Columbia* in 2003.[97] The budget spends $6 billion to turn over space transportation to commercial companies. The space agency's budget would grow to $19 billion in 2011, from $18.7 billion, under the proposed budget, with an emphasis on science and less spent on space exploration.[98] It would also get additional increases in subsequent years, reaching $21 billion in 2015. In total, NASA would receive $100 billion over the next five years. However, the budget increases come with a restructuring of NASA that also calls for a complete stop in NASA's

Constellation program, the rockets and spacecraft that NASA has been working on for the past four years to replace the space shuttles.

Some in Congress were immediately taken aback by Obama's de-funding of NASA's lunar and other space exploration programs, and promised a budgetary fight. "The president's proposed NASA budget begins the death march for the future of U.S. human space flight," said Senator Richard Shelby, the senior Republican on the appropriations subcommittee handling NASA funding. "Congress cannot and will not sit back and watch the reckless abandonment of sound principles, a proven track record, a steady path to success, and the destruction of our human space flight program," said Shelby of Alabama, whose state is home to NASA's Marshall Space Flight Center.[99]

Alongside the restructuring of NASA, Obama also committed to reducing stocks of U.S. weapons-grade plutonium and signed an agreement that will lower the country's deployed nuclear arsenals. At a two-day nuclear summit in Washington, D.C., that ended on April 14, 2010, Russia and the United States agreed to dispose of tons of surplus weapons-grade plutonium, with each side to dispose of at least thirty-four metric tons of weapons-grade plutonium, enough for seventeen thousand nuclear weapons.[100] The summit hosted forty-seven world leaders and was focused on reducing the world's stockpiles of nuclear weapons, mostly those of peaceful countries. The summit largely did not focus on Iran's suspected nuclear weapons program. That summit came less than a week after Obama signed a treaty with Russia to re-duce the nuclear stockpiles of both nations.[101]

A week before, Obama issued a strange, revised U.S. nuclear arms strategy that narrowed the conditions under which the United States would use nuclear weapons.[102] For the first time ever, an American president announced to the world a commitment to not use nuclear weapons against nonnuclear states that are in compliance with the Nuclear Non-Proliferation Treaty, even if those countries attacked the United States with biological or chemical weapons or launched a crip-pling cyberattack.

Such an announcement is very unusual. It limits our retaliatory capabilities and informs our enemies they do not need to worry about a U.S. nuclear strike if they launch certain kinds of devastating attacks on our home front. Obama argued that biological, chemical, or crippling cyberattacks could be deterred with "a series of graded options," a combination of old and new conventional weapons. "I'm going to preserve all the tools that are necessary in order to make sure that the American people are safe and secure," he said.[103] Whereas President George W. Bush—like his predecessors—reserved the right to use nuclear weapons "to deter a wide range of threats" including banned chemical and biological weapons and large-scale conventional attacks, Obama decided to change this as part of his drive toward a "nuclear-free world."[104]

All these moves—scaling back of NASA's exploration program, limiting U.S. nuclear deterrence, and downsizing American nuke arsenals—have long been petitioned by Obama's "science czar," John P. Holdren, at a magazine whose personnel, it turns out, were purportedly used for the benefit of Soviet propaganda in an attempt to disarm America. Holdren is also tied to a pro-Soviet group whose personnel are now in key defense positions in the Obama administration.[105]

Holdren's official title is Advisor to the President for Science and Technology, Director of the White House Office of Science and Technology Policy, and Co-Chair of the President's Council of Advisors on Science and Technology. In this position, Holdren is instrumental in helping to craft White House policy on key science and technology issues, including NASA and nuclear policy, in turn including nuclear energy exploration.[106]

From 1984 until right before he accepted his White House position, Holdren sat on the board of the *Bulletin of the Atomic Scientists*, a far-left nontechnical magazine that covers global security and public policy issues, especially related to the dangers posed by nuclear and other weapons of mass destruction.[107] The magazine has been published continuously since 1945, when it was founded by former Manhattan Project physicists after the atomic bombings of Hiroshima and Nagasaki, as the *Bulletin of the Atomic Scientists of Chicago.* The *Bulletin's* primary aim is to inform the public about nuclear policy debates while advocating for the international control of nuclear energy.[108]

Two of the magazine's founding sponsors, Leo Szilard and Robert Oppenheimer, were accused of passing information from the Manhattan Project to the Soviets. Both were also key initiators of the Manhattan Project.[109] In 1994, Pavel Sudoplatov, a former major general in Soviet intelligence, named Szilard and Oppenheimer as key sources of crucial atomic information to the Soviet Union. "The most vital information for developing the first Soviet atomic bomb came from scientists engaged in the Manhattan Project to build the American atomic bomb—Robert Oppenheimer, Enrico Fermi and Leo Szilard," wrote Sudoplatov. Sudoplatov said the Soviet Union "received reports on the progress of the Manhattan Project from Oppenheimer and his friends in oral form, through comments and asides, and from documents transferred through clandestine methods with their full knowledge that the information they were sharing would be passed on."[110]

Indeed, Oppenheimer was accused in Senate hearings of bringing communists into the Manhattan Project. He brought his brother Frank and three former graduate students into the project, all of whom, according to Senate hearings, were well known to him to be "members of the Communist Party or closely associated with activities of the Communist Party."[111] Oppenheimer admitted he knew by August 1943 that two of the scientists working under him were Communist Party members. Three of five scientists under Oppenheimer's direct supervision were accused of leaking secret information about the atomic bomb to the Soviets.

On October 25, 1945, Oppenheimer met with President Harry Truman at the White House, urging him to surrender the U.S. nuclear monopoly to international control. Truman was outraged, reportedly telling Secretary of State Dean Acheson, "I don't want to see that son-of-a-b*tch in this office ever again."[112] Oppenheimer and Szilard were stripped of their work in the Manhattan Project, but they continued to use the *Bulletin* to petition for the United States to surrender its nuclear arsenal to international control. According to Sudoplatov, this kind of work was for the benefit of the Soviets.

"[Soviet politician and security chief Lavrentiy] Beria said we should think how to use Oppenheimer, Szilard and others around them in the peace campaign against nuclear armament. Disarmament and the inability to impose nuclear blackmail would deprive the United States of its advantage," wrote Sudoplatov. Sudoplatov said his spymasters knew the lobby efforts of the *Bulletin* editors would be a "crucial factor in establishing the new world order after the war, and we took advantage of this."[113]

Another *Bulletin* founding sponsor, Edward U. Condon, was mentioned by FBI director J. Edgar Hoover in a May 1947 letter as having contact with an alleged spy who had passed information to the Soviets from 1941 to 1944.[114]

At the time Holdren worked on the *Bulletin* in 1984, communist and socialist sympathizers still occupied the magazine's masthead.[115] The *New Zeal* blog notes the *Bulletin*'s board of directors in 1984 included: Chairman Aaron Adler, who also served on the board of the Chicago Center for U.S./USSR Relations and Exchanges, alongside Larry McGurty of the Communist Party USA. Adler was also a member of what *New Zeal* labels a Communist Party front, the Chicago Committee to Defend the Bill of Rights. He was also involved in a committee to celebrate the hundredth birthday of Communist Party member Paul Robeson. Bernard Weissbourd, a former Manhattan Project scientist who later served on the transition oversight committee for incoming Chicago mayor Harold Washington, was active in Communist Party fronts. Weissbourd's son, Robert M. Weissbourd, later served as chairman of the Obama for America Campaign Urban and Metropolitan Policy Committee and on the Obama Transition Housing and Urban Development Agency Review Team in 2008. Ruth Adams, *Bulletin* editor, served in the 1960s on the Advisory Committee of the Hyde Park Community Peace Center. Other center members included lifelong communist front activist Robert Havighurst, communist activist and radical Trotskyist Sydney Lens, and Quentin Young, an avowed communist who has advised Obama on health care.

The *Bulletin* is not Holdren's only Soviet connection that calls into question his partiality with regard to nuclear and national security matters. These authors found that Obama's "science" czar visited the Soviet Union during the Cold War as vice chairman of a group whose founder was accused of providing vital nuclear information that helped the Soviets build an atom bomb. The original leaders of the group, the Federation of American Scientists, or FAS, also served on the board of the *Bulletin of the Atomic Scientists*.[116]

The FAS is a nonprofit organization formed in 1945 by scientists from Oppenheimer's compromised Manhattan Project. Like the *Bulletin*, the FAS has long petitioned for nuclear disarmament. Just after President Reagan's March 1983 "Star Wars" speech, in which he proposed a missile-defense shield to protect the U.S. home front, a group of Soviet academicians sent a letter to the U.S. scientific community asking about the feasibility of such a shield. The only group that responded directly to the Soviet scientists was FAS, leading to an invitation to visit the Soviet Union from Evgeny Velikhov, director of the Soviets' scientific Kurchatov Institute.[117]

Physicist David W. Hafemeister relates in his book *Physics and Nuclear Arms Today* how he was part of the FAS delegation to the USSR along with Holdren, who at the time was a professor at the University of California at Berkeley. Scientist Leo Szilard, a member of the Manhattan Project, was a principal founder of FAS. Szilard, as we just detailed, was accused of providing vital information to the Soviets that helped them build an atomic bomb.

A key group to watch is the Pugwash Conferences on Science and World Affairs (PCSWA), an international group of scientists who promote arms control. From 1987 to 1997, Holdren chaired the executive committee of Pugwash. The group has been accused of promoting the Soviet agenda at the expense of the United States. The group's official mission is to "seek ways of eliminating nuclear weapons and reducing the threat of war."[118] The first conference was held in July 1957 in Pugwash, Nova Scotia, hence the name of the organization. The group excelled at establishing communication between warring countries, playing a role in opening dialogue during the Cold War, Cuban Missile Crisis, and even the Vietnam War. The group provided background work for the Non-Proliferation Treaty of 1968, the Anti-Ballistic Missile Treaty of 1972, the Biological Weapons Convention of 1972, and the Chemical Weapons Convention in 1993. It won a Nobel Peace Prize in 1995 jointly with its founder Joseph Rotblat for efforts on nuclear disarmament.

But the group faced mounting criticism during the Cold War, including charges it was serving as a front conference for the Soviets, focusing most of its energy on disarming the United States while largely ignoring Soviet armament.[119] Indeed, it was reportedly tied to Soviet funding via the Soviet propaganda outfit World Peace Council (WPC), an organization said to have received $63 million in Soviet funding.[120] The WPC organized international "peace conferences" that focused its ire on Western armaments and weapons tests while it refrained from criticizing Russian arms, just as Pugwash was accused of doing. In 1980, the House Permanent Select Committee on Intelligence received reports of six peace groups that were "closely connected" with the World Peace Council. One of those groups was Pugwash.[121]

In 1989, Holdren, as chair of the group, organized the first Pugwash conference to be held on U.S. soil since 1970.[122] The theme of the conference, held at the Cambridge Marriott Hotel in Massachusetts, was "Building Global Security Through Cooperation."

Interestingly, in December 2008, Jayantha Dhanapala and Paolo Cotta-Ramusino, the president and secretary general of Pugwash, respectively, sent a letter to Holdren congratulating him on his appointment to the Obama administration while expressing hope that the lines of communication would be kept open. The letter also informed Holdren that their group had expanded its activities to several new fronts, including Iran, Pakistan, and the Israeli-Palestinian issue:[123]

> Your many efforts on behalf of Pugwash, beginning with your first Pugwash conference in Aulanko, Finland, in August 1973, and including your tenure as chair of the Pugwash Executive Committee [1987–97] and your acceptance speech for the Nobel Peace Prize in 1995, have been indispensable and inspirational over the years.
>
> In much the same way that you and colleagues such as Vitalii Goldanski and Yevgeni Velikhov kept open lines of communication between the US and Soviet Union during the Cold War, so is Pugwash now doing the same between the US and Iran, at the very highest levels, as well as between India and Pakistan over the Kashmir issue, between Israel, the Palestinians and the Arab countries, and between the parties involved in seeking to resolve the DPRK [North Korean] nuclear issue.
>
> We look forward to working with you and the Obama administration in the years ahead.

The hope of working together may have been further cemented in July 2010 when Obama made the stealth appointment of Pugwash participant Philip Coyle as associate director for national security in the White House Office of Science and Technology, where Coyle would answer directly to Holdren. Coyle served during the Carter administration as principal deputy assistant secretary for defense programs in the Department of Energy, where he had oversight responsibility for the nuclear weapons testing programs of the Defense Department.[124] He also served in 2005 on the nine-member Defense Base Closure and Realignment Commission; he was appointed by President George W. Bush and nominated by Nancy Pelosi. The commission was responsible for determining which U.S. military bases and facilities would be closed or realigned.[125]

In 2003, Coyle participated in the Pugwash conference, as did Holdren.

Coyle led a workshop titled "Preserving the Non-Weaponisation of Space."[126] On Coyle's new Obama administration position, the Heritage Foundation contended, "Coyle's new title may have the word 'science' in it, but he is in fact the 'high priest' of missile defense denialism."[127]

At *National Review Online*, Foreign Policy Initiative executive director Jamie Fly noted: "Coyle made a name for himself by questioning whether missile defense is technically possible, contradicting a proven track record of repeated successes by the Pentagon's Missile Defense Agency."[128]

Indeed, in 2006, just prior to North Korea test firing a volley of ballistic missiles, Coyle wrote:

> The ground-based system hasn't had a successful flight intercept test in four years. In the two most recent attempts, the interceptor never got off the ground and failed to leave its silo. And in the only other recent attempt, the kill vehicle—the pointy-end of the interceptor—failed to separate from its booster and missed its target.
>
> A question the press might ask President Bush is, "So long as you resist face-to-face meetings with North Korea, aren't you just giving them more time to develop a missile that can reach the U.S.?"
>
> Or to put it differently, "Mr. President, which do you think will take longer: North Korea to develop a missile that can reach the U.S.? Or the U.S. to develop a missile defense we can rely on?"[129]

Coyle then claimed in House testimony that deterrence will work to ensure that North Korea would never attack South Korea, Japan, or the United States.[130] Coyle must have been shocked when South Korea in May 2010 accused North Korea of torpedoing one of its warships.[131] He may have also been surprised in late November 2010 when North Korea provocatively fired dozens of artillery shells at one of South Korea's border islands, killing two marines.[132]

John Noonan of the *Weekly Standard* dubbed Coyle the "high priest of nay saying."[133]

There's an inherent danger in placing ideologues, particularly those in favor of treaties which negotiate away U.S. security, in high level defense posts. Ballistic missile defense, whether it is Obama's clumsily handled "phased, adaptive" approach or the robust system originally conceived by the Bush administration, will be our first, second, and third lines of defense as more nations develop long range missiles. Coyle's long, steadfast opposition to badly needed defensive systems, and his refusal to bend even when geo-political events dictate, make him a highly dubious candidate for such a critical White House position.

Heritage speculated that Obama pushed Coyle's appointment during a Senate recess because the administration did not want a legislative debate on Coyle's antimissile defense position at a time Obama decided to ratify the New START, the bilateral nuclear arms reduction treaty between the United States and Russia that was signed in Prague on April 8, 2010, to the likely joy of Holdren, Coyle, and their Pugwash friends.[134]

NASA, meanwhile, is not the only agency to have its budget restructured under the Obama administration. Struggling to accommodate its massive spending on bailouts, "stimulus bills," and a historic health care program, the White House has drafted plans to eliminate more than a trillion defense dollars. Already, then-Secretary of Defense Robert Gates in August 2010 canceled or cut back several dozen Pentagon weapons programs, a projected long-term savings of $330 billion, and ordered the military services and Pentagon agencies to find $100 billion in administrative cuts and efficiencies before 2015.[135]

Gates also called for the closing of the Joint Forces Command in Norfolk, Virginia. The command includes about 2,800 military and civilian positions supported by 3,000 contractors at an annual cost of $240 million. Its responsibilities include managing the allocation of global forces and running programs to press the armed services to work together on the battlefield. Gates also has proposed a 30 percent cut over three years on contractors who provide support services to the military, placed a freeze on the number of workers in his office, said he planned to eliminate at least 50 posts for generals and admirals and 150 for senior civilians, and shut down two Pentagon agencies that employ 550 more people.[136]

More massive military cutbacks may by on the way. Details of many of the proposed cuts were documented by Representative Barney Frank's Sustainable Defense Task Force in a fifty-six-page report titled *Debt, Deficits, and Defense—A Way Forward*. The task force concluded the Pentagon could cut $960 billion between 2011 and 2020. The task force recommends sweeping reductions on defense spending. The Navy will be drastically cut back to eight aircraft carriers, instead of twelve planned, and seven air wings. The overall Navy fleet will be slashed to 230 ships instead of the 313 eyed by the service. Eight ballistic missile submarines will be cut from the planned force of 14, leaving just 6. Building of nuclear attack submarines will be cut in half, leaving a force of 40 by 2020. The four active guided-missile submarines would be cut, too. Destroyer building would be frozen and the new DDG–1000 destroyer program canceled. Among other huge cuts, the naval fleet is to be reduced to 230 combat ships, eliminating 57 vessels from a current force level of 287.[137]

Army ground troops would be slashed from 562,400 to 360,000. That includes elimination of about five active-component brigade combat teams while the Army cuts back on personnel stationed in Europe and Asia, and rolling back Army and Marine Corps personnel in Iraq and Afghanistan.

The Air Force will be required to retire six fighter air wing equivalents, and at the same time build 301 fewer F-35 fighters. Procurement of the new refueling tanker and the C-17 cargo aircraft will be canceled as will the procurement of a new midair refueling tanker the Air Force has identified as one of its top acquisition priorities. Directed energy beam research and other advanced missile and space warfare defense projects will also be eliminated or curtailed.

These defense cuts contrast sharply with Obama's stated vision for the military as outlined in an April 2007 speech before the Chicago Council of Global Affairs.[138] "We must lead by building a 21st century military to ensure the security of our people and advance the security of *all people*," Obama told the crowd. His words were consistent with his endorsement of a permanent increase in the size of the military, including an additional "65,000 soldiers to the Army and 27,000 Marines."[139]

Secretary of Defense Caught in Scheme to Cede U.S. Oceans, Tied to Pro-Soviet Groups during Cold War

The drive to cut back the military and perhaps to use it for a more internationalist approach was escalated on June 22, 2011, when the Senate confirmed Leon E. Panetta to replace Robert Gates as secretary of defense. Panetta co-chaired an initiative to regulate U.S. oceans and cede them to United Nations–based international law. He is tied to several groups that form the heart of the radical network, and that, astonishingly, were accused of pro-Soviet, antiwar activity during the height of the Cold War.

Until his appointment as CIA director in 2009 by Obama, Panetta co-chaired the Joint Ocean Commission Initiative.[140] The initiative is the partner of Citizens for Global Solutions, or CGS, in a push to ratify U.S. laws and regulations governing the seas.[141]

The ocean initiative bills itself as a bipartisan, collaborative group that aims to "accelerate the pace of change that results in meaningful ocean policy reform."[142] Among its main recommendations is that the United States should put its oceans up for regulation to the UN Convention on the Law of the Sea.[143] That UN convention defines the rights and responsibilities of nations in their use of the world's oceans, establishing guidelines for businesses, the environment, and the management of marine natural resources.[144]

Other recommendations of Panetta's Joint Ocean Commission Initiative include:

★   The administration and Congress should establish a national ocean policy. The administration and Congress should support regional, ecosystem-based approaches to the management of oceans, coasts, and Great Lakes.
★   Congress should strengthen and reauthorize the Coastal Zone Management Act.
★   Congress should strengthen the Clean Water Act.

The Joint Ocean Commission Initiative Leadership Council[145] includes the former co-chair of Obama's White House transition team John Podesta, who serves as president and CEO of the Soros-funded Center for American Progress, which, as detailed in this book, is reportedly highly influential in advising the White House on policy. Podesta served as co-chair of Obama's presidential transition team.

According to its own literature, Citizens for Global Solutions, a key partner to Panetta's oceans initiative, envisions a "future in which nations work together to abolish war, protect our rights and freedoms, and solve the problems facing humanity that no nation can solve alone." CGS states it works to "build the political will in the United States" to achieve this global vision.[146] The organization currently works on issues that fall into five general areas: U.S. global engagement, global health and environment, peace and security, international law and justice, and international institutions.

CGS is a member organization and supporter of the World Federalist Movement, which seeks a one-world government.[147] The World Federalist Movement considers the CGS to be its U.S. branch.[148]

The movement openly brings together organizations and individuals that support the establishment of a global federal system of strengthened and democratized institutions with plenary constitutional power accountable to the citizens of the world and a division of international authority among separate global agencies.

The movement's headquarters are located near the UN building in New York City. A second office is near the International Criminal Court in The Hague. The locations are significant, since the movement heavily promotes the United Nations and is the coordinator of various international projects, such as the Coalition for the International Criminal Court and the Responsibility to Protect military doctrine.

U.S. Military Now Fights for United Nations?

The connection of Panetta's ocean initiative to a global center coordinating the Responsibility to Protect doctrine should have raised questions regarding his defense strategy at the time that the Senate unanimously voted to place him at the leadership of the Pentagon.

Obama has cited military doctrine as the main justification for U.S. and international air strikes against Libya. Indeed, the Libya bombings have been widely regarded as a test of Responsibility to Protect.[149]

Responsibility to Protect, or Responsibility to Act, as cited by Obama, is a set of principles, now backed by the United Nations, based on the idea that sovereignty is not a privilege but a responsibility that can be revoked if a country is accused of "war crimes," "genocide," "crimes against humanity," or "ethnic cleansing."[150]

The term "war crimes" has at times been indiscriminately used by various UN-backed international bodies, including the International Criminal Court, or ICC, which applied it to Israeli antiterror operations in the Gaza Strip. It has been feared that the ICC could be used to prosecute U.S. troops.[151]

Soros's Open Society is one of only three nongovernmental funders of the Global Centre for the Responsibility to Protect, the main body behind the doctrine. Government sponsors include Australia, Belgium, Canada, the Netherlands, Norway, Rwanda, and the United Kingdom.[152]

The center's patrons include former UN secretary-general Kofi Annan, former president of Ireland Mary Robinson, and South African activist Desmond Tutu.[153] Robinson and Tutu have made solidarity visits to the Hamas-controlled Gaza Strip as members of a group called the Elders, which includes former President Jimmy Carter.[154]

Annan once famously stated, "State sovereignty, in its most basic sense, is being redefined—not least by the forces of globalization and international cooperation. States are . . . instruments at the service of their peoples and not vice versa."[155]

The Carr Center for Human Rights Policy served on the advisory board of the 2001 commission that originally founded Responsibility to Protect. The center was led at the time by Samantha Power, the National Security Council special adviser to Obama on human rights. She reportedly heavily influenced Obama in consultations leading to the decision to bomb Libya.[156]

That 2001 commission is called the International Commission on Intervention and State Sovereignty. It invented the term "Responsibility to Protect" while defining its guidelines.[157] Also on the advisory board was Arab League secretary general Amr Moussa as well as Palestinian legislator Hanan Ashrawi, a staunch denier of the Holocaust who long served as the deputy of late Palestinian Liberation Organization leader Yasser Arafat.[158]

Soros himself outlined the fundamentals of Responsibility to Protect in a 2004 *Foreign Policy* magazine article titled "The People's Sovereignty: How a New Twist on an Old Idea Can Protect the World's Most Vulnerable Populations."[159] In the article, Soros said "true sovereignty belongs to the people, who in turn delegate it to their governments.

"If governments abuse the authority entrusted to them and citizens have no opportunity to correct such abuses, outside interference is justified," Soros wrote. "By specifying that sovereignty is based on the people, the international community can penetrate nation-states' borders to protect the rights of citizens.

"In particular, the principle of the people's sovereignty can help solve two modern challenges: the obstacles to delivering aid effectively to sovereign states, and the obstacles to global collective action dealing with states experiencing internal conflict."

Responsibility doctrine founder Ramesh Thakur recently advocated for a "global rebalancing" and "international redistribution" to create a "New World Order."

In a piece in the March 2010 issue of the *Ottawa Citizen* newspaper, Thakur wrote: "Toward a new world order, Westerners must change lifestyles and support international redistribution."[160] He was referring to a United Nations–brokered international climate treaty in which he argued, "Developing countries must reorient growth in cleaner and greener directions."

In the opinion piece, Thakur discussed recent military engagements and how the financial crisis has impacted the United States. "The West's bullying approach to developing nations won't work anymore—global power is shifting to Asia. . . . A much-needed global moral rebalancing is in train."

Thakur continued: "Westerners have lost their previous capacity to set standards and rules of behavior for the world. Unless they recognize this reality, there is little prospect of making significant progress in deadlocked international negotiations." Thakur contended "the demonstration of the limits to U.S. and NATO power in Iraq and Afghanistan has left many less fearful of 'superior' Western power."

Panetta's Concerning Record

Panetta's concerning ties, meanwhile, do not stop at his oceans initiative. He also keynoted the conference of a pro-Soviet, antiwar group during the height of the Cold War. Panetta also honored the founding member of the group, the Women's International League for Peace and

Freedom, or WILPF, which was once named by the State Department as a "Soviet front."[161]

On April 11, 1984, Panetta, then a California congressman, entered into the congressional record a tribute in honor of WILPF's founding member, Lucy Haessler. In the record, Panetta praised Haessler as "one of the most dedicated peace activists I have ever known."

Panetta recognized that Haessler traveled to the Soviet Union as a member of the WILPF: "She has also participated in peace conferences conducted by WILPF and the Woman's International Democracy Foundation in France, the Soviet Union, Poland, and East Germany," read Panetta's congressional praise.

Panetta hailed Haessler for her activism against the pending deployment of U.S. missiles to counter the Soviet buildup: "She joined thousands of dedicated peace activists where she expressed her concern about the impending deployment of Cruise missiles and Pershing II missiles in Europe," he noted.

Haessler's WILPF took on a pro-Soviet stance, although later the State Department dropped its designation as a Soviet front group. The WILPF sponsored frequent exchange visits with the Soviet Women's Committee and against "anti-Sovietism" while calling for President Reagan to "stop the arms race."

Panetta's relationship with Haessler and the WILPF goes back to at least June 1979, when he was the keynote speaker of WILPF's Biennial Conference at the University of California at Santa Cruz. The conference was arranged by Haessler. WILPF's literature notes the conference honored Ava and Linus Pauling, who were prominent supporters of ending nuclear proliferation.[162]

"This successful event elevated Santa Cruz WILPF permanently into the orbit of outstanding WILPF conferences," recalled WILPF life member Ruth Hunter in a tribute to Haessler.

Haessler, meanwhile, associated with communist activists. In April 1966, she sponsored a testimonial dinner in New York in honor of pro-communist scientist Herbert Aptheker. The dinner also marked the second anniversary of the American Institute for Marxist Studies. Most speakers, organizers, and sponsors were known members or supporters of the Communist Party USA.

Panetta later stated he was not aware of the WILPF's communist background and was merely praising Haessler's antiwar actions.

Panetta has a larger history of ties to pro-Soviet groups. He has come under newfound scrutiny for his ties to a pro-Marxist think tank accused of anti-CIA activity.[163] The Institute for Policy Studies, or IPS, has long faced criticism for positions some say attempt to undermine U.S. national security and for its cozy relationship with the Soviet Union during the Cold War.[164] A review of the voting record for Panetta, a member of Congress from 1977 to 1993, during the period in question shows an apparent affinity for IPS's agenda. The IPS is currently funded by philanthropist George Soros's Open Society Institute.

Panetta was reportedly on IPS's official 20th Anniversary Committee, celebrated on April 5, 1983. In his authoritative book *Covert Cadre: Inside the Institute for Policy Studies*, S. Steven Powell writes:

> April 5, 1983, IPS threw a large twentieth-anniversary celebration to raise funds. On the fundraising committee for the event were 14 then-current members of the U.S. House of Representatives, including Leon E. Panetta (D-Calif.), chairman of Budget Process Task Force of the House Committee on Budget (chairman of Subcommittee on Police and Personnel, Ninety-ninth Congress).[165]

Researcher Trevor Loudon, a specialist on communism, obtained and posted IPS literature documenting members of the 20th Anniversary Committee, which also included Senators Chris Dodd (D-Conn.) and Gary Hart (D-Colo.) with an endorsement by Senator Mark Hatfield(R-Ore.). Besides Panetta, congressmen on the IPS committee included Les Aspin (D-Wis.), George E Brown Jr. (D-Calif.), Philip Burton (D-Calif.), George Crockett (D-Mich.), Tom Harkin (D-Iowa), and Richard Ottinger (D-N.Y.).

In addition to serving on the IPS committee, Panetta supported the IPS's "Coalition for a New Foreign and Military Policy Line" in 1983.[166]

Powell wrote that in the 1980s Panetta commissioned the IPS to produce an "alternative" budget that dramatically cut defense spending.[167]

"The congressional supporters for the Institute for Policy Studies included many of those who biennially commission I.P.S. to produce an 'Alternative' Budget that dramatically cuts defense spending while increasing the spending for social welfare to levels only dreamed of by Karl Marx," wrote Powell in the November 1983 issue of the *American Opinion*.[168]

"In this pact of I.P.S. intimates [are] such luminaries as . . . Leon Panetta (D.-California), Chairman of the Budget Process Task Force," wrote Powell.

The IPS, meanwhile, has long maintained controversial views and its pro-Marxist line on foreign policy. It was founded in 1963 by two former governmental workers, Marcus Raskin and Richard Barnet. In his 1988 book *Far Left of Center: The American Radical Left Today*, Harvey Klehr, professor of politics and history at Emory University, said that IPS "serves as an intellectual nerve center for the radical movement, ranging from nuclear and anti-intervention issues to support for Marxist insurgencies."[169]

The FBI labeled the group a "think factory" that helps to "train extremists who incite violence in U.S. cities, and whose educational research serves as a cover for intrigue, and political agitation."[170]

IPS has been accused of serving as a propaganda arm of the USSR and even a place where agents from the Soviet embassy in Washington came to convene and strategize.[171] In his book *The KGB and Soviet Disinformation: An Insider's View*, Ladislav Bittman, a former KGB agent, called the IPS a Soviet misinformation operation at which Soviet insiders worked.[172]

Brian Crozier, director of the London-based Institute for the Study of Conflict, described IPS as the "perfect intellectual front for Soviet activities which would be resisted if they were to originate openly from the KGB."[173]

The IPS has been implicated in anti-CIA activity. The Center for Security Studies was a 1974 IPS spin-off and strove to compromise the effectiveness of U.S. intelligence agencies, according to *Discover the Networks*.[174] The mastheads of two anti-FBI and anti-CIA publications, *Counterspy* and the *Covert Action Information Bulletin*, were heavy with IPS members.[175]

Further, in 1976, the group's former director, Robert Borosage, penned the book, *The CIA File*, and co-authored *The Lawless State: The Crimes of the U.S. Intelligence Agencies*, both attacking the CIA. He also ran the so-called CIA watchdog, Center for National Security Studies.[176]

The group has been particularly concerned with researching U.S. defense industries and arms sales policies.

In March 1982, IPS's Arms Race and Nuclear Weapons Project, or ARNWP, was directed by William M. Arkin, who had been compiling a book of U.S. nuclear weapons data with "everything from where the bombs are stored to where weapons delivery systems are cooked up."[177]

In 1984, the project's activities were described thus: The IPS's ARNWP "compiles and publishes data on where bombs are stored, where delivery systems are worked on, and so on." The research was said to "serve as a data base for activist groups opposed to the development and the storage of such weapons in their geographic areas."[178]

In May 1983, at Minneapolis, ARNWP conducted a joint disarmament seminar with the Institute of the U.S.A. and Canada, which was described as "a Soviet agency promoting 'active measures' abroad," author Vojtech Mastny, a specialist in Cold War history, writes. John Barron, an expert on the KGB, said fully a third of the staff were regular KGB officers. Another participant, the U.S.S.R.-U.S.A. Friendship Society, was said by the FBI to be using "active measures" against the United States, Mastny states.[179]

Here, a quick review of Panetta's political track record is telling. Writing in the *New American* in June 2011, Christian Gomez notes, "Careful observation of former Rep. Panetta's record in the U.S. House of Representatives reveals a history of votes perceivable as in contrast with U.S. national security objectives, which if confirmed as Secretary of Defense, may compromise U.S. national defense."[180]

Indeed, as Gomez outlined, Panetta voted against the reaffirmation of the Mutual Defense Treaty with Taiwan and in support of foreign aid to the Sandinista government of communist Nicaragua. The lawmaker supported extending most-favored nation status to the Soviet Union and Warsaw Pact states during the height of the Cold War, and voted to cede control of the Panama Canal to the pro-Soviet Panamanian government.

Panetta also vocally supported various communist regimes throughout Latin America as well as Soviet-backed paramilitary groups in the region. He endorsed the IPS-supported bill H.R. 2760, known as the Boland-Zablocki bill, to terminate U.S. efforts to resist communism in Nicaragua.

Panetta slammed what he called President Ronald Reagan's "illegal and extraordinary vicious wars against the poor of Nicaragua, El Salvador, and Guatemala." He supported the Soviet satellite government of Daniel Ortega in Nicaragua and was a vocal opponent of Chile's anti-communist government.

On July 19, 1983, on the floor of the House, Panetta condemned what he called the "U.S.-sponsored covert action against Nicaragua," stating that it was "among the most dangerous aspects of the [Reagan] administration's policy in Central America."

Interestingly, Panetta, who served as the chief of the CIA since his appointment to that post in 2009, once proposed allowing Congress to conduct spot checks at its discretion of the country's sensitive intelligence agency.[181]

In 1987, Panetta as a congressman introduced the CIA Accountability Act, which would have made the CIA subject to audits by the General Accounting Office, the investigative arm of Congress.[182]

Panetta's legislation would have allowed the comptroller general, who directs the GAO, to audit any financial transactions of the CIA and evaluate all of the agency's activities either at his own initiative or at the request of the congressional intelligence committees.

The CIA is the only government agency that contests the authority of the comptroller general to audit its activities, citing the covert aspects of its operation.[183]

While the Obama administration currently is cutting defense budgets, the White House has been advocating for an increased U.S. role in the UN and other international forums. Indeed, there is evidence the Obama administration may seek to join the UN's International Criminal Court, which could place U.S. military doctrine under UN judgment and could prosecute American citizens and soldiers for "war crimes" and other offenses.[184]

Obama has long favored the use of international forums such as the UN to solve conflicts. At his 2007 speech to the Chicago foreign affairs council, Obama proposed an increase in U.S. foreign aid spending to $50 billion by 2012.[185] During a September 2009 address to the UN, Obama called for a "new era" of world engagement and challenged other nations to match his efforts to change the U.S. relationship with the rest of the world, declaring that the task of solving global crises "cannot be solely America's endeavor."[186] Hailing a new era in the United States' relationship with other nations, Obama outlined some of the major changes he said his administration has made. They include the banning of torture; the order to close the detention center at Guantanamo Bay, Cuba; the appointment of a special envoy for the Middle East with the goal of a two-state peace agreement; and the fresh investment in combating "climate change." In return, Obama said, the United States expects help from others in addressing these issues. "Those who used to chastise America for acting alone in the world cannot now stand by and wait for America to solve the world's problems alone," he said. "We have sought—in word and deed—a new era of engagement with the world. Now is the time for all of us to take our share of responsibility for a global response to global challenges."[187]

Obama's belief in global engagement has seemingly colored many of the president's foreign policy decisions, such as his call for UN sanctions against Iran as opposed to military force, or his recommending UN censure of North Korea in May 2010 after that country was accused of a deadly torpedo attack on a South Korean warship, a brazen attack against a U.S. ally.[188] There have also been reports the Obama administration may support a Palestinian declaration of statehood at the UN if the Palestinian Authority and Israel fail to reach an agreement.[189]

In examining the current U.S. approach to the UN, it is worthwhile to investigate Obama's assistant secretary of state for population, refugees and migration, Eric P. Schwartz,[190] who, it turns out, previously served as the director of a George Soros–funded organization that promoted global governance. Schwartz also coordinated meetings on behalf of Obama's transition team with a group that advocates placing more blue United Nations helmets on U.S. troops and coercing the United States to join the UN's International Criminal Court.

A 2009 report by Cliff Kincaid, president of America's Survival, Inc., warned that joining the ICC "could spark a revolt in the U.S. Armed Forces." Kincaid wrote, "Schwartz and his associates are clearly laying the groundwork for the Obama Administration's acceptance of and membership in the International Criminal Court."[191]

Prior to his appointment to the State Department last year, Schwartz served as executive director of the Connect U.S. Fund, a Soros-funded and affiliated organization. The group promotes global governance and states on its website its mission is to influence "policy through integrative collaborative grant making on human rights, non-proliferation, climate change and development, and effective foreign assistance."[192]

The Connect U.S. Fund provides grants to pro-UN groups such as Human Rights First, which states it used top military brass to secure

U.S. politicians' commitments against torture. Another grantee, the Center for Victims of Torture, produced a draft executive order against torture endorsed by prominent national security figures.[193] Months later, a virtually identical executive order was issued by Obama.[194] Groups funded by Schwartz's organization put together a January 2009 national conference call to promote a "Responsible U.S. Global Engagement" agenda for Obama's new administration.[195]

Schwartz himself has authored numerous op-eds in major national newspapers calling for more U.S. global engagement, such as a piece published in the *New York Times* in September 2007 headlined, "America's Eroding Global Leadership."[196]

Schwartz previously worked under Bill Clinton's national security adviser, Sandy Berger, in a position that, he boasted on his Connect U.S. Fund website bio, allowed him to initiate and manage "the White House review that resulted in U.S. signature of the Rome Statute of the International Criminal Court," which would subject U.S. citizens to international prosecution for "war crimes."[197]

Later, President Bush's ambassador to the UN John Bolton led the effort for the United States to pull out of the International Criminal Court, a victory Bolton touted as the "happiest moment" of his political career until that point.[198]

Schwartz's assistant at the Connect U.S. Fund, Heather B. Hamilton, who now serves as executive director at the fund, led the group's efforts to lobby against Bush's appointment of Bolton—activism about which she boasts on her official Connect U.S. Fund bio.[199]

While Schwartz was serving Obama's transition team as adviser on UN issues, he coordinated several meetings with the Washington Working Group on the International Criminal Court, which wants the United States to reenter that agreement. The Working Group is a project of the Citizens for Global Solutions, or CGS, a grassroots organization that envisions a "future in which nations work together to abolish war, protect our rights and freedoms, and solve the problems facing humanity that no nation can solve alone."[200] Hamilton, Schwartz's deputy, served as executive vice president of CGS. The CGS mission states that it seeks "More Blue (U.N.) Helmets on U.S. Troops."[201]

On a CGS blog post that has since been removed, but was documented by Kincaid's organization, the group says that in a meeting with Schwartz, it not only discussed more UN helmets on U.S. troops, but also asked that Obama pay $1.6 billion to the UN for U.S. "arrears" to the UN; lift the cap on payments to the UN for UN military operations; ensure "adequate resources" for and increase U.S. participation in UN military activities; restrict the use of the U.S. veto at the UN so UN involvement in international conflicts and situations can be increased; and support expansion of UN departments.

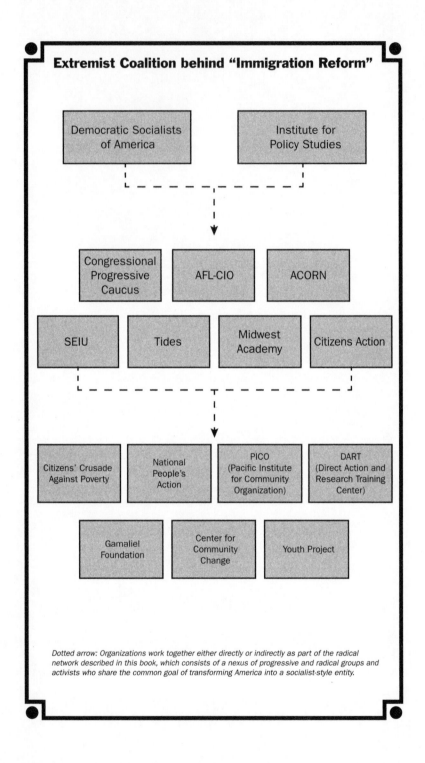

Extremist Coalition behind "Immigration Reform"

Democratic Socialists of America

Institute for Policy Studies

Congressional Progressive Caucus

AFL-CIO

ACORN

SEIU

Tides

Midwest Academy

Citizens Action

Citizens' Crusade Against Poverty

National People's Action

PICO (Pacific Institute for Community Organization)

DART (Direct Action and Research Training Center)

Gamaliel Foundation

Center for Community Change

Youth Project

Dotted arrow: Organizations work together either directly or indirectly as part of the radical network described in this book, which consists of a nexus of progressive and radical groups and activists who share the common goal of transforming America into a socialist-style entity.

chapter ten

AMNESTY SHAMNESTY

Immigration reform is one of the most important issues of our time. Documenting millions of illegal immigrants and putting them on the path to citizenship can fundamentally transform our country in so many obvious ways. The radical left network knows this and it has hijacked the issue of immigration reform as a cornerstone of its socialist goal of altering the very fabric of our nation's being.

President Obama has made clear he wants his activist agenda to include comprehensive immigration reform, or amnesty, for millions of illegal immigrants. With his poll numbers seemingly in a long-term slump, some analysts are arguing Obama's mandate for massive progressive change has been exhausted over his deeply unpopular stimulus, Obamacare, and financial reforms. The assumption seems to be Obama will have to wait for a second mandate in 2012 to attempt to advance further ideological aims, including immigration reform.

The radical network, however, excels at lying in wait, evolving and perfecting its assault so that when the right vehicle arrives, whether it's Obama or someone else, it is ready to strike, in this case to change the nation's immigration policy. Here you will see how today's immigration reform policies and the outside groups pushing that agenda originated with Marxist-socialist ideology, with much help from Saul Alinsky. We will reveal the untold history of immigration reform, a story that must be made known to understand how we arrived at the current state of affairs. Then we will thoroughly unmask the intent and radical ties of the major U.S. immigration reform groups as well as the current and future legislation aimed at remaking our country.

The backstory to movement toward immigration "reform" by progressive groups—and the Obama-Biden immigration blueprint—begins in the 1960s with the John F. Kennedy and Lyndon B. Johnson administrations and the advent of community action programs. We must first review these initiatives since it is in this tradition that the current march toward amnesty finds its roots.

During the era of the New Frontier, Robert F. Kennedy's greatest contribution was the concept of community action.[1] The Community Action Program was the centerpiece of President Lyndon B. Johnson's War on Poverty programs. However, Community Action has been described as a failure from the beginning due to a clause inserted into the poverty bill by Richard W. Boone, one of Kennedy's *guerrillas* on the President's Committee on Juvenile Delinquency (PCJD). The clause required *"maximum feasible participation* of residents of the areas and members of the groups served" (that is, a participation clause commanding involvement of the poor) in local community action agencies (CAA). The phrase is said to have been invented by Boone, who used it repeatedly until it was incorporated into the Economic Opportunity Act.[2]

Boone and fellow guerrillas who worked for David Hackett, PCJD's executive director, helped plan Kennedy's proposed National Service Corps, a project that found its way into the War on Poverty as VISTA (Volunteers in Service to America), a voluntary domestic Peace Corps. The National Service exercise led to the expansion of the CAAs, including promotion via a national tour arranged by Boone to the so-called "poverty 'pockets.'"[3]

The Community Action Program exemplified Robert Kennedy's idea that enlisting the poor to participate in the CAAs would provide them with jobs, money, and investment in the process. What was apparent to those involved with Community Action, though, was that no one really intended that the poor would actually run the programs.[4]

There was an immediate battle for resources and control of the CAAs. The War on Poverty, in one observer's view, was reduced to "an ugly series of ugly brawls."[5]

City governments nationwide accused the federal government of attempting to influence local authority. Welfare agencies asserted that involving the poor was *not feasible.* Conservatives inside and outside government branded the CAA plan as nothing more than a "blueprint for revolution."[6]

Community action was more talk than action until the passage of the Economic Opportunity Act in August 1964. LBJ put Kennedy in-law and Peace Corps director Sargent Shriver in charge of the antipoverty task force.[7]

Shriver brought in community action experts and enthusiasts, among whom were four of David Hackett's guerrillas: Boone, Jack T. Conway, Sanford Kravitz, and Frederick O'Reilly Hayes. The four had been responsible for conceptualizing and developing the new Community Action Program and necessary legislative provisions.[8]

Alinsky Organizing

Two of the guerrillas, Conway and Boone, had strong ties to Walter P. Reuther and the AFL-CIO union.

Conway had been a labor organizer from 1946 to 1961 with the United Auto Workers and was Reuther's top administrative assistant. All the men around Reuther, the late AFL-CIO labor leader Sidney Lens writes, were like him: "ex-socialists, capable, literate, devoted, [and] visionary."[9] Conway was not without experience as an organizer. In the 1930s and early 1940s, when he was a student at the University of Chicago, he had known Saul D. Alinsky, the godfather of radical community activism, although he never worked for him. It was not because Alinsky was uninterested.[10]

In an August 1980 interview, Conway said Alinsky tried to get him to go to Los Angeles for the "zoot suit riots," which broke out in 1943 between American servicemen stationed in Southern California and the Mexican-American community. Conway said he did not go because he was uninterested. He did not share Alinsky's view of community organizing and did not develop his own framework until the Community Action Program came along. He likewise turned Alinsky down when he wanted Conway to go to Minneapolis and Cleveland on community organizing efforts.

Conway describes Alinsky as a *tactician*. He says all Alinsky's methods were "organized around the devil theory, in the sense that you had to have an enemy and you had to mobilize people in opposition, and all the tactics of organizing were really built around the enemy concept."

Alinsky devoted his life to forming "organizations of the people" in hopes of giving them a voice through his agitational and coercive techniques. It is said he also hoped these types of organizations would serve as a possible basis for a future organization of society.[11]

However, the central difficulty for Alinsky organizing is "to sustain an angry mood after the initial organizing issue has passed," a March 1966 article in the *Yale Law Journal* points out. Even if a protest was successful, it did not necessarily bring fundamental change to a neighborhood. Since Alinsky groups relied upon sustained agitation, the protest group was left with nothing to do other than wait for the next protest issue to come along. Protest, the article states, becomes the organization's only business.[12]

Conway identifies himself as an institution builder. He organized key management operations for the UAW, including lobbying and public relations. Under President Kennedy he helped draft the Omnibus Housing Act of 1961. This legislation established the Department of Housing and Urban Development. During the Johnson administration, Conway was instrumental in arranging funding for both the Head Start and Job Corps programs. After two years, he left, unsurprisingly, to rejoin the labor movement.[13]

Shriver put Conway in charge of the Community Action Project in fall 1964. This included oversight, operations, and reviewing grant proposals for all CAAs.[14] Conway was left to his own devices, as the White House offered little by way of direction. Shriver relied upon his experience with the Peace Corps, while Conway relied upon his experience with the UAW to implement a plan for community action.[15]

Boone had been a member of the PCJD staff beginning in 1962. As director of policy development for the Office of Economic Opportunity, he worked closely with Conway and Shriver. Boone worked on poverty issues in both the Kennedy and Johnson administrations. He and his team had been involved in developing Head Start, Upward Bound, the Foster Grandparents Program, and Community Health Services.[16] Boone brought a special credential to his work. In Chicago, he had been an Alinsky protégé.[17]

Although it is impossible to know whether or not it was due to Boone's connection to Alinsky, Sargent Shriver invited Alinsky to participate in the study group he had formed to discuss how to organize the OEO. Also involved with the task force was modern socialist godfather Michael Harrington, then with the League for Industrial Democracy, the precursor to Students for a Democratic Society. (We discussed earlier how the modern progressive movement is modeled after Harrington's strategy of infiltration.)[18]

The Alinsky influence is a significant one. Boone held Alinsky in such high esteem that, it has been related, he kept Alinsky's picture over his desk.[19]

The question must immediately be asked why a radical community organizer, whose ideology seeks to topple the U.S. capitalist system and replace it with a socialist enterprise, would be involved in the immigrant agenda. The answer will become clear in this chapter. Indeed, a theme of our work is to demonstrate that the same radical network has infiltrated various major social and political movements with the ultimate goal of remaking our society to their socialist designs.

In 1940, direct-action activist Saul Alinsky founded the Industrial Areas Foundation in Chicago to train citizens to organize within low-income neighborhoods, particularly Mexican-American neighborhoods, often with support of a diocese of the Catholic Church. During the 1950s and 1960s, Alinsky's IAF organized in Chicago, Los Angeles, and Buffalo and Rochester, New York, and later developed national training institutes to foster a community organization network. Alinsky's work is exemplified in his two well-known books, *Reveille for Radicals* (1946) and *Rules for Radicals* (1971).[20]

Two precursors to the Community Action Program come from Chicago, Clifford Shaw's Chicago Area Project of the 1930s and Alinsky's Back of the Yards Neighborhood Council. Alinsky's Woodlawn Organization, founded in 1960, reached out during the civil rights era to the black ghetto south of the University of Chicago campus. (Woodlawn received CAP funding.)[21]

Conway talked with Alinsky a couple of times about the OEO. Alinsky, he says, was very critical; he thought the OEO was on the wrong track.[22]

Alinsky reportedly called the War on Poverty a "prize piece of political pornography" due to the dependence of CAP on the government for funding, as well as the so-called "scramble for patronage."[23]

Citizens' Crusade Against Poverty

Convinced in 1965 that the Office of Economic Opportunity was not providing social change, Boone left to become executive director of the Citizens' Crusade Against Poverty, described as an "alternative grassroots voice of the poor." CCAP, however, was not exactly a *grassroots* group. Rather, CCAP was formed from a coalition of more than one hundred liberal (progressives by today's standards) labor, civil rights, and church organizations that had been organized and were funded by the UAW to lobby for antipoverty programs.[24]

CCAP was officially founded at UAW's October 1964 convention. As early as April 1964, the UAW appropriated $100,000 to launch CCAP. In total, UAW expended $500,000 for CCAP and CAP. This was in addition to the more than $1 million the programs received from the Ford and Stern family foundations.[25]

CCAP's most significant activity was its national training program. CCAP identified and trained hundreds of ghetto and barrio leaders to function within CAP's framework. The national training program set up field sites in targeted locations (East Los Angeles, Watts in Los Angeles, and Delano in California, the Mississippi Delta, Chicago, and Newark, New Jersey).[26]

The ghettoes and barrios were familiar territory for community organizing. Alinsky's Back of the Yards organizing had been among the working-class immigrant neighborhoods—mostly Polish, but including Lithuanian and Irish—of the meatpacking houses and stockyards in Chicago.[27]

Until CCAP merged in January 1969 with the Center for Community Change, which was formed by Jack Conway, Walter P. Reuther served as CCAP chairman. Boone remained as executive director throughout.[28]

CCAP was also not without support from nonunion figures. Prominent social movement leaders such as Dr. Martin Luther King, Jr., and then League for Industrial Democracy leader and socialist icon Michael Harrington were involved. Listed among CCAP's correspondents was Saul Alinsky.[29]

When UAW spun CCAP off, the billion-dollar Ford Foundation took over full funding.[30]

It was then, as it is now, not at all unusual for private foundations to support social action groups like CCAP. Alinsky's Industrial Areas Foundation, for example, was said to depend almost entirely upon funding from other foundations and church groups.[31]

Alinsky was not averse to seeking patronage for himself. By the time his *Reveille for Radicals* came out in January 1946, he had already found his own kingmaker, Katharine Graham, whose family paper was the *Washington Post*. Six months before the book's publication, the *Post* published a six-part series, "The Orderly Revolution," on Alinsky's movement.[32]

In Chicago, Alinsky was also introduced to Bishop Bernard Sheil, who introduced him to New Yorker Marshall Field III, whose grandfather was a Chicago merchant. Field funded the beginning of Alinsky's IAF. Additionally, the *Washington Post* articles reportedly led to more funding for the IAF.[33]

The Industrial Areas Foundation is only one member of the Alinsky network of organizations. Other national organizations described as being in the Alinsky tradition are ACORN (Association for Community Reform Now), Citizen Action, National People's Action, PICO (Pacific Institute for Community Organization, now PICO National Network), Direct Action and Research Training (DART) Center, and the Chicago-based Gamaliel Foundation.

Obama Forebears

The Gamaliel Foundation is of particular interest because it provided the Alinsky tactical foundation for Barack Obama's political career in Chicago and beyond.

Like much of the radical network, Gamaliel employs coded language for socialistic redistribution of the wealth. It blandly states it believes in "shared abundance for all." The organization traces its roots to the Contract Buyers League, an African-American Group founded in 1968 to fight discrimination in housing. With its own network of affiliates in most major metropolitan areas of the Midwest, California, New York, and Pennsylvania, Gamaliel has given rise to nearly four dozen congregation-based federations, with a national clergy caucus of more than one hundred thousand members, and a women's leadership program.[34]

When Obama left New York at the end of the academic year, around June 1985, after working only three months as a community organizer for the New York Public Interest Research Group, he stepped into the Gamaliel orbit. He applied for and was hired to work as a community organizer in Chicago for the Developing Communities Project, described as a group of "about 10 poor and small black churches" that "spanned communities in Northwest Indiana, the South Suburbs and parts of the City of Chicago."[35]

While Obama provides little information about the Gamaliel Foundation—calling it nothing more than an "organizing institute working throughout the Midwest," as well as a "cooperative think tank"—there is a lot more to the story.[36]

All of Obama's trainers at Gamaliel—Gregory Galluzzo, Michael Kruglik, Gerald Kellman, and John L. McKnight—had studied Alinsky's tactics. Galluzzo, Obama's first trainer and mentor in Chicago, describes himself as an Alinsky true believer.[37]

Galluzzo writes that at the same time Gamaliel was being created, he met with Obama on a regular basis while the future U.S. president incorporated the DCP. He writes that Obama was moving DCP into action and developing its leadership structure. In July 1988 Obama told *Illinois Issues* that, while working for the DCP, he had also been a consultant and instructor for Gamaliel, which he described as the "congregation-based Alinsky-style" organization.[38]

Radical Group and Obamacare

The Center for Community Change (which brought together activists from the Community Action Program, unions, civil rights groups, and the Kennedy family) names its important partners as the Robert F. Kennedy Memorial Fund, the Ford Foundation, and leaders of the

UAW.[39] The CCAP, with its roots in the history of socialist-style immigration reform, was merged by Reuther, Conway, and the Alinskyite Boone with the Center for Community Change.[40]

Conway, CCC's founder, served as its executive director. Boone helped in the creation process of the new organization. Conway also brought David Cohen on board to lobby on behalf of the CCC. Cohen was an experienced lobbyist, having worked for the upholsterers' union and Americans for Democratic Action.[41]

Conway says at CCC he carefully tested out some of his own community organizing ideas and built what he calls community unions. He says they were very effective organizations and confirmed, in his mind, that his was a better approach to community organizing than Alinsky's.[42] When asked what the difference was between his approach and Alinsky's, Conway replied that Alinsky had intellectually shifted focus from minority groups and the disenfranchised to organizing white middle-class people.[43]

The CCC's funding comes from the Carnegie Corporation of New York, the Ford Foundation, the William Randolph Hearst Foundation, the Open Society Institute, the Rockefeller Foundation, the Tides Foundation, and others.[44] In 2002, for example, the CCC received $5.8 million from a number of foundations, including $825,000 from the Ford Foundation. The following year, CCC received in excess of $1.6 million from the Ford Foundation alone for inner-city advocacy and to train groups. Most recently, in 2010, CCC received a $1 million grant for the Ford Foundation's initiative to "increase participation of marginalized communities at all levels of civic and political life."[45]

Turning the clock back even further, to the late 1970s, CCC received generous funding from several U.S. government agencies. One source reports $2 million from the Department of Labor, $600,000 from the Community Services Administration, more than $600,000 from the Department of Housing and Urban Development (which Conway had helped create in 1961 via the Omnibus Housing Act during the Kennedy administration), and just under $1.5 million from the Department of Justice.[46]

In turn, CCC provides funding and staff support, as well as policy and organizing expertise, to inner-city groups. The CCC claims to have incubated a number of organizations.[47] CCC is currently a member of Health Care for America Now, or HCAN. The HCAN coalition not only contributed to drafting the Obamacare bill, but also lobbied for its March 2010 passage.[48]

As part of a Ford Foundation initiative, the CCC produced the 2009 book *Change Philanthropy: Candid Stories of Foundations Maximizing Results*, a road map on social justice grantmaking for foundations and nonprofits.[49]

The 2006–2007 CCC board of directors included, among others, Ron Dellums, Cecilia Muñoz, and the ever-present Obama associate and socialist activist Heather Booth, founder of the Alinsky-tactic training school, the Midwest Academy.[50]

In late November 2008, President-elect Barack Obama announced that CCC board chairman Muñoz had been selected for the position of director of intergovernmental affairs at the White House. Muñoz was senior vice president for the Office of Research, Advocacy, and Legislation at the National Council of La Raza and chairman of the board for the Coalition for Comprehensive Immigration Reform. She was also a board member of the U.S. Programs Board of the Open Society Institute and the Atlantic Philanthropies.[51]

The 2011 CCC advisory committee includes Harvard University professor Marshall Ganz and Ana Garcia-Ashley, codirector of the Civil Rights for Immigrants Department at the Gamaliel Foundation.[52] We wrote about Marshall Ganz, one of Barack Obama's advisers during the 2008 presidential campaign, in our previous book, *The Manchurian President*. Ganz is a lecturer in public policy at the Hauser Center for Nonprofit Organizations at Harvard. His background includes civil rights activism and staff membership in the Student Nonviolent Coordinating Committee. Beginning in 1965, Ganz worked with Alinsky-trained Cesar Chavez and the United Farm Workers; in 1980 Ganz became UFW's director of organizing.[53]

CCC's current board of directors includes executive director Deepak Bhargava; Heather Booth; Arlene Holt Baker, executive vice president of the AFL-CIO; Tom Chabolla, assistant to SEIU president Mary Kay Henry; and Justin Ruben, executive director of MoveOn.org.[54] Bhargava, a strong supporter of Barack Obama, for ten years worked his way around ACORN before becoming CCC executive director in 2002. Bhargava is an editorial board member for the leftist *Nation* and a National Advisory Board member of the Open Society Institute.[55]

The CCC, in conjunction with the Tides Advocacy Fund, also operates the website of Campaign to Reform Immigration for America. CRIA has a long list of campaign supporters.[56]

Please forgive us if your head is spinning by now. Once again the radical network has come full circle. A historic group with socialistic, Alinskyite origins that currently boasts ACORN, MoveOn.org activists, and Obama's socialist pal Booth not only advances immigration reform, but also had a hand in crafting Obamacare while some of its officials were appointed to the Obama administration.

And it doesn't stop there. Another Center for Community Change partner organization is the Campaign for Community Change, its voter contact and mobilization arm. The Campaign brought thousands of voters to the polls and provided programs for low-income people of color.[57]

The Campaign for Community Change claims to be an incubator organization engaged in creating *grassroots* organizations among the so-called "marginalized and disenfranchised" populations—"low-income people, immigrants and people of color." Additionally, the Campaign operates as the lobbying arm of the Center for Community Change.

The two organizations share the same staff. Deepak Bhargava doubles as the Campaign's executive director. Board members include Heather Booth; Ali Noorani, executive director of the National Immigration Forum; and Susan Sandler, daughter of philanthropists Herbert and Marion Sandler and president of Justice Matters.[58]

Spreading Young Wealth

While at Center for Community Change in the 1970s, Richard Boone established the Youth Project to help fund "anti-corporate and other elements of the left." In 1989, YP was renamed Partnership for Democracy.[59]

In his 1990 book, *Social Change Philanthropy in America*, Alan Rabinowitz focuses on the power that wealthy progressive funders have exercised since the 1960s.[60]

The Youth Project, Rabinowitz says, deserves special attention. It was created by Boone and Conway, working in conjunction with the CCC and other groups, to "provide a means by which young people with inherited wealth could channel their donations collectively and effectively."[61]

Significantly, Rabinowitz writes, those who were involved with YP in the beginning have gone on to work as leaders and executive directors in a number of organizations. Among these are Boone at the Field Foundation, Steve Kest at ACORN, the founders of the Tides Foundation and the Tides Center, Drummond Pike and Wade Rathke, a 1960s activist and founder of ACORN; Margery Tabankin, former executive director of the ARCA Foundation (R. J. Reynolds tobacco money) and current executive director of the Streisand Foundation and Steven Spielberg's Righteous Persons Foundation, and current board member with the Institute for America's Future; and Heather Booth at the Midwest Academy and Citizen Action.[62]

The YP also worked closely with the Democratic Socialists of America–linked, George Soros–funded Institute for Policy Studies.[63]

Over the years, the YP helped fund numerous organizations. In 1980, for example, the Youth Project provided financial support to the Council on Economic Priorities, Democracy Project, and Institute for Policy Studies, as well as IPS-related entities such as the socialist-leaning newspaper *In These Times*.[64]

The YP shut down in 1992 due to financial and organizational problems.[65]

Grant Money Laundering 101

The Youth Project associate director in the late 1960s was California left-wing activist Drummond Pike. The Center for Community Change/Youth Project, a pass-through operation, helped "plant the seeds of later tactics in Pike's mind of rich young heirs who financed poor young activists in anti-business community organizing," Ron Arnold writes in his *Left-Tracking Library*.[66] A long list of early progressive foundations gave Pike "his first big-money connections," Arnold writes.

Pike founded the Tides Foundation in 1976 as a public charity, not as a private foundation. Pike's operation was set up as a public charity that receives money from donors and then funnels it to the recipients of its choice. Tides has provided an almost unprecedented amount of money to organized left groups, including ACORN. Meanwhile, Tides created what Arnold characterizes as a haven for nongovernmental organizations not desirous of creating their own tax-exempt organizations. Thus Tides has "nurtured literally hundreds of new groups to plague the resource class and rural communities," Arnold writes.[67]

The Tides Foundation and the Tides Center do "two things better than any other foundation or charity in the U.S. today," reports ActivistCash.com, the creation of the Center for Consumer Freedom. Tides "routinely obscures the sources of its tax-exempt millions, and makes it difficult (if not impossible) to discern how the funds are actually being used."[68]

The Tides method is "one that strains the boundaries of U.S. tax law in the pursuit of its leftist, activist goals," ActivistCash explains. Here's how this works:

> In order to get an idea of the massive scale on which the Tides Foundation plays its shell game, consider that Tides has collected over $200 million since 1997, most of it from other foundations. The list of grantees who eventually received these funds includes many of the most notorious anti-consumer groups in U.S. history. . . .

For corporations and other organizations that eventually find themselves in these grantees' crosshairs, there is practically no way to find out where their money originated. For the general public, the money trail ends at Tides' front door. In many cases, even the eventual recipient of the funding has no idea how Tides got it in the first place.

The 2009 income tax return by the Tides Foundation states the organization's "primary exempt purpose is grantmaking." The 152-page form reveals 103 pages of grants and only 5 enumerating contributing foundations.[69]

"By using Tides to funnel its capital, a large public charity can indirectly fund a project with which it would prefer not to be directly identified in public," ActivistCash writes.

The Ruckus Society is one example of how funders can safely operate at an arm's-length from the organization's activities. Tides provided funds to the Ruckus Society, which "sees itself as a toolbox of experience, training, and skills" "designed to move a campaign forward."[70]

The organization's training offerings—while not necessarily promoting illegal activities—stress nonviolent direct-action techniques such as how to set up a blockade with or without equipment and how to use climbing gear. They also include instruction in how to conduct a "mock hanging," the "best ways to keep your action team covered legally," and "basic skills" required to be "an action medic, from caring for those dealing with trauma to treating people affected by chemical weapons."[71]

Why would a group of nonviolent grassroots activists be concerned with medical treatment? Perhaps the "radical assault" by Ruckus Society–trained activists—schooled in "confrontation tactics" and "guerrilla theater techniques"—who participated at the 1999 meeting of the World Trade Organization in Seattle will prove instructive. Activists "smashed store windows, set cars ablaze and did millions of dollars in property damage."[72]

But that's only the beginning. Ahead of the protest, leaders had made a deal with the police for a few hundred demonstrators to participate in a media photo op. However, according to one report, "when the moment for this photo op came, thousands of protestors rushed aggressively through the police security line and refused to submit to arrest." The police "responded with enough force to stop the violent protestors."[73]

At the Republican Convention in Philadelphia, more than three hundred people were arrested "during traffic-stopping demonstrations and sometimes violent conflicts with police," *Salon*'s Anthony York reported on August 8, 2000. Police officers said they "confiscated piano wire" and rags soaked in kerosene that were tied to chains, which they believed the protesters "planned to use to injure them," York wrote.[74]

Philadelphia police also claimed John Sellers, director of the Ruckus Society, who was arrested with both a cellphone and a PalmPilot in his possession, was working "behind the scenes as the puppet master." The police believed Sellers was the "wizard behind the curtain telling people what to do via cell phone," Ruckus program director Han Sham told York.[75]

Sellers's bail was set at $1 million after he was officially arrested for chaining himself to and turning over trash cans. Assistant District Attorney Cindy Martelli stated Sellers was "an admitted leader of this week's violent protests." Sellers was also charged with possession of an unnamed "instrument of crime, obstruction of justice, obstructing a highway, failure to disperse, recklessly endangering another person, and conspiracy."[76]

"He sets the groundwork. He sets the stage," Martelli said at Sellers's bail hearing. "He facilitates the more radical elements to accomplish their objective of violence and mayhem."[77]

The first week of November 2000, the district attorney's office dropped the charges: "'The evidence,' it said, 'just wasn't there . . .' against the alleged capo of 'violence and mayhem.'" It was reported the charges were "not even there for a misdemeanor."[78]

These are simply not the activities of nonviolent direct-action grassroots protesters. One has to wonder if those funneling their cash through Tides fully understand what it is they are funding.

At the time Pike founded Tides, he was executive director of the Shalan Foundation, engaged in similar activities of combining the funds of progressive donors and passing them along to progressive projects. Pike's sense of scale was grandiose, Jarol B. Manheim writes in *Biz-War and the Out-of-Power Elite*. "Pike realized that for the pooling of resources to work most effectively, someone would need to provide a variety of core management services, not only for the donors, but for the recipients as well," Manheim adds.[79]

The legitimacy of what Pike and his fellow west coast activists were doing was questionable, although not unheard of. Many Tides Foundation and Tides Center projects have followed.[80]

Pike was assisted in his activities by board member Wade Rathke, who in 1970 became the founder and chief organizer of the activist group ACORN. Rathke was also chief organizer in New Orleans of Local 100 of the Service Employees International Union. Rathke and Pike are the only Tides Foundation board members who also served on the board of the Tides Center, which was spun off in April 1996.[81]

We learn from Tides Center cofounder Drummond Pike how it was that he first connected with Rathke. In late June 2008, after Rathke announced he was stepping aside as ACORN's chief organizer, Pike wrote that he first met Rathke in 1972 when he (Pike) and Margery Tabankin were running the Youth Project. Tabankin was Pike's boss.[82]

By that time, Rathke had been running what became ACORN for about two years. Pike wrote that he went to Little Rock, Arkansas, to meet Rathke and surprisingly found "New thinking, new ambition, new methods." Pike invited Rathke to train some organizers in Montana—presumably funded via the Youth Project—at the Northern Plains Resource Council.[83]

The Tides Center was created to protect the foundation from possible legal action the groups it represented might encounter.[84] In early 2011 the Tides Center website boasted 216 projects nationwide. The majority, as depicted in the interactive Google map view, are concentrated along the East Coast from Maine southward to the Washington, D.C., area and on the west coast in California and in upper Oregon and Washington.[85]

In mid-September 2010, Drummond Pike stepped down after thirty-four years as head of Tides. Melissa L. Bradley, a Soros Justice Fellow who founded New Capitalist, an organization that "leverages human, financial, and social capital" and three programs for the Van Jones–founded Green for All, was named to replace Pike as CEO.[86]

Alinsky's Training Manual

It was during the Jimmy Carter administration that 1960s radicals, some of whom had been active with Students for a Democratic Society, from which Bill Ayers's Weatherman domestic terrorist group splintered, moved from being members of the New Left to the halls of government.[87]

Carter championed initiatives like the Home Mortgage Disclosure Act, through which neighborhoods could find out the pattern of bank lending in their areas. He backed the Consumer Protection Agency, long a chief objective of consumer activists. He appointed Monsignor Geno Baroni, Sam Brown, Marge Tabankin, Michael Pertschuk, Eleanor Holmes Norton, and many other citizen advocates to the administration.

The VISTA program, the Heritage Foundation reported in a 1982 paper on the New Left in government, is viewed as "so conceptually flawed that, no matter what the intent of its creators, it became during the Carter Administration an instrument for New Left activism rather than an agency to provide 'direct service' to America's poor."[88]

During the period 1977 through 1980, New Left radical activists used VISTA to funnel taxpayer dollars to anti-American organizations to carry out their own social and political agendas.[89]

Looking at VISTA is key. The VISTA program set the stage for how radical community organizing hijacks federal dollars, which demonstrates how ACORN and the socialist, Alinsky-style Midwest

Academy operate. It also provides insight into how the radical network continues to coordinate its multipronged assault on our country.

VISTA was administered by two antiwar radicals, Brown and Tabankin. Brown was in Chicago during the SDS violent riots at the August 1968 Democratic National Convention. He had been active in the radical Students for Democratic Action. Tabankin joined SDS while a student at the University of Wisconsin at Madison and helped coordinate the national student boycott against the Vietnam War in 1969.

In May 1972 she visited communist North Vietnam under the auspices of the People's Coalition for Peace and Justice. The historic PCPJ was affiliated with both the Socialist Workers Party and the Communist Party USA. She subsequently worked with the Indochina Peace Campaign with communist partisans and lifelong friends Tom Hayden and Jane Fonda. Following her return, in 1972, Tabankin served as executive director of the Youth Project.[90]

However, prior to graduating from the University of Wisconsin in 1969 (she finished her degree by mail), Tabankin was chosen as one of the first women trainees at Alinsky's IAF in Chicago. Tabankin reportedly studied for four months at IAF under the tutelage of Staughton Lynd before having to leave six months early, in June 1970, when she learned her mother had cancer. Lynd was a former Yale University professor hired to work for IAF following a December 1965 visit to Hanoi with Tom Hayden during the Vietnam War.[91]

Lynd subsequently assigned Tabankin to an Alinsky project. He sent her to Paul and Heather Booth, and their associate, Robert Creamer, to get them involved in the Campaign Against Pollution.[92]

By now it should be clear that there is a trend here, with Saul Alinsky and his tactical brand of community organizer training as a common thread. Alinsky mentored Richard Boone, Heather Booth, Staughton Lynd, Marge Tabankin, and many others.[93]

Alinsky was directly involved not only in training VISTA volunteers, but also in teaching Alinsky-style radical community organizing techniques, and his ideology pervades the VISTA program. His 1946 book, *Reveille for Radicals*, was used as the VISTA volunteer training manual.[94]

Interestingly, in June 2009 conservative talk radio host Mark Levin shared his own Alinsky book story with his audience. Fresh out of law school, Levin was hired by the incoming Reagan administration to work at ACTION. While taking account of the office space, Levin came across "big boxes," he says. "All kinds of radical literature that had been purchased by the federal taxpayer and sent to these poor communities by VISTA. And in those boxes were hundreds of copies of Saul Alinsky's *Rules for Radicals*."[95] "In other words," Levin continues, "our government was paying for a revolution in our inner cities through this agency." Tabankin had ordered the books.[96]

Clearly there was something else going on at ACTION and VISTA other than what taxpayers and Congress thought. Soon you shall see the same Alinskyite radicals hijacking the immigration cause, just as they have hijacked other economic and social causes.

Brown and Tabankin, director and deputy assistant director of ACTION respectively, promoted the National VISTA Grants Program to build, support, and expand organizations. Additionally, in early 1977, a process of roundtable discussion was initiated to determine which groups would receive grant funds. About one hundred organizations were represented, among them ACORN, Tom Hayden's Campaign for Economic Democracy (the parent organization of Students for Economic Democracy, which cosponsored the anti-apartheid rally at Occidental College at which Barack Obama reportedly delivered his first political speech), the CED-related Laurel Springs Training Center, and Midwest Academy—just the usual radical network suspects.[97]

ACORN, Organize Labor

The misuse of VISTA's funds and volunteers by ACORN, the Midwest Academy, and affiliated organizations was an amazing sleight of hand uncovered in October 1977 and reported to the House Appropriations Committee. Many of the same organizations and their leaders continue to accomplish the same feats.

In September 1977, ACORN, which had created the Community Organization Research and Action Project (CORAP) in July specifically to handle its VISTA funds, and socialist activist Booth's Midwest Academy received two of the first twelve national grants ($470,475 and $600,000, respectively) to train VISTA volunteers. The Youth Project received sixty VISTA volunteers and over $600,000 in cash.[98]

The CORAP grant provided for one hundred VISTAs. Of these, eighty were to be placed with ACORN to work with low-income people on local issues in seven states (Arkansas, Texas, Missouri, Tennessee, Louisiana, Florida, and South Dakota), according to a 1978 investigation by the House Appropriations Committee.[99]

Officers on the boards of ACORN and CORAP were the same individuals. The supervisor and assistant supervisor of the CORAP project—who were employed by CORAP full-time—also appeared on the ACORN payroll.

ACORN also received $347,616 in ACTION grant funds between September 1977 and December 1978.

The Midwest Academy funded two VISTA workers in Rhode Island found to be engaged full-time in organizing jewelry workers. Training materials from both CORAP and Midwest Academy were withdrawn due to the use of "'intemperate' and excessively confrontational language."[100]

The *Community Organizing Model* and *Community Organizing Handbook #2*, for example, included inflammatory language and "proscribed political activity." They were both deemed inappropriate for VISTA training.[101]

The lines between VISTA and several organizations receiving grant funds were obviously blurred. One case in point is the anticorporate Citizen/Labor Coalition, led by Heather Booth until 1981. It received $200,000 and eight volunteers from the Community Services

Administration, as well as $30,000 from VISTA to organize up to five hundred "low income consumers into energy activists."[102]

Another situation is Hayden's Laurel Springs Institute, which received VISTA funds in August 1978. LSI's function was clear: train activists for *electoral campaigning and community organizing*. An assessment of LSI's programs by officials revealed that LSI's training manual was not only "pronouncedly New Left in content," but also had been issued by the Midwest Academy. The manual's resource list recommended publications by such organizations as the Students for Democratic Society offshoot the North American Congress on Latin America, or NACLA.[103]

In 1966 SDS and other campus groups formed NACLA, which was headed by former SDSer Michael Locker. By the end of the year, NACLA was up and running, housed in uptown Manhattan. NACLA was funded by the United Methodist Church, the Presbyterian Church, and the Division of Youth Ministries of the National Council of Churches.[104]

NACLA's operation was to prepare for confrontational corporate campaigns of the type inspired by Saul Alinsky.[105]

It is obvious that many of ACORN's tactics have not changed much over the past three decades. Training funded by the grant was provided by an ACORN spin-off, the Arkansas Institute for Social Justice, which was run by two former ACORN organizers. It also appears that in October 1977 ACORN's VISTA grant was deemed *crucial* to its survival. ACORN had previously shunned receiving federal funding, but it admitted that its financial situation obviated the need to do so. For example, at one time one or two ACORN staff organizers were observed as outnumbered by thirty-two VISTA workers, with a minimum of sixteen ACORN organizers "immediately converted to the VISTA payroll upon approval of the grant."[106]

However, due to a lack of access to all ACORN/CORAP files, the House Appropriations Committee investigative staff concluded that the VISTAs comprised the majority of the ACORN organization.[107]

The Arkansas Institute for Social Justice was founded in 1972. It later changed its name to the American Institute for Social Justice.[108] AISJ was essentially a front group for ACORN. Gary Delgado, a founding ACORN organizer, writes that AISJ's intern program was used to generate trainees who would, in turn, receive stipends from AISJ. AISJ also provided a tax-exempt cover for foundations to contribute to ACORN's activities, as well as serving as a recruitment center for new activists. It also served as a way to homogenize the ACORN training model for Alinsky-style neighborhood-based organizing.[109]

A Florida incorporation profile for AISJ states it was incorporated there on September 16, 1981, by, among others, Elena Hanggi, AISJ director and former national president of ACORN, and Dale Rathke, brother of ACORN founder Wade Rathke. AISJ shared the same mailing address, 1024 Elysian Fields Avenue, New Orleans, as did its parent, ACORN. Over the years it has been the same mailing address shared by more than 290 ACORN entities. At some point AISJ relocated to Washington, D.C.[110]

In October 1977, according to the House Appropriations Committee report, not only was ACORN involved in labor organizing, but also the ACORN executive board gave its chief organizer, which would have been Wade Rathke, both the authority and responsibility to organize household workers and other unions in New Orleans. The United Labor Organizations—which ACORN was "helping get started"— was housed in the same building as ACORN. The sign on the front of the building read *ACORN* on one side and *ULO* on the other. The Household Workers Organizing Committee, said to be a ULO subsidiary, was also housed in the same building. Although it was claimed all simply rented space in the building, the investigative team could not verify it.[111]

Perhaps the team's suspicions were substantiated when it found VISTAs actively working with HWOC. The team concluded that the VISTAs were not only facilitating ACORN's labor organizing, but in fact also making it possible. Not only that, the team was concerned that the funds VISTAs solicited were ending up financing more labor organizing.

The investigative report also exposed another ACORN lie, that the VISTAs assigned to ACORN/CORAP would be "working mainly with the poor." The investigative team point out that is contrary to ACORN's stated philosophy that "takes pride in having preserved the idea of a 'majority constituency.'"

A *majority constituency* to ACORN is defined by "all people who are shut out of power or, more specifically, 'low to moderate income' families," the investigators write. They quote from ACORN's literature, which states: "It is that majority that is going to have to be organized if there is any hope for changing—for reversing—the prevailing distribution of power."

When the investigative team made site visits to Little Rock, Arkansas, and Sioux Falls, South Dakota, it discovered that work was in fact being carried out in low- and middle-income neighborhoods. A third city visited, Hot Springs, Arkansas, met the criteria for low income. Also, two of the VISTAs the team talked to—the only ones the team talked to without an ACORN staff member present—described the neighborhoods in which they worked as more middle class than poor.

Contrary to the Alinsky principle of empowering communities to become self-reliant when VISTA assistance is no longer available, the investigative team found just the opposite to be true. The team found VISTA efforts "directed toward holding groups together or building [ACORN] memberships back up."

Additionally, the VISTA Volunteer Handbook, the investigative team reports, in its "community organizing model," "spells out the ongoing role of the organizer and describes it as a 'critical process' in the continuing activities of the group." The team concluded that ACORN's "implicit goal" will only be reached when it "becomes a mass populist movement and no longer requires Federal money for its support."

Similar problems existed with the Midwest Academy, established in 1973 as a principal New Left training facility for community and group organizing. Founder Heather Booth was described in a circa 1982 Midwest Academy brochure as the "'leading social action trainer in the United States' and as a person who 'has previously worked as a civil rights and labor union organizer.'" The brochure does not mention Booth's activism with Students for a Democratic Society, nor the close relationship the Midwest Academy shares with Democratic Socialists of America.[112]

Booth's path to community organizing began with anti–death penalty work with the American Friends Service Committee, followed by sit-ins against Woolworth's with the Congress of Racial Equality (CORE), the civil rights movement, the Freedom Summer Project in 1964 with the Student Nonviolent Coordinating Committee, and the Women's Radical Action Project, or WRAP, the first campus women's organization she formed in 1965. Also in 1965, she joined SDS, where she met and married her husband, Paul Booth, national secretary of SDS, then based in Chicago. She helped found and establish work groups for the Chicago Women's Liberation Union in 1967.[113]

In 1971 Heather Booth enrolled and trained in community organizing with the IAF. Jerry Kellman, Barack Obama's training mentor at the Gamaliel Foundation in the mid-1980s, was one of Booth's classmates.[114]

Heather Booth's husband, Paul Booth, currently serves as executive assistant to American Federation of State, County and Municipal Employees (AFSCME) president Gerald McEntee, and on the Midwest Academy board of directors. Booth's pedigree as a community activist and union organizer is as long and radical as his wife's. In 1962 he coauthored the Students for a Democratic Society's Port Huron Statement with Tom Hayden. Booth is also the former president of Chicago's Citizen Action Program (CAP), which was formed in 1969 by trainees from Saul Alinsky's Industrial Areas Foundation.[115]

Alinsky created CAP (originally Campaign Against Pollution), a new *advocacy model* of organizing, to "develop allies among the middle classes, and to organize them directly." CAP is described as a "broad metropolitan and multiclass organization to address rising concerns about pollution in Chicago." The Booths and Steve Max were key leaders in CAP.[116]

CAP soon expanded from environmental issues to an agenda that included such issues as education, property taxes, mortgage lending practices, consumer issues, nuclear power plant expansion, disinvestment, and Chicago's Crosstown Expressway. Although CAP collapsed by the mid-1970s—it held its last annual convention in 1975—its coalition-building and fund-raising strategies were subsequently adopted by many of the organizations that followed in its shoes.[117]

"Almost all of CAP's success was based on smoke and mirrors. . . . There was almost no power. Just a scruffy bunch of a few hundred people," Paul Booth said in 1989.[118]

Heather Booth writes that, while working as "an editorial consultant for a market analyst," she was fired for union organizing, "defending the rights of clericals where I worked who were terribly abused." Nearly three years later, in 1972, Booth won a five-thousand-dollar award in back pay from a lawsuit filed with the National Labor Relations Board. Booth used the money to start the Midwest Academy.[119]

Since the early 1970s, Booth has served as training director for the Democratic National Committee, and worked with ACORN, SEIU, AFL-CIO, the Coalition for Democratic Values, and numerous other leftist organizations.[120]

As Mark Levin points out, all the big unions—AFSCME, AFL-CIO, SEIU—are linked with the New Left. All the ACTION leaders of the Carter era who worked with VISTA—Sam Brown, Marge Tabankin, Heather Booth—are Alinskyites.[121]

In May 2010, Booth, as head of the K Street–based Americans for Financial Reform, led a protest to shut down K Street. Ironically, K Street, the street of Washington, D.C., lobbyists' dreams, is the address for a number of progressive organizations—including USAction and Health Care for America Now, or HCAN, of which Booth is a leading member. Most recently, Booth served as senior adviser to the socialist organization One Nation Working Together: Putting America Back to Work and Pulling America Back Together.[122]

Among the resource people named in the 1982 Midwest Academy brochure is Robert Creamer, then executive director of the Illinois Public Action Council, who had been invited to the 1977 VISTA roundtable discussions. Creamer was identified in late 2009 as the author of a blueprint for universal health care—written while incarcerated for five months in 2006 in a federal prison after pleading guilty to bank fraud and withholding taxes while heading Citizen Action of Illinois. Creamer's blueprint is said to have contributed to the Obamacare plan.[123]

Another key player—although infrequently discussed—is Steve Max, who cofounded the Midwest Academy with Heather Booth in 1973. Max is Midwest's first trainer and currently serves as associate director.[124]

Steve Max was described in 1973 as a "serious, and intense young man" by Kirkpatrick Sale in his book on Students for a Democratic Society. Max, he continues, was "a true 'red-diaper baby'—his father was a former editor of the *Worker*—and he had been a member of the Communist Labor Youth League until he broke with the CP in 1956 while still in his early teens; he had graduated from high school but chose not to go on to college, devoting himself chiefly to political work and a few odd jobs."[125]

Alan Max, Steve's father, is a former managing editor of the *Daily Worker*, an official English-language Communist Party USA weekly— which supported the policies of Joseph Stalin—published in New York City. This is the same newspaper to which Barack Obama's mentor Frank Marshall Davis was a contributor.[126]

In August 1934, Communist Party delegates from the Northwest met with Socialist Party delegates to discuss forming a united front of socialists and communists to oppose fascism. The discussion was led by Voice of Action secretary Alan Max, who openly supported the CP position that socialists "merely paid 'lip service' to the united front ideal."[127]

In his testimony before the House Un-American Activities Committee regarding communist activities in the United States, Walter S. Steele, owner of the National Republic Publishing Company and managing editor of the *National Republic*, named Alan Max as "either an instructor and/or guest lecturer at the Jefferson School of Social Science." The Jefferson School operated from 1943 to 1956 as a nonprofit organization, which Steele said "enjoys benefits of the GI educational fund of the Veterans' Administration." It employed Dr. Lewis Balamuth, who formerly connected with the Manhattan Project, to teach "the rudiments of atomic power at this Communist school."[128]

In 1955, John Gates was appointed editor of the *Daily Worker*. This was following his summer 1948 indictment as one of "12 'kingpin Commies'" under the Smith Act "for being 'dedicated to the Marxist-Leninist principles of the overthrow and destruction of the Government . . . by force and violence.'" Gates was convicted in 1959 and served five years.

Steve Max was among leading Gates supporters who joined the Young Socialist Alliance, the youth affiliate of the Socialist Workers Party from 1960 to 1992. The YSA was to the left of the Young Socialist League (YSL), which in turn was affiliated with the Independent Socialist League.[129]

Max declared his path to community organizing in the late 1950s. In 1957, YSA began publishing the *Young Socialist*. In its February 1958 issue, Steve Max, using the name Steve Martin, wrote an "open defense of reformism." He proposed that the "way to fight for socialism was to fight for social reforms." In his argument, Max called for a "peaceful transition to socialism" first advocated by German Social Democrat Eduard Bernstein at the end of the nineteenth century. Max's words sound as loud a warning today of where so-called community organizers hope to take America as it did half a century ago: "The road towards socialism is a gradual step-by-step process, no part of which can be skipped or rushed. Our job begins now. We as young socialists must seek every available method of working with whatever groups—

socialist, progressive, liberal, democratic, etc—which will work with us on whatever socially desirable issue and at whatever level they are willing."[130]

Max was made a member of the *YS* editorial board in March 1958, but quickly resigned in May. Max and his supporters formed the Tom Paine Club, which soon joined the Students League for Industrial Democracy, or SLID, which a few years later became Students for a Democratic Society. Max attended the founding SDS meeting in Port Huron, Michigan.[131]

The Tom Paine Club was founded by Leo Huberman, the founding co-editor of the Marxian socialist publication *Monthly Review*, and a "passionate advocate of progressive education."[132]

Out of the New York Tom Paine Club came a political action group, the Franklin D. Roosevelt Four Freedoms Club, which organized high school and college students in New York City to support the civil rights movement. The FDR Four Freedoms Club was named after Franklin Roosevelt's 1941 statement of principles that included a social democratic blueprint for postwar America. Reportedly, the principles influenced the Port Huron Statement and the founding of SDS itself.[133]

Two other New Leftist Tom Paine members, Mickey Flacks and Bob Ross, also joined SDS. Max, long involved with both community and labor organizing since high school, became a leader with the Tom Paine Club in New York City and editor of its newsletter *Common Sense*.[134]

Camp Obama

Another Midwest Academy staffer, executive director Jackie Kendall, says that the first day she met Barack Obama in the mid-1980s, when she went home that night, she told her husband "I just met a kid who someday we're going to say *We knew him when*. He was that good."[135] Kendall is quoted in 2007 as saying Barack Obama had "given community organizing a good name."[136] Kendall has been at the Midwest Academy since 1982. Instructively, Kendall helped develop and deliver the first Camp Obama trainings for volunteers headed to Iowa during summer 2007 and for the Iowa caucuses.[137]

Although Booth and Max followed the Alinsky plan for community organizing, it differed in that Alinsky focused on local groups and the Midwest Academy works to build state and nationwide coalitions. "It's good to organize people in Chicago," says Kendall. "But it's even better if the people in Chicago can organize with a group from Detroit or Boston."[138]

In 1991, Kendall, Max, and Kimberly A. Bobo wrote the Midwest Academy's training manual, *Organizing for Social Change: Midwest Academy Manual for Activists*.

In May 1999, Kendall was honored for "more than two decades to the education and training of a generation of activists" by Democratic Socialists of America at the Eugene V. Debs–Norman Thomas–Michael Harrington Dinner held in Chicago.[139]

Kendall worked at Public Action with former director and staffer and current U.S. representative Jan Schakowsky (D-Ill.), and Schakowsky's husband, Robert Creamer.[140]

Kendall remains on the Midwest Academy board of directors although she retired at the end of 2010. Her replacement, Judy Hertz, a longtime Chicago activist, has been with Midwest since 1999.[141]

Kendall's coauthor, Kim Bobo, has known Barack Obama since at least 1992, when he headed Illinois Project Vote. Bobo served as a member of the twenty-two-member Project Vote Steering Committee, as did radical Chicago cleric Reverend Jeremiah Wright and Father Michael Pfleger; Keith Kelleher, head of SEIU Local 880; Madeline Talbott, head of Chicago ACORN; and John Owens, who succeeded Obama as head of the Developing Communities Project.[142]

It has also received funding from the Woods Fund, a nonprofit on which Obama served, alongside Bill Ayers, as paid director from 1999 to December 2002.[143]

Shakedown Artists

If *investment* (the politically correct term for *government spending*) was the new takeaway word from Barack Obama's January 2011 State of the Union address,[144] the buzzword for the kinds of activities the Center for Community Change engaged in in the late 1970s is *shakedown*. The only investing involved was in promoting CCC's bottom line.

CCC brags on its website that it helped to establish the Community Reinvestment Act, signed by President Jimmy Carter in 1977. The CCC says that, in 1978, it helped Brooklyn and St. Louis community-based groups file the first formal complaints against banks failing to meet their CRA obligations. As a result, the two cities received housing loans for low-income neighborhoods (Brooklyn, $20 million; St. Louis, $1 million).[145]

In April 1989 the CCC was one of four self-described "consumer and community groups" that circulated a letter opposing pending savings-and-loan legislation to members of the House Banking Committee. The groups demanded the legislation contain amendments that would discourage banking institutions from discrimination based on sex and race. It also encouraged housing loans for low- and moderate-income people.[146]

The other three organizations were the Consumers Union, the Consumer Federation of America, and ACORN.

ACORN, as we wrote in *The Manchurian President*, is the same organization that Barack Obama was involved with from at least 1992 forward. ACORN acted as shakedown artists descending upon Chicago banks in relation to CRA.[147]

In the winter issue of Chicago's *City Journal*, Howard Husock explains that ACORN's complaint was based on the practice of "redlining" in inner-city neighborhoods, meaning banks refused to lend to residents even while at the same time they used their deposits to finance suburban expansion. It was decreed that banks had an "affirmative obligation" to "meet the credit needs of the communities in which they are chartered, and that federal banking regulators should assess how well they do that when considering their requests to merge or to open branches."[148]

However, the banking world had changed by 2000, with bank deregulation setting off a wave of banking mega-mergers. A possible unforeseen consequence was that regulatory approval for such mergers was now in part dependent upon positive CRA ratings. Either by intervening in the CRA approval process, or just by threatening to intervene, the left-wing nonprofit groups gained control over what was described as the "eye-popping pools of bank capital." In turn, the groups parceled the money out to applicants for individual low-income mortgages.

One of these groups was ACORN Housing, which acquired access to $760 million from the Bank of New York.

Thus CRA helped ACORN enter the mortgage business. ACORN and other community groups used it "as a cudgel to force lenders to lower their mortgage underwriting standards in order to make more loans in low-income communities," Steven Malanga writes at RealClearMarkets. In exchange for ACORN to stop its CRA-related protests, banks rewarded ACORN with contracts enabling them to act as mortgage counselors in low-income areas. In 1993 alone, ACORN had as many as fourteen major banks eager to end the CRA protests. ACORN gained administrative control over $55 million in an eleven-city lending program. ACORN used similar agreements to turn ACORN, and others, into national banking players.[149]

Amnesty Shamnesty

Now we look at the issue of immigration and how it was hijacked and exploited by radical activists and groups who seek to transform our nation. Over time, these radicals evolved their assault to culminate in amnesty for millions of illegals.

The brief history of immigration amnesty begins with the immigration reform disaster following the Immigration and Nationality Act of 1965.

The immigration mess was due in great part to the change in the 1965 law that abolished the national origins quota system. "In a misguided application spirit of the civil rights era, the Kennedy and Johnson Administrations saw these ethnic quotas as an archaic form of chauvinism," Ben Johnson wrote in 2002 in *Front Page* magazine. In spite of the ill-advised assurances by Senator Ted Kennedy that the United States would not be "flooded by a million immigrants annually," we know Kennedy got it totally wrong.[150]

Prior to the 1965 legislation, immigration levels approximated 300,000 each year. In 1996 alone, however, 1,045,000 legal immigrants flooded U.S. cities.

Senator Robert Kennedy completely missed the mark by predicting only 5,000 immigrants would come to the United States from India. Attorney General Nicholas Katzenbach, who succeeded Kennedy, predicted 8,000.

However, according to the U.S. Department of Homeland Security, between 2000 and 2006 there were 421,006 Indian legal immigrants admitted, a significant increase from the decade before, which saw an influx of 352,278 legal immigrants from India. In 2006 alone, legal immigrants coming from India to the United States totaled 58,072.[151]

Not included in these statistics, naturally, is the growing number of illegal immigrants coming from India.

While Hispanics are frequently reported as coming illegally to the United States in large numbers, the second-largest percentage increase in illegal immigration since 2000 is illegal immigrants coming from India. In 2000 there were an estimated 120,000 illegal immigrant Indians. By 2006 that number had grown to about 270,000, a 125 percent increase. Because many Indians come to the United States on an H–1B non-immigrant, temporary foreign worker visa, they do not have to cross a border illegally. They are also less easy to spot than other immigrants. In general they are higher educated, can speak fluent English, and are able to blend in at the workplace, often at high-tech companies, and perform in such highly skilled jobs as engineering and computer programming.[152]

The arguments from 1965 sound familiar now. Immigrants would gain citizenship through a merit system. The bill provided for "family unification," including to extended family members, which ultimately created an "endless cycle known to sociologists as the immigration chain."[153]

In 1965, Ted Kennedy had the economics wrong as well. Johnson writes: "He confidently predicted, 'No immigrant visa will be issued to a person who is likely to become a public charge.'"

In 2010 alone, the tab for welfare benefits for children of illegal immigrants in Los Angeles County, the largest county in the United States, cost taxpayers more than $600 million. This is up from $570 million in spending for 2009.[154]

Additionally, when this is combined with public safety costs and health care costs, the total cost for illegal immigrants to Los Angeles County taxpayers exceeded $1.6 billion in 2010.

The idea of granting some form of amnesty to illegal immigrants in the United States is by no means new. Since the Immigration and Nationality Act in 1965, there have been a total of seven amnesties.[155]

The first was the Immigration Reform and Control Act of 1986 (IRCA). President Ronald Reagan granted amnesty to 2.7 million people, providing forgiveness for those who entered the United States illegally, and set them on the path to citizenship. Of the 1.3 million amnesty applications, more than 90 percent were for a specialized program for agricultural workers. The number of illegal aliens seeking amnesty exceeded expectations, however. There was widespread document fraud, with as many as a third of the applicants being granted amnesty illegally.[156]

IRCA was deemed a failure. Intended to stem the tide of illegal immigrants through the strengthening of border security and increasing immigration enforcement against employers, it did neither.[157]

During the Clinton administration, there were six more amnesties granted. In 1994 there was a temporary rolling amnesty for 578,000 illegal immigrants, with an Extension Amnesty in 1997. Also in 1997 there was the Nicaraguan Adjustment and Central American Relief Act, which granted amnesty for nearly 1 million Central American illegal immigrants. The Haitian Refugee Immigration Fairness Act amnesty in 1998 granted amnesty for 125,000 Haitian illegal immigrants.

In 2000 there were two amnesties. One, called the Late Amnesty, granted amnesty to an estimated 400,000 illegal immigrants who claimed they should have been amnestied under IRCA in 1986. The second, called the LIFE Act Amnesty, reinstated the 1994 rolling amnesty and included 900,000 more.

A non-amnesty program was created during the Clinton era to naturalize hundreds of thousands of illegal immigrants. Prior to Election Day 1996, the goal of the Citizenship USA (CUSA) program was to speedily naturalize 1 million Hispanic immigrants (presuming they would be instant Democrats). It was alleged that private contractors were responsible for a pattern of fraud in citizenship testing and that the Immigration and Naturalization Service had failed to wait for fingerprint results and background checks, resulting in "violent criminals" becoming citizens.[158]

After an investigation, in a July 2000 report the Department of Justice inspector general's office concluded that Clinton White House officials had "pressed INS to accelerate its naturalization efforts." The speeded-up citizenship process resulted in the INS doing "slipshod background checks on thousands of applicants."[159] As a result, 18 percent of those naturalized in the CUSA program between August 31, 1995, and September 30, 1996, had not been subjected by INS to a complete criminal history background check.[160]

The DOJ IG report also concluded that the crash CUSA program had been the result of a "backlog reduction initiative designed to decrease naturalization processing times."

(Coincidentally, one of the forces behind the 1996 naturalization speedup was Daniel Solis, head of the United Neighborhood Organization in Chicago, who met with President Clinton. UNO has a very close Barack Obama connection.)[161]

When Bill Clinton left office in January 2001, there were still an estimated 7 million illegal immigrants in the United States and there was little improvement during the eight years of the George W. Bush administration. Illegal immigration numbers increased as immigration enforcement decreased. By 2005, an estimated 10–20 million illegal immigrants were living in the United States.[162]

One massive immigration legalization scheme during the Bush years, the Comprehensive Immigration Reform Act of 2007, sponsored in the Senate by majority leader Reid and cosponsored by only four progressive members, failed on a vote for cloture. It had been promoted using the much worn-out sales pitch that illegal immigrants "are doing jobs Americans will not" or "are not" doing.[163]

Strong support for the bill came from the National Immigration Forum, which lobbied for "legalization opportunities" for illegal immigrants.[164] The prospect of amnesty for illegal immigrants is always just around the next legislative session corner.

In November 2009, Marco Rubio, then Speaker of the Florida House and now a Republican U.S. senator, made this valid point: "There were people trying to enter the country legally, who had done the paperwork, who were here legally, who were going through the process, who claimed, all of a sudden, 'No, no, no, no, I'm illegal.' Because it was easier to do the amnesty program than it was to do the legal process."[165]

How many illegal immigrants are there in the United States today? It depends upon whom you ask.

Half a decade ago, in February 2004, Senator John McCain cited U.S. Border Patrol information in a letter. McCain wrote that, based on illegal immigrant apprehension statistics, it was estimated nearly 4 million people had crossed the U.S. border illegally in 2002. In September 2004 *Time* magazine estimated the illegal population somewhere around 11 million. An independent study of the underground economy by Wall Street firm Bear Stearns, released in January 2005, estimated there were 18 to 20 million illegal aliens present in the United States.[166]

In what is obviously a lowball number, in May 2006 there was an estimate of 10 million people possibly eligible for legalization. The terms of a new legalization bill would include requirements for illegal immigrants to work, pay back taxes, and pay steep fines before being granted legal permanent resident status. It would also have to call for creation of a computerized verification system to help businesses verify the status of employees; stiffer penalties for employers who disregard the law; and a guest worker program to handle the expected (inevitable) future influx of new immigrant workers.[167]

During the 2008 presidential campaign, Barack Obama promised to make comprehensive immigration reform a priority. Obama reiterated his pledge in June 2009 to longtime immigration reform proponent Illinois Representative Luis Gutierrez—in exchange for the congressman's vote on the Obamacare bill.[168]

A new report in early September 2010 by the Pew Hispanic Center shows that the worsening economy had one positive effect. The number of immigrants entering the United States illegally since 2005 had decreased significantly (not stopped) for the first time in two decades.[169]

The Pew report declares the numbers of illegal immigrants entering the United States had "plunged" by almost two-thirds between 2005 and 2009. Between 2000 and 2005, Pew states, only an average 850,000 illegal immigrants per year had entered the United States. The "plunge" was allegedly even more significant between 2007 and 2009, when the numbers fell to 300,000.[170]

Another disquieting statistic was reported at the end of March 2011 by the Government Accountability Office, which pointed out to the Senate Homeland Security Committee that the federal government can actually prevent or stop illegal immigrants from entering the United States only along one 129-mile stretch of the 1,954-mile U.S.-Mexico border. The remaining 1,825 miles of the U.S.-Mexico border is wide open and the Border Patrol is helpless to prevent or stop an illegal entry. There is simply no effective way to stem the tide.[171]

Marco Rubio is correct when he says that granting amnesty is not the answer. Rubio said: "If you grant amnesty, the message that you're sending is that if you come in this country and stay here long enough, we will let you stay. And no one will ever come through the legal process if you do that."[172]

Rubio is understating things. Those currently pushing immigration reform fully intend to use the documentation of millions of illegals to not only send such a message, but also transform our country and ensure progressive rule for the long term.

Invoking the memory of Senator Ted Kennedy, President Barack Obama addressed the need for immigration reform in his March 21, 2010, video message shown at the Immigration Rally attended by more than two hundred thousand people at the National Mall in Washington, D.C. "In the end," Obama said, "our broken immigration system affects more than a single community; it affects our entire country. And as we continue to strengthen our economy and jump-start job creation, we need to do so with an immigration system that works, not the broken system we have now."[173]

Comprehensive immigration legislation—including Obama's campaign promise to make it a priority during his first year in office to formulate a "plan to make legal status possible for an estimated 12 million illegal immigrants"—has failed to emerge as anticipated by immigration reform groups.[174] Still, these organizations, including many that are centerpieces of the radical network, are quietly crafting immigration reform policy they admit is aimed at fundamentally transforming our country.

Let's take stock of where we are now. Cecilia Muñoz, a former officer with La Raza before becoming deputy assistant to the president and director of intergovernmental affairs in the White House, assured Julia Preston of the New York Times in April 2009 that a "policy reform that controls immigration and makes it an orderly system" would be forthcoming that year.[175]

Preston writes, "While acknowledging that the recession makes the political battle more difficult, President Obama plans to begin addressing the country's immigration system this year, including looking for a path for illegal immigrants to become legal."[176]

Of course, this has not happened.

The question then becomes, "What has the president done?" According to the Organizing for America website, the president has done a lot.[177]

The Obama government claims to have "provided the technical assistance to develop key elements of a bipartisan immigration bill and have taken important steps to make interior enforcement smarter, more effective, and reflective of our values, as well as addressing problems in the detention system to improve accountability and safety."

In reality, it does not seem that the Obama government has accomplished much to resolve some of the most pressing problems, such as how to deal with the burgeoning numbers of untold millions of illegal immigrants in and flooding into the United States. This situation must frustrate the immigration reform groups that contributed to the Immigration Blueprint submitted to the Obama-Biden Transition Project in November 2008.[178]

Listed contributors are several left-wing organizations, including the Center for American Progress Action Fund, the Center for Community Change's FIRM, MALDEF, National Council of La Raza, National Immigration Forum, and the National Immigration Project of the Communist Party–affiliated National Lawyers Guild.

The thirty-four-page blueprint set forth immigration policy recommendations that reflected input from the group of organizations and individuals that compiled it.

But there is more to Obama's immigration plan than what is written in the blueprint.

On July 2, 1998, on his Illinois State Legislative National Political Awareness Test, Barack Obama said "state-funded welfare benefits for legal immigrants" should be extended. He also said state funds should continue to be used for "some Medicaid coverage for legal immigrants."[179]

During the NPR–Iowa Public Radio presidential debate on December 4, 2007, at Des Moines, Iowa, Obama said "as president of the United States, I will make sure that the federal government does what it's supposed to do, which is to do a better job of closing our borders and preventing hundreds of thousands of people to pour in, have much tougher enforcement standards when it comes to employers, and create a pathway of citizenship for the 12 million people who are already here."[180]

Later in the radio debate, on the topic of what to do about illegal immigrants who are already in the United States, Obama said, as reported by Alex Newman of the *New American*, that "after illegal aliens pay their fine and get on his 'pathway,' 'they can then stay here and they can have the ability to enforce a minimum wage that they're paid, make sure the worker safety laws are available, make sure that they can join a union."[181]

Regarding the pathway to citizenship, speaking on June 3, 2007, at the Democratic debate at St. Anselm College in New Hampshire, Obama said, "We want to have a situation in which those who are already here, are playing by the rules, are willing to pay a fine and go through a rigorous process should have a pathway to legalization. . . . What [people] don't want is a situation in which there is a pathway to legalization and you've got another several hundred thousand of folks coming in every year."[182]

At the August 8, 2007, AFL-CIO Democratic primary forum, Obama modified his comments somewhat, leaving out mention of the prospects of more illegal immigrants crossing the border. He said, "We've got to give a pathway to citizenship. But people have to earn it. They're going to have to pay a fine. They've got to make sure that they're learning English. They've got to go to the back of the line so that they're not rewarded for having broken the law."

On the controversial matter of permitting driver's licenses for illegal immigrants, at the October 30, 2007, Democratic debate at Drexel University in Philadelphia Obama said, "There is a public safety concern [with denying driver's licenses to illegal immigrants]. We can make sure that drivers who are illegal come out of the shadows, that they can be tracked, that they are properly trained, and that will make our roads safer." When asked a related question at the November 15, 2007, Democratic debate in Las Vegas, on whether he supported driver's licenses for illegal immigrants, Obama was more direct. He said *yes*.

Barack Obama's U.S. Senate voting record includes support for the DREAM Act for the children of illegal immigrants, continuation of federal funds for declared "sanctuary cities," and allowing illegal aliens to participate in Social Security.

Additionally, in December 2006, U.S. Border Control, an organization founded in 1988 that is dedicated to ending illegal immigration, rated Barack Obama at 8 percent on a scale of 0–30 percent, revealing what it deemed a heavy "open-border stance."

The Obama government's failure to accommodate immigration reform advocates in a timely manner—since action was promised for 2009 to those who had not only supported his candidacy but also contributed to his Immigration Blueprint—was met in March 21, 2010, by a "March for America," yet another event organized by the Center for Community Change. It was billed as the largest protest march since Obama took office. Activist groups were expected to attend from nearly every state in a revival of the "labor-religious-community coalition" that would be "the first major mass street action for immigration reform" since the mass immigration marches in 2006.[183]

A series of marches in March 2006 had protested H.R. 4437, the Border Protection, Antiterrorism and Illegal Immigration Act of 2005, sponsored by House Judiciary Committee chairman James Sensenbrenner (R-Wis.) and Representative Peter King (R-N.Y.).[184]

In the March 2006 event, hundreds of thousands of illegal aliens and supporters marched, demanding amnesty while opposing stricter immigration enforcement.

In his description of the spectacle, *NRO*'s Mark Krikorian aptly writes that "outsiders" were exhibiting a "naked assertion of power against the American nation"—"ubiquitous Mexican flags, burning and other forms of contempt for the American flag, and widespread displays of blatant racial chauvinism and irredentism." They were demanding compliance with their wishes that *our* immigration policies should be submitted for *their* approval. If their demands are not met, he writes, they "implicitly threaten violence."[185]

In March 2010, Gabe Gonzalez, lead Center for Community Change organizer, reported that the unions and Hispanic organizations had all committed to mobilize for the march. Gonzalez said the churches were "totally on board," and "faith-based activist networks" such as the Gamaliel Foundation, PICO, and the Industrial Areas Foundation were involved.[186]

In a video message broadcast on huge screens around the Mall, Obama said he would continue working on the issue but he did not suggest a time frame: "I have always pledged to be your partner as we work to fix our broken immigration system, and that's a commitment that I reaffirm today."[187]

Again the promise of action *this year* was the message, this time delivered by the main rally speaker, Representative Luis Gutierrez, who said he was optimistic about Obama's promise. "I see a new focus on the part of this president," Gutierrez said. "That's why we are here to say we are not invisible."

The Obama administration justified that optimism on June 17, 2011, when it bypassed Congress and issued the DREAM Act and backdoor amnesty via memorandum. John T. Morton, an assistant secretary at the Department of Homeland Security and director of U.S. Immigration and Customs Enforcement (ICE), instructed all field office directors, special field agents in charge, and chief counsel to exercise prosecutorial discretion with civil immigration enforcement priorities in the apprehension, detention, and removal of aliens and the factors that should be considered.[188]

The rationale stated for the memorandum is that ICE is "confronted with more administrative violations than its resources can address," therefore it "must regularly exercise 'prosecutorial discretion' if it is to prioritize its efforts." This prosecutorial discretion allows ICE to decide to what degree it will "enforce the law against a particular individual."

This is not the first time prosecutorial discretion regarding immigration cases has been advised. A similar directive was issued by the Clinton administration in November 2000, following the Illegal Immigration Reform and Immigrant Responsibility Act in 1996, which had "limited the authority of immigration judges to provide relief from removal in many cases, and persons facing removal have sought to avoid removal by other means, including prosecutorial discretion from INS."[189]

In a June 30, 2010, memo on enforcement priorities, Morton drew from similar memos drafted by former immigration officials. The memo itemizes the factors ICE officials, agents, and counsel should take into account and provides a decision-making framework. This was followed by a similar memo on August 20, 2010.[190]

The nineteen factors listed in the June 2011 Morton memo not only are consistent with those outlined in the DREAM Act but also provide grounds to potentially grant amnesty to illegal immigrants. ICE officers, agents, and attorneys are instructed to consider all relevant factors, including those enumerated in the memo. Particular consideration is to be given to veterans and members of the U.S. armed forces, longtime lawful permanent residents, individuals present in the United States since childhood, pregnant or nursing women, victims of domestic violence, individuals who suffer from a serious mental or physical disability, and individuals with serious health conditions.

In line with the DREAM Act, consideration is to be given to a person's pursuit of education in the United States. Particular consideration is to be "given to those who have graduated from a U.S. high school or have successfully pursued or are pursuing a college or advanced degrees at a legitimate institution of higher education in the United States."

Besides those who have served in the U.S. military, reserves, or National Guard, with particular consideration given to those who served in combat, consideration is to be extended to their immediate relatives.

Other factors include a person's ties and contributions to the community, including family relationships; a person's age, with particular consideration given to minors and the elderly; whether or not a person has a U.S. citizen or permanent resident spouse, child, or parent; and whether or not a person is the primary caretaker of a person with a mental or physical disability, minor, or seriously ill relative.

This is in addition to persons "likely to be granted temporary or permanent status or other relief from removal, including as an asylum seeker, or a victim of domestic violence, human trafficking, or other crime" and a person who is "currently cooperating or has cooperated with federal, state or local law enforcement authorities, such as ICE, the U.S Attorneys or Department of Justice, the Department of Labor, or National Labor Relations Board, among others."

Also, the memo states it is "preferable" for ICE officers, agents, and attorneys to "consider prosecutorial discretion in cases without waiting for an alien or alien's advocate or counsel to request a favorable exercise of discretion." In other words, ICE officers, agents, and attorneys are to aggressively pursue resolution of pending cases, period: "ICE officers, agents, and attorneys should examine each such case independently to determine whether a favorable exercise of discretion may be appropriate."

Based on these guidelines, and any other non-itemized factors ICE should decide to include, it would seem almost impossible for ICE officers, agents, and attorneys, in exercising prosecutorial discretion, to *not* rule favorably for and to *not* prosecute and/or deport millions of illegal immigrants—and prospective Democrat voters.

Also noteworthy is that, in the summer of 2010, the American Federation of Government Employees Council 118, which represents about 7,000 ICE workers, cast a vote of no confidence in Morton's leadership. The council accused Morton of "abandoning ICE's 'core mission' of enforcing immigration laws and focusing on 'policies related to amnesty.'"[191]

While, in essence, ICE officials are being encouraged by Morton to not enforce immigration law—using prosecutorial discretion—his memo leaves the status of the illegal immigrants who will not be prosecuted or deported in limbo. Will the Obama administration issue an amnesty memo next?

Obama Adviser: Amnesty to Ensure Progressive Rule

Immigration reform is without a doubt the key issue for unions such as the Service Employees International Union. Not only would the union possibly add millions of members, but it would also receive much-needed funds. The SEIU's pension plans are headed toward insolvency.[192]

If any one person in the SEIU is pushing for immigration reform to help solve the union's problems, it is Eliseo Medina, SEIU's international secretary-treasurer. Medina began on September 15, 2010, serving at least until 2012, as he completes the term of Anna Burger, who resigned in August 2010 after losing her bid to succeed retiring president Andy Stern.[193] Medina was appointed in November 2008 to serve on Obama's transition team committee on immigration.[194]

Medina has made his way up the ranks. When he was ten years old he was brought from Mexico to the United States legally by his mother. His career as a labor activist began in 1965 when, at the age of nineteen, he participated with fellow grape pickers in the historic United Farm Workers' strike in Delano, California. Medina spent the next thirteen years working with Cesar Chavez—whom Saul Alinsky called his greatest success story—and worked as a union organizer. Medina rose through the ranks to become national president of the United Farm Workers. He joined SEIU in 1986 and ten years later was elected SEIU's international executive vice president.[195]

In 2001, Eliseo Medina delivered the keynote address at the Democratic Socialists of America annual convention. He was honored at the May 14, 2004, 48th Annual Eugene V. Debs–Norman Thomas–Michael Harrington Dinner for, among other things, his "vital role in the AFL-CIO's reassessment of its immigration policy." The following August, Medina was named a DSA honorary chair for his "key role in the AFL-CIO's decision to adopt a new policy on immigration."[196]

Also at the Debs Dinner it was announced that the politically active union group UNITE! had met at a "regional political action conference at Lake Geneva over the weekend to dump Bush and elect Barack Obama." On March 16, 2004, Obama had won the Illinois primary for the Democratic nomination to the U.S. Senate.[197]

Upon hearing the news of Medina's pending election, DSA vice chair Harold Meyerson wrote on August 18, 2010, in the *American Prospect*, "Medina also was a key negotiator on behalf of labor in the immigration-reform deliberations with the Bush administration, a leader in Hispanic voter mobilization efforts for Barack Obama in 2008, and one of the foremost advocates for comprehensive immigration reform—and against the Obama administration's stepped-up deportations of immigrants—during the past two years."[198]

Speaking on June 2, 2009, in Washington, D.C., at the America's Future Now! Conference—the annual progressive conference organized by Campaign for America's Future—Medina said of Latino voters, "when they voted in November [2008], they voted overwhelmingly for progressive candidates. Barack Obama got two out of every three voters that showed up."[199]

Medina continues:

So I think there's two things, very quickly, that matter for the progressive community.

Number one. If we are to expand this electorate to win, the progressive community needs to solidly be on the side of immigrants, then we'll solidify and expand the progressive coalition for the future. . . . When you are in the middle of a fight for your life you will remember who was there with you. And immigrants count on progressives to be able to do that.

Number two. We reform the immigration laws, it puts 12 million people on the path to citizenship and eventually voters. Can you imagine if we have, even the same ratio, two out of three? If we have eight million new voters that care about our [ratio?] and be voting, we will be creating a governing coalition for the long term, not just for an election cycle.

Just to restate here: Medina openly declared that granting citizenship to millions of illegal immigrants would expand the *progressive* electorate and help ensure a *progressive* governing coalition for the long term.

Barack Obama boasted during his 2008 presidential campaign of his track record of working with SEIU, promising he would help to "paint the nation purple with SEIU."[200]

A January 15, 2008, video, which surfaced after the election, was posted online in October 2009. It reveals the longtime close relationship of SEIU and Obama. Obama told a group of SEIU workers that all political candidates "claim they are pro-union when they are looking for endorsements." Obama continued:[201]

They'll all say, "We love SEIU." But the question you've got to ask yourself is, do they have it in their gut? Do they have a track record of standing alongside you on picket lines? Do they have a track record of going after the companies that aren't letting you organize? Do they have a track record of voting the right way but also helping you organize to build more and more power? . . . I've been working with SEIU before I was elected to anything. When I was a community organizer, SEIU local 880 and myself, we organized people to make sure that home-care workers had the basic right to organize.

We organized voting registration drives. That's how we built political power on the south side of Chicago. . . . And now the time has come for us to do it all across this country. We are going to paint the nation purple with SEIU. . . . I would not be a United States senator had it not been for the support of your brothers and sisters in Illinois. They supported me early. They supported me often. I've got my purple windbreaker from my campaign in 2004.

At the end of his speech, Obama raised his fist and chanted, "SEIU! SEIU! SEIU!"

"SEIU's political loyalties are solid, reaching back to the 2004 Illinois Senate race, when Obama was a long shot but earned the union's endorsement," Andrew Stern told Peter Nicholas of the *Los Angeles Times* in June 2009.[202]

It was no exaggeration when Stern announced the 1.9 million member union's endorsement of Obama's presidential candidacy on February 15, 2008, saying: "There has never been a fight in Illinois or a fight in the nation where our members have not asked Barack Obama for assistance and he has not done everything he could to help us."[203]

And, of course, SEIU expected a lot in return for all its support. "Any one of them could stall, if not derail, President Obama's overhauling of the U.S. healthcare system," Peter Nicholas reports on June 18, 2009, in the *Los Angeles Times*. However, they showed their solidarity, standing shoulder to shoulder with Obama in front of the TV cameras.[204]

Nearly a year earlier, in August 2008, Barack Obama had rewarded SEIU by including Eliseo Medina on his National Latino Advisory Council. The council coincidentally also included several members of the Congressional Hispanic Congress: Gutierrez (D-N.Y.), Nydia Velazquez (D-N.Y.), Xavier Becerra (D-Calif.), Hilda Solis (D-Calif.) (now secretary of labor), Linda T. Sanchez (D-Calif.), Charles Gonzalez (D-Texas), and Raul Grijalva (D-Ariz.).[205]

In a video clip that made the rounds on the Internet, President Obama is captured telling union members:[206]

Your agenda has been my agenda in the United States Senate. Before debating health care, I talked to Andy Stern and SEIU members. Before immigration debates took place in Washington, I talked with Eliseo Medina and SEIU members. Before the EFCA [Employees Freedom of Choice Act/Card Check], I talked to SEIU. So, we've worked together over these last few years and I am proud of what we've done. I'm just not satisfied.

Eliseo Medina and SEIU are top supporters of Representative Gutierrez's Comprehensive Immigration Reform for America's Security and Prosperity Bill, "which seeks to document up to 12 million illegal immigrants inside the U.S.," Aaron Klein pointed out in February 2010.[207]

SEIU's determination for immigration reform is clearly spelled out in a January 17, 2007, letter to Senator Kennedy. SEIU president Andy Stern, Anna Burger, and Medina noted how SEIU had worked diligently with him and members of the Senate and their staff. SEIU said it was willing to consider "any fair, practical and tough proposal" that would "bring out of the shadows an estimated 12 million undocumented individuals" and had rededicated its efforts and resources to "make reform a reality."[208]

In March 2010, SEIU announced that it was "stepping up its immigration reform efforts as a national campaign the same way we did for healthcare." Javier Morillo, SEIU immigration campaign director, said, "We are full-bore working on this. We are moving to get this done this year."[209]

SEIU's immigration "war room" was set to "use member education, canvassing and paid media as part of its effort." Morillo said the White House "reassured union officials it considers immigration reform a legislative priority. 'We've had assurances from the very beginning that they're serious about getting it done,' he said. 'The White House can't move this alone, they understand this.'"[210]

Surprisingly, analysis of what President Barack Obama really wants when it comes to immigration reform has been discussed by members of the media from both the left and the right. Unsurprisingly, however, it is likely that too many Latinos and members of the media will have forgotten by the 2012 presidential campaign that, in 2007, Barack Obama voted to kill immigration reform.

Noel Sheppard, at the conservative *NewsBusters*, responded in April 2010 to liberal David Broder's *Washington Post* article, "How Congress Botched Immigration Reform."[211] Sheppard wrote: "Broder curiously chose to ignore the fact that Barack Obama was, for all intents and purposes, the fateful deciding vote."[212]

Another leftist, Michael D. Shear, misdirected his readers with a July 2010 *Washington Post* headline "Republican Immigration Position Likely to Alienate Latinos, Dems Say."[213]

Fortunately, conservative journalist Jennifer Rubin, then with *Commentary* magazine, walked right past this and went straight to the heart of the matter. It was all a game of smoke and mirrors. Obama was to call for legislation, which would be good for the Democrat-Hispanic relationship. In reality, however, he was unlikely to press for immigration reform in 2010. At the same time, the strategy was for his allies to keep nudging Republicans toward immigration reform.[214]

Rubin writes, "Because, you see, if he passed a bill, the issue would go away. And then Hispanics wouldn't be mad at the GOP. It is quite a buried lode." The headline, Rubin says, should have read, "Obama Wants Divisive Racial Issue, Not Immigration Reform," then adds: "Hispanic activists actually wanted the president to work on comprehensive immigration reform. But during a White House meeting, they learned that's not the game here."

But that's okay. They're willing to wait. Shear reported that, while the takeaway for activists was that Obama could be doing more, they walked away satisfied that the president would "use the immigration debate to punish the GOP and aggressively seek the Latino vote in 2012."[215]

What this means could not be clearer. The National Council of La

Raza, which was represented at the meeting, was willing to put immigration reform on the back burner now, in spite of the years of pushing for it, so Barack Obama can use it as a reelection ploy to pull in Latino voters—again—in 2012.

In July 2010, Shear also wrote: "Democrats must deliver not only on Obama's promise of immigration reform, but also on improving the economic conditions of Latinos. Unemployment among Hispanics is at 12.4 percent, well above the 9.5 percent rate for the rest of the country."[216]

It is difficult to imagine how legislation like the stimulus bill, which did not, as repeatedly promised, *save or create* jobs, sits well with Hispanic voters. Additionally, the rising cost of health insurance and health care will contribute to raising the unemployment rate among Hispanics.

The March 2011 unemployment rate for all Hispanics was 11.9 percent. This is down from the year before, when unemployment was at 13.3 percent.[217]

It may well be the West Wing's strategy is to cross its collective fingers and hope that Latinos—*the ones who are in this country legally, and eligible to vote legally*—will not notice how the immigration reform football has already been kicked miles down the road from the 2008 campaign trail and that those goalposts are no longer in sight.

MEMBERS OF THE CONGRESSIONAL PROGRESSIVE CAUCUS (CPC)

As of May 22, 2011, the CPC listed seventy-five declared members in the 112th Congress:

CO-CHAIRS: Keith Ellison (Minn.) and Raúl M. Grijalva (Ariz.)

VICE CHAIRS: Tammy Baldwin (Wis.), Judy Chu (Calif.), William "Lacy" Clay, Jr. (Mo.), Sheila Jackson-Lee (Tex.), Chellie Pingree (Me.)

WHIP: Henry C. "Hank" Johnson, Jr. (Ga.)

SENATE MEMBER: Bernie Sanders (Vt.)

HOUSE MEMBERS: Karen Bass (Calif.), Xavier Becerra (Calif.), Earl Blumenauer (Ore.), Robert A. Brady (Penn.), Corrine Brown (Fla.), Michael E. Capuano (Mass.), André Carson (Ind.), Donna M. Christensen (Del. V.I.), Yvette D. Clarke (N.Y.), David Cicilline (R.I.), Emanuel Cleaver II (Mo.), Steve Cohen (Tenn.), John Conyers, Jr. (Mich.), Elijah E. Cummings (Md.), Danny K. Davis (Ill.), Peter A. DeFazio (Ore.), Rosa DeLauro (Conn.), Sam Farr (Calif.), Chaka Fattah (Penn.), Bob Filner (Calif.), Barney Frank (Mass.), Marcia L. Fudge (Ohio), Luis V. Gutiérrez (Ill.), Maurice Hinchey (N.Y.), Mazie Hirono (Hi.), Michael Honda (Calif.), Jesse L. Jackson, Jr. (Ill.),

Eddie Bernice Johnson (Texas), Marcy Kaptur (Ohio), Dennis Kucinich (Ohio), Barbara Lee (Calif.), John Lewis (Ga.), David Loebsack (Iowa), Ben R. Luján (N.M.), Carolyn Maloney (N.Y.), Edward J. Markey (Mass.), James McDermott (Wash.), James P. McGovern (Mass.), George Miller (Calif.), Gwendolynne Moore (Wis.), James P. Moran (Va.), Jerrold Nadler (N.Y.), Eleanor Holmes-Norton (Del. D.C.), John Olver (Mass.), Frank Pallone (N.J.), Edward Pastor (Ariz.), Donald M. Payne (N.J.), Chellie Pingree (Me.), Jared Polis (Colo.), Charles Rangel (N.Y.), Laura Richardson (Calif.), Lucille Roybal-Allard (Calif.), Bobby L. Rush (Ill.), Linda T. Sánchez (Calif.), Jan Schakowsky (Ill.), José Serrano (N.Y.), Louise Slaughter (N.Y.), Fortney Pete Stark (Calif.), Bennie G. Thompson (Miss.), John Tierney (Mass.), Nydia Velazquez (N.Y.), Maxine Waters (Calif.), Melvin L. Watt (N.C.), Peter Welch (Vt.), Frederica Wilson (Fla.), and Lynn Woolsey (Calif.)

MEMBERS OF THE CONGRESSIONAL BLACK CAUCUS (CBC)

Members of the CBC listed for the 112th Congress include:

CHAIR: Rep. Emanuel Cleaver II (Mo.)

HOUSE MEMBERS: Karen Bass (Calif.), Sanford D. Bishop, Jr. (Ga.), Corrine Brown (Fla.), George K. Butterfield (N.C.), Andre Carson (Ind.), Donna M. Christensen (Del. V.I.), Hansen Clark (Mich.), Yvette D. Clarke (N.Y.), William Lacy Clay, Jr. (Mo.), James E. Clyburn (S.C.), John Conyers, Jr. (Mich.), Elijah E. Cummings (Md.), Danny K. Davis (Ill.), Donna Edwards (Md.), Keith Ellison (Minn.), Chaka Fattah (Penn.), Marcia L. Fudge (Ohio), Al Green (Texas), Alcee L. Hastings (Fla.), Jesse L. Jackson, Jr. (Ill.), Sheila Jackson Lee (Texas), Henry C. "Hank" Johnson, Jr., (Ga.), Eddie Bernice Johnson (Texas), Barbara Lee (Calif.), John Lewis (Ga.), Gregory Meeks (N.Y.), Gwendolynne Moore (Wis.), Eleanor Holmes-Norton (Del. D.C.), Donald M. Payne (N.J.), Charles B. Rangel (N.Y.), Laura Richardson (Calif.), Cedric Richmond (Calif.), Bobby L. Rush (Ill.), David Scott (Ga.), Robert C. Scott (Va.), Terri A. Sewell (Ala.), Bennie G. Thompson (Miss.), Edolphus Towns (N.Y.), Maxine Waters (Calif.), Melvin L. Watt (N.C.), Alan West (Fla.), Frederica Wilson (Fla.)

MEMBERS OF THE CONGRESSIONAL HISPANIC CAUCUS (CHC)

Members of the Congressional Hispanic Caucus (CHC) for the 112th Congress include:

CHAIR: Charles A. Gonzalez (Texas)

1ST VICE CHAIR: Rubén Hinojosa (Texas)

2ND VICE CHAIR: Ben Ray Luján (N.M.)

WHIP: Dennis Cardoza (Calif.)

HOUSE MEMBERS: Joe Baca (Calif.), Xavier Becerra (Calif.), Jim Costa (Calif.), Henry Cuellar (Texas), Raúl M. Grijalva (Ariz.), Luis V. Gutiérrez (Ill.), Robert Menendez (N.J.), Grace F. Napolitano (Calif.), Edward Pastor (Ariz.), Pedro Pierluisi (P.R.), Silvestre Reyes (Texas), Lucille Roybal-Allard (Calif.), Gregorio "Kilili" Camacho Sablan (Northern Mariana Islands), Linda T. Sánchez (Calif.), José Serrano (Calif.), Albio Sires (N.J.), Nydia Velázquez (N.Y.)

APPENDIX D:
MEMBERS OF THE CONGRESSIONAL ASIAN PACIFIC AMERICAN CAUCUS (CAPAC)

Members of the Congressional Asian Pacific American Caucus (CA-PAC) for the 112th Congress include:

EXECUTIVE BOARD: Chair—Rep. Judy Chu (Calif.); Vice Chair—Rep. Madeleine Z. Bordallo (Guam); Whip—Rep. Colleen Hanabusa (Hi.); Chair Emeritus—Rep. Michael Honda (Calif.)

SENATE: Daniel Akaka (Hi.) and Daniel Inouye (Hi.)

HOUSE: Xavier Becerra (Calif.), Hansen Clarke (Mich.), Eni Faleomavaega (Del. American Samoa), Al Green (Texas), Mazie K. Hirono (Hi.), Doris O. Matsui (Calif.), Gregorio "Kilili" Camacho Sablan (Northern Mariana Islands), Robert C. Scott (Va.), David Wu (Ore.)

MEMBERS OF THE SUSTAINABLE ENERGY AND ENVIRONMENT COALITION (SEEC)

Only Sustainable Energy and Environment Coalition members who are also members of the Congressional Progressive Caucus, Congressional Black Caucus, Congressional Hispanic Caucus, and/or Congressional Asian Pacific American Caucus are listed below. All SEEC members are members of the House of Representatives.

CO-CHAIRS: Jay Inslee (Wash.) and Steve Israel (N.Y.)

VICE CHAIRS: Gerald Connolly (Va.), Rush Holt (D-N.J.), Chellie Pingree (Me.), Jared Polis (Colo.), and Paul Tonko (D-N.Y.)

MEMBERS: Tammy Baldwin (Wis.), Earl Blumenauer (Ore.), Donna M. Christensen (Del. V.I.), Steve Cohen (Tenn.), Maurice Hinchey (N.Y.), Mazie K. Hirono (Hi.), Michael Honda (Calif.), Barbara Lee (Calif.), David Loebsack (Iowa), Ben Ray Luján (N.M.), Doris O. Matsui (Calif.), James McDermott (Wash.), James P. McGovern (Mass.), George Miller (Calif.), Jan Schakowsky (Ill.), Louise Slaughter (N.Y.), Peter Welch (Vt.), Lynn C. Woolsey (Calif.)

AGRICULTURE: Joe Baca, Dennis A. Cardoza, Jim Costa, Henry Cuellar, David Scott

APPROPRIATIONS: Sanford D. Bishop, Jr., Rose DeLauro, Sam Farr, Chaka Fattah, Maurice Hinchey, Michael M. Honda, Jesse L. Jackson, Jr., Marcy Kaptur, Carolyn Cheeks Kilpatrick, Barbara Lee, James P. Moran, John Olver, Edward Pastor, Ciro D. Rodriguez, Lucille Roybal-Allard, John T. Salazar, José E. Serrano

ARMED SERVICES: Madeleine Z. Bordallo, Robert A. Brady, Henry C. "Hank" Johnson, Jr., David Loebsack, Solomon P. Ortiz, Chellie Pingree, Silvestre Reyes

BUDGET: Xavier Becerra, Earl Blumenauer, Rosa DeLauro, Marcy Kaptur, James P. McGovern, Gwendolynne Moore, Robert C. Scott

EDUCATION AND LABOR: George Miller, *Chairman*. Judy Chu, Yvette D. Clark, Marcia Fudge, Raúl M. Grijalva, Phil Hare, Rubén Hinojosa, Mazie K. Hirono, Dennis J. Kucinich, David Loebsack, Donald M. Payne, Pedro Pierluisi, Jared Polis, Gregorio "Kilili" Camacho Sablan, Robert C. Scott, John F. Tierney, Lynn C. Woolsey, David Wu

ENERGY AND COMMERCE: Henry A. Waxman, *Chairman.* Tammy Baldwin, George K. Butterfield, Donna M. Christensen, Charles A. Gonzalez, Edward J. Markey, Doris O. Matsui, Frank Pallone, Bobby L. Rush, Jan Schakowsky, Peter Welch

FINANCIAL SERVICES: Barney Frank, *Chairman.* Joe Baca, Michael E. Capuano, André Carson, William Lacy Clay, Emanuel Cleaver II, Keith Ellison, Alan Grayson, Al Green, Luis V. Gutiérrez, Rubén Hinojosa, Carolyn B. Maloney, Gregory W. Meeks, Gwendolynne Moore, David Scott, Nydia M. Velázquez, Maxine Waters, Melvin L. Watt

FOREIGN AFFAIRS: Jim Costa, Keith Ellison, Eni Faleomavaega, Sheila Jackson-Lee, Barbara Lee, Gregory W. Meeks, Donald M. Payne, David Scott, Albio Sires, Diane E. Watson, Lynn C. Woolsey

HOMELAND SECURITY: Bennie G. Thompson, *Chairman.* Anh "Joseph" Cao, Yvette D. Clarke, Emanuel Cleaver II, Henry Cuellar, Peter A. DeFazio, Al Green, Sheila Jackson-Lee, Eleanor Holmes Norton, Laura Richardson

HOUSE ADMINISTRATION: Robert A. Brady, *Chairman.* Michael Capuano, Artur Davis, Charles A. Gonzalez

JUDICIARY: John Conyers, Jr., *Chairman.* Tammy Baldwin, Judy Chu, Steve Cohen, Charles A. Gonzalez, Luis V. Gutiérrez, Sheila Jackson-Lee, Henry C. "Hank" Johnson, Jr., Jerrold Nadler, Pedro Pierluisi, Jared Polis, Linda T. Sanchez, Robert C. Scott, Maxine Waters, Melvin L. Watt

NATURAL RESOURCES: Joe Baca, Madeleine Z. Bordallo, Donna M. Christensen, Jim Costa, Peter A. DeFazio, Eni Faleomavaega,

Raúl M. Grijalva, Maurice Hinchey, Ben Ray Luján, Edward J. Markey, George Miller, Grace F. Napolitano, Frank Pallone, Pedro Pierluisi, Gregorio "Kilili" Camacho Sablan

OVERSIGHT AND GOVERNMENT REFORM: Edolphus Towns, *Chairman*. Anh "Joseph" Cao, Judy Chu, William Lacy Clay, Henry Cuellar, Elijah E. Cummings, Danny K. Davis, Marcy Kaptur, Dennis J. Kucinich, Carolyn B. Maloney, Eleanor Holmes Norton, John F. Tierney, Diane E. Watson, Peter Welch

PERMANENT SELECT COMMITTEE ON INTELLIGENCE: Silvestre Reyes, *Chairman*. Alcee L. Hastings, Jan Schakowsky, John F. Tierney

RULES: Louise M. Slaughter, *Chairman*. Dennis Cardoza, Alcee L. Hastings, Doris O. Matsui, James P. McGovern, Chellie Pingree, Jared Polis

SCIENCE AND TECHNOLOGY: Donna F. Edwards, Marcia L. Fudge, Alan Grayson, Eddie Bernice Johnson, Ben Ray Luján, Lynn C. Woolsey, David Wu

SELECT COMMITTEE ON ENERGY INDEPENDENCE AND GLOBAL WARMING: Edward J. Markey, Chairman. Earl Blumenauer, Emanuel Cleaver II, John J. Hall

SMALL BUSINESS: Nydia Velázquez, *Chairman*. Yvette D. Clarke

STANDARDS OF OFFICIAL CONDUCT: George K. Butterfield, Peter Welch

TRANSPORTATION AND INFRASTRUCTURE: Corrine Brown, Anh "Joseph" Cao, Michael E. Capuano, Steve Cohen, Elijah E.

Cummings, Peter A. DeFazio, Donna F. Edwards, Bob Filner, John J. Hall, Phil Hare, Mazie K. Hirono, Eddie Bernice Johnson, Henry C. "Hank" Johnson, Jr., Jerrold Nadler, Grace F. Napolitano, Eleanor Holmes Norton, Solomon P. Ortiz, Laura Richardson, Albio Sires

VETERANS AFFAIRS: Bob Filner, *Chairman*. Corrine Brown, John J. Hall, Ciro D. Rodriguez

WAYS AND MEANS: Xavier Becerra, Earl Blumenauer, Artur Davis, Danny K. Davis, John Lewis, James McDermott, Kendrick B. Meek, Charles B. Rangel, Linda T. Sanchez, Fortney Pete Stark

MEMBERS OF THE CONGRESSIONAL POPULIST CAUCUS (CPC)

The Congressional Populist Caucus (CPC) lists the following Democratic House members in the 112th Congress.

Founding members include:

CHAIR: Bruce Braley (Ia.)

VICE-CHAIRS: Peter DeFazio (Ore.), Rosa DeLauro (Conn.), Donna Edwards (Md.), Betty Sutton (Ohio)

MEMBERS: Leonard Boswell (Ia.), Steve Cohen (Tenn.), Joe Courtney (Conn.), Keith Ellison (Minn.), Bob Filner (Calif.), John Garamendi (Calif.), Mazie Hirono (Hi.), Hank Johnson (Ga.), David Loebsack (Iowa), Ben Ray Luján, Jr. (N.M.), Michael Michaud (Me.), Linda Sanchez (Calif.), Jan Schakowsky (Ill.), Brad Sherman (Calif.), Louise Slaughter (N.Y.), Jackie Speier (Calif.), Paul Tonko (N.Y.), Henry Waxman (Calif.), Peter Welch (Vt.), John Yarmuth (Ky.)

NOTES

Chapter One: Congressional Red Army

1. See Leon Wieseltier, "The Unreal World of Cornel West. All and Nothing at All," *New Republic Online*, March 6, 1995, http://www.discoverthenetworks.org/Articles/allor.html. Wieseltier does not give a link for his quote.

2. "About the Fabian Society," *Fabians.org.uk*, http://www.fabians.org.uk/about-the-fabian-society.

3. "Eduard Bernstein," *Marxists.org*, http://www.marxists.org/reference/archive/bernstein/index.htm. Socialism Time Line, "Heaven and Earth."

4. Ibid.

5. William F. Jasper, "The Grasp of Socialist International," *The New American*, March 1, 2010, http://files.meetup.com/1013239/The%20New%20American%20March%201,%202010%20State%20vs%20Federal.pdf.

6. Bernie Sanders with Huck Gutman, *Outsider in the House* (New York: Verso, 1998), 153.

7. Ibid., 154.

8. Ron Baiman, "Reorganized Illinois Citizen Action," *New Ground* 56 (January–February 1998), http://www.chicagodsa.org/ngarchive/ng56.html#anchor1041720.

9. "Executive Committee, Progressive Caucus of the U.S. House of Representatives," Democratic Socialists of America website, July 1997, http://web.archive.org/web/19970706174935; www.dsausa.org/Dems/ProgCauc.html.

10. "Members of the Progressive Caucus of the U.S. House of Representatives," Democratic Socialists of America website, July 1997, http://web.archive.org/web/19970706182044; www.dsausa.org/Dems/PCMembers.html.

11. Jennifer G. Hickey, "Clinton and Carey: Scratching backs. (President Bill Clinton; International Brotherhood of Teamsters president Ron Carey)," *Insight on the News*, November 10, 1997; Bill Sammon, "Teamsters crisis may shift labor leanings," *Washington Times*, January 5, 1998.

12. Geoff Metcalf, "The enemy within," *WND.com*, November 23, 1998.

13. Robert W. Lee, "Totally Radical!" *New American*, March 29, 1998, http://web.
     archive.org/web/20011201011123; www.thenewamerican.com/tna/1999/03-29-
     99/totally_radical.htm.

14. "Poverty and Policy," *Washington Post*, October 14, 1987.

15. Herbert Mitgang, "Saluting Veteran of War on Poverty," *New York Times*,
     July 2, 1988.

16. Ibid.; Paula Span, "The Harrington Perspective; In N.Y. a Salute to the Ail-
     ing Activist," *Washington Post*, July 2, 1988.

17. Ibid. See "Michael Harrington, at 61; Author, Social Reformer, Political Ac-
     tivist," *Boston Globe*, August 2, 1989.

18. Span, "The Harrington Perspective," July 2, 1988.

19. "RNC Chairman Hits Democrat-Socialist Links; Nicholson Says Gephardt's
     Offer to Socialist Sanders Is 'Outrageous,'" PRNewswire, December 1, 1999.

20. Juliet Eilperin, "In Session: Congress; In House Spat on F-22, Angry Rheto-
     ric Flies," *Washington Post*, June 12, 2000.

21. "West Coast: DSA at LA," *Democratic Left*, October 1, 2000.

22. Balint Vazsonyi, "The riddle that isn't," *Washington Times*, April 23, 2002.

23. Balint Vazsonyi, "Putting Pelosi's cards on the table," *Washington Times*, No-
     vember 12, 2002.

24. Democratic Socialists of America PAC (ID: C00419572), Federal Elec-
     tions Commission, 2006–2010, http://query.nictusa.com/cgi-bin/fecimg/?
     C00419572.

25. Vazsonyi, "Putting Pelosi's cards on the table," November 12, 2002.

26. Ibid.

27. Lincoln Cushing, "A brief history of the 'clenched fist' image," *DocsPopuli
     .org*, January 25, 2006; updated May 22, 2009; "The Red Rose as a Progres-
     sive Symbol," Tamiment Library and Robert F. Wagner Labor Archive, New
     York University.

28. Site Map for Democratic Socialists of America, archived February 1998,
     http://web.archive.org/web/19980206053457; www.dsausa.org/index/index
     .html.

29. E. J. Dionne, "Washington Talk: Politics," *Washington Post*, August 15, 1989.

30. Herbert Mitgang, "Michael Harrington, Socialist and Author, Is Dead,"
     New York Times, August 2, 1989.

31. "A Progressive Agenda. Democratic Socialists of America (1992)," archived
     July 1997, http://web.archive.org/web/19970706174148; www.dsausa.org/
     Lit/ProgPlat.html.

32. "A Budget for New World Realities and for Rebuilding America—FY 1993," PRRAC.org, July/August 1993.

33. Representative Bernie Sanders, "Sanders and Progressive Caucus Launch 'Cancel the Contract' Campaign/Offer 11-Part Comprehensive Alternative—'The Progressive Promise,'" *govt.eserver.org*, January 19, 1995.

34. "A New DSA Campaign for Economic Justice: An Overview," *New Ground* 50 (January/February 1997), http://www.chicagodsa.org/ngarchive/ng50.html#anchor465058.

35. Baiman, *New Ground*, 56. See "Agenda."

36. Ibid. See "Strategy."

37. Greg Pierce, "Inside Politics," *Washington Times*, November 10, 1998.

38. James C. Lucier, "Extremism in Defense of Virtue (Republicans accused of being extremists)," *Insight on the News*, February 22, 1999.

39. Jennifer Steinhauer, "On a Senate Call, a Glimpse of Marching Orders," *The Caucus* (blog), *New York Times*, March 29, 2011.

40. Lucier, "Extremism in Defense of Virtue," February 22, 1999.

41. Matthew Robinson, "Democrats scramble for tax strategy," *Human Events*, February 26, 2001.

42. Ibid.

43. Lucier, "Extremism in Defense of Virtue," February 22, 1999.

44. The New Party, and Barack Obama's connections to it, are discussed at length in chapter 6 of the authors' 2010 book, *The Manchurian President*.

45. John Nichols, "Building a Progressive Caucus," *Nation*, July 5, 1999.

46. Adam Doster, "Dancing into the Majority," *ZNet*, May 24, 2007; Grassroots for America, "New Political Organization to be Launched in Boston: Progressive Democrats of America," PRNewswire, July 22, 2004.

47. Progressive Democrats of America, "Progressive Wing of the Democratic Party Announces First Policy Statement and Ongoing Mission; Organization Pledges to Hold Democrats and Republicans Responsible to 57 Million Voters," PRNewswire, November 14, 2004; Chris Cillizza, "The decline and fall of the Democratic Leadership Council," *The Fix* (blog), *Washington Post*, February 7, 2011.

48. Grassroots for America, "New Political Organization to Be Launched in Boston," July 22, 2004.

49. Ibid.; Steve Miller, "Nader is persona non grata in Boston," *Washington Times*, July 26, 2004.

50. Doster, "Dancing into the Majority," May 24, 2007.

51. Tim Carpenter, "PDA is working to build the Democratic Wing of the

Democratic Party!" *Democratic Left* (Fall 2006): 9, http://www.dsausa.org/dl/Fall_2006.pdf.

52. "Advisory board," Progressive Democrats of America, accessed September 3, 2010, http://pdamerica.org/about/board.php; Doster, "Dancing into the Majority," May 24, 2007.

53. Alan Gomez, "Obama could change relations with Cuba," *USA Today*, December 7, 2008.

54. "IPS History," Institute for Policy Studies/ips-dc.org.

55. Murray N. Rothbard, "Where the Left Goes Wrong on Foreign Policy," *Inquiry*, July 1982 (LewRockwell.com).

56. Dateline D.C., "Bill Clinton and the IPS," *Pittsburgh Tribune-Review*, April 1, 2007; Saul Landau, "The Forever Fidel Obsession," *Truthdig.com*, September 19, 2010.

57. "Institute for Policy Studies," Institutional Analysis #2, Heritage Foundation, April 19, 1977.

58. Jo-Ann Mort, "Secular Saints," *TPMCafe/TalkingPointsMemo.com*, August 29, 2009.

59. Heritage Foundation, "Institute for Policy Studies," April 19, 1977.

60. "Board of Trustees," Institute for Policy Studies/ips-dc.org.

61. Bob Roman, "A Town Meeting on Economic Insecurity: Employment and Survival in Urban America," *New Ground* 45 (March–April 1996), http://www.chicagodsa.org/ngarchive/ng45.html#anchor1078705.

62. "DSA News: Dr. Quentin Young in the Wikipedia," *New Ground* 106.3 (June 13, 2006), Chicago Democratic Socialists of America, http://www.chicagodsa.org/ngarchive/ng106.html; "Quentin D. Young," Debs-Thomas-Harrington Annual Dinner, Chicago Democratic Socialists of America, May 1, 1992, http://www.chicagodsa.org/d1992/index.html; PA Staff, "Steps Toward Health Care Reform," *Political Affairs*, November 13, 2008.

63. Ibid.

64. Roy, "Obama neighbors head to D.C.," January 16, 2009.

65. Lynn Sweet, "McCain misleading public in role Ayers played in Obama political career," *Chicago Sun-Times*, October 15, 2008; Andrew Ferguson, "Mr. Obama's Neighborhood. The Democratic candidate has made his home in Chicago's Hyde Park, a place that's not like any other in America," *Weekly Standard* 13, no. 38 (June 16, 2008); Gabrielle Birkner, Obituary: "Rabbi Arnold Wolf, 84, Was Progressive Leader," *Forward*, December 26, 2008; Doni Remba, "Rabbi Arnold Jacob Wolf, z'l—'Obama's Rabbi'—A Remembrance," Jewish Alliance for Change website, n.d.

66. "Our Structure. Honorary Chairs," Democratic Socialists of America, accessed October 4, 2010, http://www.dsausa.org/about/structure.html; "Eliseo Medina," *DiscovertheNetworks.org.*

67. Democratic Socialists of America, "Resolution on the 2008 Presidential Election," *Democratic Left* (Summer 2008), http://www.dsausa.org/dl/Summer_2008.pdf.

68. "Members, Congressional Progressive Caucus," Democratic Socialists of America website, June 2001, Internet Archive, http://web.archive.org/web/20010602181018/http:/www.mmcw.homestead.com/DSA.html.

69. Vazsonyi, "Putting Pelosi's cards on the table," November 12, 2002.

70. Cliff Kincaid, "Speaker Pelosi's Controversial Marxist Connections," *Accuracy in Media*/aim.org, May 24, 2009.

71. "Pelosi Elected Speaker, First Woman to Lead House," *FoxNews.com*, January 4, 2007.

72. Cheryl K. Chumley, "Fringe-Left Democrats Wield New Influence," *HumanEvents.com*, March 13, 2007.

73. Shaw, "Speaker Pelosi and the Revival of Progressive Politics in America," May 7, 2010; Nick Burt and Joel Bleifuss, "Progressive Caucus Rising. This election was no victory for centrists," *In These Times* 8 (2006).

74. "PDA Working with CPC to Elect More Progressives," Progressive Democrats of America/pdamerica.org, November 3, 2006.

75. Chumley, "Fringe-Left Democrats Wield New Influence," March 13, 2007.

76. Other coalition members are Americans United for Separation of Church and State, League of Conservation Voters, National Education Association, National Council of Churches, National Organization for Women, and People for the American Way.

77. Edward Epstein, "Liberal legislative caucus envisions post-Bush era," *San Francisco Chronicle*, July 5, 2005; Congressional Progressive Caucus, "Congressional Progressive Caucus Comes Out Strong," *AfterDowningStreet.org*, November 5, 2008; Congressional Progressive Caucus, "Progressive Caucus Offers 'Progressive Promise' as Alternative to President Bush's 'Ownership Society,'" posted on Progressive Democrats of America website, June 25, 2005.

78. Congressional Progressive Caucus, "The Progressive Promise: Fairness for All," circa November 2008, *AfterDowningStreet.org*, http://www.afterdowningstreet.org/downloads/progprom.pdf; Nick Burt and Joel Bleifuss, "This election was no victory for centrists," *In These Times*, November 10, 2006.

79. Anna Cameron, "Congressional Black Caucus Releases Their Own Budget

Proposal," TalkRadioNews.com, April 14, 2011, http://www.talkradionews
.com/news/2011/4/14/congressional-black-caucus-releases-their-own-budget
-proposa.html; The 2012 Budget, Congressional Black Caucus, http://the-
congressionalblackcaucus.com/issues/the-2012-budget/; Chad Pergram,
"House Defeats Alternative 2012 Budget Plans," *Politico*, April 15, 2011,
href=http://politics.blogs.foxnews.com/2011/04/15/house-defeats-cbc-
2012-budget-plan.

80. Brenda J. Elliott, "Is American Liberalism Really in Retreat?" *RBO*, April 10,
2011, http://therealbarackobama.wordpress.com/2011/04/10/rbo-rant-is-
american-liberalism-really-in-retreat/. Pete Kasperowicz, "Chaos on House
floor as Democrats try to unsettle GOP budget," *The Hill*, April 15, 2011,
http://thehill.com/blogs/floor-action/house/156333-house-democrats-try-
to-force-passage-of-conservative-rsc-budget.

Chapter Two: Radicals in the Halls

1. Nick Burt and Joel Bleifuss, "Progressive Caucus Rising. This election was
no victory for centrists," *In These Times*, November 8, 2006; Chris Bowers,
"Congressional Progressive Caucus Rising," *MyDD.com*, August 14, 2008.

2. Brian Montopoli, "Nancy Pelosi Elected to Lead House Dems in New Congress; Boehner to Lead GOP," *CBSNews.com*, November 17, 2010.

3. "Origins and the History of the Congressional Black Caucus," Congressional
Black Caucus Foundation, http://www.cbcfinc.org/cbc.html. Congressional
Black Caucus members, 111th Congress, Congressional Black Caucus Foundation, accessed August 26, 2010, http://www.cbcfinc.org/cbc/cbc-members
.html. The CBC website is located at http://www.thecongressionalblackcau
cus.com/; Kenneth J. Cooper, "For Enlarged Congressional Black Caucus, a
New Kind of Impact," *Washington Post*, September 19, 1993. See appendix B
for a list of members.

4. Congressional Hispanic Caucus members, 111th Congress, http://chc.
velazquez.house.gov/about/members.shtml; "History of the Congressional
Hispanic Caucus," accessed August 26, 2010, http://chc.velazquez.house
.gov/CHC%20General%20Info.pdf; "Congressional Hispanic Caucus Has
New Leadership," *Hispanically Speaking News*, November 19, 2010, http://
www.hispanicallyspeakingnews.com/notitas-de-noticias/details/congressio
nal-hispanic-caucus-has-new-leadership/3062/. See appendix C for a list of
members.

5. Congressional Asian Pacific American Caucus website, http://www.honda
    .house.gov/index.php?option=com_content&view=article&id=65&Ite
    mid=57; Congressional Asian Pacific American Caucus members, 111th
    Congress, http://www.honda.house.gov/index.php?option=com_content
    &view=article&id=762&Itemid=318. See appendix D for a list of mem-
    bers.

6. Bruce Braley, "23 Democratic members of Congress joined together to form
    the Populist Caucus," official House website of Bruce Braley (D-Iowa),
    March 12, 2009, http://www.braley.house.gov/index.php?option=com_cont
    ent&task=view&id=304&Itemid=1; Ryan Grim, "Populist Caucus To Form
    In House: Braley," *Huffington Post*, February 10, 2009. See appendix G for a
    list of members.

7. "About Us," Progressive Congress, accessed November 1, 2010, http://action
    .progressivecongress.org/t/5866/content.jsp?key=3360.

8. Grantee: American Progressive Caucus Policy Foundation, Open Society In-
    stitute, 2009 and 2010.

9. "Keith Ellison," *Discover the Networks.org*. See also Jay Baggett, "New Mus-
    lim Congressman Called for Terrorist's Release," *WorldNetDaily*, January 21,
    2007 http://www.wnd.com/news/article.asp?ARTICLE_ID=53796.

10. Toby Harnden, "Bush like Hitler, says first Muslim in Congress," *Tele-
    graph* (UK), July 14, 2007; Joel Roberts, "Congressman Admits 9/11 Error,"
    CBSNews.com, July 18, 2007.

11. Alan Cooperman, "Muslim Candidate Plays Defense: Lead Shrinks as Min-
    nesota Democrat Repudiates Association with Farrakhan," *Washington Post*,
    September 11, 2006.

12. Ibid.

13. Scott W. Johnson, "Louis Farrakhan's First Congressman," *Weekly Stan-
    dard*, Oct. 9, 2006. http://www.weeklystandard.com/Content/Public/
    Articles/000/000/012/764obcsx.asp.

14. "DHS official Daniel Sutherland spoke at recent ISNA conference," *Militant
    IslamMonitor.org*, September 23, 2008.

15. *United States of America v. Holy Land Foundation for Relief and Development*,
    CR NO. 3:04-CR-240-G. List of Unindicted Co-conspirators and/or Joint
    Venturers. Court documents posted online at http://www.investigative
    project.org/documents/case_docs/423.pdf.

16. Statement of J. Michael Waller, Annenberg Professor of International Com-
    munication, Institute of World Politics Before the Subcommittee on Terror-
    ism, Technology and Homeland Security, Senate Committee on the Judiciary,

October 14, 2003, http://kyl.senate.gov/legis_center/subdocs/101403_wallerl.pdf.

17. 44th Annual ISNA Convention, Community Service Recognition Luncheon, Chicago, IL, September 1, 2007, http://web.archive.org/web/20070821040947/http://www.isna.net/conferences/annualconvention2007/csrl.html.

18. "DHS official Daniel Sutherland spoke at recent ISNA conference," September 23, 2008.

19. "Ellison Inspires Voters at 1st 'Rock the Muslim Vote' Townhall Forum," Muslim Public Affairs Council, September 24, 2008. Quote posted by Dennis MacEoin, "Keith Ellison's Stealth Jihad," *Middle East Quarterly* (Summer 2010), 31–40.

20. Session 4A: "Stand Up and Be Heard: Effective Strategies for Muslim Political Advocacy," 46th Annual ISNA Convention, Washington, DC, July 6, 2009, http://www.muslimadvocates.org/isnaconventionprgramwebsite.pdf.

21. 47th Annual ISNA Convention, "Nurturing, Compassionate Communities: Connecting Faith and Service," Chicago, IL, July 2–4, 2010, http://www.isna.net/assets/conventions/2010/program/conventionprogram_websiteversion.pdf.

22. "Halal Accreditation," Australian Federation of Islamic Councils, http://www.afic.com.au/?p=465.

23. 47th Annual ISNA Convention, July 2–4, 2010.

24. "ISNA Conference Again Features Conspiracy Theories," Investigative Project on Terrorism, July 6, 2010, http://www.investigativeproject.org/2044/isna-conference-again-features-conspiracy-theories.

25. Mitch Anderson, "Ellison: Hajj was transformative," *Minneapolis–St. Paul Star Tribune*, December 18, 2008.

26. Robert Spencer, "Muslim Congressman's Hajj paid for by Muslim Brotherhood front group," *Jihad Watch*, December 2008; Robert Spencer, "Ellison reveals cost of trip to Mecca: $13.5K," *Jihad Watch*, October 8, 2009. See also: Muslim American Society–Investigative Project dossier, http://www.investigativeproject.org/documents/misc/44.pdf (accessed June 16, 2011).

27. Noreen S. Ahmed-Ullah, Sam Roe, and Laurie Cohen, "A Rare Look at Secretive Brotherhood in America," *Chicago Tribune*, Sept. 19, 2004.

28. Ibid.; Mohamed Akram, "An Explanatory Memorandum on the General Strategic Goal for the Brotherhood in North America," May 19, 1991, Investigative Project on Terrorism, http://www.investigativeproject.org/document/id/20.

29. "Founding Advisors," Middle East Children's Alliance, accessed December 10, 2010, https://www.mecaforpeace.org/staff-board-and-advisors; "History," Middle East Children's Alliance," accessed December 10, 2010, https://www.mecaforpeace.org/history.

30. "History," MECA; "Barbara Lubin," *DiscovertheNetworks.org.*

31. "Middle East Children's Alliance," *DiscovertheNetworks.org.*

32. "Barbara Lubin," *DiscovertheNetworks.org.*

33. Jordan Fabian, "Black Caucus members want Gaza blockade lifted in light of flotilla incident," *Hill*, June 4, 2010.

34. "H. Res. 34: Recognizing Israel's right to defend itself against attacks," *Gov Track.us*, January 9, 2009.

35. *Washington Report on Middle East Affairs*, November 2001, 63. http://www.wrmea.com/archives/november01/0111063.html.

36. "Middle East Children's Alliance," *DiscovertheNetworks.org.*

37. Ibid.

38. Ed Lasky, "The Said-Khalidi-Obama Connection," *American Thinker*, October 22, 2008, http://www.campus-watch.org/article/id/5897.

39. "Barack Obama's Islamist ties to Rashid Khalidi, Edward Said and Ali Abunimah," *MilitantIslamMonitor.org*, September 10, 2008.

40. "Background," *VenceremosBrigade.org*, http://www.venceremosbrigade.org/background.htm.

41. State Sponsors of Terrorism, U.S. Department of State, http://www.state.gov/s/ct/c14151.htm.

42. Country Reports, Chapter 3: State Sponsors of Terrorism, U.S. Department of State, August 5, 2010, http://www.state.gov/s/ct/rls/crt/2009/140889.htm.

43. Background Note: Cuba, U.S. Department of State, March 25, 2010, http://www.state.gov/r/pa/ei/bgn/2886.htm.

44. Ibid.; Emile Schepers, "Cuba travel bill vote delayed," *People's World*, October 15, 2010.

45. S. 428 Freedom to Travel to Cuba Act, 111th Congress (2009–2010), introduced February 12, 2010, by Senator Byron Dorgan (D-N.D.) with thirty-nine cosponsors; H.R. 4645, Travel Restriction Reform and Export Enhancement Act, 111th Congress, 2d Session, February 23, 2010.

46. CNN Staff, "Cuban-American politicians against loosening travel, aid rules," *CNN.com*, August 21, 2010.

47. Representative Barbara Lee, "Mr. President: Lift the travel ban," *Hill*, August 23, 2010.

48. Mark Hemingway, "Comrade Barbara: A California congresswoman's new book reveals a lot," *National Review Online*, April 17, 2009.

49. J. Michael Waller, "Congresswoman Barbara Lee: Still stuck in the Cold War," *Political Warfare*, April 7, 2009, http://jmw.typepad.com/political_warfare/2009/04/congresswoman-barbara-lee-still-stuck-in-the-cold-war.html.

50. "Raúl meets with members of the U.S. Congressional Black Caucus," *Granma .cu*, April 7, 2009.

51. Alex Isenstadt, "CBC members praise Castro," *Politico*, April 9, 2009.

52. Patricia Grogg, "Cuba: 'It's time to talk' say US lawmakers," *People's World*, April 9, 2009.

53. Jack Tierney, "Return of the Radical Left?" Capital Research, [sixties@lists.village.virginia.edu Listserv], December 17, 2001, http://lists.village.virginia.edu/lists_archive/sixties-l/3892.html.

54. Robert W. Lee, "Totally Radical!" *New American*, March 29, 1999, Internet Archive, http://web.archive.org/web/20000818223401/; http://www.thenewamerican.com/tna/1999/03-29-99/totally_radical.htm; William P. Hoar, "Barbara Lee's Background," *New American* 17, no. 24 (November 19, 2001), 42.

55. Hoar, "Barbara Lee's Background," November 19, 2001.

56. "PWW events salute peoples leaders," *People's Weekly World*, December 15, 2006.

57. John Elvin, "Hey, Fidel, Don't Forget the Cigars," *Insight on the News* 15, no. 38 (October 18, 1999), 34.

58. J. A. Sierra, *History of Cuba Timeline, 1980–1999*, 2, *HistoryofCuba.com*. "Info on Info on Cuba 2/99 delegation" and Andres Petit, "Black Caucus Delegation visits Cuba, meets with Castro, Robaina," *La Habana, AfroCubaWeb.com*, February 19, 1999.

59. Petit, "Black Caucus Delegation visits Cuba," February 19, 1999.

60. "Congressional Black Caucus Meeting Marks a Turning Point," Radio Habana Cuba, *AfroCubaWeb.com*, September 21, 2000.

61. Vote number 2001-270 keeping Cuba travel ban until political prisoners released July 25, 2001, regarding bill HR 2590; Amendment adopted, 240–186, *On the Issues*, http://www.ontheissues.org/HouseVote/Party_2001-270.htm.

62. Brendan Farrington, "Obama to ease Cuba travel restrictions," Associated Press (*Washington Post*), January 14, 2010.

63. Ibid.

64. John Otis, Michelle Mittelstadt, and Bennett Roth, "Jackson Lee tries to

smooth Chavez ties. Her Venezuela trip, she says, was an attempt to protect jobs here," *Houston Chronicle*, February 23, 2007.

65. Richard Connelly, "Funeral, Cameras: Yep, Sheila Jackson Lee Is in the House," *Hair Balls/HoustonPress.com*, July 7, 2009.

66. "Rep. Sheila Jackson Lee insists South Vietnam is still a thing," *Daily Caller*, July 16, 2010.

67. Jim Hoft, "Dem Rep Sheila Jackson Lee Tells NAACP: 'All Those Who Wore Sheets a Long Time Ago Lifted Them Off to Wear Tea Party Clothing' (Applause!)," *Gateway Pundit*, July 15, 2010.

68. Simmi Aujula, "Sheila Jackson Lee wants DOJ to monitor tea partiers at polls," *Politico*, November 28, 2010.

69. Philip Klein, "Sheila Jackson Lee Says Repealing ObamaCare Violates Constitution," *American Spectator*, January 18, 2010.

70. "John Conyers," *DiscovertheNetworks.org*.

71. Addison Ross, "Rep. Conyers: Patriot or something else?" *BrookesNews.com*, February 18, 2003, http://www.brookesnews.com/031802conyers.html.

72. Ibid.

73. Ibid.

74. Ibid. Michael Parenti, "Kozy with the Klan," *MichaelParenti.org*, undated, http://www.michaelparenti.org/KozyWithKlan.html.

75. Lee, "Totally Radical!" March 29, 1999.

76. 3 Leslie Feinberg, "Jan. 18 Protest Tells Bush: No War, No Way. D.C.: Largest U.S. protest yet against Iraq war," *Workers World*, January 18, 2003.

77. Ibid.

78. "Conyers blasts Bush, Ashcroft," *People's World*, April 3, 2003.

79. Ibid.

80. John Hogan, Kathy Quinn, and John Strauss, "The DSA 2003 Convention: November 14-17, 2003," Democratic Socialists of America, accessed October 13, 2010, http://www.dsausa.org/convention2003/report/index.html.

81. "The Call to Drive Out the Bush Regime," The World Can't Wait website, July 13, 2006; "US Rep. John Conyers, Jr. speaking at the rally in Detroit in Oct. 5," World Can't Wait website, October 5, 2006; "Voice of the Revolutionary Communist Party, USA," http://rwor.org/a/rwlink/links.htm.

82. Eric Ebel, "Detroit-area progressives push back," *Talking Union* (blog), Democratic Socialists of America, February 21, 2010.

83. Frank Llewellyn, "March for Jobs, Justice and Education: 10.2.10," Democratic Socialists of America website, October 8, 2010; YouTube video posted October 11, 2010, http://www.youtube.com/watch?v=MkZCHhr_u0c.

84. "Endorsing Organizations," One Nation Working Together website.

85. Aaron Klein, "Shock video: Top Dem, socialists plot '1-world' scheme. Plan calls for unions, clergy, civil rights leaders to 'strengthen' Obama," *WND.com*, October 17, 2010.

86. Jonathan Allen, "Waters chooses ethics trial," *Politico*, July 30, 2010.

87. "Charles B. Rangel," *WhoRunsGov.com*, undated, http://www.whorunsgov .com/Profiles/Charles_B._Rangel/; Brody Mullins and Devlin Barrett, "House to Try Top Democrat. Rangel, Ex-Head of Tax-Writing Committee, Is Accused of Breaking Ethics Rules," *Wall Street Journal*, July 23, 2010; Billy House, "Rangel Found Guilty," *National Journal* website, November 16, 2010.

88. Michael Mcauliff and Corky Siemaszko, "Rep. Charles Rangel gets recommended punishment from House: Censure, apologizes and pleads for mercy," New York *Daily News*, November 18, 2010.

89. Michael Winter, "House votes to censure Rangel," *USA Today*, December 2, 2010.

90. Susan Crabtree, "After electoral drubbing, Democrats must now deal with ethics trials," *Hill*, November 3, 2010; Associated Press, "New documents in Waters case, ethics hearing off," *Google.com*, November 19, 2010; John Bresnahan and Jonathan Allen, "Maxine Waters ethics trial delayed," *Politico*, November 19, 2010.

91. R. Jeffrey Smith and Carol D. Leonnig, "Ethics probe of Rep. Waters derailed by infighting, sources say," *Washington Post*, December 16, 2010.

92. Perry Bacon, Jr., "Rep. Maxine Waters blasts ethics panel and media, defends links to OneUnited," *Washington Post*, August 13, 2010.

93. Bacon, "Rep. Maxine Waters blasts ethics panel and media," August 13, 2010.

94. RedState Insider, "Maxine & Barbara Sitting In A Tree," *RedState.com*, August 3 2010. See Citizens for Responsibility and Ethics in Washington's 2010 report, "CREW's Most Corrupt. Unfinished Business," http://www .citizensforethics.org/page/-/PDFs/Reports/CREWs_Most_ Corrupt_2010.pdf?nocdn=1.

95. "Rep. Maxine Waters Unmasks the Democrats—Wants to Nationalize the Oil Industry," *Neville Awards*, May 24, 2008, http://www.nevilleawards .com/maxine.shtml. The YouTube video clip, "Maxine Waters threatens to nationalize U.S. oil industries," May 22, 2008, can be viewed at http://www .youtube.com/watch?v=PUaY3LhJ-IQ.

96. "Maxine Waters Under Investigation," *Corruption Chronicles*/Judicial Watch website, September 17, 2009.

97. Editorial, "The Story of Joanne Chesimard," *NJLawman.com*, May 2003, http://www.njlawman.com/Feature%20Pieces/Joanne%20Chesimard .htm; "Congresswoman Waters issues statement on U.S. Freedom Fighter Assata Shakur," September 29, 1998, http://www.hartford-hwp.com/ archives/45a/089.html.

98. "Maxine Waters," *DiscovertheNetworks.org*.

99. "Charles Rangel," *DiscovertheNetworks.org*; Congressman Charles B. Rangel, U.S. House of Representatives, *AfroCubaWeb.com*, undated.

100. Warner Todd Huston, "New Evidence of Nancy Pelosi Associate Supporting Chavez, Marxists, & Terrorists," *NewsBusters.org*, October 15, 2008.

101. Antonio Sosa, "Can the United States Survive a Marxist President?" *American Daughter*, October 18, 2008, http://frontpage.americandaughter. com/?p=2066; "Colombian Senator Piedad Cordoba: 'Hugo Chavez is a good human being,'" *Colombia Reports*, November 23, 2009; Judi McLeod, "Senator Piedad Cordoba Colombia's Mata Hari," *Canada Free Press*, March 7, 2008.

102. Sosa, "Can the United States Survive a Marxist President?" October 18, 2008; "Revolutionary Armed Forces of Colombia. Fuerzas Armadas Revolucionarias de Colombia - FARC," *GlobalSecurity.org*, undated, http://www .globalsecurity.org/military/world/para/farc.htm.

103. Adriann Alsema, "Piedad Cordoba authorized to mediate release of FARC hostages," *Colombia Reports*, September 19, 2009; Kirsten Begg, "'FARC-politics' charges announced against Piedad Cordoba," *Colombia Reports*, April 10, 2010; Adriann Alsema, "Probe into alleged rebel ties a 'farce': Cordoba," *Colombia Reports*, June 20, 2009.

104. Sosa, "Can the United States Survive a Marxist President?" October 18, 2008; Mary Anastasia O'Grady, "FARC's 'Human Rights' Friends," *Wall Street Journal*, July 7, 2008.

105. Larry Jones, "Congressman John Lewis, Civil Rights Leader, Keynotes Conference African American History Month Program," United States Conference of Mayors, March 8, 1999, http://usmayors.org/usmayornewspaper/ documents/03_08_99/lewis.htm; William T. Poole, *New Left in Government: From Protest to Policy-Making*, Institution Report #9, Heritage Foundation, November 1978.

106. Poole, *New Left in Government: From Protest to Policy-Making*, November 1978.

107. *Student Non-Violent Coordinating Committee (SNCC)*, Department of Defense, 1967, http://www.aavw.org/protest/carmichael_sncc_abstract06_full .html.

108. Ibid; *Records of the Southern Christian Leadership Conference, 1954–1970, Records of the Executive Director and Treasurer*, A Microfilm Guide: Black Studies Research Sources, Part 2 (Bethesda, MD: University Publications of America), xiv, http://www.lexisnexis.com/documents/academic/upa_cis/1564_RecsSouthChrLeadConfPt2.pdf; "Fair Play for Cuba Committee," *Spartacus Educational*, http://www.spartacus.schoolnet.co.uk/JFKfairplay.htm.

109. *Student Non-Violent Coordinating Committee (SNCC)*, Department of Defense, 1967.

110. Abstract: *Subversive Influences in Riots, Looting, and Burning (Los Angeles–Watts)*, House Un-American Activities Committee, 90th Congress, 1st Session (Washington, DC: GPO, 1967, 1968), Part 3 (November 28, 29, 30, 1967).

111. Ibid.

112. Tony Pecinovsky, "History of YCL (Young Communist League)," YCLUSA website, November 19, 2002.

113. Poole, *New Left in Government: From Protest to Policy-Making*, November 1978; *The nationwide drive against law enforcement intelligence operations: Hearing before the Subcommittee to Investigate the Administration of the Internal Security Act and Other Internal Security Laws of the Committee on the Judiciary*, United States Senate, Ninety-Fourth Congress, first session, Part 2, July 11, 1975; "National Committee against Repressive Legislation (NCARL)," in Michael A. Hallett and Dennis J. Palumbo, U.S. Criminal Justice Interest Groups: Institutional Profiles (Westport, CT: Greenwood Press, 1993), 66.

114. *The nationwide drive against law enforcement intelligence operations*, July 11, 1975.

115. Chicago Committee to Defend the Bill of Rights website, http://www.ccdbr.org/; "Celebration of the Dynamic Life of Frank Wilkinson (1914–2006)," CCDBR, October 29, 2006, http://www.ccdbr.org/events/wilkinson/Wilkinson_Committee.html; "Frank Wilkinson (1914–2006)," *CCDBR.org*.

116. Poole, *New Left in Government: From Protest to Policy-Making*, November 1978; "John Lewis," *DiscovertheNetworks.org*.

117. "David Dellinger," *Spartacus*, http://www.spartacus.schoolnet.co.uk/JFK-dillinger.htm; John Michael Schell, Jr., "Tom Hayden and the Climate of SDS," *Journal of Undergraduate History*, archive, University of Wisconsin, n.d., http://uwho.rso.wisc.edu/Archive/John%20Michael%20Schell%20volume%205.pdf.

118. "John Lewis," *DiscovertheNetworks.org*; website of Congressman John Lewis, http://johnlewis.house.gov/index.php?option=com_content&task=view&id=156.

119. William Douglas, "Tea party protesters scream 'nigger' at black congress-man," McClatchy Newspapers, March 20, 2010.

120. Patrick O'Connor and James Hohmann, "Dems say protesters used N-word," *Politico*, March 20, 2010.

121. Martin Knight, "John Lewis: Civil Rights Icon . . . and a Liar. Because Liars Need To Be Called Out," *RedState.com*, March 23, 2010.

122. Mike Allen and Jonathan Martin, "Civil rights icon says McCain stirs hate," *Politico*, October 11, 2008.

123. Ibid. John Lewis's full statement is posted on his official campaign website: http://www.johnlewisforcongress.com/node/219.

124. Bennett Roth, "Union Brass Making No Overtures to the GOP, Trumka: Elections Not a Mandate for 'John Boehner's America,'" *Roll Call*, November 17, 2010.

125. Ceci Connolly and R. Jeffrey Smith, "Obama Positioned to Quickly Reverse Bush Actions. Stem Cell, Climate Rules Among Targets of President-Elect's Team," *Washington Post*, November 9, 2008.

126. Transcript: "John Podesta on 'FNS,'" *FoxNews.com*, November 9, 2008.

127. Ibid.

128. John D. Podesta, *The Power of the President*, Center for American Progress website, November 15, 2010.

129. Sarah Rosen Wartell, comp., *The Power of the President* (Full Report), Center for American Progress website, November 2010; Sarah Rosen Wartell, comp., *The Power of the President* (Executive Summary), Center for American Progress website, November 2010.

Chapter Three: The Radical Origins of Obamacare

1. Marguerite Higgins, "Video of the Week: 'We have to pass the bill so you can find out what is in it,'" *The Foundry* (blog), Heritage Foundation, March 10, 2010; Nancy Pelosi, "We have to pass the health care bill so that you can find out what is in it," YouTube, March 9, 2010, http://www.youtube.com/watch?v=KoE1R-xH5To.

2. Dwyer Arce, "US House passes health care reform legislation," *Jurist/Paper Chase*, March 22, 2010; Bill Summary and Status, H.R. 3590 Patient Protection and Affordable Care Act, 111th Congress (2009–2010), http://thomas.loc.gov/cgi-bin/bdquery/z?d111:H.R.3590; "The House and Senate Bills," *The Scoop*, Heritage Foundation, January 29, 2010,

http://fixhealthcarepolicy.com/key-documents/the-house-and-senate-bills/.

3. "Momentum Builds for Public Health Insurance Option!!! Caucuses Unite Behind Public Health Insurance Plan Option," Health Care for America Now website, April 30, 2009.

4. "Charles Rangel on Health Care," *On the Issues*, accessed October 19, 2010, http://www.ontheissues.org/NY/Charles_Rangel_Health_Care.htm; Jedediah Bila, "ACORN and The Working Families Party: Another Connection," *HumanEvents.com*, September 25, 2009.

5. "Jacob S. Hacker," Political Science, Yale University, accessed October 18, 2010, http://www.yale.edu/polisci/people/jhacker.html; "Jacob S. Hacker. Keynote Speaker at NASI's 21st Conference," National Academy of Social Insurance, nasi.org.

6. Staff, "Queens College to toast beloved poli-sci professor, 82," New York *Daily News*, November 10, 2010; "Distinguished Achievement Award Recipients, 1992: Andrew Hacker '47," Horace Mann School/horacemann.org.

7. "Andrew Hacker," Macmillan Books, http://us.macmillan.com/author/andrewhacker.

8. Staff, "Queens College to toast beloved poli-sci professor, 82," November 10, 2010; "Andrew Hacker," Queens College, New York City, http://qcpages.qc.edu/Political_Science/hacker.html.

9. Obituaries, "Louis M. Hacker, 88, Leading Advocate of Adult Education," *New York Times*, March 22, 1987.

10. Scott C. Zeman, "Historian Louis M. Hacker's 'Coincidental Conversion' to the Truth," *The Historian* (Phi Alpha Theta, History Honor Society, 1998).

11. Jacob S. Hacker, "A mandate isn't mandatory," *Los Angeles Times*, February 26, 2008; Press Release: "Health Care for America Would Save Billions. Lewin Analysis Shows Immediate Savings, Rein on Costs," Economic Policy Institute, February 15, 2008, http://www.sharedprosperity.org/hcfa/news_release.pdf; Speaker's Profile: "Jacob Hacker," Leigh Bureau, accessed October 18, 2010, http://www.leighbureau.com/speaker.asp?id=387.

12. Jacob S. Hacker, "Health care for America: A proposal for guaranteed, affordable health care for all Americans building on Medicare and employment-based insurance," EPI Briefing Paper No. 180, Economic Policy Institute, January 11, 2007, http://www.sharedprosperity.org/bp180.html.

13. John Sheils and Randall Haught, *Covering America: Real Remedies for the Uninsured. Cost and Coverage Analysis of Ten Proposals to Expand Health Insur-*

ance Coverage, Lewin Group, 2003, http://www.esresearch.org/publications/SheilsLewinall/E-Hacker.pdf.

14. "Jacob S. Hacker," former fellow, New America Foundation, accessed October 19, 2010, http://www.newamerica.net/people/jacob_hacker; H.R. 676—Expanded and Improved Medicare for All Act, Bill Summary & Status, 109th Congress (2005–2006), http://thomas.loc.gov/cgi-bin/bdquery/z?d109:h.r.00676; "A Brief Summary: The 'United States National Health Insurance Act,' H.R. 676 ('Expanded and Improved Medicare For All Bill')," http://web.archive.org/web/20070219075523/http://www.healthcare-now.org/resources/hr676.htm.

15. "A Brief Summary: The United States National Health Insurance Act."

16. "Healthcare-NOW," *DiscovertheNetworks.org.*

17. "Single-payer system," National Library of Medicine, Medical Subject Headings, 2008 MeSH, http://www.nlm.nih.gov/cgi/mesh/2008/MB_cgi?mode=&index=17627&field=all&HM=&II=&PA=&form=&input=.

18. "Our Board," *Healthcare-NOW.org.*

19. "Medea Benjamin," *DiscovertheNetworks.org.*

20. Roger Hickey, "Lewin Findings on Hacker-EPI Health Plan: Good News for Obama and Clinton," Campaign for America's Future website, February 15, 2008.

21. Paul Howard and David Gratzer, "The Road to Rationing," *New Atlantis* 24 (Spring 2009), 95–102.

22. Jacob S. Hacker, "Better Medicine. Fixing the left's health-care prescription," *Slate.com*, October 10, 2006.

23. Kip Sullivan, "Bait and switch: How the 'public option' was sold," Physicians for a National Health Program website, July 20, 2009.

24. Mark Schmitt, "The History of the Public Option," *TAPPED/ American Prospect*, August 18, 2009.

25. Sullivan, "Bait and switch," July 20, 2009.

26. Jacob S. Hacker, "Why I Still Believe in This Bill," *New Republic*, December 20, 2009.

27. John Nichols, "How to Push Obama," *Progressive*, January 2009.

28. Ibid.; "Standing Room Only Crowd Greets Obama at Cobb Town Hall Meeting," *wsbtv.com*, July 8, 2008.

29. Amy Chozick, "Obama Touts Single-Payer System for Health Care," *Wall Street Journal*, August 19, 2008.

30. David Sirota, "Obama for Single-Payer Before He Was Against It: How Political Elites Have Made Single Payer 'Politically Impossible,'" *AlterNet.org*, May 11, 2009.

31. "Barack Obama on single payer in 2003," Physicians for a National Health Program, June 4, 2008, http://www.pnhp.org/news/2008/june/barack_obama_on_sing.php.

32. Sirota, "Obama for Single-Payer," May 11, 2009.

33. Larissa MacFarquhar, "The Conciliator," *New Yorker*, May 7, 2007.

34. Associated Press, "Health insurers offer to accept close regulation: Reduced rates for women discussed amid fear of new government plan," *MSNBC.com*, May 5, 2009.

35. David Shalleck-Klein, "Dems backtrack on single-payer bill," *Hill*, August 30, 2010.

36. "Issues 2000: Health Care," Campaign for America's Future, October 6, 1999, Internet Archive, http://web.archive.org/web/20000522005145; www.ourfuture.org/readarticle.asp?ID=519.

37. "About Us," Health Care for America Now website.

38. Press Conference: Launch of Health Care for America Now by Jeffrey D. Blum, director, USAction, Washington, DC, YouTube, August 8, 2009, http://www.youtube.com/watch?v=1xZ35qCKcTg; Press Release: "Health Care for America Now Launch," Health Care for America Now website, July 8, 2008.

39. Ibid.; Jeff Patch, "Liberal Beachhead Established on K Street," *Politico*, February 26, 2007.

40. Dan Eggen, "How interest groups behind health-care legislation are financed is often unclear," *Washington Post*, January 7, 2010; Lee-Lee Prina, "Health Reform: What Foundations Are Saying and Funding," *HealthAffairs GrantWatch Blog*, April 9, 2010, http://healthaffairs.org/blog/2010/04/09/health-reform-what-foundations-are-saying-and-funding/ (see section, "$26.5 Million in Grants to Health Care for America Now"); Suzanne Perry, "Advocates Plot Next Steps Even as Ink Dries on Health-Care Overhaul Law," *Chronicle of Philanthropies*, March 23, 2010.

41. "Open Society Institute," *DiscovertheNetworks.org*.

42. "Health Care for America Now State Contact List," accessed October 18, 2010, http://www.scribd.com/doc/19925391/ACORNHealthcare-for-American-Now-State-Contact-List.

43. "About Us," Health Care for America Now.

44. "Senator Obama Signs Onto Health Care for America Now Campaign," Health Care for America Now website; "Obama Backs Health Care for America Now," Atlantic Philanthropies, October 8, 2008.

45. Kip Sullivan, "An analysis of Celinda Lake's slide show, 'How to talk to voters

about health care,'" Physicians for a National Health Program website, November 29, 2008; "About PNHP," Physicians for a National Health Program website.

46. Carrie Budoff Brown, "Obscure group shapes reform fight," *Politico*, April 2, 2009.

47. "History of Herndon Alliance," Herndon Alliance website, June 21, 2010.

48. Brown, "Obscure group shapes reform fight," April 2, 2009.

49. "NGRC Principals," National Grassroots and Communication, n.d. (this Web page was cached by Zoom Information on March 2, 2007); "Past Events," Center for American Progress website, August 2006. (See Van Vranken's bio near bottom of page.)

50. Ibid. "Board and Staff," Herndon Alliance website.

51. "Philippe Villers, President, Board of Directors," Families USA website; "Families USA," *DiscovertheNetworks.org*.

52. Sheryl Gay Stolberg, "White House and Allies Set to Build Up Health Law," *New York Times*, June 6, 2010.

53. "Ron Pollack," Families USA website.

54. Brown, "Obscure group shapes reform fight," April 2, 2009.

55. "Celinda Lake," *LakeResearch.com*.

56. "Board of Directors," Progressive Congress Action Fund website.

57. "Herndon Alliance Partners," *HerndonAlliance.org*.

58. "History," American Environics website.

59. "American Environics Staff," American Environics website.

60. Ibid.; Garance Franke-Ruta, "Remapping the culture debate: Can the Democrats finally learn to talk culture? Fascinating new research challenges some cherished assumptions—and offers clues about the future," *American Prospect*, February 1, 2006; "The Death of Environmentalism and the Politics of Possibility," *La Prensa*, February 8, 2008; Arnold, *Freezing in the Dark*, 368, 382 and 386–87.

61. Arnold, *Freezing in the Dark*, 377–78, 382.

62. Franke-Ruta, "Remapping the culture debate," February 1, 2006.

63. Aaron Klein and Brenda J. Elliott, *The Manchurian President: Barack Obama's Ties to Communists, Socialists and Other Anti-American Extremists* (Washington, D.C.: WND Books, 2010), 233–37.

64. Ibid.

65. American Environics, *Road Map for a Health Justice Majority*, American Environics website, May 2006.

66. Sullivan, "An analysis of Celinda Lake's slide show," November 29, 2008.

67. Brown, "Obscure group shapes reform fight," April 2, 2009.

68. "History of Herndon Alliance."

69. Brown, "Obscure group shapes reform fight," April 2, 2009.

70. "Words We Use," Herndon Alliance website, July 7, 2010.

71. "Q = A + 1," Herndon Alliance website, July 13, 2010.

72. "Resources. Grid: Individual Mandate," Herndon Alliance website, October 13, 2010.

73. "History of Herndon Alliance."

74. "Services," Herndon Alliance website, June 21, 2010.

75. "Resources. Grid: Opposing Repeal," Herndon Alliance website, October 13, 2010.

76. "Post Passage Messaging Guide," Herndon Alliance website, August 18, 2010.

77. Brown, "Obscure group shapes reform fight," April 2, 2009.

78. Huma Khan, "House Passes Bill Repealing Health Care Law: Republicans Say Bill Sends a Strong Message, Urge Debate in Senate," *ABCNews.com*, January 19, 2011; "House Passes Health Care Repeal Bill," *DCEmployment LawUpdate.com*, January 19, 2011.

79. Khan, "House Passes Bill Repealing Health Care Law," January 19, 2011.

80. Matthew Jaffe, "Senate GOP to Attach Health Care Repeal as Amendment to FAA Reauthorization Bill," *The Note/ABCNews.com*, February 1, 2011.

81. "Senate Dems block GOP's health bill repeal," *WMICentral.com*, February 5, 2011; "Healthcare Repeal Bill Amendment Gets Waived in the Senate," *Ham Report*, February 3, 2011.

82. Eugene Kiely, "Senate GOP introduces bill to repeal new health care law," *USA Today*, March 23, 2010.

83. "Michigan AG praises Florida court health care ruling," WJRT ABCNews, February 1, 2011; Case No.: 3:10-cv-91-RV/EMT, *Attorney General Pam Bondi et al. v. United States Department of Health and Human Services*, United States District Court for the Northern District of Florida, Pensacola Division, State of Florida, http://www.scag.gov/newsroom/pdf/2011/healthcare-summaryjudgement.pdf.

84. Case No.3-10-cv-91-RV/EMT.

85. "Herndon Alliance 2011 Work Plan," Herndon Alliance website, December 13, 2010.

86. Dobbs, "American Fabianism." Cited from *Report of the Joint Legislative Committee Investigating Seditious Activities, April 24, 1920, Senate of the State of New York*, 1088.

87. Jennifer Haberkorn, "Democrats coordinate health messaging," *Politico*, February 4, 2011.

Chapter Four: Making It in America

1. John Bresnahan and Jonathan Allen, "At White House, Nancy Pelosi leverages tension," *Politico*, July 14, 2010.
2. "Ask the Speaker with Speaker Nancy Pelosi," Netroots Nation Agenda for 2010, n.d., http://www.netrootsnation.org/agenda/2010?day=&type=keynote&sort=cron; "Make It In America – AAM," YouTube, posted July 24, 2010, http://www.youtube.com/watch?v=qWNXGcHhjm0.
3. Leo Gerard, "For the Strength of Rosie the Riveter: Make It in America," *AlterNet.org*, July 28, 2010.
4. Dave Johnson, "Pelosi: Congress' Coming 'Making It In America' Initiative," Campaign for America's Future website, July 24, 2010.
5. Gerard, "For the Strength of Rosie the Riveter," July 28, 2010.
6. Lori Montgomery and Brady Dennis, "New Democratic strategy for creating jobs focuses on a boost in manufacturing," *Washington Post*, August 4, 2010.
7. Ibid.; Stephanie Condon, "Mark Critz Defeats Tim Burns in Pennsylvania Special Election for Murtha's Seat," *CBSNews.com*, May 18, 2010.
8. Montgomery and Dennis, "New Democratic strategy," August 4, 2010; Rick Haglund, "While Obama celebrates new manufacturing jobs in Michigan, factory workers shouldn't get their hopes up," *mlive.com*, July 31, 2010.
9. Condon, "Mark Critz," May 18, 2010; Gerard, "For the Strength of Rosie the Riveter," July 28, 2010.
10. Montgomery and Dennis, "New Democratic strategy," August 4, 2010.
11. Ibid.
12. Ibid.; James Parks, "House Democrats Push 'Make It in America' Agenda," AFL-CIO Blog, August 3, 2010.
13. Press Release: Matthew Beck, "House Votes to Strengthen U.S. Manufacturing Jobs," House Committee on Ways and Means, U. S. House of Representatives, July 21, 2010; Press Release: "Making It in America Builds Our Economy," official House website of Representative Charles B. Rangel, U.S. House of Representatives, September 9, 2010; Montgomery and Dennis, "New Democratic Strategy," August 4, 2010.
14. "2010 Supplemental Appropriations, U.S. Patent and Trademark Office," House Committee on Appropriations, U.S. House of Representatives, July 28, 2010.
15. "House Approves Legislation to Improve Public-Private Sector Economic Development," House Committee on Education and Labor, U.S. House of Representatives, July 19, 2010.

16. H.R. 1875, End the Trade Deficit Act, *OpenCongress.org*, July 18, 2010.

17. Speaker of the House, "Pelosi: 'When We Make It In America, We Create Jobs, Promote Competitiveness, and Lead the World Economy,'" PRNewswire, September 15, 2010; H.R. Congressional Made in America Act, official House website of Representative Marcy Kaptur, U.S. House of Representatives, n.d.; Press Release: "Kaptur's 'Made in America' Promise Act Passes House," official House website of Representative Marcy Kaptur, U.S. House of Representatives, September 15, 2010.

18. H.R. 3116, Berry Amendment Extension Act, *GovTrack.us*, September 16, 2010.

19. H.R. 4678, Foreign Manufacturers Legal Accountability Act of 2010, introduced February 24, 2010, *Thomas.loc.gov*.

20. "H.R. 4692, The National Manufacturing Strategy Act, passed in the House of Representatives," official House website of Representative Daniel Lipinski, U.S. House of Representatives, July 28, 2010.

21. H.R. 5156, Clean Energy Technology Manufacturing and Export Assistance Act of 2010, *GovTrack.us*, July 28, 2010.

22. H.R. 5893, Investing in American Jobs and Closing Tax Loopholes Act, *GOP.gov*, July 30, 2010.

23. Representative Charles Rangel (D-N.Y.), "Making It in America Builds Our Economy," official U.S. House of Representatives website, September 9, 2010.

24. Representative Bruce Braley (D-Iowa), "Populist Caucus Announces American Jobs First Platform," official U.S. House of Representatives website, April 19, 2010.

25. Scapozzola, "Hoyer, Democratic Leaders and Members Hold Press Conference on the 'Make It in America' Agenda," *AmericanManufacturing.org*, July 22, 2010.

26. Ibid.

27. Scapozzola, "The Alliance for American Manufacturing," *AmericanManufacturing.org*, August 4, 2010.

28. Ibid.

29. Peter Nicholas, "Democrats divided on Obama's political tactic," *Los Angeles Times*, November 21, 2010.

30. "Senate Democrats Roll Out Agenda For Winning The Future By Cutting Spending, Creating High-Paying Jobs And Keeping America Competitive," *Democrats.Senate.gov*, February 16, 2011.

31. Scapozzola, "Senate Democrats Offer Manufacturing, Trade, and Infrastructure Plans," February 17, 2011, *AmericanManufacturing.org*.

32. Scott N. Paul, "We're Number Two: Why America Is Losing its Lead in Manufacturing," *USW.org* blog, March 20, 2011.

33. Robert Borosage, "Ryan's Roadmap To Ruin," Campaign for America's Future website, April 5, 2011.

34. Representatives Keith Ellison and Raul Grijalva, "People's budget or roadmap to ruin?" *Politico*, April 5, 2011.

35. Philip Klein, "House progressives to release liberal alternative to Ryan budget plan," *Washington Examiner*, April 7, 2011.

36. Russell Berman, "Hoyer Pushes 'Make It in America,'" *Hill*, May 4, 2011.

37. "Pelosi issues rallying call," CNN Political Ticker, January 21, 2011.

38. Berman, "Hoyer Pushes 'Make It in America,'" May 4, 2011.

39. "Keep It Made In America [Tour]," *AmericanManufacturing.org*.

40. Vriz, "Keep It Made In America Tour–Day One," *MadeInAmericaTour.org*, May 12, 2009.

41. H.R. 2378, Currency Reform for Fair Trade Act, Introduced in U.S. House of Representatives, May 12, 2010, *OpenCongress.org*, H.R. 2378, Currency Reform for Fair Trade Act, *GovTrack.us*, last action September 29, 2010.

42. Howard Schneider, "House slaps China on currency policy, deepening trade dispute," *Washington Post*, September 29, 2010.

43. Copies of letters to the House of Representatives posted by the Fair Currency Coalition on its website, with various dates in September 2010, http://www.faircurrency.org/presscenter/2010%2009%2029%20Press%20Package%20Letters%20supporting%20HR%202378.pdf; "Members," Fair Currency Coalition website, February 19, 2010.

44. S. 3134, Currency Exchange Rate Oversight Reform Act of 2010, introduced in the U.S. Senate, *GovTrack.us*, March 17, 2010.

45. Greg Sargent, "Obama Camp Unveils 'Buy American, Vote Obama' Campaign," *TPM Central /TalkingPointsMemo.com*, August 15, 2008.

46. Brenda J. Elliott, "Buy American, Vote Obama. What?," *RBO*, August 16, 2008, http://therealbarackobama.wordpress.com/2008/08/16/buy-american-vote-obama-what/.

47. John Batchelor, "Canada Goes to War," *RBO*, February 3, 2009, http://therealbarackobama.wordpress.com/2009/02/03/batchelor-canada-goes-to-war/.

48. Ibid.

49. John Batchelor, "'Buy American,'" *RBO*, February 4, 2009, http://therealbarackobama.wordpress.com/2009/02/04/batchelor-buy-american/.

50. Ibid.

51. "Canada should pursue 'Buy Canadian' strategy: Layton," CBC News, Feb-

ruary 3, 2009; David Charter, Rory Watson, and Philip Webster, "President Obama to water down 'Buy American' plan after EU trade war threat," *Times Online* (UK), February 4, 2009.

52. Carol E. Lee, "Obama backs off 'Buy American,'" *Politico*, February 13, 2009; "Canada-U.S. agreement on Buy American came into force," Foreign Affairs and International Trade Canada, February 16, 2009.

53. "About Us. Scott Paul," Alliance for American Manufacturing website.

54. "Leo W. Gerard," *Huffington Post*.

55. Bob Roman, "Chicago Anti-FTAA Action," *New Ground* 76 (May–June 2001), Chicago Democratic Socialists of America, http://www.chicagodsa .org/ngarchive/ng76.html#anchor423866; "Member Parties of the Socialist International," Socialist International, accessed November 1, 2010, http:// www.socialistinternational.org/viewArticle.cfm?ArticlePageID=931.

56. "2007 Eugene V. Debs–Norman Thomas–Michael Harrington Dinner," Chicago Democratic Socialists of America, May 4, 2007, http://www.chica godsa.org/d2007/index.html.

57. "Project Partners," Alliance for American Manufacturing website; "Who We Are," Alliance for American Manufacturing website.

58. *Buy America Works: Longstanding United States Policy Enhances the Job Creating Effect of Government Spending*, Alliance for American Manufacturing web- site, February 2010.

59. Vicki Needham, "Manufacturing sector continues expansion," *Hill*, April 1, 2011.

60. Jarol B. Manheim, *Biz-War and the Out-Of-Power Elite: The Progressive-Left Attack on the Corporation* (Psychology Press, 2004), 134; Arnold, *Freezing in the Dark*, 205: Heather Booth, longtime Democratic operative and cofounder of the Midwest Academy, "trained many activist members" of Campaign for America's Future.

61. Dave Johnson, "Manufacturing Strategy Idea Gets a Boost," Campaign for America's Future website, July 26, 2010; Eric Lotke and Armand Biroonak, "Where We're Going. How We'll Get There," Institute for America's Future website, October 29, 2009.

62. "Making It In America: Building the New Economy," Campaign for Ameri- ca's Future website, October 29, 2009.

63. Ibid.

64. Robert L. Borosage, "Making It In America," Institute for America's Future website, July 22, 2010.

65. Dave Johnson, "Making Sense: Making It In America," Campaign for Amer- ica's Future website, October 13, 2010.

66. Ibid.

67. Robert E. Scott, "'Make it in America' bills will advance U.S. manufacturing," Economic Policy Institute website, August 2, 2010; "Who We Are," Alliance for American Manufacturing.

68. Paul Taylor, "Analyzing Alternatives In Labor's Think Tank; Liberal Economists Study Government's Role," *Washington Post*, February 19, 1987, Final Edition, A25.

69. John B. Judis, "The Pressure Elite: Inside the Narrow World of Advocacy Group Politics," *American Prospect* 2 (Spring 1992), 24, cited in Richard Magat, *Unlikely Partners: Philanthropic Foundations and the Labor Movement* (Ithaca, NY: Cornell University Press, 1999), 74.

70. Magat, *Unlikely Partners*, 74: Roger Hickey, interview with author, November 10, 1993.

71. Ibid.; "Lester Thurow," *nndb.com*; "Barry Bluestone, Dean, School of Social Science, Urban Affairs, and Public Policy," Northeastern University, accessed October 27, 2010, http://www.polisci.neu.edu/faculty_staff/fulltime_faculty/bluestone/.

72. EPI Board of Directors, Economic Policy Institute website.

73. EPI Board of Directors; "R. Thomas Buffenbarger," Theodore Roosevelt Conservation Partnership/trcp.org.

74. EPI Board of Directors; Doug Cunningham, "Change To Win Chair Anna Burger Retires," *Workers Independent News*, August 12, 2010, http://www.laborradio.org/node/14010; "About Us," *Change to Win*, changetowin.org/.

75. EPI Board of Directors; "About," Communications Workers of America/cwa-union.org.

76. EPI Board of Directors; "Leo W. Gerard," United Steel Workers/usw.org.

77. "President Gerald W. McEntee" section in "About AFSCME," *afscme.org.*

78. "UNITE HERE General President Bruce Raynor Suspended from Union," *Talking Union*, April 21, 2009; Steven Greenhouse, "Union Accuses a Leader of Financial Misconduct," *New York Times*, March 31, 2011; Daniel Massey, "Bruce Raynor Leaving Workers United," *CrainsNewYork.com*, April 26, 2011.

79. EPI Board of Directors; Alec MacGillis, "Officials say SEIU president is stepping down from post," *Washington Post*, April 13, 2010.

80. EPI Board of Directors.

81. "$40 Million Health Care Campaign to Launch, Announce New National Ad," PRNewswire, July 7, 2008.

82. Aaron Klein and Brenda J. Elliott, *The Manchurian President: Barack Obama's*

Ties to Communists, Socialists and Other Anti-American Extremists (Washington, DC: WND Books, 2010), chapter 14.

83. Board members, Campaign for America's Future," http://www.ourfuture.org/page/2009052122/campaign-americas-future-board-members; Advisors, Campaign for America's Future, Internet Archive, http://web.archive.org/web/20030218054424/http://www.ourfuture.org/aboutus/founders.cfm.

84. Manheim, *Biz-War and the Out-of-Power Elite*, 134–35.

85. Tula Connell, "Trumka Named to Obama Economic Advisory Panel," AFL-CIO NOW Blog, February 6, 2009.

86. Holly Rosenkrantz and Stephanie Armour, "Union Enthusiasm for Obama Re-Election Fades, AFL-CIO's Chief Trumka Says," Bloomberg, June 1, 2011, http://www.bloomberg.com/news/2011-06-01/union-enthusiasm-for-obama-re-election-fades-afl-cio-s-chief-trumka-says.html.

87. "Board," Apollo Alliance/apolloalliance.org.

88. Jim Grossfeld, "Leo the Linchpin: Steelworker President Leo Gerard Looks Like an Old-Time Union Leader, but He's Put Together a Labor-Environmentalist Alliance That Bridges Some Growing Democratic Fissures," *American Prospect* 18 (October 2007).

89. Keith Schneider, "Clean Energy Breakthrough in Stimulus, Next Steps," Apollo News Service, February 20, 2009, http://www.cows.org/about_newsroom_detail.asp?id=970.

90. Dani Rodrik, "The Return of Industrial Policy," *ProjectSyndicate.org*, May 12, 2010.

91. Ilya Podolyako, "Guest Post: A Closer Look at Industrial Policy," *Baseline Scenario* website, April 15, 2009.

92. Taylor, "Analyzing Alternatives," February 19, 1987.

93. Magat, *Unlikely Partners*, 74.

94. Marilyn Marks, "What experts say candidates should be discussing," *St. Petersburg Times* (Florida), March 1, 1988, City Edition, A4.

95. Andrew Rosenthal, "Taking Cue from Reaganites, Liberals Are Drafting Blueprints," *New York Times*, July 6, 1988, Late City Final Edition, A14.

96. Bailey Morris, "Hunt for a winning economic formula; US presidential election," *Times* (London), July 21 1988. The author is also known as Bailey Morris-Eck.

97. Rosenthal, "Taking Cue from Reaganites," July 6, 1988.

98. David R. Francis, "Shift to Left Seen in US Public," *Christian Science Monitor*, January 31, 1990, p. 9.

99. Stephen Klaidman, "Group Advocates Environmental Trusts," *Washington Post*, March 28, 1977, A3.

100. Rael Jean Isaac and Erich Isaac, *The Coercive Utopians: Social Deception by America's Power Players* (Washington, DC: Regnery Publishing, 1984), 130; Eric Miller, *Hope in a Scattering Time: A Life of Christopher Lasch* (Grand Rapids, MI: Eerdmans, 2010), 162; Constance Curry et al., *Deep in Our Hearts: Nine White Women in the Freedom Movement* (Athens: University of Georgia Press, 2000), 205.

101. Isaac and Isaac, *The Coercive Utopians*, 130, 131.

102. High Road Service Center website, May 2, 2003, Internet Archive, http://web.archive.org/web/20030502002647/http://www.highroadnow.org/; "Take the High Road," High Road Service Center, ALICE, May 2, 2003, Internet Archive, http://web.archive.org/web/20030502163556/www.highroadnow.org/about/index.cfm.

103. "About," Economic Analysis and Research Network (EARN)/earncentral.org.

104. "National Organizations," Economic Analysis and Research Network (EARN)/earncentral.org.

105. "Wisconsin's Job Base Shifting Away from Provision of Health Care," *COWS Notes*/cows.org, May 2004.

106. High Road Service Center website, May 2, 2003.

107. Katrina Vanden Heuvel, "Meet ALICE," *Nation*, April 24, 2004.

108. Ruth Conniff, "Send in Mr. Rogers?" *Progressive*, January 1, 2005.

109. High Road Service Center website, May 31, 2008, Internet Archive, http://web.archive.org/web/20080531051855/http://www.highroadnow.org/.

110. H.R. 5156, Clean Energy Technology Manufacturing and Export Assistance Act of 2010, *GovTrack.us*, July 28, 2010, http://www.govtrack.us/congress/bill.xpd?bill=h111-5156; Press Release: "House Energy and Commerce Committee Passes Matsui Clean Tech Manufacturing and Export Promotion Legislation; Floor Consideration Possible Before August Recess," official website of Speaker Nancy Pelosi, U.S. House of Representatives, July 21, 2010.

111. Apollo Alliance, *Make It in America: The Apollo Clean Transportation Manufacturing Action Plan*, Apollo Alliance website, October 2010.

112. Apollo Alliance, "Making It In America: 3.7 Million Jobs, 600,000 in Manufacturing, Through Infrastructure Investments," Apollo Alliance website, October 26, 2010.

113. Apollo Alliance, *Make It in America: The Apollo Clean Transportation Manufacturing Action Plan*, Apollo Alliance, October 2010, 3–4.

114. Ibid., 2.

115. Apollo Alliance, "TMAP Policy Recommendation Endorsers," Apollo Alliance website.

116. Apollo Alliance, *Make It in America*, October 2010, 6.

117. Ibid.; Apollo Alliance, *Make It in America: The Apollo Green Manufacturing Action Plan*, Apollo Alliance website, March 2009.

118. Apollo Alliance, *Make It in America*, October 2010, 6.

119. Apollo Alliance, Executive Summary, *Make It in America: The Apollo Clean Transportation Manufacturing Action Plan*, Apollo Alliance website, October 2010.

120. Sarah Goodyear, "Building lots of infrastructure sounds great. Paying for it won't be easy," *Grist*, January 26, 2011.

121. "Who We Are," Transportation for America website, *t4america.org*.

122. "Equity Caucus," Transportation for America website, *t4america.org*.

123. Art Levine, "Beset by GOP, Obama and Labor Mount Quixotic Drive for Infrastructure Bills," *In These Times*, October 21, 2010.

Chapter Five: Bill Ayers—Education Czar?

1. Dinitia Smith, "No Regrets for a Love of Explosives; In a Memoir of Sorts, a War Protester Talks of Life with the Weathermen," *New York Times*, September 11, 2001.

2. Max Horn, *The Intercollegiate Socialist Society, 1905–1921: Origins of the Modern American Student Movement* (Boulder, CO: Westview Press, 1979), 53.

3. Zygmund Dobbs, "Keynesism in the United States," chapter 6 in *Keynes at Harvard. Economic Deception as a Political Credo*, 2009 Web version transcribed from the revised and enlarged edition (1969), http://www.keynesatharvard.org/book/KeynesatHarvard-ch06.html; "Alvin Hansen (1887–1975)," *EconomyProfessor.com*.

4. Brown University News Bureau, "A Half-Billion-Dollar to the Nation. Annenberg Challenge Will Support and Energize National Efforts To Redesign and Improve Schools," *News from Brown*, Brown University, December 17, 1993, http://brown.edu/Administration/News_Bureau/1987-95/93-075.html.

5. Alexander Russo, "From Frontline Leader to Rearguard Action: The Chicago Annenberg Challenge," in Russo et al., "Can Philanthropy Fix Our Schools? Appraising Walter Annenberg's $500 Million Gift to Public Education," Thomas B. Fordham Institute, April 1, 2000, http://www.edexcellence.net/detail/news.cfm?news_id=41&pubsubid=619#619.

6. Stanley Kurtz, "Obama and Ayers Pushed Radicalism on Schools," *Wall Street Journal*, September 23, 2008.

7. Stanley Kurtz, "Chicago Annenberg Challenge Shutdown? A cover-up in the making?" *National Review Online*, August 18, 2008.

8. The Chicago Annenberg Challenge 1999 Annual Report to the Annenberg Foundation, January 31, 2000, http://sonatabio.com/CAC/CAC-1999-annual.pdf.

9. October League (Marxist-Leninist), "Building a new Communist Party in the U.S.," October League (Marxist-Leninist), Los Angeles, 1973; Aaron Klein, "Obama worked closely with terrorist Bill Ayers: Records show collaboration on funding leftists despite claim he's just 'a guy' in neighborhood," *WND.com*, September 23, 2008.

10. Mike Klonsky's response at "Targeting Obama/Ayers and Chicago school reform," *Small Talk* (blog), September 20, 2008.

11. Marvin Martin, "Schools Offer A New Perspective: In Alternative Program, Less Equals More For Pupils," *Chicago Tribune*, November 20, 1994, 3.

12. "Staff: Pat Ford," Stearns Family Foundation, http://www.steansfamilyfoundation.org/bio_ford.shtml; Curriculum Vitae: Michael K. Klonsky, University of Illinois at Chicago, http://www.oce.uic.edu/oce/ocepublic/courses/viewResume.asp?CIID=1954.

13. Mike Klonsky and Pat Ford, "One Urban Solution: Small Schools," *Educational Leadership* 51, no. 8 (May 1994), 64–67. An abstract can be viewed here: http://www.ascd.org/publications/educational-leadership/may94/vol51/num08/One-Urban-Solution@-Small-Schools.aspx; William Ayers and Patricia Ford, eds., *City Kids, City Teachers: Reports from the Front Row* (New York: New Press, 1996).

14. Rachel Rosenblit, "New small schools picking their leaders," *Catalyst*, May 2002; "Staff: Pat Ford," Stearns Family Foundation.

15. Martin, "Schools Offer A New Perspective: In Alternative Program, Less Equals More For Pupils," November 20, 1994.

16. Ibid.

17. Kurtz, "Obama and Ayers Pushed Radicalism on Schools," *Wall Street Journal*, September 2008; Small Schools Workshop in "A descriptive list of thirteen Implementation Grants awarded by the Chicago Annenberg Challenge in 1995 and the list of twenty-two Planning Grants also awarded," Chicago Annenberg Challenge, May 7, 1996, 10, http://www.verumserum.com/media/2008/10/cac-1995-docs.pdf.

18. Martin, "Schools Offer A New Perspective: In Alternative Program, Less Equals More For Pupils," November 20, 1994.

19. "Chicago Annenberg Challenge," Annenberg Foundation, undated, http://

www.annenbergfoundation.org/usr_doc/The_Chicago_Annenberg_Chal lenge_External_Partners.pdf.

20. Ibid.

21. Russo, "From Frontline Leader to Rearguard Action," April 1, 2000.

22. Kurtz, *Radical-in-Chief*, 120.

23. "Carnegie Names John Ayers New Vice President," Carnegie Foundation for the Advancement of Teaching/carnegiefoundation.org, n.d.; "Innovation in high schools: New Talent Development high school strives to nurture and prepare students for the future," Chicago Public Schools, December 1, 2008, http://www.cps.edu/Spotlight/Pages/Spotlight32.aspx.

24. Russo, "From Frontline Leader to Rearguard Action," April 1, 2000.

25. Margalit Fox, "Theodore R. Sizer, Leading Education-Reform Advocate, Dies," *New York Times*, October 23, 2009.

26. Bryan Marquard, "Theodore Sizer, 77; leader in effort to overhaul education," *Boston Globe*, October 25, 2009.

27. "The Coalition of Essential Schools," *StateUniversity.com*, accessed October 11, 2010, http://education.stateuniversity.com/pages/1839/Coalition-Essen tial-Schools.html; "Coalition of Essential Schools Common Principles," *State University.com*, accessed October 11, 2010, http://education.stateuniversity .com/pages/1840/Coalition-Essential-Schools-Common-Principles.html.

28. "Coalition of Essential Schools Common Principles," *StateUniversity.com*.

29. William Ayers, "Schooling for 'Good Rebels': Socialist Education for Children in the United States, 1900–1920," *Nation*, May 10, 1993.

30. "Executive Board," Coalition of Essential Schools, accessed October 12, 2010, http://www.essentialschools.org/items/26.

31. "The Coalition of Essential Schools," *StateUniversity.com*.

32. Jim Cullen, "Opening the Academy: Theodore R. Sizer, 1932–2009," *Common-Place* 10, no. 2 (January 2010), http://www.common-place.org/vol-10/no-02/school/.

33. "Teacher-Centered Philosophies: Excerpt from David Miller Sadker and Karen R. Zittleman, *Teachers, Schools, and Society: A Brief Introduction to Education*," *Education.com*, n.d.

34. Kathleen Cushman, "Developing Curriculum in Essential Schools," Coalition of Essential Schools, 1996, http://www.essentialschools.org/re sources/82.

35. "Resources. Essential Questions," Coalition of Essential Schools, accessed October 11, 2010, http://www.essentialschools.org/benchmarks/8.

36. Cushman, "Developing Curriculum in Essential Schools," 1996; Bobby Ann

Starnes, "The Foxfire Approach to Teaching and Learning: John Dewey, Experiential Learning, and the Core Practices," *ERIC Digest*, January 1999.

37. Cushman, "Developing Curriculum in Essential Schools," 1996.

38. "Teaching Awards: List of 2006 Awardees," Center for the Scholarship of Teaching, College of Education, Michigan State University/educ.msu.edu.

39. Jill Davidson, "Radical Math: Creating Balance in an Unjust World, Conference Report," Coalition for Essential Schools, 2007, http://www.essentialschools.org/resources/385.

40. Eric Gutstein and Bob Peterson, *Rethinking Mathematics: Teaching Social Justice by the Numbers*, Rethinking Schools website, 2005.

41. Matthew Cardinale, "Social Justice Schools Shape New Wave of Activists," Inter Press Service, November 29, 2009, http://www.noras.no/galdu/web/index.php?odas=4178&giella1=eng.

42. Daniel J. Flynn, "Howard Zinn's Biased History," History News Network, June 9, 2003.

43. Michael Kazin, "Howard Zinn's History Lessons," *Dissent*, Spring 2004.

44. Cliff Kincaid, "Leftist 'Historian' Howard Zinn Lied About Red Ties," *Accuracy in Media/aim.org*, July 30, 2010.

45. Cigi Ross, "Political guru urges kids to be activists," *Courier News* (Elgin, IL), February 6, 2009.

46. John Perazzo, "Howard Zinn's History of Hate," *FrontPageMag.com*, February 2, 2010.

47. Mary Grabar, "The Sociopath Professors Part II: 'We Are Terrorizing Ourselves,'" *Townhall.com*, September 17, 2010.

48. Ibid.; Howard Zinn, *A People's History of the United States* (1980; reprint, New York: Harper Perennial, 2001), 425.

49. Ibid., 425.

50. Ron Radosh, "America the Awful—Howard Zinn's History," *Mindingthe Campus.com*, January 28, 2010.

51. Ibid.

52. Chuck Rogér, "Pushing Junk Science on Children," *AmericanThinker.com*, October 6, 2010.

53. Nicholas Ballasy, "Congressman Calls for Schools to 'Promote the Agenda' of Climate Change, Population Limitation; Rep. John Sarbanes says more environmental education in public schools will promote the agenda of climate change and population growth," *CNSNews.com*, September 22, 2010.

54. Rogér, "Pushing Junk Science on Children," October 6, 2010.

55. Ross Douthat, "The 'Insights' of Paul Ehrlich," *Atlantic*, December 19, 2008.

56. Rogér, "Pushing Junk Science on Children," October 6, 2010.

57. "About," American Association for the Advancement of Science (AAAS)/ *aaas.org*.

58. "Programs: Education," American Association for the Advancement of Science (AAAS) website/*aaas.org*.

59. "Project 2061 Curriculum," American Association for the Advancement of Science (AAAS)/project2061.org; "The Physical Setting: Weather and Climate," *project2061.org*.

60. Kathleen Cushman, "Math and Science in the Essential School," Coalition for Essential Schools, 1992, http://www.essentialschools.org/resources/150; "*Atlas of Science Literacy*, Volumes 1 and 2. Mapping K–12 science learning," American Association for the Advancement of Science (AAAS)/*project2061.org*.

61. News Release: "AAAS Board Releases New Statement on Climate Change," American Association for the Advancement of Science (AAAS) website, February 18, 2007.

62. "AAAS Climate Change Town Hall," *Worldchanging.com*, February 24, 2007.

63. Kathleen Cushman, "What's Out There? Curricula that Support Essential School Ideas. (Section) Worth Checking Out: Across the Curriculum: Frameworks with a Coherent, Student-Centered Emphasis," Coalition of Essential Schools, 1998, http://www.essentialschools.org/resources/84.

64. "A Half-Billion-Dollar to the Nation," December 17, 1993.

65. "The Challenge Sites: New York Networks for School Renewal," Annenberg Challenge, accessed October 13, 2010, http://www.annenberginstitute.org/ Challenge/sites/nynsr.html.

66. Final Report of the Evaluation of New York Networks for School Renewal: An Annenberg Foundation Challenge for New York City, 1996–2001, Education Resources Information Center ED464164/eric.ed.gov.

67. Ibid., 7.

68. "Bertha Lewis," *Huffington Post*.

69. New York ACORN, *Secret Apartheid: A Report on Racial Discrimination Against Black and Latino Parents and Children in the New York City Public Schools*, 1995, Internet Archive, accessed October 13, 2010, http://web.archive.org/ web/20040716190148/http://www.acorn.org/ACORNarchives/studies/ secretapartheid/.

70. John M. Beam and Sharmeen Irani, *ACORN Education Reform Organizing: Evolution of a Model*, National Center for Schools and Communities, Fordham University; *ncscatfordham.org*, April 8, 2003, 5.

71. "A Commentary on the Campaign for Human Development," prepared for the Catholic Bishops of the United States by the Wanderer Forum Foundation, *wandererforum.org*, circa 1996.

72. ACORN Community High School (K499), Brooklyn, http://www.acornchs.net/home.aspx and http://schools.nyc.gov/SchoolPortals/13/K499/default.htm.

73. Dennis Shirley, *Community Organizing for Urban School Reform* (Austin: University of Texas Press, 1997), 289.

74. Barbara A. Taveras, "Transforming Public Schools," *Shelterforce Online*, May/June 1998.

75. Shirley, *Community Organizing for Urban School Reform*, 289.

76. Kurtz, *Radical-in-Chief*, 235.

77. Ibid., 235 and 267.

78. Ibid., 284.

79. Woods Fund of Chicago attachments to Illinois Annual Reports 1997–2001 to Illinois Secretary of State, obtained by *JudicialWatch.org*, http://www.judicialwatch.org/documents/2008/Woods_Fund.pdf. Woods Fund of Chicago, Donors Forum, Illinois, http://ifs.donorsforum.org/ (subscription required); "Obama and Acorn. Community organizers, phony voters, and your tax dollars," *Wall Street Journal*, October 14, 2008.

80. "The attraction of charter schools," *nwitimes.com* (northwest Indiana), December 7, 1997.

81. "Guides: Grants 1997," *Catalyst-Chicago.org*; "Guides: Grants 1998," *Catalyst-Chicago.org*; Form 990-PF, Return of Private Foundation, Chicago Annenberg Challenge, Tax Year 2001, 17, http://globallabor.info/Annenberg%20Documents/CAC%20990PF%202001.pdf/.

82. Brett Schaeffer, "Funding program sought for bricks and mortar," *Catalyst-Chicago.org*, October 2000; Rosalind Rossi, "Charter schools popular; test results 'mixed,'" *Chicago Sun-Times*, December 15, 2000.

83. Mario Ortiz, "ACORN, UNO: Schools Stumble," *Catalyst-Chicago.org*, November 2000.

84. Gregory A. Galluzzo, "Gamaliel and the Barack Obama Connection," Gamaliel Foundation/*gamaliel.org*, n.d.

85. Ibid.; Phil Davidson, "Community organizer Jerry Kellman trained the man who would become president," *IllinoisIssues.uis.edu*, March 2009.

86. United Neighborhood Organization (UNO) /uno-online.org.

87. Jim Cavallero, "Civil Rights Groups Delay Release of 'Framework for Education Reform' Critical of Obama and Duncan Education Policies . . . Release

delayed due to 'scheduling conflicts'?" *SubstanceNews.net*, August 2, 2010. See photo box there for info.

88. Alexander Russo, "AM News: Not Much News," *ChicagoNow.com*, September 27, 2010. See comment by Russo.

89. "Donors," *TeachForAmerica.org*.

90. Noreen Ahmed-Ullah, "CPS hearing draws charter school officials," *Chicago Tribune*, January 18, 2011.

91. Samuel Totten, "Review: Facing History and Ourselves," *Holocaust and Genocide Studies* 5, no. 4 (1990): 463, http://hgs.oxfordjournals.org/content/5/4/463.extract.

92. "More on Evaluation," Facing History and Ourselves, http://www.facinghistory.org/more-evaluation. "For sixteen years, the U.S. Department of Education selected Facing History as an 'exemplary program' worthy of dissemination through the federal government's National Diffusion Network (Program Effectiveness Panel, 1980,1985, 1993)."

93. "FHAO offices," Facing History and Ourselves */facinghistory.org*; "Where We Work," Facing History and Ourselves */facinghistory.org*.

94. "Our Partners and Supporters," Facing History and Ourselves/facinghistory.org.

95. Peter Schworm, "Mosque says students weren't pressed to pray: Parents defend school as trip ignites debate," *Boston Globe*, September 10, 2008.

96. Charles Jacobs, "Video Shows Mosque which Hosted Wellesley Public School Students also Sponsored Hate Speakers," *BigPeace.com*, September 27, 2010; screenshot of Muslim Society of America, *BigPeace.com*, http://www.peaceandtolerance.org/images/masiau.jpg.

97. Ibid.

98. "Participating Schools, New England," Facing History and Ourselves/facinghistory.org; "Social Studies for All Students: History/Social Science Vision," Wellesley Public Schools, May 2003, http://www.wellesley.k12.ma.us/curriculum/elem-ss/socialstudies.pdf.

99. Fred Lucas, "Obama-Run Foundation Gave Millions to Liberal Groups, Including One Run by Bill Ayers," Associated Press/*CNSNews.com*, October 13, 2008.

100. "Guides: Grants 1997," *Catalyst-Chicago.org*; Joyce Foundation Annual Report 1999, http://www.joycefdn.org/resources/content/1/0/0/documents/99_AnnualReport.pdf.

101. Curriculum vitae for William C. Ayers.

102. "Senator Barack Obama Addresses Youth at Chicago Benefit," Facing History and Ourselves, *facinghistory.org*, May 15, 2006.

103. "Michelle Obama Speaks on the Importance of Facing History and Ourselves," Facing History and Ourselves, facinghistory.org, May 4, 2007; "Terrence Roberts and Michelle Obama at Chicago Benefit Dinner," Facing History and Ourselves /facinghistory.org, May 10, 2007.

104. "Profiles," Facing History and Ourselves, facinghistory.org.

105. "Eboo Patel," Facing History and Ourselves, facinghistory.org, March 12, 2009.

106. "Samantha Power," Facing History and Ourselves, facinghistory.org, April 27, 2007.

107. Jeremy Nesoff, "Choosing to Participate," Coalition for Essential Schools, 2008 (accessed October 24, 2010), http://www.essentialschools.org/resources/483.

108. "North America Project," Facing History and Ourselves, facinghistory.org.

109. Ibid.

110. "Small Schools Network," Facing History and Ourselves, facinghistory.org; "Facing History and Ourselves Announces Small Schools Network," Facing History and Ourselves /facinghistory.org, October 10, 2008.

111. Jeff Jacoby, "What 'Facing History' really teaches," Boston Globe, July 17, 1995.

112. Ibid.; Lucy S. Dawidowicz, "How They Teach the Holocaust," Commentary-Magazine.com, December 1990.

113. Jacoby, "What 'Facing History' really teaches," July 17, 1995.

114. Ibid.

115. Ibid.; Marian Wright Edelman, The Measure of Our Success: A Letter to My Children and Yours (New York: Harper Paperbacks, 1993), 81.

116. Jacoby, "What 'Facing History' really teaches," July 17, 1995.

117. John Spritzler, "'Falsifying History and Ourselves': Anti-Democratic Propaganda in the Classroom," newdemocracyworld.org, June 2001.

118. Sandra Stotsky, "Part I. Supplemental Curricula: Civics Gone Awry," "The Stealth Curriculum: Manipulating America's History Teachers," Thomas B. Fordham Foundation, April 13, 2004, http://www.edexcellence.net/detail/news.cfm?news_id=331&pubsubid=1002#1002.

Chapter Six: Red-ucation

1. Jesse Gordon, "The Blueprint for Change: Barack Obama's Plan for America," On the Issues, February 2008, http://www.ontheissues.org/Blueprint_Obama.htm.

2. Gordon, February 2008; "Education" in *Blueprint for Change: Obama and Biden's Plan for America*, Obama '08, http://www.barackobama.com/pdf; ObamaBlueprintForChange.pdf.

3. Lynn Sweet, "Transcript: Obama education speech in Ohio," *Chicago Sun-Times*, September 9, 2008; "Facts for Education Advocates: International Comparison," Alliance for Excellent Education, January 2009, http://con nection-collegeboard.com/09jan/pdf/adv-fact-sheet-CM_09jan26.pdf.

4. Fact Sheet: "American Recovery and Reinvestment Act: The Largest Investment in Education in Our Nation's History—to Prevent Teacher Layoffs, Make Key Education Improvements and Help Make College Affordable," *whitehouse.gov*, February 17, 2009.

5. Press Release: "Secretary Duncan Releases Application for $650 Million to Support Innovation," U.S. Department of Education, *ed.gov*, March 8, 2010.

6. Sam Dillon, "Education Department Deals Out Big Awards," *New York Times*, August 5, 2010.

7. Press Release: "All Winning i3 Applicants Secure Private Match; More Than Half Successfully Used Foundation Registry," U.S. Department of Education/*ed.gov*, September 20, 2010; "i3 2010 Highest-Rated Applications," U.S. Department of Education/ed.gov; "Faculty," Erikson Institute, http://www.erikson.edu/default/faculty/faclistings.aspx; "Faculty: Barbara T. Bowman," Erikson Institute, http://www.erikson.edu/default/faculty/faclistings/barbara_bowman.aspx.

8. "Faculty: Barbara T. Bowman."

9. Steven Hicks, "Duncan Honors Legendary Early Childhood Education Expert Barbara T. Bowman at Georgetown National Summit on Professional Development," U.S. Department of Education/*ed.gov*, December 2009.

10. Lorraine Forte, "35 networks get first Annenberg funds," *Catalyst-Chicago .org*, February 1996.

11. "Tribute to Late Mr. Thomas Ayers," *Chicago City Council Journal*, June 13, 2007, 3335–36, http://www.chicityclerk.com/citycouncil/journals/061307meeting/16A greedCalendar/pgs3296-3345.pdf; Brad O'Leary, "Obama's sweetheart-deal home loan," *WND.com*, October 15, 2008; "Stewardship: Members of the Board," Erikson Institute, 2001, Internet Archive, http://web.archive.org/web/20010210204217/ www.erikson.edu/About/Stewardship/stewardship.html; "Stewardship: Executive Committee," Erikson Institute, updated September 16, 2001, Internet Archive, http://web.archive.org/web/20020213160301/erikson.edu/About/ Stewardship/stewardship.html; William Ayers, *A Kind and Just Parent: The Children of Juvenile Court* (Boston: Beacon Press, 1998), 82; Testimony of

Walter S. Steele regarding Communist activities in the United States. Hearings before the Committee on Un-American Activities, House of Representatives, 80th Congress, first session, on H.R. 1884 and H.R. 2122, bills to curb or outlaw the Communist Party in the United States.

12. Charles Leroux, "Should she now be teaching law? Northwestern alumnus Sean O'Shea doesn't think so," *Chicago Tribune*, December 28, 2001, 3.

13. Brenda J. Elliott, "A Chicago Marxist Family History Mystery," *RBO*, February 24, 2010, http://therealbarackobama.wordpress.com/2010/02/24/a-chicago-marxist-family-history-mystery/; Kathryn Waddell Takara, "Frank Marshall Davis: A Forgotten Voice in the Chicago Black Renaissance," *Western Journal of Black Studies* 26, no. 4 (2002) 215 ff.; Bill Mullen, "Popular Fronts: 'Negro Story' Magazine and the African American Literary Response to World War II," *African American Review* 20, no. 1 (1996), 5 ff.; James Edward Smethurst, *The New Red Negro: The Literary Left and African American Poetry, 1930–1946* (New York: Oxford University Press, 1999), 35; Gerald Home, *Communist Front? The Civil Rights Congress, 1946–1956* (Rutherford, NJ: Associated University Presses, 1988), 35; Frank Marshall Davis and John Edgar Tidwell, *Livin' the Blues: Memoirs of a Black Journalist and Poet* (Madison: University of Wisconsin Press, 2003), xxii, 283–84.

14. Robert Cohen, "Student Activism in the 1930s," New Deal Network, http://newdeal.feri.org/students/index.htm.

15. Elliott, "A Chicago Marxist Family History Mystery," February 24, 2010; Sabrina L. Miller and James Janega, "Bernard Weissbourd, 78, Scientist, Attorney, Real Estate Developer," *Chicago Tribune*, November 5, 2000; "Board of Directors," *Bulletin of the Atomic Scientists* (1945–85, 40th Anniversary Issue), August 1985, 1.

16. Ibid.

17. Fran Spielman, "Daley rips Race to the Top education funding process," *Chicago Sun-Times*, September 15, 2010.

18. "Race to the Top Winners: Snapshots," *Education Week* 30, no. 2; Round 2 of winners in millions of dollars: District of Columbia, 75; Hawaii, 75; Florida, 700; Georgia, 400; Maryland, 250; Massachusetts, 250; New York, 700; North Carolina, 400; Ohio, 400; and Rhode Island, 7.

19. Lindsey Burke, "Education Spending in the American Recovery and Reinvestment Act: Stimulating the Status Quo," Heritage Foundation, April 16, 2010.

20. Ibid.

21. Ibid.; U.S. Department of Education, National Center for Education Sta-

tistics, "What Are the Enrollment Trends in Public and Private Elementary and Secondary Schools?" April 15, 2010, http://nces.ed.gov/fastfacts/display .asp?id=65.

22. Israel Ortega, "Prolonging Education's Race to the Bottom," Heritage Foundation, June 11, 2010, http://blog.heritage.org/2010/06/11/morning-bell-prolonging-educations-race-to-the-bottom/. Statistics for per pupil spending since 1985 found in Dan Lips, Shanea Watkins, and John Fleming, "Does Spending More on Education Improve Academic Achievement?" Heritage Foundation Backgrounder #2179, September 8, 2008. Information for per pupil spending comes from Lindsey Burke, "Creating a Crisis: Schools Gain Staff, Not Educational Achievement," Heritage Foundation, May 26, 2010, and Lindsey Burke, "D.C. Opportunity Scholarship Program: Study Supports Expansion," Heritage Foundation, February 18, 2009.

23. Burke, "Education Spending in the American Recovery and Reinvestment Act," April 16, 2010. Burke quotes from Andy Smarick, "$100 Billion for Reform . . . or to Subsidize the Status Quo?" American Enterprise Institute, June 23, 2009.

24. Neal McCluskey, "More and More Caution Flags Race to the Top," *At Liberty*/Cato Institute, April 28, 2010.

25. Trip Jennings, "UPDATED: More states drop out of Race to the Top," *Independent* (New Mexico), April 23, 2010.

26. Peterson and Rothstein, "Let's Do Numbers," April 20, 2010.

27. Burke, "Education Spending in the American Recovery and Reinvestment Act," April 16, 2010.

28. Diane Ravitch, Curriculum Vitae, *dianeravitch.com*, accessed October 6, 2010; Diane Ravitch, "The Race to Nowhere," *EdWeek*, December 15, 2009.

29. Ravitch, "The Race to Nowhere," December 15, 2009.

30. Fernanda Santos, "On Upper West Side, Hurdles for Charter School," *New York Times*, January 21, 2010.

31. Press Release: "Education Secretary Arne Duncan Announces Twelve Grants for $50 Million to Charter School Management Organizations," U.S. Department of Education, *ed.gov*, September 29, 2010.

32. Jeff Coplon, "The Patron Saint (and Scourge) of Lost Schools," *New York*, April 25, 2010.

33. Ibid.

34. Glen Ford, "Obama and the Charter School Sugar Daddies," *Black Agenda Report*, June 2, 2010.

35. "Board of Directors," Success Charter Schools, successcharters.org.

36. Nancy Hass, "Scholarly Investments," *New York Times*, December 6, 2009.

37. Trip Gabriel and Jennifer Median, "Charter Schools' New Cheerleaders: Financiers," *New York Times*, May 9, 2010.

38. Ford, "Obama and the Charter School Sugar Daddies," June 2, 2010.

39. Department of Education, Charter Schools Program (CSP); Office of Innovation and Improvement; Overview Information; Charter Schools Program (CSP): State Educational Agencies Notice Inviting Applications for New Awards for Fiscal Year (FY) 2011, Federal Register 76, no. 16 (Tuesday, January 25, 2011), 4322 ff., http://www.gpo.gov/fdsys/pkg/FR-2011-01-25/pdf/2011-1518.pdf.

40. Douglas O. Staiger, Robert Gordon, and Thomas J. Kane, *Identifying Effective Teachers Using Performance on the Job*, Hamilton Project/Brookings Institution, brookings.edu, April 2006.

41. Aaron Collier, "Race to the Rocky Top," *Chattarati.com*, January 12, 2010.

42. Sam Dillon, "Administration Takes Aim at State Laws on Teachers," *New York Times*, July 23, 2009.

43. Kim Chipman and Matthew Benjamin, "Obama Names Rubin Ally Furman to Economic Policy Post," Bloomberg News, June 9, 2008.

44. fflambeau, "Obama's 'Smoking Gun': His Hamilton Project Speech shows his links to Goldman, Entitlement Cuts (Part 1)," *Firedoglake* (blog), December 7, 2009.

45. "Democrats Defend Opposition-Party Role," *All Things Considered*, NPR, April 5, 2006.

46. "Peter Orszag," Who Runs Government/*Washington Post*, *Who RunsGov .com*, http://www.whorunsgov.com/Profiles/Peter_Orszag; Brenda J. Elliott, "Unprez's 'economic recovery' advisers include two top union officials and failed subprime lender," *RBO*, February 6, 2009, http://therealbarackobama .wordpress.com/2009/02/06/unprezs-economic-recovery-advisers-include-two-top-union-officials-and-failed-subprime-lender/.

47. EEP Team, "EEP Weighs in on Race to the Top Guidelines," Education Equality Project, *edequality.org*, August 28, 2009.

48. Ibid.

49. "Statement of Principles," Education Equality Project, *edequality.org*.

50. "What is the Elementary and Secondary Education Act?" U.S. Department of Education, accessed October 4, 2010, https://answers.ed.gov/app/answers/detail/a_id/4; "Fact Sheet on the Major Provisions of the Conference Report to H.R. 1, the No Child Left Behind Act," archived, U.S. Depart-

ment of Education/ed.gov; "'Leave No Child Behind' Bill Introduced," *Precinct Reporter*, June 14, 2001.

51. Lindsey Burke, "School Choice is First Casualty of Obama Education Overhaul," *The Foundry* (blog), Heritage Foundation, March 18, 2010.

52. Alyson Klein and Michele McNeil, "Administration Unveils ESEA Reauthorization Blueprint; Aims to Address Concerns About NCLB Inflexibility, Look Beyond Test Scores," *Education Week*, March 17, 2010.

53. Burke, "School Choice is First Casualty of Obama Education Overhaul," March 18, 2010.

54. Clay Burell, "Obama's Town Hall Charter School Remarks: Your Take?" Education/*Change.org*, March 27, 2009.

55. Press Release: "Charter Schools Are Focus of First ESEA Reauthorization Hearing," *Thompson.com*, February 26, 2010 (posted March 4, 2010).

56. *FY 2010 Obama Education Budget;* "Charter Schools Grants. Fiscal Year 2010 Budget Summary," U.S. Department of Education, *ed.gov*, May 7, 2009.

57. Press Release, U.S. Department of Education, August 16, 2010.

58. Grover Whitehurst and Michelle Croft, "The Harlem Children's Zone, Promise Neighborhoods, and the Broader, Bolder Approach to Education," Brookings Institution/*brookings.edu*, July 20, 2010.

59. Press Release: "President Obama to Highlight Innovative Programs that are Transforming Communities Across the Nation," Office of the White House Press Secretary, *whitehouse.gov*, June 30, 2009.

60. Press Release: "U.S. Department of Education Opens Competition for Promise Neighborhoods," U.S. Department of Education, *ed.gov*, April 30, 2010.

61. Ibid.

62. Press Release: "Expert Task Force Charges School Reform Alone Will Fail in Closing Achievement Gap; Diverse Bipartisan Group Launches Campaign for 'Broader, Bolder' Policies to Improve Education, Bridge Achievement Gaps," A Broader Bolder Approach to Education, June 10, 2008, http://www.boldapproach.org/20080610_broader_bolder_release.pdf.

63. "BBA Leaders and Signatories," BBA, accessed October 6, 2010, http://www.boldapproach.org/bios.html; "Promise Neighborhoods," Fiscal Year 2010 Budget Summary, U.S. Department of Education, *ed.gov*, May 7, 2009.

64. Press Release: "U.S. Department of Education Awards Promise Neighborhoods Planning Grants; 21 Communities Win Funding to Build Effective Schools with Strong Support Systems," U.S. Department of Education, ed.gov, September 21, 2010.

65. Sharon Otterman, "Two New York City Groups Win 'Promise Neighborhood' Grants," *New York Times*, September 21, 2010.

66. Bread and Roses HS. 05M685; 2009–2010 School Comprehensive Educational Plan (CEP), http://schools.nyc.gov/documents/oaosi/cep/2009-10/cep_M685.pdf.

67. Sol Stern, "ACORN's Nutty Regime for Cities," *City Journal*, Spring 2003.

68. "Our Presence in New York Area Schools and Universities," Facing History and Ourselves/*facinghistory.org.*

69. "Universal Community Homes," *data.ed.gov*, accessed October 6, 2010, http://data.ed.gov/node/17206.

70. Ibid.; "About Us," Universal Companies, accessed October 5, 2010, http://www.universalcompanies.org/AboutUs/NewsEvents/.

71. "Universal Community Homes," accessed October 6, 2010.

72. David J. Rusin, "Obama Office Operates in Philly's Islamist Corridor," Pajamas Media, October 22, 2008.

73. Joe Kaufman and Beila Rabinowitz, "Philadelphia's Islamist Boy Scouts," *FrontPageMag.com*, July 13, 2010.

74. Joe Kaufman, "Kenny Gamble the United Muslim Movement and Universal; Islamist payola in the City of Brotherly Love," *MilitantIslamMonitor.org*, December 31, 2007; Steven Emerson, "New Disclosures Tighten ISNA–Muslim Brotherhood Bonds," IPT News, *InvestigativeProject.org*, July 22, 2008.

75. Kaufman and Rabinowitz, "Philadelphia's Islamist Boy Scouts," July 13, 2010; Rusin, "Obama Office Operates in Philly's Islamist Corridor," October 22, 2008.

76. Kaufman and Rabinowitz, "Philadelphia's Islamist Boy Scouts," July 13, 2010.

77. In June 2011, the Jawala Scouts website (http://jawalascouts.com/) was under construction. The United Muslim Masjid website (http://ummonline.org/jawalamuslimah-scouts/) states that the scouting program consists of "Principals *[sic]* of Islam such as Salat, Adab, basic Aqeedah (Islamic Beliefs) and other Islamic essentials," with a program "tailored for Muslim girls ages 6 thru 16 years old." Boy scouts ages seven through seventeen years old "receive training in Islamic education, adab, manhood and self reliance." Also see Sharon Rondeau, "'Humanitarianism' in Big Cities Funded by Islamic Organizations, Some Radical Ties, and Your Tax Dollars," *Post & Mail*, July 19, 2010, http://www.thepostemail.com/2010/07/19/islam-moves-to-take-over-u-s-neighborhoods/.

78. Kaufman and Rabinowitz, "Philadelphia's Islamist Boy Scouts," July 13, 2010.

79. Daniel Pipes, "Is Kenny Gamble Building a Muslim-only Enclave in Philadelphia?" *danielpipes.com*, November 1, 2007, updated April 1, 2008; Matthew Teague, "King Kenny," *PhillyMag.com*, November 20, 2007, 2.

80. "The Universal Plan: Universal Companies, Philadelphia, PA," Muslim Alliance in North America, accessed October 6, 2010, http://www.mana-net .org/pages.php?ID=activism&ID2=&NUM=18.

81. Daryl Gale, "Let My People Go," *Philadelphia City Paper*, April 11–17, 2002.

82. Pipes, "Is Kenny Gamble Building a Muslim-only Enclave in Philadelphia?" April 1, 2008.

83. "The Universal Plan," MANA.

84. Jacqueline L. Salmon, "With a Hefty Education Grant Come Equally Great Expectations: Gates Foundation Provides Money, and Mandates," *Washington Post*, December 4, 2006.

85. "About the DC Promise Neighborhood Initiative," Urban Institute, 2010, accessed October 9, 2010, http://www2.urban.org/nnip/ meet2010_05%5CDCPN%20Overview.pdf.

86. Ibid.

87. "Urban Institute (UI): A Guide to the Political Left," *DiscovertheNetworks .org*.

88. Keith Schneider, "Boston Green Justice Coalition Joins Apollo Alliance," Apollo Alliance website, December 7, 2008.

89. *Mapping the Field of Organizing for School Improvement: A report on Education Organizing in Baltimore, Chicago, Los Angeles, the Mississippi Delta, New York City, Philadelphia, San Francisco and Washington, D.C.*, Institute for Education and Social Policy, New York University/*nyu.edu*, August 2001.

90. Fact Sheet: Barack Obama's Education Reform Speech in Dayton, Ohio: "Reforming and Strengthening America's Schools for the 21st Century," Obama for America, September 9, 2008, http://www.barackobama.com/ pdf/issues/education/Fact_Sheet_Education_Reform_Speech_FINAL .pdf; Amanda Scott, "Barack in Dayton: 'A new vision for a 21st century education,'" *MyBarackObama.com*, September 9, 2008, http://my.barackobama .com/page/community/post/amandascott/gG5pB4.

91. Ibid.; William J. Symonds, "A School Makeover in Mapleton: A school district outside Denver has galvanized students and parents with a daring experiment in public school choice," *Bloomberg BusinessWeek*, June 16, 2006.

92. Karen E. Crummy, "Obama praises successful Thornton school; Candidate

awards high marks to Mapleton, outlines education goals," *Denver Post*, May 29, 2008.

93. David O. Williams, "Obama talks up Thornton school in 30-minute ad," *Colorado Independent*, October 30, 2008; David O. Williams, "Denver Principal Among Obama's Top Education Advisers," *Colorado Independent*, May 15, 2008; "About Us," New Leaders for New Schools, *nlns.org*; Joe Williams, "DFER-CO Press Release on US Secretary of Education Arne Duncan Visit to Colorado," Democrats for Education Reform–Colorado, dfer.org, April 9, 2009.

94. Todd Felton, "President Obama Visits Capital City Charter School," Expeditionary Learning, February 3, 2009, http://elschools.org/press-center/president-obama-visits-capital-city-charter-school.

95. Macon Phillips, "How our schools should be," Office of Social Innovation and Civic Participation, *whitehouse.gov*, February 4, 2009; Press Release: "President Barack Obama, First Lady Michelle Obama & Education Secretary Arne Duncan Visit Capital City Public Charter School," Expeditionary Schools, February 3, 2009, http://elschools.org/sites/default/files/obama-visit-capital-city.pdf.

96. Peter Baker and Campbell Robertson, "Flood of questions for Obama in New Orleans," *Seattle Times*, October 22, 2009.

97. Diane Demee-Benoit, "A Passion for Knowledge: An Introduction to Expeditionary Learning," *edutopia.org*, June 27, 2007.

98. Press Release, Expeditionary Learning, February 3, 2009.

99. Sam Stringfield, Steven M. Ross, and Lana Smith, *Bold Plans for School Restructuring: The New American Schools Designs* (Mahwah, NJ: Lawrence Erlbaum, 1996), 110.

100. Ibid.

101. Fiscal Year 2011 Budget Summary—February 1, 2010, U.S. Department of Education, *ed.gov*.

102. Major credit for exposing the IB agenda goes to Lisa McLoughlin, who maintains the Truth About IB website, truthaboutib.com/; Chicago Annenberg Challenge Records (Boxes 5 and 6), Special Collections, University Library, University of Illinois at Chicago, http://www.uic.edu/depts/lib/specialcoll/services/rjd/findingaids/AnnenbergChallenge.pdf.

103. Lisa McLoughlin, "Annenberg Challenge Funds IB MYP in Chicago," Truth About IB, *truthaboutib.com*.

104. *Case Study: Building a Continuum of Excellence: Linking the MYP and the Diploma Programme in the Chicago Public School System*, International Baccalaure-

ate, 2007–2008, accessed November 10, 2010, http://www.dekalb.k12.ga.us/support/ib/files/5AAE0260180A499CA46D04D455FCEBCC.pdf.

105. *Case Study: Building a Continuum of Excellence.*

106. Lisa McLoughlin, "How Much Does Duncan Like IB? Lots!" Truth About IB, accessed November 1, 2010, http://truthaboutib.com/obamaduncanib.html; CPS staff website, April 2009, http://www.cps.k12.il.us/aboutcps/PressReleases/March_2005/IB_schools.htm.

107. "Enrollment Management and Marketing: International Baccalaureate Program," Center for Access and Attainment, DePaul University, accessed November 10, 2010, http://www.depaul.edu/emm/caa/hsPrograms/ib.asp.

108. "Magnet and Selective Enrollment Schools and Programs for the 2010–2011 School Years," *Chicago Public Schools Policy Manual*, December 16, 2009, http://policy.cps.k12.il.us/documents/602.2.pdf.

109. George N. Schmidt, "Mayor, minions sabotaging Chicago's remaining public high schools," *SubstanceNews.com*, October 2005.

110. Paul Street, "Arne Duncan and Neoliberal Racism," *BlackAgendaReport.com*, December 30, 2008.

111. Subscripts Staff, "Subscript: If Oscar Mayer needs changing why doesn't the Board use the Mulligan or Near North buildings?" *SubstanceNews.com*, April 2008.

112. World Conference for Heads of IB World Schools, International Baccalaureate in Cooperation with California International Baccalaureate Organization (CIBO) Heads Standing Association (HSA), Hyatt Regency Hotel, San Francisco, October 11–14, 2007, http://www.ibo.org/heads/conference2007/documents/IBGH-comp.pdf; Arne Duncan, "Tackling District Reform: The Chicago Story," IB Americas Conference, Quebec City, Quebec, Canada, July 9–12, 2009, http://www.ibamericasconference.org/en/node/80.

113. Austin Kline, "International Baccalaureate is Anti-American & Anti-Christian?" *Pittsburgh.About.com*, February 22, 2006.

114. Seana Cranston, "Internationalist Curriculum Infiltrates U.S. Schools," *Catholic Family and Human Rights Institute* 13, no. 49, November 18, 2010.

115. Lisa McLoughlin, "IB's Muslim Agenda and Slush Fund," Truth About IB, *truthaboutib.com*, October 29, 2010.

116. Cranston, "Internationalist Curriculum Infiltrates U.S. Schools," November 18, 2010.

117. Ibid.

118. Cranston, "Internationalist Curriculum Infiltrates U.S. Schools," November

18, 2010. "About UNICEF. Carol Bellamy," UNICEF/unicef.org, "Carol Bellamy delivers the Peterson Lecture, 23 April 2009," IBO.org, April 2009.

119. Carey Roberts, "When the Sisterhood Rules the World: The Sad Tale of UNICEF," *Free Republic*, December 21, 2004.

120. Ibid.

121. Cranston, "Internationalist Curriculum Infiltrates U.S. Schools," November 18, 2010.

122. "Council Members, Carol Bellamy," IBO.org, http://www.ibo.org/coun cil/members/documents/CAROLBELLAMYbio.pdf; START Network Funders, *WorldLearning.org*.

123. Debra K. Niwa, "International Baccalaureate (IB) Program Unraveled," *NHTeaPartyCoalition.org*, March 2010, 2. Niwa's report is exhaustively researched and a treasure trove of details.

124. Fiscal Year 2011 Budget Summary—February 1, 2010, U.S. Department of Education.

125. *The American Recovery and Reinvestment Act (ARRA): Capitalize on Federal Education Funding Opportunities with the International Baccalaureate (IB)*, International Baccalaureate, ibo.org, 2009–2010.

Chapter Seven: Reds Turning America Green?

1. Presidential Climate Action Project, *Climate Action Plan in Brief*, November 2008, http://www.climateactionproject.com/docs/PCAP_Brief_11_08.pdf.

2. Laura Blumenfeld, "Soros's Deep Pockets vs. Bush: Financier Contributes $5 Million More in Effort to Oust President," *Washington Post*, November 11, 2003; David Von Drehle, "Liberals Get a Think Tank of Their Own," *Washington Post*, October 23, 2003.

3. Michael Scherer, "Inside Obama's Idea Factory in Washington," *Time*, November 21, 2008.

4. Sarah Rosen Wartell with foreword by John Podesta , "The Power of the President: Recommendations to Advance Progressive Change," Center for American Progress website, November 2010.

5. Ibid.

6. Aaron Klein, "White House still listening to Van Jones 'green' advice; Communist-group founder on team influencing environmental policies," *WND .com*, November 30, 2009.

7. Ibid.

8. Presidential Climate Action Project, *Plan B: Near-Term Presidential Actions for Energy & Environmental Leadership*, *ClimateActionProject.com*, August 2010, http://www.climateactionproject.com/plan2010/PCAP-Report_August2010.pdf.

9. Adam D. Krauss, "Obama announces low carbon fuel plan at UNH," *Foster's Daily Democrat* (Dover, NH), April 21, 2007.

10. S.1324: National Low-Carbon Fuel Standard Act of 2007, 110th Congress, *GovTrack.us*, May 7, 2007; "Obama Introduces National Low-Carbon Fuel Standard," *RenewableEnergyWorld.com*, May 9, 2007.

11. "Obama Introduces National Low-Carbon Fuel Standard," May 9, 2007; Krauss, "Obama announces low carbon fuel plan at UNH," April 21, 2007.

12. "Obama Introduces National Low-Carbon Fuel Standard," May 9, 2007.

13. Derrick Penner, "Government brings in low-carbon fuel bill," *Vancouver Sun/Canada.com*, April 2, 2008.

14. "Monitoring and reduction of greenhouse gas emissions from fuels (road transport and inland waterway vessels)," European Parliament, December 17, 2008, http://www.europarl.europa.eu/sides/getDoc.do?pubRef=-//EP//TEXT+TA+20081217+ITEMS+DOC+XML+V0//EN&language=EN#sdocta5.

15. Presidential Climate Action Project, *Plan B*, August 2010.

16. Ibid.

17. "PCAP: Sign the State of the Climate," accessed April 13, 2010, http://www.climateactionproject.com/sign/sign_statement.php.

18. "PCAP Advisory Committee," Presidential Climate Action Project, accessed April 13, 2010, http://www.climateactionproject.com/advisory.php.

19. Aaron Klein and Brenda J. Elliott, *The Manchurian President: Barack Obama's Ties to Communists, Socialists and Other Anti-American Extremists* (Washington, DC: Regnery Publishing, 2010), 152–55.

20. "Tides Foundation and the Tides Center," *DiscovertheNetworks.org*; "Apollo Alliance," *UndueInfluence.com*.

21. *Tides Foundation Annual Report 2001/2002*, http://www.tidesfoundation.org/fileadmin/tf_pdfs/TidesFoundation_AnnualReport_2001-2002.pdf.

22. Ibid.; Ben Johnson, "57 Varieties of Radical Causes, Part I," *FrontPageMagazine.com*, September 16, 2004.

23. Rep. Jay Inslee and Bracken Hendricks, *Apollo's Fire: Igniting America's Clean Energy Economy*, CalCars Initiative, http://www.calcars.org/books.html#af.

24. Apollo Alliance board members in 2006, *DemocraticUnderground.com*, http://www.democraticunderground.com/discuss/duboard.php?az=view_all&address=115x37653.

25. "BlueGreen and Apollo Join Forces to Strengthen Movement for Good, 21st Century Clean Energy Jobs," Apollo Alliance press release, May 26, 2011, http://apolloalliance.org/communications/bluegreen-alliance-apollo-alliance-join-forces-to-strengthen-movement-for-good-21st-century-clean-energy-jobs/.

26. "Achievements," Apollo Alliance website.

27. Ibid.

28. Press Release: "Brown Announces New Bill Providing $30 Billion in Funds to Help Auto Suppliers, Manufacturers Retool for Clean Energy Jobs," official website of Senator Sherrod Brown, U.S. Senate, June 17, 2009.

29. The press release for "Apollo Alliance Joins Sen. Sherrod Brown to Introduce Bill to Help Manufacturers Retool for Clean Energy Economy," Apollo Alliance website, June 17, 2009. This article is no longer available.

30. "Sen. Brown IMPACT Legislation: Brown Proposes $30 Billion Plan To Strengthen Green Energy Manufacturers," Apollo Alliance website, n.d.

31. "Brown Announces New Bill Providing $30 Billion in Funds," June 17, 2009.

32. Andrea Buffa, "Greencollar Association," Facebook, circa June 2010, http://www.facebook.com/topic.php?uid=112817996094&topic=13820.

33. "H.R. 3534, Consolidated Land, Energy, and Aquatic Resources (CLEAR) Act," Committee on Energy and Commerce, U.S. House of Representatives, July 30, 2010.

34. S. 2877, Carbon Limits and Energy for America's Renewal (CLEAR) Act, introduced December 11, 2009, by Senator Maria Cantwell, (D-Wash.).

35. "Founding Board Members," Apollo Alliance, February 19, 2006, Internet Archive, http://web.archive.org/web/20060219050705/www.apolloalliance.org/about_the_alliance/; "Founding Board Members," Apollo Alliance, February 6, 2005, Internet Archive, http://web.archive.org/web/20050206163710/http://www.apolloalliance.org/about_the_alliance/#1.

36. "Apollo Alliance," *Discover the Networks.org.*

37. Lynn Sweet, "Obama's politically expedient ethics conversions: Earmarks latest example," *Chicago Sun-Times*, March 14, 2008.

38. Brenda J. Elliott, "Friends and Neighbors for Obama: The Center for Neighborhood Technology," *RBO*, September 17, 2008, http://therealbarackobama.wordpress.com/2008/09/17/friends-and-neighbors-for-obama-the-center-for-neighborhood-technology/.

39. Jennifer Rubin, "Obama and the Woods Fund; As a board member, Obama helped scratch a lot of backs with grants to politically connected groups," *Pajamas Media*, September 13, 2008.

40. Aaron Klein, "Obama worked with terrorist," *WND.com*, February 24, 2008.

41. Jennifer Rubin, "Obama and the Woods Fund," *Pajamas Media*, September 13, 2008.

42. Isabel Wilkerson, "With Chicago Calm, Daley Glides Toward Primary," *New York Times*, February 19, 1991; Mick Dumke, "Where is Dorothy?" *Chicago Reader*, April 4, 2007; Fran Spielman, "Daley is finally ready to run," *Chicago Sun-Times*, December 11, 2006, http://www.suntimes.com/news/metro/167594,CST-NWS-daley11.article.

43. Press Release: "Blagojevich Unveils List of Chairs, Vice-Chairs of Issues-Based Transition Committees," Illinois Government News Network, December 3, 2002.

44. "Illinois' Democratic Convention Delegation Complete," CapitalFax Blog/Illinoize website, May 5, 2008.

45. "Perlmutter's Livable Communities Act Receives Financial Services Committee Hearing," official House website of Representative Ed Perlmutter, September 23, 2010.

46. "Livable Communities Act Endorsed by the U.S. Senate Banking Committee," Center for Neighborhood Technology, August 5, 2010, http://www.cnt.org/news/2010/08/05/livable-communities-act-endorsed-by-the-u-s-senate-banking-committee/.

47. Ibid.

48. Experts: "Bracken Hendricks," Center for American Progress website.

49. "Our Team. Board," 1Sky.org, http://www.1sky.org/about/ourteam/board.

50. "Bracken Hendricks," Center for American Progress website.

51. "About the Network," Efficiency Cities /*efficiencycities.org.*

52. "Past Calls" section (with list of presenters), Efficiency Cities/*efficiencycities.org.*

53. Ibid.

54. "Retrofit America's Cities" section, Green For All/*greenforall.com.*

55. "Mission statement," Emerald Cities Collaborative/*emeraldcities.org.*

56. "Board Member Organizations," Emerald Cities Collaborative/*emeraldcities.org.*

57. Jonathan Leake, "Climate change data dumped," *Sunday Times* (UK), November 29, 2009, http://www.timesonline.co.uk/tol/news/environment/article6936328.ece.

58. Harrison Schmitt, "The Central Role Of The Sun In Climate Change," *ClimatePhysics.com*, July 10, 2010, http://climatephysics.com/2010/07/10/the-central-role-of-the-sun-in-climate-change/.

59. Jonathan Petre, "Climategate U-turn as scientist at centre of row admits: There has been no global warming since 1995," *Daily Mail*, February 14, 2010.

60. "Report: Antarctic Ice Growing, Not Shrinking," *FoxNews.com*, April 18, 2009.

61. Manfred Wenzel and Jens Schroter, "Reconstruction of regional mean sea level anomalies from tide gauges using neural networks," *Journal of Geophysical Research* 115 (2010).

62. Jerome Ringo, "Testimony before the Senate Committee on Environment and Public Works: 'Green Collar Jobs in the Clean Energy Economy,'" *Senate.gov*, September 25, 2007, http://epw.senate.gov/public/index.cfm?FuseAction=Files. View&FileStore_id=50fcf19e-652a-4fa5-810a-485f1d36f396.

63. News Release: "Proposed Apollo Economic Recovery Act Will Yield 650,000 Green-Collar Jobs ," Apollo Alliance, December 6, 2009, http://apolloalliance.org/programs/full-proposal/apollo-economic-recovery-act/.

64. Faiz Shakir, "Al Gore leads new 'Reality' Coalition to debunk 'clean coal' myth," *Think Progress.org*, December 4, 2008.

65. Rachel Weiner, "Gore's 'Reality Coalition' Fighting 'Clean Coal,'" *Huffington Post*, December 4, 2008.

66. Al Gore, "The Climate for Change," *New York Times*, November 9, 2008.

67. See "About" section on Reality Coalition website, http://action.thisisreality.org/about/reality_coalition/.

68. See list of Apollo endorsers, http://apolloalliance.org/about/endorsers/.

69. Press Release: "'Reality' Coalition Launches Campaign Debunking 'Clean Coal' Myth," *NRDC.org*, December 4, 2008, http://www.nrdc.org/media/2008/081204a.asp.

70. Ibid.

71. Alister Bull, "Obama: Copenhagen paves way for action on climate," Reuters, December 19, 2009.

72. Kim Chipman, "Agencies Urged to Plan for 'Inevitable Effects' of Warming in U.S. Report," Bloomberg News, October 14, 2010.

73. Gerald B. Seib, "In Crisis, Opportunity for Obama," *Wall Street Journal*, November 21, 2008.

74. Helene Cooper and Jackie Calmes, "In Oval Office Speech, Obama Calls for New Focus on Energy Policy," *New York Times*, June 15, 2010.

75. "Remarks by the President to the Nation on the BP Oil Spill," *White House.gov*, June 15, 2010.

76. Ibid.

77. Text, "PRESIDENT OBAMA'S DEVELOPMENT POLICY AND THE GLOBAL CLIMATE CHANGE INITIATIVE," http://usun.state.gov/documents/organization/148452.pdf.

78. "Who's On Board With The Copenhagen Accord?" U.S. Climate Action Network, January 31, 2010, http://www.usclimatenetwork.org/policy/copenhagen-accord-commitments.

79. "NGO's write benchmark Copenhagen climate treaty," Press Release, IndyACT, June 8, 2009, http://www.indyact.org/news_details.php?news_id=NDA.

80. "NGO's Climate Treaty and the Real Deal," WWF, June 8, 2009 (updated November 2009), http://wwf.panda.org/what_we_do/footprint/climate_carbon_energy/climate_agreement/?166141.

81. Ibid.

82. "A Copenhagen Climate Treaty, Version 1.0: A Proposal for a Copenhagen Agreement by Members of the NGO Community," text of treaty listing draft organizations available online at http://assets.wwf.ca/downloads/wwf_proposal_copenhagen_climatetreaty.pdf.

83. See "Team" at IndyACT website, http://www.indyact.org/team.php.

84. Van Jones listed as "Messenger" on list at 350.org site, http://www.350.org/en/messengers.

Chapter Eight: Red Media Army

1. "Katie Couric rhymes a health care message," *Storyballoon.org*, November 23, 2009, http://storyballoon.org/blog/2009/11/23/katie-couric-rhymes-a-health-care-message/.

2. CBSNews.com, "Katie Couric's Notebook: Fear and Frustration," August 13, 2009, http://www.cbsnews.com/8301-500803_162-5242830-500803.html.

3. Executive Summary: *Obama the Taxcutter: A Network Fairy Tale*, Media Research Center, October 19, 2010, http://www.mrc.org/bmi/reports/2010/Obama_the_Tax_Cutter_A_Network_Fairy_Tale.html.

4. "See which media stars dis book exposing Obama *unread;* Editors, reporters trash Obama project as 'sensational rubbish,'" *WorldNetDaily.com*, May 6, 2010.

5. Jonathan Strong, "Documents show media plotting to kill stories about Rev. Jeremiah Wright," *Daily Caller*, July 20, 2010.

6. Transcript: "Obama and Clinton Debate," *ABCNews.go.com*, April 16, 2008.

7. Ibid.

8. Rand Simberg, "'Fred Barnes, Karl Rove, Who Cares? Call Them Racists,'" *Pajamas Media*, July 20, 2010.

9. Jonathan Strong, "When McCain picked Palin, liberal journalists coordinated the best line of attack," *Daily Caller*, July 23, 2010.

10. Jonathan Strong, "Obama wins! And JournoListers rejoice," *Daily Caller*, July 28, 2010.

11. Jonathan Strong, "Liberal journalists suggest government shut down of Fox News," *Daily Caller*, July 29, 2010.

12. Ibid.

13. Clarice Feldman, "New additions make for 107 JournoList names," *American Thinker*, July 24, 2010.

14. James Nuechterlein, "Whose Left," in *First Things: A Monthly Journal of Religion and Public Life*, January 2001, 7.

15. "Frida Berrigan," New America Foundation, http://www.newamerica.net/people/frida_berrigan; "About," *In These Times*, http://www.inthesetimes.com/about/.

16. New America Foundation website, http://www.newamerica.net/.

17. New America Foundation website, http://www.newamerica.net/; "Eric Schmidt," New America Foundation, http://www.newamerica.net/people/eric_schmidt.

18. Thomas Lifson, "JournoList update," *American Thinker*, August 10, 2010.

19. "Funding," New America Foundation, http://www.newamerica.net/about/funding.

20. "Robert Kuttner," *American Prospect*, http://www.prospect.org/cs/about_tap/about_the_editors#kuttner.

21. Phyllis Bennis and Chuck Collins, "Secretary of Commerce: Margot Dorfman; Secretary of State: Jim McDermott. Our Picks for an Obama Cabinet: Parts 1 & 2," Institute for Policy Studies, September 26, 2008, http://www.ips-dc.org/articles/742.

22. "Demos Backgrounder," *Demos.org*, http://www.demos.org/backgrounder.cfm.

23. Bennis and Collins, "Our picks for an Obama cabinet—Parts 1 & 2," September 26, 2008.

24. "Chuck Collins," Institute for Policy Studies, http://www.ips-dc.org/staff/chuck.

25. "Partner Organizations," Institute for Policy Studies, http://www.ips-dc.org/about/partners.

26. "Chuck Collins," *KeyWiki.org*, http://www.keywiki.org/index.php/Chuck_ Collins; . Klein, *The Manchurian President*, 84.

27. Trevor Loudon, "Pro-Obama JournoList outed," *New Zeal Blog*, July 27, 2010.

28. Robert Kuttner, "Saving Progressivism from Obama," *AlterNet.org*, November 28, 2010.

29. Loudon, "Pro-Obama JournoList outed," July 27, 2010.

30. Jonathan Strong, "Political operatives on JournoList worked to shape news coverage," *Daily Caller*, December 1, 2010.

31. See Brandzel's biography at *Huffington Post*, http://www.huffingtonpost .com/ben-brandzel, also at http://otb.huffingtonpost.com/wiki/index.php/ John_Edwards_Staff.

32. Brandzel listed as a speaker alongside Klein at the conference of the Social Democratic Movement. See schedule at http://www.netrootsnation.org/ node/826. Netroots agenda viewable at the group's website, http://www.net-rootsnation.org/about.

33. Ibid.

34. See Brandzel's *Huffington Post* bio.

35. Ben Brandzel, "MoveOn: It's All About The Members," *TPM Café/Talking-PointsMemo.com*, July 30, 2008.

36. Mission statement listed in "About Us" section at http://www.avaaz.org/en/ about.php.

37. "Gaza: Investigate the raid, lift the blockade," petition online at https:// secure.avaaz.org/en/gaza_flotilla/?fp.

38. Lifson, "JournoList update," August 10, 2010.

39. "FLOWERING JUDIS! Journalists threw their support to Obama, Judis says, in a vast gaffe," *Daily Howler*, May 22, 2008, http://www.charm .net/~somerby/dh052208.html.

40. "Free Press calls on Obama administration to resist extremism in the media," *FreePress.com*, September 8, 2009.

41. "New Public Media: A Plan for Action," *Free Press.com*, May 2010.

42. Peter Suderman, "Media Watchdogs Ask FCC to Track Internet Hate Speech," *Reason.com*, June 1, 2010.

43. "Comments of National Hispanic Media Coalition," Federal Communications Commission written testimony on the manner of Future of Media and Information Needs of Communities in a Digital Age, FCC GN Dkt. No. 10-25, http://fjallfoss.fcc.gov/ecfs/document/view?id=7020450549.

44. "Biography of Chairman Julius Genachowski," Federal Communications

Commission, http://www.fcc.gov/commissioners/genachowski/biography
.html.

45. Klein and Elliott, *The Manchurian President*, 35–36, 198–99, 200–201.

46. "Susan Crawford," Advisory Committee to the Congressional Internet Caucus, http://netcaucus.org/biography/susan-crawford.shtml; Cecilia Kang, "Obama tech adviser Susan Crawford plans departure," *Washington Post*, October 27, 2009.

47. John Eggerton, "Free Press' Ben Scott exits for State Department post," *Broadcasting & Cable*, May 27, 2010.

48. Ben Scott and Robert W. McChesney, eds., *The Future of Media: Resistance and Reform in the 20th Century* (New York: Seven Stories Press, 2005).

49. "Susan Crawford at Free Press Summit: Changing Media. Government intervention in newspapers and bandwidth," *Canada Free Press*, October 9, 2009. Transcript was expanded by the authors from the video posted with the article.

50. "Participating organizations," *OneWebDay.org*, http://onewebday.org/partic
ipating-organizations/.

51. "Obama's Internet Czar Susan Crawford has ties to ACORN," *FireAndrea
Mitchell.com*, September 27, 2009.

52. "Advisory Board," *PublicKnowledge.org;* "About. Funders," *PublicKnowledge
.org*.

53. "Organizations We Work With," *Public Knowledge.org*.

54. "Tim Wu," *TimWu.org*.

55. "Tim Wu on Network Neutrality," *GeekEntertainment.TV*, April 21, 2009; "Net Neutrality: A Historical Timeline," *Sidecut Reports*, November 16, 2008.

56. Cliff Kincaid, "'Media Reform' Activists Cheer Obama," Accuracy in Media, June 8, 2008.

57. "Lawrence Lessig—Creative Commons & Tech advisor ties to Mohammad Nanabhay," *Freedomist*, October 10, 2009, http://freedomist
.com/2009/10/10/lawrence-lessig-creative-commons-obama-tech-advisor-
ties-2-mohamed-nanabhay/; Mark Polege, "Robert McChesney and the Free Press," *Examiner*, November 3, 2009, http://www.examiner.com/conserva-
tive-in-st-louis/robert-mcchesney-and-the-free-press.

58. Lawrence Lessig, "The Dems get Net Neutrality," *Lessig.org*, July 30, 2006.

59. Warner Todd Huston, "Obama tech advisor introduces video of gay, singed Jesus who gets hit by a car," *NewsBusters.org*, April 21, 2008.

60. "The Arena Profile: Lawrence Lessig," *Politico.com*, http://www.politico
.com/arena/bio/lawrence_lessig.html.

61. Elizabeth Montalbano, "Microsoft, Lessig get new copyright tool," *InfoWorld.com*, June 21, 2006.

62. Noam Cohen, "Few in U.S. See Jazeera's Coverage of Gaza War," *New York Times*, January 11, 2009.

63. Fred Benenson, "Recovery.gov Following WhiteHouse.gov's Lead," *Creative Commons.com*, March 20, 2009.

64. David Folkenflik, "NPR ends Juan Williams contract after Muslim remarks," *NPR.org*, October 21, 2010.

65. Liz Goodwin, "Fox News offers Juan Williams $2 million contract," Yahoo! News, October 21, 2010.

66. "NPR Launches New Online Local Journalism Venture with CPB and Knight Foundation Funding," *NPR.org*, October 2, 2009.

67. "New Knight Grant Accelerates Center for Public Integrity's Digital Transformation," Center for Public Integrity, October 7, 2010, http://www.public integrity.org/news/entry/2505/.

68. Cliff Kincaid, "The hidden Soros agenda: Drugs, money and political power," Accuracy in Media, *aim.org*, October 27, 2004.

69. Elizabeth Jensen, "With Grant, NPR to Step Up State Government Reporting," *New York Times*, October 17, 2010, http://www.nytimes .com/2010/10/18/business/media/18npr.html?_r=2.

70. Joe Pompeo, "Huffington Post And Center For Public Integrity Create "One Of The Largest Investigative Newsrooms In The Country," *BusinessInsider .com*, October 19, 2010.

71. "Soros Gives $1 Million to Target Fox News," *Newsmax.com*, October 27, 2010.

72. Center for Public Integrity, http://www.publicintegrity.org/about/.

73. See Soros Initiatives grantees: http://www.soros.org/initiatives/justice/focus_ar eas/gideon/grantees/cpi_2000; http://www.soros.org/initiatives/justice/focus_ areas/gideon/grantees/cpi_2001; http://www.soros.org/grants?id=102; and http://www.soros.org/grants?id=101.

74. Aaron Klein, "Gates lawyer was young Obama's mentor," *WorldNetDaily.com*, July 24, 2009.

75. Cynthia Gordy, "Obama Mentor Charles Ogletree Shares Insight on Our President," *Essence*, February 12, 2009.

76. Ibid.

77. Aaron Klein, "Gates lawyer was young Obama's mentor," *WorldNetDaily.com*, July 24, 2009.

78. David Horowitz, "Uncivil Wars: Alan Dershowitz's Capitulation to the Racial Left," *FrontPageMag.com*, July 7, 2002.

79. "Ogletree Charles Jr. Biography—Selected writings," *Biography.com*, http://biography.jrank.org/pages/2366/Ogletree-Jr-Charles.html.

80. Ibid.

81. Dennis Drabelle, "Charles Ogletree's book on the arrest of Henry Louis Gates," *Washington Post*, July 27, 2010.

82. James Crawley, "Obama: Police who arrested professor 'acted stupidly'" *CNN.com*, July 22, 2009.

83. Press Release: "AP to distribute content from nonprofit journalism organizations," Associated Press, June 13, 2009, http://www.ap.org/pages/about/pressreleases/pr_061309a.html.

84. "About Us," *ProPublica.com*.

85. "Herb and Marion Sandler," *DiscoverTheNetworks.org*.

86. Ibid.

87. Cheryl K. Chumley, "ProPublica: Investigative Journalism or Liberal Spin?" Capital Research Center's Foundation Watch, http://www.capitalresearch.org/pubs/pdf/v1241117859.pdf.

88. Shafer, "What Do Herbert and Marion Sandler Want?" October 15, 2007.

89. "Pro Publica," *UndueInfluence.com*.

90. Associated Press, "Study: Bush led U.S. to war on 'false pretenses,'" *MSNBC.com*, January 23, 2008, http://www.msnbc.msn.com/id/22794451/ns/world_news . . . /n_africa.

91. Richard Poe, "Soros Shadow Party Stalks DeLay," *FrontPageMag.com*, April 12, 2005.

92. "AP to distribute content from nonprofit journalism organizations," Associated Press, January 13, 2009.

93. Cliff Kincaid, "The hidden Soros agenda: Drugs, money and political power," October 27, 2004.

94. Brenda J. Elliott, "Mark Lloyd: Redistribution of Wealth Czar at the FCC," *RBO*, August 17, 2009, http://therealbarackobama.wordpress.com/2009/08/17/mark-lloyd-redistribution-of-wealth-czar-at-the-fcc/.

95. Seton Motley on Glenn Beck about Mark Lloyd: "Assault on Conservative and Christian Talk Radio," *FoxNews.com*, August 14, 2009; Mark Lloyd, "Forget the Fairness Doctrine," Center for American Progress, July 27, 2007, http://www.americanprogress.org/issues/2007/07/lloyd_fairness.html.

96. Ibid.

97. Klein and Elliott, *The Manchurian President*, 188–89.

98. Matt Cover, "FCC's Chief Diversity Officer Wants Private Broadcasters to

Pay a Sum Equal to Their Total Operating Costs to Fund Public Broadcasting," *CNSNews.com*, August 13, 2009.

99. Ibid.

100. George Fallon, "Mark Lloyd: FCC Chief Diversity Officer Seeks to Punish Conservative Broadcasters," *RightPundits.com*, August 14, 2009.

101. Cover, "FCC's Chief Diversity Officer," August 13, 2009.

102. Cecilia Kang, "FCC chair announces net neutrality push without re-asserting role over broadband Internet," *Washington Post*, December 1, 2010.

103. Katrina vanden Heuvel, "Obama Blasts FCC Media Ownership Decision," *Nation*, December 18, 2007.

104. Ibid.

105. Ibid. Vanden Heuvel quotes from her December 12, 2007, Editor's Cut, "On the Media."

106. Ben Compaine, "Senate's Media Ownership Crusade: Ignores Research, Will Have Unintended Consequences," *Who Owns the Media?* November 9, 2007, http://wotmedia.blogspot.com/2007/11/senates-media-ownership-crusade-ignores.html.

107. Ibid.

108. Peter Suderman, "Top FCC Staffer Says Commissioner Copps 'would love to have jurisdiction over everything,'" *Reason.com*, May 19, 2010.

109. "Michael J. Copps: Why He Matters," *Washington Post*, *WhoRunsGov.com*, http://www.whorunsgov.com/Profiles/Michael_J._Copps.

110. Ibid.

111. Edward Wyatt, "U.S. Court Curbs F.C.C. Authority on Web Traffic," *New York Times*, April 6, 2010.

112. Susan Crawford, op-ed, "An Internet for Everybody," *New York Times*, April 10, 2010.

113. Susan Jones, "FCC Commissioner Wants to Test the 'Public Value' of Every Broadcast Station," *CNSNews.com*, December 3, 2010.

114. Brian Stelter, "F.C.C. Commissioner Proposes 'Public Values Test,'" *New York Times*, December 2, 2010.

115. Steven Vass, "Auntie's value for money test; In the face of a new, multichannel age, the BBC must show that its service is worth the licence fee. Can it succeed?" *Sunday Herald*, June 27, 2004.

116. Ibid.

117. "UK regulator mulls BBC on-demand proposals (Office of Communications analyses BBC's broadcast services)," *Screen Digest*, October 1, 2006.

118. "Likely market impact of BBC's proposed on-demand services," M2 Presswire, January 23, 2007.

119. Clinton Manning, ed., "Beeb Cyber Plan Gets Slammed," *Mirror* (London), January 24, 2007.

120. "Broadcasting: New Tests for Aid for New Media," *European Report*, July 14, 2009.

121. Wolfgang Kleinwæchter, "Public Broadcasting in Europe, the EU Amsterdam Protocol of 1997 and the GATS Negotiations within the WTO," Universit of Aarhus/NETCOM Institute Leipzig, accessed December 6, 2010, http://www.medialaw.ru/e_pages/laws/project/k3-6.htm. See Pre-Conference #2 for identification of Wolfgang Kleinwæchter, http://www.icahdq.org/conferences/preconference_info_pf.asp.

122. Ibid.

123. "What is Pluralism?" Pluralism Project, Harvard University, *Pluralism.org*.

124. Kleinwæchter, "Public Broadcasting in Europe."

125. Daniel Burke, "Saguaro seminar stays with Obama," *ReligionNewsService.com*, June 11, 2009.

126. "About Us," Saguaro Seminar, Harvard University, Kennedy School of Government, accessed April 14, 2010, http://www.hks.harvard.edu/saguaro/.

127. Thomas Sander, "Watering the Obama grassroots post-election," *Social Capital* (blog), January 14, 2009, http://socialcapital.wordpress.com/2009/01/14/watering-the-obama-grassroots-post-election/.

128. Ibid.

129. "Background," Saguaro Seminar, Harvard University, Kennedy School of Government, accessed November 1, 2010, http://www.hks.harvard.edu/saguaro/background.htm; *Better Together* (report), December 2000, with additions after September 11, 2001, http://www.bettertogether.org/thereport.htm.

130. Mark K. Smith, "Robert Putnam, Social Capital and Civic Community," accessed November 1, 2010, http://www.infed.org/thinkers/putnam.htm; Robert D. Putnam, "Bowling Alone: America's Declining Social Capital. An Interview with Robert Putnam," *Journal of Democracy* 6, no. 1 (January 1995), 65–78, http://xroads.virginia.edu/~HYPER/DETOC/assoc/bowling.html.

131. Bowling Alone website, http://www.bowlingalone.com/.

132. David Moberg, "Not Quite Bowled Over," *In These Times*, January 22, 2001.

133. Burke, "Saguaro seminar stays with Obama," June 11, 2009.

134. Ibid.

135. Klein, *The Manchurian President*, 62.

136. Sabrina L. Miller, "Schools Get Big Bucks to Fund Reform: 35 Clusters in City Sharing $2.5 Million," *Chicago Tribune*, December 20, 1995.

137. Bliss W. Browne, *A Chicago Case Study in Intergenerational Appreciative Inquiry, childrenfriendlycities.org*, 1999, 3; Lorraine Forte, "35 networks get first Annenberg funds," *Catalyst-Chicago.org*, February 1996.

138. Ibid., 10.

139. Patti Villacorta, "The Originators of Obama-speak: Public Allies and the ABCD Institute. Want to make sense of the first couple's oratory? Examine their involvement with these two groups," *Pajamas Media*, October 25, 2009.

140. Bob Roman, "A Town Meeting on Economic Insecurity: Employment and Survival in Urban America," Chicago DSA, *New Ground* 45 (March–April 1996), http://www.chicagodsa.org/ngarchive/ng45.html.

141. Richard D. Heffner, Transcript: "Michael Harrington: The Long Distance Runner," *Open Mind*, July 6, 1988, http://www.thirteen.org/openmind/history/michael-harrington-the-long-distance-runner/637/; Michael Pugliese, "SDUSA, part 1," LBO-Talk Archives, July 6, 2001, http://mailman.lbotalk.org/2001/2001-July/012817.html.

142. "National Advisory Council," Social Democrats USA, April 30, 2008, Internet Archive, http://web.archive.org/web/20080430091952/www.socialdemocrats.org/natcom.html.

143. "Executive Committee," W.E.B. DuBois Institute for African and African American Research, accessed November 10, 2010, http://dubois.fas.harvard.edu/executive-committee; "Board of Directors," Center on Budget and Policy Priorities, accessed November 1, 2010, http://www.cbpp.org/cms/?fa=view&id=715; "William Julius Wilson," *UndueInfluence.com*.

144. Lynn Sweet, "Obama taps Martha Minow, John G. Levi for Legal Service Corporation Board," *Chicago Sun-Times*, August 6, 2009; Liza Mundy, "When Michelle Met Barack," *Washington Post*, October 5, 2008.

145. Carrie Budoff Brown, "Obama: The journey of a confident man," *Politico*, August 28, 2008.

146. Sweet, "Obama taps Martha Minow, John G. Levi for Legal Service Corporation Board," August 6, 2009.

147. "DUSP's Briggs joins Obama administration," *MIT News*, January 20, 2009, http://web.mit.edu/newsoffice/2009/briggs-0120.html.

148. Ibid.; Department of Health and Human Services Team Leads, *Change.gov*, accessed November 1, 2010, http://change.gov/learn/department_of_health_and_human_services_team_leads.

149. Roger Kimball, "E. J. Dionne, Obama, and the return of socialism," *Roger's Rules*, PajamasMedia.com, July 11, 2008.

150. Ibid.

151. E. J. Dionne, "A World Safe for Socialism," *Washington Post*, April 27, 1999.

152. Ibid.

153. "EXCLUSIVE: George Stephanopoulos Interviews Presidential Hopeful Barack Obama. Obama Sits Down for First Sunday Morning Interview with ABC News' George Stephanopoulos," ABC News, May 9, 2007; "Interview with George Stephanopoulos of ABC News," American Presidency Project, January 27, 2008, http://www.presidency.ucsb.edu/ws/index.php?pid=77313.

154. Robin Abcarian, "Stephanopoulos defends his questions to Obama," *Los Angeles Times*, April 17, 2008.

155. Ibid.

156. Lynn Sweet, "Oops! Barack Obama says 'my Muslim faith' in interview with ABC's George Stephanopoulos; he was discussing false rumors when he slipped up," *Chicago Sun-Times*, September 8, 2008.

157. "TRANSCRIPT: George Stephanopoulos' Exclusive Interview with President Obama," ABC News, January 20, 2010, http://blogs.abcnews.com/george/2010/01/transcript-george-stephanopoulos-exclusive-interview-with-president-obama.html; "Transcript: George Stephanopoulos Interviews President Obama. 'Good Morning America' Anchor Sat Down for Exclusive Interview Following START Treaty Signing," ABC News, April 17, 2010.

158. Scott Whitlock, "ABC's George Stephanopoulos Spins for Obama: 'Set Aside' Last Two Terror Attacks," Media Research Center, July 19, 2010, http://www.mrc.org/biasalert/2010/20100719125647.aspx.

159. Ibid.

160. NB Staff, "MRC's Bozell: Stephanopoulos Must Recuse Himself From Obama Reporting," *NewsBusters.org*, January 29, 2009.

161. Executive Order, Amendments to Executive Order 13199 and Establishment of the President's Advisory Council for Faith-Based and Neighborhood Partnerships, *WhiteHouse.gov*, February 5, 2009, http://www.whitehouse.gov/the_press_office/AmendmentstoExecutiveOrder13199andEstablishmentofthePresidentsAdvisoryCouncilforFaith-BasedandNeighborhoodPartnerships/.

162. Eli Saslow, "Obama's Path to Faith Was Eclectic; President-Elect Will Reach Out to Diverse Set of Religious Leaders for Advice," *Washington Post*, January 18, 2009.

163. "Brookings Institution Launches The Hamilton Project," Brookings Institution, April 5, 2006, http://www.brookings.edu/media/NewsReleases/2006/20060405_hamilton.aspx.

164. Barack Obama, "Restoring America's Promise of Opportunity, Prosperity and Growth," Hamilton Project, Brookings Institution, Washington, DC, April 5, 2006, http://www.brookings.edu/comm/events/20060405obama .pdf; Jim Wallis, "Restoring America's Promise of Opportunity, Prosperity and Growth," Hamilton Project, Brookings Institution, Washington, DC, April 5, 2006, http://www.brookings.edu/comm/events/20060405wallis .pdf.

165. "Jim Wallis," *DiscovertheNetworks.org.*

166. Ibid.

167. Ibid.

168. M. Danielson, "Sojourners Founder Jim Wallis' Revolutionary Anti-Christian 'Gospel.' Will Christian Leaders Stand with Wallis?" Lighthouse Trails Research, June 2, 2010, http://www.crossroad.to/Quotes/spirituality/ lighthousetrails/010/6-wallis.htm.

169. "Jim Wallis," *DiscovertheNetworks.org.*

170. Book Review: Jim Wallis, "Agenda for Biblical People," *Theology Today*, July 1977, http://theologytoday.ptsem.edu/jul1977/v34-2-bookreview2.htm.

171. Greg Hengler, "Jim Wallis on MSNBC: Social Justice, Economic Justice, & H'care 'Are At The Heart Of The Gospel,'" *Townhall.com*, April 9, 2010.

Chapter Nine: Disarming America

1. Sheryl Gay Stolberg, "Obama Offers Sympathy and Urges No 'Jump to Conclusions," *New York Times*, November 17, 2009.

2. Ibid.

3. "Fort Hood shootings: The meaning of 'Allahu Akbar,'" *Telegraph* (UK), November 6, 2009.

4. Philip Sherwell and Alex Spillius, "Fort Hood shooting: Texas army killer linked to September 11 terrorists," *Telegraph* (UK), November 7, 2009.

5. "Treasury designates Anwar al-Awlaki key leader of AQAP," *CNN.com*, July 16, 2010.

6. Brian Ross and Rhonda Schwartz, "Major Hasan's E-Mail: 'I Can't Wait to Join You' in Afterlife," *ABCNews.go.com*, November 19, 2009.

7. Bryan Bender, "Ft. Hood suspect was Army dilemma," *Boston Globe*, February 22, 2010.

8. Dana Priest, "Fort Hood suspect warned of threats within the ranks," *Washington Post*, November 10, 2009.

9. Ibid.

10. Mark Schone, "The Army Asks If Major Nidal Hasan Is Insane," *ABCNews .go.com*, December 2, 2009.

11. U.S. District Court, Eastern District of Michigan, Southern Division, Case 2:10-cr-20005-NGE-DAS Document 7 Filed 01/06/2010, available at http://www.cbsnews.com/htdocs/pdf/Abdulmutallab_Indictment.pdf.

12. "EDITORIAL: Obama denies crotch bomber conspiracy," *Washington Times*, December 29, 2009.

13. Adam Nossiter, "Lonely Trek to Radicalism for Terror Suspect," *New York Times*, January 16, 2010.

14. Matthew Cole, Brian Ross, and Nasser Atta, "Underwear Bomber: New Video of Training, Martyrdom Statements," *ABCNews.go.com*, April 26, 2010.

15. David Gardner, "Obama: 'We're at war with Al-Qaeda and we'll do whatever it takes to defeat them,'" *Daily Mail* (UK), January 8, 2010.

16. Editorial, "'Islamic terrorism' and the Obama administration: Critics on the right say the administration is deliberately denying the existence of 'radical Islam' and 'Islamic terrorism,'" *Los Angeles Times*, June 8, 2010.

17. "Obama Bans Islam, Jihad From National Security Strategy Document," *FoxNews.com*, April 7, 2010.

18. Thomas Donnelly, "The Underpinnings of the Bush Doctrine," American Enterprise Institute for Public Policy Research, February 2003, http://www .aei.org/outlook/15845.

19. "'I am Muslim soldier ready to plead guilty 100 times over': Failed bomber admits bungled Times Square attack," *Daily Mail* (UK), June 22, 2010.

20. Aaron Klein, *Schmoozing with Terrorists: From Hollywood to the Holy Land, Jihadists Reveal their Real Plans—To a Jew!* (New York: WND Books, 2007).

21. *MideastWeb.com*, "Who is Osama Bin Laden?"

22. Hilary Leila Krieger, "Top US security official: Our enemy isn't terrorism, jihad," *Jerusalem Post*, May 27, 2010.

23. Kamran Pasha, "Anwar Al-Awlaki: The Jim Jones of Islam," *Huffington Post*, May 23, 2010.

24. Krieger, "Top US security official," May 27, 2010.

25. Barry Rubin, "Brennan on Hezbollah: They Can't Be Terrorists! They Have Lawyers!" *GlobalPolitician.com*, August 19, 2009.

26. Jarrett Murphy, "Beirut Barracks Attack Remembered," *CBSNews.com*, October 23, 2003.

27. "PM 'says Israel pre-planned war,'" *BBC Online*, March 8, 2007, http://news .bbc.co.uk/2/hi/middle_east/6431637.stm.

28. Ibid.

29. Adam Cassandra, "Brennan: U.S. Should Foster 'Moderate Elements' of the Terrorist Group Hezbollah," *CNSNews.com*, May 23, 2010.

30. Center for Special Studies, Intelligence and Terrorism Information Center, "The Hamas civilian infrastructure in PA territories," http://www.terrorism-info.org.il, July 10, 2006.

31. Video available at http://www.youtube.com/watch?v=pVP7Y54rdVE; Aaron Klein, "Counter-terror adviser: U.S. should 'never' profile. Declares himself 'citizen of the world,' compares Muslims to 'bias' against Irish, Italians," *WND.com*, February 18, 2010.

32. Editorial, "Will Profiling Make a Difference?" *New York Times*, January 4, 2010.

33. Josh Gerstein, "Brennan, unruffled, talks terror at NYU," *Politico*, February 14, 2010.

34. Aaron Klein, "Hamas-linked group set up meeting with Obama adviser," *WND.com*, February 19, 2010.

35. Press Release: "ISNA President Opens Townhall Meeting on the Nation's Security with John Brennan," ISNA, http://www.isna.net/articles/News/ISNA-President-Opens-Dialogue-on-the-Nations-Security-with-John-Brennan.aspx.

36. "ISNA President Opens Townhall Meeting on the Nation's Security with John Brennan," *Tri-State Muslim/*tsmmedia.net, February 16, 2010.

37. Josh Gerstein, "Islamic Groups Named in Hamas Funding Case," *New York Sun*, June 4, 2007.

38. "Holy Land founders get life sentences," *Jewish Telegraphic Agency, jta.org*, May 28, 2009.

39. "Islamic Society of North America (ISNA)," *DiscovertheNetworks.org*.

40. Ibid.

41. Aaron Klein, "Soda, Pizza and the Destruction of America," *WND.com*, March 18, 2003.

42. Stephen Schwartz, "Wahhabism & Islam in the U.S.: Two-faced policy fosters danger," *NationalReview.com*, June 30, 2003.

43. "ISNA," *DiscovertheNetworks.org*.

44. Ibid.

45. "Leaders of Hamas linked group met with Obama's Transition Team," *Militant Islam Monitor*, January 18, 2009, http://www.militantislammonitor.org/article/id/3820.

46. Josh Gerstein, "Obama prayer speaker has Hamas tie?" *Politico*, January 17, 2009.

47. Michael A. Fletcher, "Ramadan Dinner at the White House: The Guest List," *Washington Post*, September 1, 2009.

48. Steven Emerson, "Top Obama aide invites head of terrorist-linked org to join administration task force," *JewishWorldReview.com*, June 29, 2009.

49. Jennifer Rubin, "Why Is the Justice Department Cozying Up to Islamic Radicals?" *PajamasMedia.com*, June 22, 2009.

50. Hammad Hammad, "Valerie Jarrett Addresses the Islamic Society of North America," White House blog, June 6, 2009, http://www.whitehouse.gov/blog/Valerie-Jarrett-Addresses-the-Islamic-Society-of-North-America.

51. Joseph Klein, "Obama's radical guests," *FrontPageMag.com*, August 19, 2010.

52. Katelyn Sabochik, "President Obama Celebrates Ramadan at White House Iftar Dinner," White House blog, August 14, 2010, http://www.whitehouse.gov/blog/2010/08/14/president-obama-celebrates-ramadan-white-house-iftar-dinner.

53. Toby Harnden, "Barack Obama backtracks over Ground Zero mosque support," *Telegraph* (UK), August 15, 2010.

54. Eboo Patel, "Saving Each Other, Saving Ourselves," *Reconstructionist* 72, no. 1 (Fall 2007), 37–41, http://bjpa.org/Publications/downloadPublication.cfm?PublicationID=4017. The piece is from Patel's book *Acts of Faith* (2007).

55. Press Release: "Obama Announces White House Office of Faith-based and Neighborhood Partnerships," *WhiteHouse.gov*, February 5, 2009, http://www.whitehouse.gov/the_press_office/ObamaAnnouncesWhiteHouseOfficeofFaith-basedandNeighborhoodPartnerships/.

56. "Local students share meals, faith," *Morton Grove Champion* (IL), November 27, 2003.

57. Eboo Patel, Patrice Brodeur, and Imam Feisal Abdul Rauf, *Building the Interfaith Youth Movement: Beyond Dialogue to Action* (Lanham, MD: Rowman & Littlefield, 2006).

58. "ASMA: American Society for the Advancement of Muslims—faux moderates promoting Islamisation by 'Muslim Leaders of Tomorrow,'" *Militant Islam Monitor*, May 2, 2007.

59. Specific except of book available online at http://bjpa.org/Publications/downloadPublication.cfm?PublicationID=4017.

60. Eboo Patel, "Saving Each Other, Saving Ourselves," Fall 2007.

61. Eboo Patel, "Van Jones, Faith Hero," *Huffington Post*, March 5, 2010.

62. Tom Topousis, "Imam terror error: Ground Zero mosque leader hedges on Hamas," *New York Post*, June 19, 2010; Aaron Klein, "'Ground Zero' imam

makes stunning terror comments. Claims to support peace but refuses to condemn violent jihad groups," *WND.com*, June 21, 2010.

63. Klein, "'Ground Zero' imam," June 21, 2010.

64. Anne Barnard, "Parsing the Record of Feisal Abdul Rauf," *New York Times*, August 21, 2010.

65. Ibid.

66. Alyssa A. Lappen, "The Ground Zero Mosque Developer: Muslim Brotherhood Roots, Radical Dreams," *Pajamas Media*, May 14, 2010.

67. James Zumwalt, "Muslims Know the Symbolism of the Ground Zero Mosque," *HumanEvents.com*, August 3, 2010.

68. "Napolitano Appoints Islamist To Homeland Security Panel," ITP News, October 21, 2010.

69. Homeland Security Press Release, "Secretary Napolitano Swears in Homeland Security Advisory Council Members," *dhs.gov*, October 15, 2010.

70. Rod Dreher, "If She Knew, Would She Care?," *BeliefNet.com*, August 16, 2007.

71. "Inside Al-Qaeda, the Islamist Terrorist Network," *MideastWeb.org*, n.d.

72. Mollie, "The long arc of Sayyid Qutb," *GetReligion.org*, December 15, 2009.

73. Mohamed Elibiary, "OPINION: Mohamed Elibiary: Verdict misinterprets 'material support,'" *Dallas Morning News*, June 24, 2010.

74. News Release: "Homeland Security Council Executive Order," *WhiteHouse.gov*, March 21, 2002, http://georgewbush-whitehouse.archives.gov/news/releases/2002/03/20020321-9.html.

75. Sayyid Qutb, "A Muslim's Nationality and His Belief," *Islaam.com*, n.d.

76. Ibid.

77. Paul Berman, "The Philosopher of Islamic Terror," *New York Times Magazine*, March 23, 2003.

78. Rod Dreher, "Unreliable advice from this Muslim group," *DallasNews.com*, November 11, 2009, http://dallasmorningviewsblog.dallasnews.com/archives/2009/11/unreliable-advi.html.

79. Jihad Watch: "Dallas: A tribute to the great Islamic visionary, Ayatollah Khomeini," *JihadWatch.com*, December 14, 2004.

80. Ibid.

81. Todd Bensman and Robert Riggs, "Texas Muslims Host Ayatollah Khomeini Tribute," CBS-11 News, December 17, 2004, http://iranvajahan.net/cgi-bin/printarticle.pl?l=en&y=2004&m=12&d=18&a=1.

82. "Text: Obama's Speech in Cairo," *New York Times*, June 4, 2009, http://www.nytimes.com/2009/06/04/us/politics/04obama.text.html?_r=2.

83. "Muslim Americans: Middle Class and Mostly Mainstream," Pew Research Center, May 22, 2007, http://pewresearch.org/assets/pdf/muslim-ameri cans.pdf.

84. Robert Spencer, "Most Muslims Reject Terrorism?" International Analyst Network, November 2, 2007, http://www.analyst-network.com/article .php?art_id=1148.

85. Ibid.

86. "Support for Terror Wanes Among Muslim Publics. Islamic Extremism: Common Concern for Muslim and Western Publics," Pew Global Attitudes Project at the Pew Research Center, July 14, 2005, http://pewglobal .org/2005/07/14/islamic-extremism-common-concern-for-muslim-and-western-publics/.

87. Associated Press, "Poll: Majority of Palestinians support kidnappings," *Jerusalem Post*, July 9, 2006.

88. "Obama's Speech in Cairo," June 4, 2009.

89. "NASA Chief: Next Frontier Better Relations With Muslim World," *FoxNews.com*, July 5, 2010.

90. Judson Berger, "Former NASA Director Says Muslim Outreach Push 'Deeply Flawed,'" *FoxNews.com*, July 6, 2010.

91. Jack Tapper, "White House Now Says NASA Administrator Not Tasked with Muslim Outreach," *ABCNews.com*, July 12, 2010.

92. Ibid.

93. "NASA Outreach Program 'Confirmed' Despite White House Denial, Rep Says," *FoxNews.com*, July 14, 2010.

94. Howard E. McCurdy, "Inside NASA at 50," ch. 2 in *NASA's First 50 Years*, 2010, http://ntrs.nasa.gov/archive/nasa/casi.ntrs.nasa.gov/20100025882_2010028370 .pdf.

95. "Special Message to the Congress on Urgent National Needs—Page 4," Speech of President John F. Kennedy as delivered in person before a joint session of Congress, May 25, 1961, http://www.jfklibrary .org/Historical+Resources/Archives/Reference+Desk/Speeches/JFK/ Urgent+National+Needs+Page+4.htm.

96. Press Release: "News Conference by President Obama," Palaiz de la Musique et Des Congres Strasbourg, France, on April 4, 2009, *whitehouse.gov*.

97. Kenneth Chang, "Obama Calls for End to NASA's Moon Program," *New York Times*, February 1, 2010.

98. Irene Klotz, "Obama budget would cut NASA moon plan," Reuters, February 1, 2010, http://www.reuters.com/article/idUSTRE6101XF20100201.

99. Ibid.

100. CNN Wire staff, "Obama: 'Real progress' at nuclear summit," *CNN.com*, April 14, 2010.

101. Ibid.

102. David E. Sanger and Peter Baker, "Obama Limits When U.S. Would Use Nuclear Arms," *New York Times*, April 5, 2010.

103. Ibid.

104. Toby Harnden, "Barack Obama pledges to limit nuclear attacks," *Telegraph* (UK), April 6, 2010.

105. Aaron Klein, "U.S. czar in Cold War: Smack in the USSR," *WND.com*, March 4, 2010.

106. "Director John P. Holdren," Office of Science and Technology Policy, *white house.gov*.

107. "The Bulletin and the Scientists' Movement," *Bulletin of the Atomic Scientists*, December 1985, 23.

108. "About Us," *Bulletin of the Atomic Scientists* website, http://www.thebulletin .org/content/about-us/purpose.

109. Aaron Klein, "Obama's nuke agreements meant to disarm U.S.?," *WND.com*, April 13, 2010. See also: *NationMaster.com Encyclopedia*, s.v. "Federation of American Scientists," http://www.statemaster.com/encyclopedia/Federa tion-of-American-Scientists.

110. "Pavel Sudoplatov on the Atomic Spies who helped Russia get the bomb" and assorted source materials accessed October 26, 2010, http://mailstar.net/ atomic-spies.html.

111. Kenneth D. Nichols, "Indictment of J. Robert Oppenheimer," Manhattan Project Heritage Preservation Association, http://www.mphpa.org/classic/ JRO/02.htm.

112. Peter J. Kuznick, "A Tragic Life: Oppenheimer and the Bomb," http://www .armscontrol.org/print/1851.

113. "Pavel Sudoplatov on the Atomic Spies who helped Russia get the bomb," accessed October 26, 2010, http://mailstar.net/atomic-spies.html.

114. "Notes on Hoover Spy Letter," Federal Bureau of Investigation, United States Department of Justice, May 29, 1946, http://www.spongobongo.com/ no9940.htm; Trevor Loudon, "Obama File 98 Obama Science Czar Hold- ren's Pro-Soviet Associations," *New Zeal Blog*, May 2, 2010.

115. Ibid.

116. FAS, June 1988, http://www.mit.edu/people/jeffrey/JEH_FAS_Hetero_ AIDS_June_1988.pdf; FAS, January/February 2002, http://www.fas.org/

faspir/2002/v55n1/v55n1.pdf; FAS, March/April 2002, http://ftp.fas.org/faspir/2002/v55n2/v55n2.pdf; FAS, Summer 2003, http://www.fas.org/faspir/2003/v56n2/v56n2.pdf.

117. David W. Hafemeister, *Physics and Nuclear Arms Today: Readings from Physics Today* (New York: American Institute of Physics, 1991), 379. See also John Greenwald, Jordan Bonfante, and Ken Olsen, "Soviet Union Wooing The West," *Time*, March 2, 1987.

118. Mission statement at Pugwash website, www.pugwash.org.

119. Richard Felix Staar, *Foreign Policies of the Soviet Union* (Stanford, CA: Hoover Institution Press, 1991).

120. Ibid.

121. U.S. Congress, House Select Committee on Intelligence, *Soviet Covert Action: The Forgery Offensive*, Feb. 6 and 19, 1980, 96th Cong., 2d sess., 1963 (Washington, DC: GPO, 1980).

122. Press Release: "The 39th Pugwash Conference on Science and World Affairs," PRNewswire, July 19, 1989.

123. Letter of congratulations to Holdren printed at the website for the Pugwash Conferences on Science and World Affairs, http://www.pugwash.org/congratulations-john-holdren.htm.

124. "About Us: Philip Coyle," Nieman Foundation for Journalism at Harvard University, http://www.niemanwatchdog.org/index.cfm?fuseaction=about.viewcontributors&bioid=115.

125. Defense Base Closure and Realignment Commission, "About the Commission" section, http://www.brac.gov/About.html.

126. Schedule posted at Pugwash.org; "U.S. participation in Pugwash Conference Workshops: American Participants in International Pugwash Meetings, 2003," http://www.pugwash.org/organization/usa/intl.htm.

127. "Obama's Other Audacious Stealth Appointment," Heritage Foundation blog, July 7, 2010, http://blog.heritage.org/2010/07/07/obamas-other-audacious-stealth-appointment/.

128. Jamie M. Fly, "On Missile Defense, Obama Strikes a Strange Balance," *NationalReview.com*, March 10, 2010.

129. Philip E. Coyle, "Our missile defense system is seen as an expensive bluff," Nieman Watchdog of Nieman Foundation of Journalism at Harvard University, July 12, 2006, http://www.niemanwatchdog.org/index.cfm?fuseaction=background.view&backgroundid=00101.

130. Prepared Remarks before the House Committee on Armed Services, Subcommittee on Strategic Forces, *The Future of Missile Defense Testing*, Philip E.

Coyle, III, Senior Advisor, World Security Institute, Wednesday, February 25, 2009, http://armedservices.house.gov/pdfs/STRAT022509/Coyle_Testimony022509.pdf.

131. Jack Kim and Ross Colvin, "South Korea says North torpedoed ship," Reuters, May 20, 2010.

132. "North Korean artillery hits South Korean island," BBC News, November 23, 2010, http://www.bbc.co.uk/news/world-asia-pacific-11818005.

133. John Noonan, "Obama Nominates Missile Defense Critic to Key White House Spot," *Weekly Standard*, March 4, 2010, http://www.weeklystandard.com/blogs/obama-nominates-missile-defense-critic-key-dod-spot.

134. "Obama's Other Audacious Stealth Appointment," Heritage Foundation blog, July 7, 2010.

135. Editorial, "Mr. Gates Makes a Start," *New York Times*, August 14, 2010.

136. Ibid.

137. "Debt, Deficits, and Defense: A Way Forward," June 11, 2010, Sustainable Defense Task Force, http://www.comw.org/pda/fulltext/1006SDTFreport.pdf.

138. Christopher Preble, "Barack Obama's American Exceptionalism," *Globalist*, May 25, 2007, http://www.cato.org/pub_display.php?pub_id=8380.

139. Ibid.

140. Leon Panetta bio at Joint Ocean Commission website, accessed June 26, 2011, http://www.jointoceancommission.org/cgi-bin/bios.cgi?panetta.

141. Interview: Leon Panetta, Joint Ocean Commission Initiative, Citizens for Global Solutions website, undated, http://archive2.globalsolutions.org/publications/interview_leon_panetta_joint_ocean_commission_initiative.

142. Main page of Joint Ocean Commission website, accessed June 26, 2011, www.jointoceancommission.org/.

143. Interview: Leon Panetta, undated.

144. Oceans and Law of the Sea. Division for Ocean Affairs and Law of the Sea, United Nations, 2011, http://www.un.org/Depts/los/index.htm.

145. Leadership Council, Joint Ocean Commission Initiative, http://www.jointoceancommission.org/leadership-council.html.

146. "About," Pittsburgh chapter of Citizens for Global Solutions website, http://www.globalsolutionspgh.org/about/.

147. Ibid.

148. World Federalist Association Mansfield (Connecticut) Chapter Records, Archives and Special Collections at the Thomas J. Dodd Research Center at the University of Connecticut, http://doddcenter.uconn.edu/findaids/wfa/MSS19890006.html.

149. President Barack Obama, "Remarks by the President in Address to the Nation on Libya," delivered at National Defense University, Washington, D.C., March 28, 2011, http://www.whitehouse.gov/the-press-office/2011/03/28/remarks-president-address-nation-libya.

150. International Commission on Intervention and State Sovereignty, *The Responsibility to Protect*, December 2001, at http://www.iciss.ca/pdf/Commission-Report.pdf.

151. Peter Beaumont, "Israel May Face War Crimes Trials over Gaza. Court Looks at Whether Palestinians Can Bring Case. International Pressure Grows over Conflict," *Guardian* (UK), March 2, 2009, http://www.guardian.co.uk/world/2009/mar/02/israel-war-crimes-gaza; Daniel Schwammenthal, "War Crimes: The International Criminal Court claims jurisdiction over U.S. soldiers in Afghanistan," *Wall Street Journal*, November 26, 2009, http://online.wsj.com/article/SB10001424052748704013004574519253095440312.html.

152. See "Donors" page of Global Center for the Responsibility to Protect website, accessed June 26, 2011, http://globalr2p.org/whoweare/donors.php.

153. "Patrons," Global Center for the Responsibility to Protect, http://globalr2p.org/whoweare/patrons.php.

154. "About The Elders," The Elders website, http://www.theelders.org/elders.

155. Kofi A. Annan, "Two Concepts of Sovereignty," *The Economist*, September 18, 1999, http://www.un.org/News/ossg/sg/stories/kaecon.html.

156. "Advisory board," Responsibility to Protect website, http://www.iciss.ca/advisory_board-en.asp.

157. "Annan Calls for Responsibility to Protect," International Commission on Intervention and State Sovereignty website, undated, http://www.iciss.ca/menu-en.asp.

158. "Advisory Board," International Commission on Intervention and State Sovereignty, http://www.iciss.ca/advisory_board-en.asp.

159. George Soros, "The People's Sovereignty: How a New Twist on an Old Idea Can Protect the World's Most Vulnerable Populations," *Foreign Policy*, January 1, 2004, http://www.foreignpolicy.com/articles/2004/01/01/the_peoples_sovereignty.

160. Ramesh Thakur, "Toward a New World Order," *Ottawa Citizen*, March 1, 2010, reprinted at http://www.cigionline.org/articles/2010/03/toward-new-world-order.

161. Information for this section comes from Trevor Loudon, "Panetta Report 2: Leon Panetta Paid Tribute to Pro-Communist Peace Activist," *Trevor Loudon.com*, June 16, 2011, http://trevorloudon.com/2011/06/panetta-

report-2-leon-panetta-paid-tribute-to-pro-communist-peace-activist/; Trevor Loudon, "Panetta Report 3: Leon Panetta and the Santa Cruz Socialists," *TrevorLoudon.com*, June 18, 2011, http://trevorloudon.com/2011/06/panetta-report-3-leon-panetta-and-the-santa-cruz-socialists/; and Cliff Kincaid, "Who Checked Out Leon Panetta?" *NewsWithViews.com*, June 17, 2011, http://www.newswithviews.com/Kincaid/cliff529.htm.

162. "Undaunted Dove," official newsletter of Women's International League for Peace and Freedom, June 2010 edition, accessed June 27, 2011, http://wilpf.got.net/PDFs/Dove_June_10.pdf.

163. Profile: Institute for Policy Studies, *knology.net*, undated, http://www.knology.net/~bilrum/ips1.htm. "Leon Panetta and the Marxist Institute for Policy Studies," USA Survival News, http://www.usasurvival.org/ck06.14.2011.html.

164. Emerson Vermaat, "Obama's Preferred Future Spy Chief Leon Panetta Supported Communist-Linked Anti-CIA Think Tank," PipeLineNews.org, January 9, 2009, reprinted at http://www.militantislammonitor.org/article/id/3807.

165. S. Stephen Powell, *Covert Cadre: Inside the Institute for Policy Studies* (Ottawa, Ill.: Green Hill Publishers, Inc., 1987), 249–50 (quoted from in "Kerry, the Sandinistas, and the Institute for Policy Studies [IPS]," *FreeRepublic.com*, February 11, 2004, http://www.freerepublic.com/focus/f-news/1076375/posts); event also reported by Warren Mass, "The Trouble with Leon Panetta," *The New American*, January 7, 2009, http://www.thenewamerican.com/usnews/election/655.

166. Vermaat, "Obama's Preferred Future Spy Chief Leon Panetta Supported Communist-Linked Anti-CIA Think Tank," January 9, 2009.

167. Profile: Institute for Policy Studies, *knology.net*.

168. S. Stephen Powell, "Moscow's Friends at the Institute for Policy Studies," *American Opinion*, November 1983, quoted in Christian Gomez, "Leon Panetta and the Institute for Policy Studies," *The New American*, June 11, 2011, http://www.thenewamerican.com/usnews/congress/7819-panetta-unfit-for-sec-of-defense.

169. Harvey E. Klehr, *Far Left of Center: The American Radical Left Today* (Piscataway, NJ: Transaction Publishers, 1988), 177.

170. Robert W. Chandler, *Shadow World: Resurgent Russia, the Global New Left, and Radical Islam* (Washington, DC: Regnery Publishing, 2008), 203.

171. Gomez, "Leon Panettta and the Institute for Policy Studies," June 11, 2011.

172. Ladislav Bittman, *The KGB and Soviet Disinformation: An Insider's View* (Dulles, VA: Potomac Books, 1985), 204, 205.

173. Trevor Loudon, "Panetta Report 1: Leon Panetta Paid Tribute to Two Long-time Communists," *TrevorLoudon.com*, June 14, 2011, http://trevorloudon .com/2011/06/panetta-report-1-leon-panetta-paid-tribute-to-two-long-time-communists/.

174. "Institute for Policy Studies," *Discover the Networks*, http://www.discover thenetworks.org/groupProfile.asp?grpid=6991.

175. Ibid.

176. "Robert Borosage," *Discover the Networks*, http://www.discoverthenetworks .org/individualProfile.asp?indid=1170.

177. "Glossary" for *The War Called Peace. The Soviet Peace Offensive* on Americans for Southern Heritage website, 1982, http://chasvoice.co.cc/PeaceGrpGloss .htm. See section "European Nuclear Disarmament (END)" as well as section on IPS.

178. Vojtech Mastny, *Power and Policy in Transition: Essays Presented on the Tenth Anniversary of the National Committee on American Foreign Policy in Honor of Its Founder, Hans J. Morgenthau* (Westport, CT: Greenwood Press, 1984), 110.

179. Ibid.

180. Gomez, "Leon Panettta and the Institute for Policy Studies," June 11, 2011.

181. David B. Ottaway, "GAO Audits of CIA Proposed by 33 in House," *Washington Post*, November 4, 1987.

182. "Lawmakers Urge More Scrutiny of CIA by Congress," *Boston Globe*, November 4, 1987.

183. Steven Aftergood, "Admin Threatens Veto Over GAO Role in Intel Oversight," *FAS.org*, March 17, 2010, http://www.fas.org/blog/secrecy/2010/03/ veto_over_gao.html.

184. Press Release: "Advancing U.S. Interests at the United Nations," Office of the White House Press Secretary, *whitehouse.gov*, September 20, 2010.

185. Preble, "Barack Obama's American Exceptionalism," May 25, 2007.

186. Michael D. Shear and Dan Balz, "Obama Appeals for Global Cooperation: U.S. Can't Face International Crises Alone, He Tells U.N. in Effort to Strengthen Ties," *Washington Post*, September 24, 2009.

187. Ibid.

188. Tania Branigan, "Barack Obama backs South Korea in torpedo dispute; Barack Obama orders US military to 'ensure readiness' to help deter future aggression by North," *Guardian* (UK), May 24, 2010.

189. Natasha Mozgovaya and Barak Ravid, "PM heads to U.S. under threat of Palestinian statehood declaration," *Haaretz.com*, August 11, 2009.

190. "Eric P. Schwartz," Assistant Secretary, Bureau of Population, Refugees,

and Migration, U.S. Department of State, http://www.state.gov/r/pa/ei/biog/125768.htm.

191. Cliff Kincaid, "Obama Advisers Demand 'More Blue Helmets on U.S. Troops,'" America's Survival, Inc., http://www.usasurvival.org/docs/ASI_Rprt_Obama_n_UN.pdf.

192. "About," Connect Fund website, *connectusfund.org*.

193. Connect U.S. Fund PowerPoint Presentation, www.connectusfund.org/ . . . /Connect%20U.S.%20Fund%20Power%20Point%20Presentation.ppt.

194. Michael Isikoff, "The End of Torture: Obama banishes Bush's interrogation tactics," *Newsweek*, January 22, 2009.

195. "New Era, New Openings: FCNL's 2009 Annual Meeting," Conference Call Event Summary at Connect U.S. Fund website, http://www.connectusfund.org/events/new-era-new-openings-fcnls-2009-annual-meeting.

196. Samuel R. Berger and Eric P. Schwartz, "America's eroding global leadership," *New York Times*, September 5, 2007.

197. Kincaid, "Obama Advisers Demand 'More Blue Helmets on U.S. Troops."

198. "Let the child live: The world's first permanent war-crimes tribunal is proving more robust than expected; even skeptical America is softening its line," *Economist*, January 25, 2007.

199. "Biographical Information: Heather B. Hamilton," Connect Fund website, *connectusfund.org*.

200. Biography: "Don Kraus: Chief Executive Officer," Citizens for Global Solutions, http://globalsolutions.org/users/dkraus.

201. "Our accomplishments," Citizens for Global Solutions, http://archive2.globalsolutions.org/about/our_accomplishments.

Chapter Ten: Amnesty Shamnesty

1. Jeff Shesol, *Mutual Contempt: Lyndon Johnson, Robert Kennedy, and the Feud That Defined a Decade* (New York: Norton, 1998), 241.

2. Ibid.; Edward Zigler and Sally J. Styfco, *The Hidden History of Head Start* (New York: Oxford University Press, 2010), 49.

3. Alice O'Connor, *Poverty Knowledge: Social Science, Social Policy, and the Poor in Twentieth-Century U.S. History* (Princeton, NJ: Princeton University Press, 2000), 160.

4. Shesol, *Mutual Contempt*, 241.

5. Ibid.

6. Lillian B. Rubin, "Maximum Feasible Participation: The Origins, Implications, and Present Status," *Annals of the American Academy of Political and Social Science* 385 (September 1969), 15.

7. O'Connor, *Poverty Knowledge*, 161; Lyndon B. Johnson, "Remarks Upon Signing the Economic Opportunity Act. August 20, 1964," American Presidency Project, http://www.presidency.ucsb.edu/ws/index.php?pid=26452.

8. O'Connor, *Poverty Knowledge*, 168.

9. Sidney Lens, *The Crisis of American Labor* (New York: Sagamore Press, 1959), 168; Myrna Oliver, "Obituaries: Jack Conway; Labor Leader, Social Activist," *Los Angeles Times*, January 18, 1998.

10. Oral History Interview with Jack T. Conway with Michael L. Gillette, August 13, 1980, General Services Administration, National Archives and Records Service, Lyndon Baines Johnson Library, 2, 3. Available online in Google Docs.

11. Dwight D. Murphey, "What the Businessman Should Know About the 'New Left,'" *Business Journal* (College of Business Administration at Wichita State University), Summer 1970, 5–10, http://www.dwightmurphey-collected-writings.info/A6-Business&NewLeft.htm.

12. "Participation of the Poor: Section 202(a)(3) Organizations under the Economic Opportunity Act of 1964," *Yale Law Journal* 75, no. 4 (March 1966), 609, http://www.jstor.org/stable/794866.

13. Oliver, "Obituaries: Jack Conway," January 18, 1998; Andrew S. McFarland, *Common Cause: Lobbying in the Public Interest* (Chatham, NJ: Chatham House, 1984), 87; Oral History Interview with Jack T. Conway with Michael L. Gillette, August 13, 1980, 7.

14. Richard M. Flanagan, "Lyndon Johnson, Community Action and Management of the Administrative State," *Presidential Studies Quarterly* 31, no. 4 (2001), 585 ff..

15. Ibid.

16. Polly Greenberg, Brief Professional Bio, http://pollygreenberg.net/bio.htm; "25th Anniversary: Tuesday, April 24, 2007," Center on Budget and Policy Priorities, http://www.cbpp.org/anniversary/; Southern Rural Poverty Collection, DeWitt Wallace Center for Media and Democracy, Sanford School of Public Policy, Duke University, 621, fn. 79, http://dewitt.sanford.duke.edu/index.php/rutherfurd-living-history/southern_rural_poverty_collection/.

17. Gara LaMarche, "Richard Boone and the Field Foundation: Beacons of Leadership for Social Justice Philanthropy," Atlantic Philanthropies, April 14, 2009.

18. Maureen O'Connor, *Knocking on Doors: VISTA Volunteers Remember 1965–1971* (Cambridge, MA: Harvard Book Store), x, 36.

19. Edward R. Schmitt, *President of the Other America: Robert Kennedy and the Politics of Poverty* (Amherst: University of Massachusetts Press, 2010), 83.

20. *A Guide to the Industrial Areas Foundation Records*, [ca. 1938–1995] (bulk 1951–1987), Center for American History, University of Texas at Austin, http://www.lib.utexas.edu/taro/utcah/00172.xml; G. William Domhoff, "The Ford Foundation in the Inner City: Forging an Alliance with Neighborhood Activists," *Who Rules America*, September 2005.

21. Rubin, "Maximum Feasible Participation: The Origins, Implications, and Present Status," September 1969, 18; Oral History Interview with Jack T. Conway with Michael L. Gillette, August 13, 1980, 6.

22. Oral History Interview with Jack T. Conway with Michael L. Gillette, August 13, 1980, 4.

23. Carmen Sirianni and Lewis Friedland, *Civic Innovation in America: Community Empowerment, Public Policy, and the Movement for Civic Renewal* (Berkeley: University of California Press, 2001), 44.

24. O'Connor, *Poverty Knowledge*, 172; Southern Rural Poverty Collection, Duke University, 621; David Zarefsky, *President Johnson's War on Poverty: Rhetoric and History* (University: University of Alabama Press, 1986), 72; Taylor E. Dark, *The Unions and the Democrats: An Enduring Alliance* (Ithaca, NY: Cornell University Press, 1999), 58.

25. Citizens' Crusade Against Poverty Collection, Papers, 1964–1970 (Predominantly 1965–1968), Archives of Labor and Urban Affairs, Wayne University; Nelson Lichtenstein, *The Most Dangerous Man in Detroit: Walter Reuther and the Fate of American Labor* (New York: Basic Books, 1995), 390.

26. John R. Chávez, *Eastside Landmark: A History of the East Los Angeles Community Union, 1968–1993* (Stanford, Calif.: Stanford University Press, 1998), 31; CCAP Papers, Wayne University; Lichtenstein, *The Most Dangerous Man in Detroit*, 390.

27. "Saul Alinsky," in George R. Goethals et al., eds., *Encyclopedia of Leadership*, vol. 2 (Thousand Oaks, CA: Sage, 2004), 26–27.

28. Chávez, 27; CCAP Papers, Wayne University.

29. Ibid.

30. Lichtenstein, *The Most Dangerous Man in Detroit*, 433.

31. "Participation of the Poor: Section 202(a)(3) Organizations under the Economic Opportunity Act of 1964," *Yale Law Journal* 75, no. 4 (March 1966), 625, http://www.jstor.org/stable/794866.

32. David Horowitz and Richard Poe, *The Shadow Party: How George Soros, Hillary Clinton, and Sixties Radicals Seized Control of the Democratic Party* (Nashville, TN: Thomas Nelson, 2006), 58–59.

33. Ibid.; "Saul Alinsky," *Encyclopedia of Leadership*, 27.

34. "The Gamaliel Foundation's Faith and Democracy Platform," Gamaliel Foundation, *gamaliel.org*; Sirianni and Friedland, *Civic Innovation in America*, 54–55. Information comes from *Gamaliel Foundation, Jubilee: A Time for Metropolitan Equities and the Common Good* (Chicago: Gamaliel Foundation, 1999).

35. Brian DeBose, "Obama's Early Near-Miss; 2008 Hopeful Initially Rejected for Chicago Job," *Washington Times*, July 26, 2007; Gregory A. Galluzzo, "Gamaliel and the Barack Obama Connection," Gamaliel Foundation, *gamaliel.org*, n.d. (post–general election).

36. Galluzzo, "Gamaliel and the Barack Obama Connection," n.d.; Barack Obama, "Why Organize? Problems and Promise in the Inner City?" *Illinois Issues* (July/August 1988). The essay was included as a chapter in *After Alinsky: Community Organizing in Illinois* (Springfield, IL: Sangamon State University, 1990), 35–40.

37. Lizza, "The Agitator;" Galluzzo, "Gamaliel and the Barack Obama Connection," *Investor's Business Daily*, September 29, 2008.

38. Obama, July/August 1988; Woods Fund of Chicago Evaluation of the Fund's Community Organizing Grant Program: Executive Summary and Findings and Recommendations of the Evaluation Team, April 1995, 5, http://www.nfg.org/cotb/42woods.pdf.

39. "About Us, Our History," Center for Community Change, Internet Archive, October 25, 2004, http://web.archive.org/web/20041025172706/http://www.communitychange.org/about/history/; "Center for Community Change," *DiscovertheNetworks.org;* Sirianni and Friedland, *Civic Innovation in America*, 60.

40. Footnote 39 in Kevin Boyle, *The UAW and the Heyday of American Liberalism, 1945–1968* (Ithaca, NY: Cornell University Press, 1995), 327. Boyle cites UAW, CCAP, and CCC records.

41. Carmen Sirianni and Lewis Friedland write that the Center for Community Change was founded in 1967. See their *Civic Innovation in America*, 60; Loree Bykerk and Ardith Maney, *U.S. Consumer Interest Groups: Institutional Profiles* (Westport, CT: Greenwood Press, 1995), 62; Southern Rural Poverty Collection; McFarland, *Common Cause: Lobbying in the Public Interest*, 87.

42. Oral History Interview with Jack T. Conway with Michael L. Gillette, August 13, 1980, 4.

43. Ibid., 5.

44. Ben Johnson, "Who's Behind the Immigration Rallies?" *FrontPageMagazine .com*, March 29, 2006.

45. Domhoff, "The Ford Foundation in the Inner City: Forging an Alliance with Neighborhood Activists," September 2005; Grantee: "Center for Community Change," Ford Foundation, http://www.fordfoundation.org/grants/grantdetails?grantid=80645; "GrantMaking Issues: 'To increase participation of marginalized communities at all levels of civic and political life,'" Ford Foundation, http://www.fordfoundation.org/issues/democratic-and-accountable-government/increasing-civic-and-political-participation/grant-making.

46. Rael Jean Isaac and Erich Isaac, *The Coercive Utopians: Social Deception by America's Power Players* (Washington, DC: Regnery Publishing, 1984), 189.

47. Domhoff, "The Ford Foundation in the Inner City," September 2005; "Our History," Center for Community Change, n.d., *A Katrina Reader*, http://katrinareader.org/center-community-change.

48. "Who We Are (Our Coalition Updated—Dec. 1, 2009)," Health Care for America Now, http://healthcareforamericanow.org/site/content/who_we_are/.

49. "The Linchpin Campaign. Our Method," Center for Community Change, 2010, http://www.communitychange.org/our-projects/linchpin/what-we-do/our-method; Alicia Epstein Korten, with Kim Klein, ed., *Change Philanthropy: Candid Stories of Foundations Maximizing Results through Social Justice* (San Francisco: Jossey-Bass, 2009).

50. CCC Board in 2006, Center for Community Change, February 4, 2007, Internet Archive, http://web.archive.org/web/20070204131306/community change.org/about/board/.

51. "LULAC Congratulates President-Elect Barack Obama On The Appointment Of Cecilia Munoz For White House Director Of Intergovernmental Affairs," Targeted News Service, November 26, 2008.

52. "Advisory Committee," Center for Community Change, accessed January 30, 2011, http://www.communitychange.org/our-projects/generationchange/our-team/advisory-committee.

53. Aaron Klein and Brenda J. Elliott, *The Manchurian President: Barack Obama's Ties to Communists, Socialists and Other Anti-American Extremists* (Washington, DC: WND Books, 2010), 60.

54. "Our Board," Center for Community Change, accessed January 30, 2011, http://www.communitychange.org/who-we-are/our-board.

55. "Deepak Bhargava," *DiscovertheNetworks.org*; "Who We Are: Deepak Bhargava," Center for Community Change, http://www.communitychange.org/who-we-are/our-staff/bios/deepak-bhargava.

56. "Campaign Supporters," Campaign to Reform Immigration for America, accessed October 7, 2010, http://reformimmigrationforamerica.org/about/organizations/.

57. "Our Work," Campaign for Community Change, accessed October 7, 2010, http://www.campaignforcommunities.org/about-us/our-work.

58. "Who We Are: Staff," Campaign for Community Change, accessed October 7, 2010, http://www.campaignforcommunities.org/about-us/who-we-are.

59. "Young Leaders in the Spotlight, 25th Anniversary: Tuesday, April 24, 2007," Center on Budget and Policy Priorities, http://www.cbpp.org/anniversary/?fa=youth; William T. Poole, *The Environmental Complex—Part III*, Institutional Analysis #19, Heritage Foundation, June 1, 1982.

60. Alan Rabinowitz, *Social Change Philanthropy in America* (New York: Quorum Books, 1990), xi.

61. Ibid., 49.

62. Ibid., 50. "About: Board," Righteous Persons Foundation, http://www.righteouspersons.org/about/board.php; "Board of Directors," Institute for America's Future, http://www.ourfuture.org/page/2009052122/institute-america-board-members.

63. Rabinowitz, *Social Change Philanthropy*, 50.

64. Ibid.; Poole, *The Environmental Complex—Part III*, June 1, 1982.

65. Magat, *Unlikely Partners*, 174.

66. "Dummond Pike," *Left-Tracking Library, UndueInfluence.com*.

67. Ron Arnold, *Undue Influence: Wealthy Foundations, Grant-Driven Environmental Groups, and Zealous Bureaucrats That Control Your Future* (Bellevue, WA: Free Enterprise Press, 1999), 76.

68. "Tides Foundation & Tides Center," *ActivistCash.com*, http://activistcash.com/organization_overview.cfm/o/225-tides-foundation—tides-center.

69. Form 990, Return of Organization Tax Exempt From Income Tax, 1990m, http://www.tides.org/fileadmin/user/990/990-Tides-Foundation-2009.pdf.

70. "What We Do," The Ruckus Society, http://www.ruckus.org/section.php?id=71.

71. "Trainings We Offer," The Ruckus Society, http://www.ruckus.org/section.php?id=91.

72. Lowell Ponte, "Ruckus at the Republican Convention," *FrontPageMag.org*, http://archive.frontpagemag.com/readArticle.aspx?ARTID=11627.

73. Ibid.

74. Anthony York, "Do Not Pass Go. Are the Philadelphia Police Using High Bail to Keep an Activist Leader away from the Democratic Convention?" *Salon*, August 8, 2000, http://dir.salon.com/news/feature/2000/08/08/ruckus; "The Week That Was: Some Random Thoughts On The Republican National Convention," *Philly.com*, August 7, 2000, http://articles.philly.com/2000-08-07/news/25595368_1_ruckus-society-violent-protesters-pr-war/.

75. York, "Do Not Pass Go," August 8, 2000.

76. "Catalyst for Chaos, or Singled Out Unfairly? John Sellers Was Arrested on Misdemeanor Charges in Center City. His Bail Has Been Set at $1 Million," *Philly.com*, August 4, 2000, http://articles.philly.com/2000-08-04/news/25594855_1_ruckus-society-violent-protests-john-sellers.

77. Ibid.

78. "Rock-a-bye, Constitutional Rights? When Police Rounded Up the Usual Suspect This Summer, the Cradle of Liberty Got Rocked," *Philly.com*, November 16, 2000, http://articles.philly.com/2000-11-16/news/25613771_1_ruckus-society-protests-secret-police.

79. Manheim, *Biz-War and the Out-of-Power Elite: The Progressive-Left Attack on the Corporation*, 44.

80. Ibid., 44, 45.

81. Ibid., 48; Arnold, *Undue Influence*, 79–80.

82. Drummond Pike, "Saul . . . time to step aside," *Notes from the Left Coast*, June 25, 2008.

83. Ibid.

84. Arnold, *Undue Influence*, 80.

85. "Project Directory," Tides Center, January 25, 2011,

86. Press Release: "Tides Taps Social Entrepreneur and Progressive Thought Leader as New CEO," Tides Center, September 16, 2010.

87. Harry C. Boyte, Heather Booth, and Steve Max, *Citizen Action and the New American Populism* (Philadelphia: Temple University Press, 1986), 17.

88. "Institution Building," in *The New Left in Government Part II: The VISTA Program*, Heritage Foundation, February 19, 1982.

89. Ibid.

90. Ibid.; audio clip from *The Mark Levin Show*, June 19, 2009, http://vocalminority.typepad.com/blog/2009/06/listen-learn-mark-levin-exposes-how-your-tax-money-funding-radical-left-orgs-for-decades-61909.html; William T. Poole,

New Left in Government: From Protest to Policy-Making, Institution Report #9, Heritage Foundation, November 1978; "The ACORN Files: Community Organization Research Action Project," http://www.conservativeusa.org/CommunityOrganizingResearchActionProject.pdf; Nikki Finke, "A Radical Move: Margery Tabankin Has Fled the Center of Power for the Center of Status, but Without Missing an Activist Beat," *Los Angeles Times*, August 13, 1989.

91. Poole, *New Left in Government: From Protest to Policy-Making*, November 1978; Arnold, *Freezing in the Dark*, 217. Arnold's source is Gary Delgado, *Organizing the Movement: The Roots and Growth of ACORN* (Philadelphia: Temple University Press, 1986), 23; Finke, "A Radical Move," August 13, 1989.

92. Poole, *New Left in Government: From Protest to Policy-Making*, November 1978.

93. Linda Sunde, "Stories of Service: VISTA," AmeriCorps (nationalservice .gov), n.d.

94. O'Connor, *Knocking on Doors*, 36.

95. Mark Levin, "This Is What We Are Up Against," *The Mark Levin Show*, June 19, 2009, http://www.freerepublic.com/focus/bloggers/2276524/posts.

96. Ibid.

97. Poole, *New Left in Government: From Protest to Policy-Making*, November 1978.

98. Isaac and Isaac, *The Coercive Utopians*, 188; House Appropriations Committee, "The ACORN Files," circa 1978.

99. House Appropriations Committee, "The ACORN Files," circa 1978.

100. *The New Left in Government Part II: The VISTA Program.*

101. House Appropriations Committee, "The ACORN Files," circa 1978.

102. Isaac and Isaac, *The Coercive Utopians*, 189.

103. *The New Left in Government Part II: The VISTA Program.*

104. Arnold, *Freezing in the Dark*, 216.

105. Ibid., 217–18.

106. *The New Left in Government Part II: The VISTA Program.*

107. House Appropriations Committee, "The ACORN Files," circa 1978.

108. "The American Institute for Social Justice," in Directory of Environmental Justice Organizations, MELDI, accessed October 22, 2010, http://meldi .snre.umich.edu/ej_orgs?page=3.

109. Delgado, *Organizing the Movement: The Roots and Growth of ACORN*, 101–2.

110. "Arkansas Institute for Social Justice Inc.," *CorporationWiki.com.*; Larry Johnson, "Obama's Campaign Lies About ACORN," *NoQuarterUSA.net*, October 14, 2008; Cindy Rauckhorst, "The making of an activist: Acorn chief learns to

roar," *American Banker*, July 28, 1986; "Arkansas Institute for Social Justice," Training Directory, Shelterforce Online 101 (September–October 1998).

111. House Appropriations Committee, "The ACORN Files," circa 1978.

112. According to the Heritage Foundation report, the date and mission of the Midwest Academy was reported in the Winter 1974 issue of *Working Papers for a New Society*.

113. "Heather Booth, Feminist Icon, Organizer, Fighter for Justice and Democracy," VFA Board Member, Veteran Feminists of America, http://www.vfa .us/#HEATHER%20BOOTH,%20FEMINIST%20ICON.

114. "Heather Booth," *DiscovertheNetworks.org*.

115. "Paul Booth," *DiscovertheNetworks.org*; James Warren, "A '60s SDS Radical Turned Labor Leader Is Moving On," *Chicago Tribune*, December 29, 1988.

116. "Paul Booth," *DiscovertheNetworks.org*; Mark R. Warren, *Dry Bones Rattling: Community Building to Revitalize American Democracy* (Princeton, NJ: Princeton University Press, 2001), 44; Abraham Monk, *Handbook of Gerontological Services* (New York: Columbia University Press, 1990), 179; Gregory Squires, *Chicago: Race, Class, and the Response to Urban Decline* (Philadelphia: Temple University Press, 1989), 141.

117. Jean-Paul D. Addie, Department of Geography, York University, *A Century of Chicago's Crosstown Corridor: From Daniel Burnham's City Beautiful to Richard M. Daley's Global City*, 11, http://www.transportchicago.org/ uploads/5/7/2/0/5720074/6-a_century_of_chicagos_crosstown_corridor .pdf; Larry Bennett, "Community Organizing," *The Electronic Encyclopedia of Chicago* (Chicago: Chicago Historical Society, 2005); Squires, *Chicago: Race, Class, and the Response to Urban Decline*, 141.

118. Squires, *Chicago: Race, Class, and the Response to Urban Decline*, 142.

119. "Heather Booth," *DiscovertheNetworks.org*; Ben Joravsky, "She's leaving home: Heather Booth looks back on 25 years of struggle," *Chicago Reader*, April 27, 1989.

120. "Heather Booth," *DiscovertheNetworks.org*.

121. Levin, "This Is What We Are Up Against," June 19, 2009.

122. Brenda J. Elliott, "Anti-Capitalist Progressive Astroturf K Streeters to Protest K Street?" *RBO*, May 15, 2010, http://therealbarackobama.wordpress .com/2010/05/15/anti-capitalist-progressive-astroturf-k-streeters-to-pro test-k-street/; Brenda J. Elliott, "Faux Roots Rally October 2 in DC—'One Nation Working Together,'" *RBO*, September 30, 2010, http://thereal barackobama.wordpress.com/2010/09/30/faux-roots-rally-october-2-in-dc- one-nation-working-together/.

123. *The New Left in Government Part II: The VISTA Program;* Klein, *The Manchurian President*, 250.

124. "About Us," *MidwestAcademy.com*.

125. Kirkpatrick Sale, *SDS* (New York: Vintage Books, 1973), 27.

126. "The Daily Worker," *Spartacus Educational*, http://www.spartacus.schoolnet.co.uk/USAworkerD.htm.

127. Seth Goodkind, "The Voice of Action: A Paper for Workers and the Disenfranchised," *The Great Depression in Washington State*, Washington State Department of Education, http://depts.washington.edu/depress/voice_of_action.shtml; *Voice of Action*, March 25, 1933, 2; Alan Max, *Voice of Action*, August 17, 1934, 1; *Voice of Action*, September 14, 1934, 131.

128. Testimony of Walter S. Steele regarding Communist activities in the United States. Hearings before the Committee on Un-American Activities, House of Representatives, 80th Congress, 1st sess., on H.R. 1884 and H.R. 2122, bills to curb or outlaw the Communist Party in the United States, 7.

129. Guy Williams, *YSA: How It Began*, Ozleft, May 3, 2005, http://ozleft.wordpress.com/2005/05/03/ysahowitbegan/; "Young Socialist Alliance," *Infoshop Wiki*, http://wiki.infoshop.org/Young_Socialist_Alliance.

130. Williams, *YSA: How It Began*, May 3, 2005; *Young Socialist* 1, no. 5 (February 1958).

131. Ibid.

132. John J. Simon, "Leo Huberman: Radical Agitator, Socialist Teacher," *Monthly Review* 55, no. 5 (October 2003); Comment by Chris Horton at Helen Thomas, "44 Takes Office with Blunt Rejection of 43," *Seattle Post-Intelligencer, CommonDreams.org*, January 21, 2009.

133. Comment by Chris Horton, January 21, 2009; Douglas Charles Rossinow, *Visions of Progress: The Left-Liberal Tradition in America* (Philadelphia: University of Pennsylvania Press, 2007), 202; Tina Braxton, "H-1960s: SDS Talk in Boulder, CO," *h-net.msu.edu*, February 26, 2006.

134. Harvey J. Kaye, *Thomas Paine and the Promise of America* (New York: Hill & Wang, 2006), 243–44.

135. Sasha Abramsky, *Inside Obama's Brain* (New York: Portfolio, 2009), ch. 5.

136. David Moberg, "Obama's Third Way," *Shelterforce Online*, Spring 2007.

137. "Board of Directors," *MidwestAcademy.com*; Mark Wiznitzer, "Camp Obama—The Training," Organizing for America, June 10, 2007, http://my.barackobama.com/page/community/post/markwiznitzer/CtKz.

138. Joravsky, "She's leaving home: Heather Booth looks back on 25 years of struggle," *Chicago Reader*, April 27, 1989.

139. The 1999 Debs–Thomas–Harrington Dinner, Chicago Democratic Socialists of America, May 7, 1999, http://www.chicagodsa.org/d1999 .html#anchor703644.

140. Laurie Cohen, "For A Public Watchdog, Questions Of Politics, Principle," *Chicago Tribune*, June 5, 2003.

141. "Jackie Kendall to retire, Midwest Academy seeks new Executive Director," *MidwestAcademy.com*.

142. Stanley Kurtz, *Radical-in-Chief: Barack Obama and the Untold Story of American Socialism* (New York: Threshold Editions, 2010), 194.

143. Richard Henry Lee, "Obama and the Woods Fund of Chicago," *American Thinker*, July 7, 2008; "Midwest Academy," *UndueInfluence.com;* Stephen D. Lerner, "Paul Booth: Silhouette," *Harvard Crimson*, November 2, 1965.

144. Richard Wolf and Gregory Korte, "State of the Union: Fact-checking Obama's speech," *USA Today*, January 25, 2011.

145. "Our History," Center for Community Change, accessed October 7, 2010, http://www.communitychange.org/who-we-are/our-history.

146. Dave Skidmore, "Administration Tries Squelching Effort to Weaken Plan for S&Ls," Associated Press, April 11, 1989.

147. Klein, *The Manchurian President*, 117.

148. Howard Husock, "The Trillion-Dollar Bank Shakedown That Bodes Ill for Cities," *City Journal* (Chicago), Winter 2000.

149. Steven Malanga, "Acorn's a Creature of the CRA," *RealClearMarkets.com*, September 16, 2009.

150. Ben Johnson, "The 1965 Immigration Act: Anatomy of a Disaster," *FrontPageMag.com*, December 10, 2002.

151. *Yearbook of Immigration Statistics 2006*, U.S. Department of Homeland Security, http://www.dhs.gov/files/statistics/publications/LPR06.shtm.

152. "Illegal immigrants from India Increasing at a High Rate," *Rediff India Abroad (rediff.com)*, February 19, 2008; "Illegal immigrants from India Increasing at a High Rate," U.S. Immigration Support, n.d. [2008], http:// www.usimmigrationsupport.org/indian-immigration.html.

153. Johnson, "The 1965 Immigration Act," December 10, 2002.

154. "Welfare Tab for Children of Illegal Immigrants Estimated at $600M in L.A. County," *FoxNews.com*, January 19, 2011.

155. "A Brief History of Illegal Immigration in the United States," *EndIllegal Immigration.com*.

156. Ibid.; Rachel L. Swarns, "Failed Amnesty Legislation of 1986 Haunts the Current Immigration Bills in Congress," *New York Times*, May 23, 2006.

157. "A Brief History of Illegal Immigration in the United States," *EndIllegal Immigration.com*.

158. Dirk Kirschten, "The Politics of Citizenship," *GovExec.com*, January 1, 1997.

159. Tom Curry, "Parties wrangle over election-year citizenship: 1996 deja vu: Can immigrants become citizens in time to vote in the fall?" *MSNBC.com*, July 1, 2008.

160. Robert L. Ashbaugh, Acting Inspector General, "Executive Summary," Office of the Inspector General, U.S. Department of Justice, http://www.justice.gov/oig/special/0007/exec.htm.

161. Curry, "Parties wrangle over election-year citizenship," July 1, 2008.

162. "A Brief History of Illegal Immigration in the United States," *EndIllegal Immigration.com*.

163. S.1348—Comprehensive Immigration Reform Act of 2007, *OpenCongress .org*.

164. Michelle Mittelstadt, "Kennedy, McCain keep immigration bill closeted; Cornyn, Specter are openly critical of being shut out," *Houston Chronicle*, March 1, 2007.

165. George Bennett, "Rubio: Reagan erred in supporting 1986 amnesty for illegal immigrants," *Palm Beach Post*, November 17, 2009.

166. "Overview—illegal aliens in the United States," *TheAmericanResistance.com*, n.d.; letter from Sen. John McCain can be read at http://www.theamerican resistance.com/ref/letter_mccain_2004feb10.html.

167. Swarns, "Failed Amnesty Legislation of 1986," May 23, 2006.

168. Lynn Sweet, "Luis Gutierrez a yes on Obama health care bill," *Chicago Sun-Times*, March 18, 2010; Joshua Hoyt, "Obama risks alienating Latinos with lack of immigration reform," *Washington Post*, March 5, 2010.

169. Tara Bahrampour, "Number of illegal immigrants in U.S. drops, report says," *Washington Post*, September 1, 2010. For more details on the report, see Jeffrey Passel and D'Vera Cohn, "U.S. Unauthorized Immigration Flows Are Down Sharply Since Mid-Decade," Pew Hispanic Center, September 1, 2010.

170. Ibid.

171. Terence P. Jeffrey, "Federal Auditor: Border Patrol Can Stop Illegal Entries Along Only 129 Miles of 1,954-Mile Mexican Border," *Newsmax.com*, March 31, 2011.

172. Bennett, "Rubio: Reagan erred in supporting 1986 amnesty for illegal immigrants," November 17, 2009.

173. Jennifer McFadyen, "March for America: Change Takes Courage," DeCosmo LLP, March 21, 2010.

174. Julia Preston, "Obama to Push Immigration Bill as One Priority," *New York Times*, April 9, 2009.

175. Ibid.

176. Ibid.

177. "What the Administration Has Done to Date," in "Comprehensive Immigration Reform," Organizing for America, accessed October 7, 2010, http://www.barackobama.com/issues/immigrationreform/index.php.

178. "Immigration Policy: Transition Blueprint," Obama-Biden Transition Project, November 16, 2008, http://otrans.3cdn.net/1414e4fb31bb801ef0_ww m6i6uks.pdf.

179. "Barack Obama on Immigration," *On the Issues*, accessed October 7, 2010, http://www.ontheissues.org/2008/barack_obama_immigration.htm.

180. Transcript: NPR Democratic Candidates' Debate, *npr.org*, December 4, 2007.

181. NPR, Democratic Candidates' Debate, December 4, 2007; Alex Newman, "Obama's Plan for Immigration 'Reform,'" *TheNewAmerican.com*, December 1, 2008.

182. "Barack Obama on Immigration," *On the Issues.*

183. Randy Shaw, "New Immigrant Rights Campaign to Mount Largest March of Obama Era," *Huffington Post*, March 14, 2010; Yani Kunichoff, "Tens of Thousands March on Washington, DC, for Immigration Reform," *truthout .org*, March 23, 2010.

184. "DC Immigrants March," Revolution #040, March 26, 2006, http://rwor .org/a/040/dc-immigrants-march.htm.

185. Mark Krikorian (Director, Center for Immigration Studies), "American Dhimmitude: The road from amnesty," *National Review Online*, March 30, 2006, http://old.nationalreview.com/krikorian/krikorian200603301130.asp.

186. Shaw, "New Immigrant Rights Campaign to Mount Largest March of Obama Era," March 14, 2010.

187. Kunichoff, "Tens of Thousands March on Washington, DC, for Immigration Reform," March 23, 2010.

188. John Morton, Director of U.S. Immigration and Customs Enforcement, Memorandum: Exercising Prosecutorial Discretion Consistent with the Civil Immigration Enforcement Priorities of the Agency for the Apprehension, Detention, and Removal of Aliens, U.S. Department of Homeland Security, June 17, 2011, http://www.ice.gov/doclib/secure-communities/pdf/prosecu torial-discretion-memo.pdf.

189. U.S. Department of Justice Immigration and Naturalization Service Fact

Sheet: Prosecutorial Discretion Guidelines, November 28, 2000, http://shusterman.com/prosecutorialdiscretion-insfactsheet.html.

190. Shoba Sivaprasad Wadhia, "Reading the Morton Memo: Federal Priorities and Prosecutorial Discretion," Immigration Policy Center, December 1, 2010, http://www.immigrationpolicy.org/special-reports/reading-morton-memo-federal-priorities-and-prosecutorial-discretion; Mary Giovagnoli, "What ICE's Latest Memo on Prosecutorial Discretion Means for Future Immigration Cases," *ImmigrationImpact.com*, June 21, 2011, http://immigrationimpact.com/2011/06/21/what-ice%E2%80%99s-latest-memo-on-prosecutorial-discretion-means-for-future-immigration-cases/; "Prosecutorial Discretion Memos Provide Immigration Officers Guidance, Promote Family Unity, and Save Government Resources," *ImmigrantJustice.org*, August 27, 2011, http://www.immigrantjustice.org/press_releases/prosecutorial-discretion-memos-provide-immigration-officers-guidance-promote-family-u.

191. Jerry Markon, "Calls for His Resignation 'Just Part of the Territory,' Says ICE Director Morton," *Washington Post*, July 19, 2010, http://www.washingtonpost.com/wp-dyn/content/article/2010/07/18/AR2010071803017.html.

192. Jeff Dunetz, "SEIU Exec VP: 'White Workers Are So F***ing Rabidly Racist,'" *Yid with Lid*, April 11, 2010, http://yidwithlid.blogspot.com/2010/04/blog-post.html.

193. David Moberg, "New SEIU Sec.-Treas. Eliseo Medina Sets Plans for Organizing, Immigration Reform," *In These Times*, September 20, 2010; "Our Union. Anna Burger, Secretary-Treasurer," *SEIU.org*.

194. "Latinos pin hopes of immigration reform on Obama; After helping Barack Obama win the election, Latinos seek to remind him to enact comprehensive immigration reform," McClatchy Newspapers, November 24, 2008; "Patricia Madrid Named to Obama's National Latino Advisory Council," *RootsWire.org*, August 22, 2008.

195. "Our Union: Eliseo Medina," *SEIU.org*, accessed October 7, 2010.

196. DSA 2001 Convention Keynote Address, Eliseo Medina, International Executive Vice President Service Employees International Union, http://www.dsausa.org/convention2k1/eliseo.html; "46th Annual Eugene V. Debs–Norman Thomas–Michael Harrington Dinner," Chicago, Democratic Socialists of America, May 7, 2004, http://www.chicagodsa.org/d2004.html; "Eliseo Medina named an Honorary Chair of DSA," Democratic Socialists of America, August 9, 2004, http://www.dsausa.org/LatestNews/2004/medina.html.

197. Ron Baiman, "The Dump Bush Dinner," *New Ground* 94 (May/June 2004), http://www.chicagodsa.org/ngarchive/ng94.html#anchor346820.

198. Harold Meyerson, "Meet Eliseo Medina," *American Prospect, prospect.org*, August 18, 2010.

199. "Eliseo Medina Speaks on Immigrants for Votes [June 2, 2009]," YouTube, added January 25, 2010, http://www.youtube.com/watch?v=AK7K0itgQt0.

200. Chelsea Schilling, "Obama: 'We're going to paint nation purple with SEIU'; Explains how he 'built political power on south side of Chicago,'" *WND.com*, October 13, 2009.

201. Ibid.; Andrew Breitbart, "Uncovered Video Obama Leads SEIU Chant After Vowing to Paint the Nation Purple," YouTube, posted October 12, 2009, http://www.youtube.com/watch?v=DQj-xBH30-I.

202. Peter Nicholas, "Obama's curiously close labor friendship: SEIU chief Andy Stern enjoys unusual access to the White House, but some in the fractious labor movement question its value," *Los Angeles Times*, June 28, 2009.

203. Foon Rhee, "Obama gets big union nod," *Boston Globe*, February 15, 2008.

204. Nicholas, "Obama's curiously close labor friendship," June 28, 2009.

205. "Patricia Madrid Named to Obama's National Latino Advisory Council," August 22, 2008.

206. "Glenn Beck: Time to Re-found America," *GlennBeck.com*, September 15, 2009. There does not appear to be any other printed record of Obama's remarks.

207. Aaron Klein, "Obama adviser: Amnesty to ensure 'progressive' rule.' 'Imagine 8 million new voters who care about our issues?'" *WND.com*, February 2, 2010.

208. Eliseo Medina, "SEIU on immigration reform," *workingimmigrants.com*, January 17, 2007.

209. Sean J. Miller, "Union sees immigration reform as winning issue for Democrats," *Hill*, May 10, 2010.

210. Ibid.

211. Noel Sheppard, "Obama Helped Kill Immigration Reform In 2007—Will Media Remember?" *NewsBusters.com*, April 29, 2010.

212. Ibid.

213. Michael D. Shear, "Republican immigration position likely to alienate Latinos, Democrats say," *Washington Post*, July 20, 2010.

214. Jennifer Rubin, "Obama Tips His Hand: No Reform, Just an Issue," *Commentary*, July 20, 2010, http://www.commentarymagazine.com/blogs/index.php/rubin/330756.

215. Shear, "Republican immigration position likely to alienate Latinos, Democrats say," July 20, 2010.

216. Ibid.

217. Employment Situation Summary, Bureau of Labor Statistics, U.S. Department of Labor, January 7, 2011, http://www.bls.gov/news.release/empsit.nr0.htm.

GLOSSARY

ALLIANCE FOR AMERICAN MANUFACTURING. AAM is a union-dominated organizatin that claims to be a nonpartisan partnership forged to strengthen manufacturing in the United States.

AMERICAN ENVIRONICS. Describing itself as a consulting firm, AE uses social values surveys, cognitive linguistics, and political psychology to help foundations and nonprofits develop breakthrough social change initiatives.

AMERICAN FEDERATION OF LABOR AND CONGRESS OF INDUSTRIAL ORGANIZATIONS. The AFL-CIO is a national trade union center, the largest federation of unions in the United States, made up of fifty-six national and international unions, together representing more than 11 million workers. John Sweeney, the union's president emeritus and longtime leader, is a socialist activist and a card-carrying member of the Democratic Socialists of America.

AMERICAN LEGISLATIVE ISSUE CAMPAIGN EXCHANGE. ALICE is perhaps the mother organization to progressive legislation-writing efforts. Self-described as a "pro-labor, pro-environment, pro-good-government educational organization," ALICE launched in early 2003 as a collaborative project of several progressive organizations.

ANNENBERG CHALLENGE. The largest gift ever made to American public education, the group is a $500 million, five-year "challenge to the nation designed to energize and support promising efforts at school reform throughout the country." Funds came from the late Honorable Walter H. Annenberg, former U.S. ambassador to Great Britain during the Richard Nixon administration. Barack Obama was appointed as the Chicago Annenberg Challenge's first chairman in 1995. The CAC was cofounded by Bill Ayers, who also served as an ex officio board member. It granted money to radical leftist activist causes, including ACORN.

APOLLO ALLIANCE. AA is a coalition of labor, business, environmental, and community leaders working to catalyze what it calls a clean energy revolution. The group is led by a slew of radicals, including the founder of a communist revolutionary organization and a former top leader of the Weatherman terrorist organization.

BROADER, BOLDER APPROACH TO EDUCATION. An arm of the Economic Policy Institute, the Broader, Bolder Approach to Education, or BBA, was founded as a task force of national policy experts to "consider the broader context" of No Child Left Behind in the "nation's approach to education and youth development policy."

CAMPAIGN FOR AMERICA'S FUTURE. CAF is a progressive political organization that purports to concern itself with issues of the environment, energy independence, health care reform, Social Security, and education. Its sister organization is the Institute for America's Future.

CAMPAIGN FOR COMMUNITY CHANGE. CCC claims to be an incubator organization engaged in creating *grassroots* organizations among the so-called marginalized and disenfranchised populations— "low-income people, immigrants and people of color." Additionally, the Campaign operates as the lobbying arm of the Center for Community Change. The two organizations share the same staff.

CENTER FOR AMERICAN PROGRESS. CAP is a progressive public policy research and advocacy organization led by John Podesta, who served as cochair of Barack Obama's presidential transition team. CAP was founded in 2003 with seed money from George Soros, who also donated $3 million to its sister organization, the Project Action Fund. Podesta and CAP are heavily influential in helping the Obama White House craft legislation.

CENTER FOR COMMUNITY CHANGE. A large, so-called community-building organization founded with the purpose, according to its website, "to help establish and develop community organizations across the country, bring attention to major national issues related to poverty, and help insure that government programs are responsive to community needs."

CENTER FOR PUBLIC INTEGRITY. A George Soros–funded organization that claims to be dedicated to producing "responsible investigative journalism" on issues of public concern.

CENTER ON WISCONSIN STRATEGY. COWS is a progressive policy institute housed on the campus of the University of Wisconsin–Madison and founded as a center organized around the concept of "high road" economic development through so-called environmental sustainability.

CHICAGO WOODS FUND. A grant-making foundation whose goal is to increase opportunities for less advantaged people and communities in the Chicago metropolitan area. Barack Obama sat as a paid director on the board of the Chicago Woods Fund alongside Bill Ayers.

CITIZENS' CRUSADE AGAINST POVERTY. Described as an "alternative grass-roots voice of the poor," the group was formed from a coalition of more than one hundred liberal labor, civil rights, and church organizations.

COALITION OF ESSENTIAL SCHOOLS. Guided by a set of socialist-style principles, as we expose, the CES curriculum is based on the concept of essentialism, which "strives to teach students the accumulated knowledge of our civilization through core courses in the traditional academic disciplines."

CODEPINK. A radical women-led organization, CODEPINK purports to concern itself with antiwar activities. Yet we expose how the group's leadership serves on boards that had a hand in Obama's health care and economic initiatives.

COMMUNIST PARTY USA. The CPUSA is a Marxist political party in the United States.

CONGRESSIONAL BLACK CAUCUS. An organization that represents the black members of the United States Congress. Membership is exclusive to blacks. While the caucus officially presents itself as nonpartisan, the group functions as a progressive lobbying group within the wider Democratic Party. The CBC includes many Congressional Progressive Caucus members. The two caucuses work largely in tandem, as we document.

CONGRESSIONAL PROGRESSIVE CAUCUS. Originally founded as an arm of Democratic Socialists of America, the CPC is the largest caucus within the Democratic caucus in the United States Congress, currently with eighty-three declared members. The CPC says it works to advance progressive issues and positions. We expose how the CPC functions as a vehicle to carry out the Democratic Socialists of America's agenda and how multiple CPC members to this day are openly affiliated with the DSA. The CPC includes two other arms: the Progressive Congress Action Fund, an advocacy organization to engage the American public with progressives in Congress, and a research and education arm, the ProgressiveCongress.org

CONNECT U.S. FUND. A George Soros–funded organization that promotes global governance and states on its website that its mission is to influence "policy through integrative collaborative grant making on human rights, nonproliferation, climate change and development, and effective foreign assistance."

COUNCIL ON AMERICAN-ISLAMIC RELATIONS. CAIR is America's largest Muslim civil liberties advocacy organization. It is an unindicted co-conspirator in a Hamas funding case involving the Holy Land Foundation charity.

CREATIVE COMMONS. A nonprofit organization that says it is devoted to expanding the range of creative works available for others to build upon legally and to share.

DEMOCRATIC SOCIALISTS OF AMERICA. The largest socialist group in America, the DSA is the principal U.S. affiliate of the Socialist International. DSA's website explains, "We are socialists because we reject an international economic order sustained by private profit, alienated labor, race and gender discrimination, environmental destruction, and brutality and violence in defense of the status quo."

The site further advises, "To achieve a more just society, many structures of our government and economy must be radically transformed. . . . Democracy and socialism go hand in hand. All over the world, wherever the idea of democracy has taken root, the vision of socialism has taken root as well—everywhere but in the United States." The DSA spawned multiple U.S. progressive groups, some of which, as we document, attempt to disguise their socialist agenda.

DEMOS. A far-left think tank that purports to be a nonpartisan public policy research and advocacy organization with four stated goals: a more equitable economy with widely shared prosperity and opportunity; a vibrant and inclusive democracy with high levels of voting and civic engagement; an empowered public sector that works for the common good; and responsible U.S. engagement in an interdependent world.

ECONOMIC POLICY INSTITUTE. EPI is a liberal think tank funded by George Soros's Open Society Institute. According to EPI's website, the institute was established to "broaden the discussion about economic policy to include the interests of low- and middle-income workers." EPI focuses on "the economic condition of low- and middle-income Americans and their families."

EFFICIENCY CITIES NETWORK. ECN describes itself as an "informal policy learning network of government staff, researchers and technical assistance providers, and NGOs currently active in or committed to making scaled efforts at high-road energy retrofits of urban building stock." The group holds regular sessions on energy and environmental policy issues with officials from Congress, the Department of Energy, and local governmental agencies.

ELLA BAKER CENTER FOR HUMAN RIGHTS. Named after a little-known socialist firebrand and led by Van Jones, the group is an action center with the stated aim of working for "justice, opportunity and peace" in urban America.

EMERALD CITIES COLLABORATIVE. A "consortium of diverse organizations—businesses, unions, community organizations, development intermediaries, social justice advocates, research and technical assistance providers—united around the goal of 'greening' our metropolitan areas in high-road ways that advance equal opportunity, shared wealth, and democracy within them."

ERIKSON INSTITUTE. Served as a training ground for both teachers and staff to "develop comprehensive curriculum for early childhood education in a network of Chicago public schools." The Institute was partnered with a program called Building Early Childhood Centers of Excellence to develop and improve curriculum and assessment in preschool through third grade in six Chicago schools. We thoroughly expose the radical ties and aims of this group.

EXPEDITIONARY LEARNING (EL). A nonprofit group founded by radicals that partners with schools and/or school districts to "implement and assess the best curriculum and practices." The EL School network claims to serve 150 schools in twenty-eight states and the District of Columbia and to support 50,000 students and 4,000 teachers.

EXPLORATORY PROJECT FOR ECONOMIC ALTERNATIVES. The group says its goal was to "develop economic alternatives which move us away from a future dominated by the values of giant corporate and bureaucratic institutions." The evolution of EPEA begins with the Democratic Socialists of America–affiliated Institute for Policy Studies.

FACING HISTORY AND OURSELVES. The group's stated focus is on "bringing ethical and moral philosophy to history and social studies classes, particularly regarding issues of racism, civic responsibility and tolerance." We expose how this group was founded and funded by radicals and is intimately tied to the "Radical Network."

FREE PRESS. A George Soros–funded, Marxist-founded organization with close ties to the White House. Free Press published petitions for more government control of the news media. It recently published a study advocating the development of a "world class" government-run media system in the United States.

GREEN FOR ALL. This is an environmental activist group founded by Van Jones.

HEALTH CARE FOR AMERICA NOW. HCAN purports to be a national grassroots campaign of more than one thousand organizations in forty-six states dedicated to winning "quality, affordable health care we all can count on in 2010 and beyond."

HEALTHCARE-NOW. An organization not to be confused with the organization Health Care for America Now, it was established in 2004 to lobby on behalf of single-payer health care. Healthcare-NOW's broad base includes socialist, labor, church, and community organizations.

HERNDON ALLIANCE. This is the marketing outfit that helped to rebrand Obamacare. When it fails to successfully rebrand radical policies, it takes a step back, repackages those policies, and tries again, ever careful to use the kind of language the public wants to hear to sell the same idea it has previously rejected.

INDUSTRIAL AREAS FOUNDATION. A direct-action activist group founded by Saul Alinsky to train citizens to organize within low-income neighborhoods, particularly Mexican-American neighborhoods, often with support of a diocese of the Catholic Church.

INSTITUTE FOR POLICY STUDIES. A think tank funded by philanthropist George Soros, the IPS has been described as an idea factory for the left. It has carried out projects in support of leftist dictators and revolutionary nationalists and various social movements. The IPS is a crucial component of the Radical Network, helping to formulate ideas that, we expose, ultimately become congressional legislation or, under President Obama, White House legislation.

ISLAMIC SOCIETY OF NORTH AMERICA. A major Islamic umbrella group established in the United States by the Muslim Brotherhood–associated Muslim Students' Association. It has been described in the media as the largest Muslim organization in North America. Through its affiliate, the North American Islamic Trust—a Saudi government–backed organization created to fund Islamist enterprises in North America—the ISNA reportedly holds the mortgages on 50 to 80 percent of all mosques in the United States and Canada. It is an unindicted co-conspirator in the largest terror financing case in U.S. history.

JOURNOLIST. An e-mail listserv comprised of several hundred journalists and activists that used the online group to discuss minimizing negative publicity surrounding Obama's radical ties. The list was founded by *Washington Post* blogger Ezra Klein, formerly an associate editor for the *American Prospect* political magazine, who worked on former Vermont governor Howard Dean's 2004 presidential primary campaign.

MIDDLE EAST CHILDREN'S ALLIANCE. MECA is a nongovernmental organization that purports to work for peace and justice for "Palestine, Israel, Lebanon and Iraq."

MIDWEST ACADEMY. Founded by socialist activist Heather Booth as a principal New Left training facility for community and group organizing modeled on Saul Alinsky tactics.

MOVEON.ORG. A George Soros–funded nonprofit, progressive public policy advocacy group and political action committee that has raised millions of dollars for political candidates it identifies as "moderates" or "progressives."

NATIONAL ASSOCIATION FOR THE ADVANCEMENT OF COLORED PEOPLE. The NAACP is an African-American civil rights organization that states its goal is to "ensure the political, educational, social, and economic equality of rights of all persons and to eliminate racial hatred and racial discrimination."

NATION OF ISLAM. An Afrocentric extremist movement founded by Wallace D. Fard Muhammad and currently run by Louis Farrakhan, who has spoken out against "white devils" and Jewish "bloodsuckers."

NEW PARTY. A controversial 1990s political party that sought to elect members to public office with the aim of moving the Democratic Party far leftward to ultimately form a new political party with a socialist agenda. We cited evidence in our previous book, *The Man-churian President*, documenting that Obama was a member of the New Party and that many New Party leaders are currently associated with Obama. The New Party took advantage of what was known as electoral "fusion," which enabled candidates to run on two tickets simultaneously, attracting voters from both parties. Although the New Party still exists, it went defunct as a political party in 1998, one year after fusion was halted by the Supreme Court.

OPEN SOCIETY INSTITUTE. OSI is the main funding arm of philan-thropist George Soros. The group is aimed at shaping public policy to promote democratic governance, human rights, and economic, legal, and social reform.

POPULIST CAUCUS. The group's plank has been described as typically progressive, but with more of a rural farmer and union feel than the Congressional Progressive Caucus, and with a heavily New Left and multi-ethnic approach. The caucus comes most recently from the farm crisis of the early 1980s. Membership in the Populist Caucus overlaps with that of the CPC, although there are several non-CPC members. In many ways, we find, the Populist Caucus's agenda re-sembles that of CPC.

PRESIDENTIAL CLIMATE ACTION PROJECT. PCAP is a group that re-leases recommendation papers to help guide the White House and other U.S. government arms in fighting so-called global warming and other energy concerns.

PROGRESSIVE DEMOCRATS OF AMERICA. Works to carve out a space for progressives in the Democratic Party. The PDA is another orga-nization created by progressives to counterbalance the Democratic Leadership Council, which was formed in 1985 following Ronald Reagan's sweeping win. Viewed as politically too far to the right and much too conservative, the DLC shut down in early February 2011. Progressive Democrats of America works closely with the Democratic Socialists of America and the Congressional Progres-sive Caucus.

PROPUBLICA. Defines itself as "an independent, non-profit newsroom that produces investigative journalism in the public interest." ProPublica was founded with a $10 million annual grant from Herbert and Marion Sandler. The journalistic integrity of ProPublica has been repeatedly called into question. A report by the Capital Research Center concluded ProPublica "churns out little more than left-wing hit pieces about Sarah Palin and blames the U.S. government for giving out too little foreign aid."

PUBLIC KNOWLEDGE. A George Soros–funded public interest group that is involved in Internet advocacy, intellectual property law, competition, and choice in the digital marketplace.

SERVICE EMPLOYEES INTERNATIONAL UNION. Claiming 2.2 million members, SEIU is the fastest-growing union in North America. SEIU is focused on organizing workers in health care, public services, and property services. The group donates millions of dollars to Democratic lawmakers and politicians. The SEIU is a crucial organizing and lobbying component of the Radical Network. It serves as a de facto socialist-leaning union army. The group works closely with ACORN and multiple major progressive and socialist organizations.

SMALL SCHOOLS WORKSHOP. Cofounded by Bill Ayers and communist activist Mike Klonsky, the group has been the main provider of research, training, and support for teachers and principals in Chicago who were trying to redesign and restructure their large, overcrowded high schools into smaller learning communities.

SOCIAL DEMOCRATIC MOVEMENT OF NETROOTS NATION. A group whose agenda is to amplify "progressive voices by providing an online and in-person campus for exchanging ideas and learning how to be more effective in using technology to influence the public debate."

SOCIALIST INTERNATIONAL. Arguably the largest organized socialist organization in the world. This global umbrella group consists of social democratic, socialist, and labor parties. It currently brings together 162 political parties and organizations from all continents. It has existed in its present form since 1951, when it was reestablished at the Frankfurt Congress. Since then it has been increasingly active and grown considerably in membership, more than doubling the number of its members in recent years. SI's "organizing document" cites capitalism as the cause of "devastating crises," "mass unemployment," "imperialist expansion," and "colonial exploitation" worldwide.

STUDENT NONVIOLENT COORDINATING COMMITTEE. SNCC is one of the 1960s' most active black revolutionary groups.

STUDENTS FOR A DEMOCRATIC SOCIETY. A leftist student activist and antiwar movement representative of the country's New Left, it was reincarnated on college campuses in 2006.

SUSTAINABLE ENERGY AND ENVIRONMENT COALITION. Initiated in Congress concurrently with both Barack Obama's inauguration and his administration's stated goals of a *green economy*, the group was founded to be a strong voice in the U.S. House of Representatives in advancing policies that promote "clean energy innovation," create "green collar" jobs, and help arrest "global warming." The group clearly leans toward the Congressional Progressive Caucus agenda.

TIDES CENTER. A spin-off of the Tides Foundation, a George Soros–funded organization, makes very clear its openly leftist agenda: "We strengthen community-based organizations and the progressive movement by providing an innovative and cost-effective framework for your philanthropy."

UNITED NEIGHBORHOOD ORGANIZATION OF CHICAGO. UNO is modeled on Alinsky-style community organizing. Its mission was to build grassroots leadership in Chicago's Hispanic neighborhoods, "organize for power," and address such local issues as street violence, the Hispanic dropout rate, and overcrowding in schools.

WEATHERMAN. Known colloquially as the Weathermen, and later the Weather Underground Organization, this was an American radical left organization that carried out domestic terrorist attacks aimed at bringing down the U.S. capitalist system.

WORKING FAMILIES PARTY. WFP is a far-left political party supported by the Democratic Socialists of America and closely affiliated with ACORN.

YOUTH PROJECT. Founded by radicals, the group worked in conjunction with the Center for Community Change with the stated goal of providing a means by which young people with inherited wealth could channel their donations collectively and effectively.

INDEX